PATERNOSTER THEOLOGICAL MONOGRAPHS

Grace and Global Justice

The Socio-Political Mission of the Church in an Age of Globalization

Commendations

"This wide-ranging study in political theology explores how the Christian community should respond to the challenges posed by globalization. Claiming that the church must be engaged in a 'multidimensional liberating activity in the contemporary world,' Richard Gibb argues that the church must not accept existing global structures and institutions but seek to reform and transform them. More particularly, he argues that the church, in pursuing the cause of global justice, should approach its task from a cosmopolitan perspective that deemphasizes the moral significance of state boundaries. A major strength of this book is its careful synthesis and critique of the theology and political ethics of three major contemporary Christian thinkers - Jürgen Moltmann, Stanley Hauerwas, and Oliver O'Donovan. This study is warmly recommended for its theological insights and its careful integration of international political theory and biblical faith."
Mark Amstutz, Professor of Political Science, Wheaton College

"Globalization is a vital issue for the church today, and Richard Gibb has important things to say about it. Especially prominent in his lucid argument is a concern that the church's approach to issues of global justice be rooted in the theology of grace. This is interdisciplinary thinking from a thoroughly Christian theological base."
Richard Bauckham, Professor of New Testament, University of St. Andrews

"Debates over the proper way (if any) to engage in socio-political mission have long divided the Evangelical world. Here is a study that takes a broad view of mission but a precise and distinctively Evangelical view of its theological rationale – in the doctrine of grace."
David Bebbington, Professor of History, University of Stirling

"A thoughtful and most welcome attempt to present a Christian theology of responsible globalization. It is an excellent scholarly treatise and deserves to be read by everyone interested in making global capitalism more inclusive and socially acceptable."
John H. Dunning, Emeritus Professor of International Business, University of Reading and Emeritus Professor of International Business, Rutgers University

"Too often, Christian commentary on pressing economic and political matters fails. The task is a difficult one, requiring both an understanding of complex issues in the contemporary world, and a sound grasp of Christian theology. Richard Gibb not only proves himself expert in both areas, but brings an enviable gift in relating one to the other, demonstrating how apparently abstruse theological debates about grace make real differences to socio-political ethics, and, more importantly, how the gospel of Christ has something distinctive and urgent to contribute to the question of

globalization, arguably the single most important feature of the political and economic landscape today."
Stephen Holmes, Lecturer in Theology, University of St. Andrews

"In this important book Richard Gibb provides an illuminating critical survey of key theological explorations of topics relating to political-economic concerns. But unlike so many theological explorations of such matters, that stay mostly on the level of generalization, he demonstrates – in ways that I found extremely insightful – the actual connections of theology to urgent issues of economic justice, globalization, and political authority."
Richard Mouw, President and Professor of Christian Philosophy, Fuller Theological Seminary

"In his systematic study, Richard Gibb brings into debates over the ethics of globalization a hitherto missing perspective – that of evangelical Christian theology. At the outset, he vows to conduct his analysis from the distinctive standpoint of the Christian gospel as narrated in Scripture. By the end, he delivers on what he promises, offering readers a unique position on globalization that emphasizes servant leadership, a privileged position for the marginalized, and the uncompromising role of the church as a community of grace. His position is one that neither theological ethicists nor students of globalization of any stripe ought to ignore."
Dan Philpott, Associate Professor of Political Science, University of Notre Dame

"This important book supplies further evidence of an awakening interest in social and political theology among Evangelicals. Further, it challenges Christians in the Reformed tradition to abandon the pietistic cul-de-sac within which many of them became trapped in the twentieth century and shows how the doctrine of grace actually provides a foundation for the practice of radical discipleship in the era of globalization. This is a very important contribution to ongoing debate and it deserves a wide readership."
David Smith, Lecturer in Urban Mission and World Christianity, International Christian College, Glasgow

"Globalization is one of the most pressing challenges facing the church today. This book offers a timely theological reflection on how the church can be a voice for justice on behalf of the global poor by affirming its mission as a community of grace."
William F. Storrar, Director, Center of Theological Inquiry, Princeton

"When theologians engage with questions of politics and social justice, the temptation is to allow a concern with ethics to eclipse theological insight and, ultimately, an easy legalism to displace a theology of grace. Far from enhancing the relevance of Christian theology, this serves to diminish its distinctive insights and the profound contribution which the Gospel can make to these all-important debates.

What is particularly impressive about this volume is the author's lucid and clear-headed articulation of the light which the doctrine of our participation by grace in God's covenant purposes serves to shed on the nature of our participation in a globalized world. This goes hand in hand with an analysis couched in a scholarly and informed expertise in politics and economics which is admirably free from emotive rhetoric.

The end result is an insightful and pertinent analysis of a field of growing international concern which, precisely by virtue of its being theologically driven, sheds fresh light on the nature and implications of globalization as also on the risks which attend it and the resulting ethical obligations."
Alan Torrance, Chair of Systematic Theology, University of St. Andrews

"Christians have a deplorable tendency to polarize over grace or law, evangelism or social action, personal piety or public and political witness. Richard Gibb rightly roots every dimension of our Christian response to the world and all its needs in our doctrine and experience of God's grace. No other foundation is possible if Christian social engagement is to be consistent with the biblical Gospel."
Christopher J.H. Wright, International Director, Langham Partnership International

"In much evangelical theology the terms 'grace' and 'global justice' are rarely teamed together, but it is the basis of Richard Gibb's forceful and richly-resourced argument that they must. The key links are the definition of the church as a community determined by the grace of the gospel and a biblical view of its mission as inclusive of the social and political dimensions of human life – now inescapably global. Dr. Gibb evaluates three eminent theologians standing in Reformation traditions, Moltmann, Hauerwas and O'Donovan, as guides to the accomplishing of the church's task today. This is vigorous theology grounded in remarkably wide reading, not least on the theme of globalization itself. It provides a model for others to follow in its relentless fidelity to starting always with the central doctrines of the gospel and kingdom of Christ."
David F. Wright, Emeritus Professor of Patristic and Reformed Christianity, University of Edinburgh

A complete listing of all titles in both this series and
Paternoster Biblical Monographs
will be found at the close of this book

Grace and Global Justice

The Socio-Political Mission of the Church in an Age of Globalization

Richard Gibb

Foreword by Bruce Milne

Paternoster:
thinking faith

First published 2006 by Paternoster

Paternoster is an imprint of Authentic Media
9 Holdom Avenue, Bletchley, Milton Keynes, MK1 1QR, UK
and
PO Box 1047, Waynesboro, GA 30830–2047, USA

12 11 10 09 08 07 06   7 6 5 4 3 2 1

British Library Cataloguing in Publication Data
A catalogue record for this book is available from the British Library

ISBN-13: 978-1-84227-459-0
ISBN-10: 1-84227-459-7

Typeset by R. Gibb and A.R. Cross
Printed and bound in Great Britain
by Nottingham Alphagraphics

Series Preface

In the West the churches may be declining, but theology—serious, academic (mostly doctoral level) and mainstream orthodox in evaluative commitment—shows no sign of withering on the vine. This series of *Paternoster Theological Monographs* extends the expertise of the Press especially to first-time authors whose work stands broadly within the parameters created by fidelity to Scripture and has satisfied the critical scrutiny of respected assessors in the academy. Such theology may come in several distinct intellectual disciplines—historical, dogmatic, pastoral, apologetic, missional, aesthetic and no doubt others also. The series will be particularly hospitable to promising constructive theology within an evangelical frame, for it is of this that the church's need seems to be greatest. Quality writing will be published across the confessions—Anabaptist, Episcopalian, Reformed, Arminian and Orthodox—across the ages—patristic, medieval, reformation, modern and counter-modern—and across the continents. The aim of the series is theology written in the twofold conviction that the church needs theology and theology needs the church—which in reality means theology done for the glory of God.

Series Editors

David F. Wright, Emeritus Professor of Patristic and Reformed Christianity, University of Edinburgh, Scotland, UK

Trevor A. Hart, Head of School and Principal of St Mary's College School of Divinity, University of St Andrews, Scotland, UK

Anthony N.S. Lane, Professor of Historical Theology and Director of Research, London School of Theology, UK

Anthony C. Thiselton, Emeritus Professor of Christian Theology, University of Nottingham, Research Professor in Christian Theology, University College Chester, and Canon Theologian of Leicester Cathedral and Southwell Minster, UK

Kevin J. Vanhoozer, Research Professor of Systematic Theology, Trinity Evangelical Divinity School, Deerfield, Illinois, USA

To
the two most significant women in my life:
my mother, Daphne, and my wife, Alison

Contents

Foreword by Bruce Milne xv

Preface xvii

PART ONE: The Methodology and Foundations 1

Chapter 1
The Strategy of this Study and Theological Scholarship 3
A Theology of Grace and the Mission of the Church in a Globalized World 3
Introduction to the Research Project 3
Some Studies Pertaining to the Church's Socio-Political Involvement 4
The Fundamental Theological Questions of this Study 6
The Method of Investigation 8
Limitations to the Scope of Study 9
Survey of Theological Scholarship Pertaining to the Study 11
Introduction 11
Christian Pacifism and the Anabaptist Position 12
Calvinism and Preserving God's Justice in Society 13
The German Context and the Development of a Public Theology 16
Christian Realism and Socio-Political Engagement 18
The Political Content of the Biblical Text 21
The Social Conscience of the Evangelical Churches 24
A Need for Further Study 27
Concluding Remarks 29

Chapter 2
The Church as a Grace-Defined Community 30
Introduction 30
Grace as the Context of Knowledge of God 33
The Anthropocentric Culture of the West 33
Modernity and its Influence on Socio-Political Engagement 35
The Being of God as Prior to All Theological Questioning 37
Grace and General Revelation 39
Divine Self-Revelation and the Incarnate Word of God 44
Grace and Covenant Relationship with God 47
The Covenant of Grace and the Kingdom of God 47
The Nature of the Covenant 50
Grace and the Dynamics of Community 55
Divine Affirmation of Human Value 58
The Will of God and the Mission of the Church 60

Conclusion..62

PART TWO: The Comparison 63

Chapter 3
Grace and Jürgen Moltmann's Political Theology.....................................65
Introduction..65
The Eschatological Kingdom of God and a Vision of Transformation 67
   The Resurrection of Christ and Christian Hope...67
   Human Rights and a Theology of Liberation 69
   The Glory of God in Creation 71
   The Lordship of Christ Over His Church..73
The Servanthood of Christ and the Universal Mission of the Church 74
   The Implications of Christology for Christopraxis...74
   The Cross of Christ and Solidarity with the Powerless...................................76
   Freedom to Serve and Socio-Political Involvement..78
Critical Reflection 81
   Christ as the Foundation for Social and Political Action................................81
   The Concept of Servanthood for the Social Witness of the Church....................82
   Eschatology and Universal Justice 83
   Grace and the Freedom of God 86
   A Victim-Orientated Soteriology and the Covenant of Grace...........................88
Conclusion..91

Chapter 4
Grace and Stanley Hauerwas' Political Theology 92
Introduction..92
Narrative as a Mode of Moral Reflection...94
   Postliberal Theology and the Particularity of Christian Faith 94
   Theological Ethics and the Narrative of Scripture...96
   Narrative and Divine Self-Communication 99
   Virtues and the Communal Nature of the Christian Life...............................100
Christian Distinctiveness and Socio-Political Involvement..................................103
   Contemporary Culture and a Separated Christian Community.......................103
   Power, Politics, and the Witness of the Church 105
   Understanding Justice in a Secular Society...108
Critical Reflection 110
   Grace, Revelation, and the Self-Manifestation of God 110
   Christology and the Political Existence of the Christian 113
   The Use of Narrative as a Hermeneutical Tool...116
   The Politics of the World and the Politics of the Church................................117
Conclusion..119

Chapter 5
Grace and Oliver O'Donovan's Political Theology.. 120
Introduction.. 120
The Gospel of Jesus Christ and Ethical Directions 122
Scripture as the Source of Socio-Political Debate............................... 122
The Ethical Implications of the Resurrection and the Created Order 124
Love as the Human Response to Divine Act... 127
The Unfolding of God's Reign and Political Activity in the World.................... 129
Christian Tradition and the Notion of Authority................................ 129
The Promised Unity of God's All-Sovereign Rule 132
The Church as a Political Society... 135
Critical Reflection 139
The Reign of God and Political Authority 139
The Servanthood of Christ and the Church's Socio-Political Witness.............. 141
Covenant and Kingship as Political Concepts.................................... 143
The Gospel and the Eschatological Hope of World Justice................... 146
Conclusion 147

PART THREE: The Test Case 149

Chapter 6
Power and the Dynamics of Global Transformations................................ 151
Introduction.. 151
The Globalization Debate 152
The Hyperglobalizers, the Sceptics, and the Transformationalists.................... 152
Contemporary Globalization and the Transformation of Power 154
Forces of Global Transformation in the Contemporary World 156
The Post-War World Economy.. 156
Trade Liberalization and a New Global Framework........................... 158
World Financial Markets and Global Interconnectedness 161
Production and the Changing Competitive Landscape for Business.................. 163
Transforming Power Relations and the Implications for Global Justice 167
Opportunities and Challenges of Globalization 167
The Transforming Nature of Nation-States... 170
Power and the Contemporary Global Order 173
Conclusion 176

Chapter 7
Grace and Agents of Justice in a Globalized World 177
Introduction.. 177
International Political Theory and Global Justice 178
Recognizing the Need for an "Ethical Globalization" 178
The Question of Justice.. 182

Human Rights and International Distributive Justice 185
The Moral Demands of Cosmopolitanism 188
State Boundaries and Agents of Justice in a Globalized World 191
Grace and Servant-Leadership in the Globalized Socio-Political Arena 194
Servanthood in a Power Dominated World 194
Faithful Christian Witness in a Culture of Economism 197
Global Integration and the Unified Kingdom of God 200
Being a Community of Grace in the Globalized Socio-Political Arena 202
Conclsuion 206

Chapter 8
Conclusion 207

Bibliography 209

General Index 241

Foreword

"For the first time in history children are coming to adulthood with a global consciousness", observes Howard Snyder, and therein captures the essential, and irreversible, context of life on planet earth today and tomorrow. Globalization is here to stay. Its influence on life across the planet is already far-reaching, and will only increase in the future.

For Christians, no less than other earth-dwellers, the implications are major ones. Indeed, as adherents of a faith which claims world-wide significance and which is a response to the world's only Lord and God, the arrival of the age of globalization inevitably stirs our imagination, and puts fresh nerve into our endeavours.

But it also challenges us to identify an authentic Biblical-ethical response. For not all the effects of living in 'one world' are benign, and that needs to concern us. The economic and social impact of the way the global forces are developed over the next period has the potential to determine the quality of life for vast multitudes all around the world.

One of the most immediate implications of globalization is a redefinition of our 'neighbour', that vulnerable individual lying by the roadside, whom Jesus summons to minister to and help. He is no longer merely the social casualty in our immediate neighbourhood. 'Neighbour' is also that subsistence, peasant farmer in Sichuan Province in China, that HIV-Aids infected mother of eight in Lusaka, Zambia, or that penniless family trapped in the *favela* in Rio de Janeiro, all of whom stand to be significantly impacted by how globalization functions in the next years. To ignore the issues of global justice which are raised here is to find ourselves in the company of James' cynical 'Christian observer', "Go, I wish you well; keep warm and well fed", but "does nothing about his physical needs", the man "whose faith is dead" (James 2:15-17).

But what *can* we do in face of the dauntingly massive forces involved here? Richard Gibb's book is a 'must read' response. Representing the substance of his interdisciplinary, doctoral thesis presented to the University of St. Andrews, it is in many ways a pioneering exploration of this very issue.

In the first of its three sections Richard offers a masterly over-view of post-reformation, evangelical theology structured around the central motif of the grace of God. The second sees this criterion insightfully applied, with the help of enviably resourced research, to three seminal Christian ethicists, Jürgen Moltmann, Stanley Hauerwas, and Oliver O'Donovan.

In the third, closing section, Richard courageously faces the challenge of bringing the fruits of his consistently biblical analysis in the earlier sections into focus in a viable Christian response to the globalization challenge, which latter he expounds with commendable fairness and scholarly rigour.

Why ought this book to be bought, read and studied? Firstly, because it takes us to a place where we all need to go – to ignore the issues posed by globalization is to consign ourselves to moral and spiritual irrelevance in today's world. Secondly, because it will help evangelical Christians move beyond the crippling, unbiblical polarities of evangelism *or* social action, personal piety *or* public witness, to an inclusiveness which is truly honouring to God and powerfully authenticating of the gospel in this twenty-first century world. (Richard himself nicely modeled this holistic perspective by dividing his time in preparing this manuscript on global justice with giving leadership to the "Christianity Explored" evangelism programme at Charlotte Chapel, Edinburgh). Thirdly, *Grace and Global Justice* is to be bought, read and studied because it will stimulate further thinking, debate and writing. Many aspects of the highly complex phenomenon which is globalization are necessarily only touched upon here. The best tribute to this landmark writing is for it to become a starting-point for the emergence of an unashamedly evangelical lobby for global justice, which will both authenticate our faith, and make a difference around the world.

No prizes will be issued on the judgment day for spending our lives engaging with the issues of generations no longer peopling planet earth. Loving, compassionate and God-pleasing witness means engagement with the issues of our own time, and here is arguably the largest of them all – globalization. Let Richard Gibb walk you into it in this passionate, informed, and finally deeply hopeful study. It is a genuine privilege to be invited to commend it.

Bruce Milne,
Vancouver, 2006

Preface

This is a book about the holistic mission of the Christian community in a globalized world. Specifically, it is an exploration of two fundamental theological questions: first, what does it mean for the Christian community to conceive of itself as a community defined by the covenant of grace; and second, what are the implications of this distinctiveness for its socio-political mission in an age of globalization.

The desire to commence this study was birthed during my career as a consultant with the global business advisory firm Ernst & Young. Globalization, it became increasingly apparent, not only was having an intensifying impact within and among nation-states, but it was also evident that the challenge for the church with respect to how it interprets its thoughts and policies in response to this multidimensional phenomenon is significant. Yet there is presently a scarcity of theological literature relating to the social and political concerns intrinsic to this whole field. It is the aim of this book to help redress this through engaging in interdisciplinary research, which seeks to articulate the key theological ingredients of the socio-political witness of the church in this specific historical and cultural context, and to do so with particular reference to the theological insights constitutive of the Reformation tradition.

In completing this study, which is in fact a slightly revised and updated edition of my doctoral dissertation, produced in St. Andrews, U.K., and submitted in 2005, I was extremely fortunate in benefiting from the supervision and encouragement of Professor Alan Torrance and Dr. Stephen Holmes. I look back on those days of lively discussion late in the evenings at the University of St. Andrews with much fondness. I also wish to express my particular thanks to Professor Richard Bauckham who helped me at several points along the way. Mention must likewise be made of my good friend Dr. James Dixon Douglas, who until his call home to be with the Lord, was a delight to visit in St. Andrews. I learned much from his wide experience and similarly appreciated his good cooking!

My formal theological education actually began over the Atlantic at Wheaton College, Illinois. Heartfelt thanks are due to Professor Walter Elwell for his guidance and supervision throughout these formative years studying at Wheaton College. One never grows tired of acknowledging how much we owe our teachers.

Additionally, I am indebted to Dr. Bruce Milne for his friendship, wise counsel, and for graciously being willing to write the Foreword to this book. His example of integrating theological scholarship with practical ministry is one that I greatly admire and which provides a marvelous model to emulate.

Throughout the completion of this study I was fortunate in having a number of distinguished scholars from a variety of academic disciplines and institutions read over different sections, and I am particularly grateful to Professor David Wright (Ecclesiastical History, University of Edinburgh) and Dr. David Smith (Urban Mission and World Christianity, International Christian College, Glasgow) who read through the entire draft version of this work in its earlier form, and Professor William Storrar (Center of Theological Inquiry, Princeton) and Professor Mario Aguilar (Religion and Politics, University of St. Andrews) who examined the final manuscript. Additionally, I would like to acknowledge my debt of gratitude to the following scholars for commenting on individual chapters: Chapter 1: Professor David Bebbington (History, University of Stirling); Professor Nicholas Wolterstorff (Philosophical Theology, Yale University); Chapter 2: Dr. Bruce Milne (theological writer and former Senior Minister of First Baptist Church, Vancouver); Professor Christopher Seitz (Old Testament, University of St. Andrews); Dr. Nathan MacDonald (Old Testament, University of St. Andrews); Professor John Walton (Old Testament, Wheaton College); Chapter 3: Dr. Tom Smail (former Pastor and Vice-Principal of St. John's College, Nottingham); Chapter 4: Dr. Samuel Wells (Priest-in-Charge of St Mark's, Newnham, Cambridge); Chapter 5: Dr. Jonathan Chaplin (Political Theory, Institute for Christian Studies, Toronto); Chapter 6: Professor John Dunning (International Business, University of Reading); Dr. Alison Watson (International Relations, University of St. Andrews); Professor Peter McKiernan (Management, University of St. Andrews); Chapter 7: Professor Mark Amstutz (Political Science, Wheaton College); Professor Duncan Forrester (Christian Ethics and Practical Theology, University of Edinburgh); Dr. Dan Philpott (Political Science, University of Notre Dame); Professor Nicholas Rengger (International Relations, University of St. Andrews). In considering the practical implications of the church's mission in the context of a globalized world, particular help was also given by Gary Edmonds, former Secretary General of the World Evangelical Alliance.

Similarly, I would like to thank Jeremy Mudditt, Dr. Robin Parry, and Dr. Anthony R. Cross from Paternoster for their patience and perseverance.

My brother, Jonathan Gibb, and Rutherford House, a Christian theological study and research centre, generously made funding available for this research project. Without their support, this study would not have been completed.

And most importantly, I am indebted to two significant women in my life. One is my mother, who along with my father, impressed upon me at a young age the profound implications of the gospel of grace in all aspects of life. And the other is my wife, Alison, who has been a constant source of encouragement and support throughout the completion of this work. In love and gratitude it is dedicated to them both.

Richard Gibb
Edinburgh
August 2006

PART 1

The Methodology and Foundations

CHAPTER 1

The Strategy of this Study and Theological Scholarship

Our main tasks in this chapter are to state the central theological questions of the study, to explain the method of research employed, to outline the limitations of the study, to survey the theological scholarship from the turn of the twentieth century relevant to Christian involvement in the socio-political arena, and to identify the contributions and deficiencies of that scholarship. As such, this chapter will give the reader an idea of the main argument of this book and of its significance in relation to contemporary biblical and theological academic research - an argument that leads us to consider what it is to be the church in the context of a globalized world.

A Theology of Grace and the Mission of the Church in a Globalized World

Introduction to the Research Project

In referring to the phenomenon of globalization, we refer to the power transformations that have taken place and continue to take place in the contemporary world.[1] Indeed, the concept of globalization is now a defining feature of the twenty-first century. With the removal of barriers to free trade and the closer integration of national economies, this has had a significant impact on people's lives throughout the world. This global interconnectedness, which presents both opportunities and challenges, results in effects in one part of the world having increasing effects on peoples and societies in other parts of the world. Globalization is not simply an economic dynamic, but involves all facets of political and societal life. Integral to contemporary globalization are the forces of interdependence and integration that operate within states, yet have little or no respect for political boundaries. Therefore the far-reaching dynamics presented by the emergence of this new global political and economic system has shaped the whole discussion of the church's involvement in the contemporary issues of the twenty-first century world.

In defining political involvement, William Cavanaugh and Peter Scott state: "Politics may be understood for the purpose of a political theology in terms of the self-governance of communities and individuals."[2] Specifically, when we refer to the church's socio-political involvement, we are referring to members of the Christian

---

[1] This will be discussed in greater depth in chapter 6.

[2] William T. Cavanaugh and Peter Scott, "Introduction," in *The Blackwell Companion to Political Theology*, ed. Peter Scott and William T. Cavanaugh (Malden, MA: Blackwell Publishing, 2004), 1.

community engaging with contemporary issues. Consistent with this focus, our aim is to help identify how Christians can effectively relate their biblical faith to the realities of the contemporary world. George Forell points out the significance of such a concern at the start of his historical survey of Christian social teachings: "The most persistent and disturbing problem confronting the Christian community since its birth in Palestine two thousand years ago to the very present has been and continues to be its relationship to the surrounding world."[3] Yet within the more recent history of theological scholarship that has been undertaken in analyzing the socio-political involvement of the church, relatively few studies have been successful in integrating this theology in an informed manner with the challenges that are found in the surrounding world. Additionally, with the transforming impact of globalization in practically all spheres of life, not least in the role of nation-states, there has yet to be undertaken a comprehensive analysis in assessing what involvement Christians should have, if any, in seeking to shape the future direction of globalization.

There are two possible reasons for this lack of theological scholarship. The first is simply that the level of interconnectedness across the globe is unprecedented in world history. Only in comparatively recent years has globalization become of importance in the academic community and in the public sphere. The second is due to the complex nature of this contentious issue and the level of interdisciplinary engagement required in integrating a political theology with this multidimensional phenomenon. Globalization is indeed one of the most interdisciplinary of all subjects. Richard Bauckham remarks on this aspect of complexity as a possible reason why Christians have tended to disengage from political and social reality: "The adaptations needed to transfer biblical teaching on personal morality from its cultural situation to ours are comparatively easily made, but a more imaginative and creative hermeneutic is necessary for the Bible to speak to modern political life."[4]

In endeavoring to overcome some of these weaknesses in previous studies, our own way of analyzing a Christian response to globalization involves interdisciplinary engagement. This, we believe, is a promising way of developing an informed theology as to the holistic mission of the church in the context of a globalized world.

Some Studies Pertaining to the Church's Socio-Political Involvement

Despite the absence of studies devoted to assessing the implications of a world of transforming global power relations for the church's mission, some of the best treatments in assessing what the socio-political involvement of the church should be have contributed significantly to the task of developing an informed theology of Christian witness in this particular context. Three leading contemporary thinkers, who share common roots in what is broadly described as the Reformation tradition,

---

[3] George W. Forell (ed.), *Christian Social Teachings: A Reader in Christian Ethics from the Bible to the Present* (Minneapolis: Augsburg, 1971), ix.

[4] Richard J. Bauckham, *The Bible in Politics: How to Read the Bible Politically* (London: SPCK, 1989), 12.

but who are nevertheless interestingly different, have been particularly helpful.[5] All three scholars have been widely influential voices in the church.

First, Jürgen Moltmann, Professor of Systematic Theology at the University of Tübingen from 1967 to 1994, is one of the most important contemporary German theologians. Through his extensive works, and especially in his three major volumes, *Theology of Hope*, *The Crucified God*, and *The Church in the Power of the Spirit*, Moltmann has been highly influential in calling the church to rediscover its holistic mission of service to the contemporary world.[6] Reexamining theology from an eschatological perspective, he emphasizes that the church is tasked with being an agent of transformation in the world in anticipation of the eschatological kingdom of God. In undertaking this mission, the ethical teachings of Jesus Christ, whose priority was the kingdom of God, cannot be separated from Christian praxis. Arguing that the church exists for the sake of the kingdom, Moltmann urges the church to serve those who lack power and influence in the contemporary world.

Second, Stanley Hauerwas, Gilbert T. Rowe Professor of Theological Ethics at Duke University, presents an alternative perspective on the witness of the church. In being a severe critic of political liberalism, Hauerwas argues that the church is to be a distinct community in a secular world, which includes the rejection of the use of force in social and political action. The works of John Howard Yoder and Alasdair MacIntyre have been particularly significant in shaping Hauerwas' thought, and this is evident throughout his entire theological project. Maintaining the significance of narrative for Christian ethics in his prolific works, Hauerwas presents a sharp contrast to the individualistic rationalism of post-Enlightenment thought. Two of Hauerwas' most popular works that highlight these essential aspects of his theology are *The Peaceable Kingdom* and *Resident Aliens*.[7]

Third, Oliver O'Donovan, Chair of Christian Ethics and Practical Theology at the University of Edinburgh, has furthered theological academic debate concerning the socio-political mission of the church, particularly within the evangelical movement. His two main works in this field are *Resurrection and Moral Order* and *The Desire of the Nations*, in which he highlights political aspects of christology.[8] O'Donovan,

---

[5] It should also be noted that the Roman Catholic Church does appear to have developed a more effective stance on socio-political issues than that offered by the Protestant Church.

[6] Jürgen Moltmann, *Theology of Hope: On the Ground and the Implications of a Christian Eschatology* (London: SCM Press, 1967); *The Crucified God: The Cross of Christ as the Foundation and Criticism of Christian Theology* (London: SCM Press, 1974); and *The Church in the Power of the Spirit: A Contribution to Messianic Ecclesiology* (London: SCM Press, 1975).

[7] Stanley M. Hauerwas, *The Peaceable Kingdom: A Primer in Christian Ethics* (London: SCM Press, 1984); and Stanley M. Hauerwas and William H. Willimon, *Resident Aliens: A Provocative Christian Assessment of Culture and Ministry for People who Know that Something is Wrong* (Nashville: Abingdon Press, 1989).

[8] Oliver O'Donovan, *Resurrection and Moral Order: An Outline for Evangelical Ethics* (Leicester: InterVarsity, 1986); and *The Desire of the Nations: Rediscovering the Roots of Political Theology* (Cambridge: Cambridge University Press, 1996).

whose position has been inspired and developed from the theology of St. Augustine of Hippo, is emphatic that "theology must be political if it is to be evangelical." To rule out political questions from the church's involvement in the world is to "cut short the proclamation of God's saving power."[9] Therefore O'Donovan contends that to achieve a positive reconstruction of political thought, we must have a fuller and less selective reading of the Scriptures. Central to these political discussions are the questions of authority generated by Jesus' proclamation of the kingdom of God.

The Fundamental Theological Questions of this Study

In this book, we will seek to complement and develop studies relating to Christian involvement in the socio-political arena. Our specific focus will involve exploring the fundamental theological question: *what does it mean for the Christian community to conceive of itself as a community defined by the covenant of grace?* Indeed as we shall seek to demonstrate in subsequent chapters, how one perceives of the distinctiveness of the church depends upon how one understands the grace of God, and the inextricably related comprehension of the catholicity of its nature and mission in the world. In his analysis of the idea of grace in the history of Christian theology, Philip Watson states: "Christianity is pre-eminently a religion of grace...So much is this the case, that in any attempt to explain the meaning of grace, it is almost necessary to give an account, at least in outline, of the entire Christian faith."[10] Indeed it is a truism to state that an emphasis on the grace of God also lay at the heart of the Protestant Reformation.[11] Colin Gunton highlights succinctly this constitutive feature of Christian theology by declaring: "Theology is dependent upon grace for its very possibility."[12] Summing up the relationship of the triune God with creation, the doctrine of grace, Christoph Schwöbel explains, is "the nerve-centre" of Christianity:

> Christian doctrine, worship, and life are shaped in all their dimensions by the way in which grace is understood. Since the concept of grace determines our understanding of divine action and its relationship to human action it is a highly contentious concept.

---

[9] O'Donovan, *The Desire of the Nations*, 3.

[10] Philip S. Watson, *The Concept of Grace: Essays on the Way of Divine Love in Human Life* (London: Epworth, 1959), 5.

[11] See Robert D. Linder, "The Reformation," in *The New International Dictionary of the Christian Church*, ed. James D. Douglas and Earle E. Cairns, 2nd edn (Grand Rapids: Zondervan, 1978), 830-831; and R. Tudor Jones, "Reformation Theology," in *New Dictionary of Theology*, ed. Sinclair B. Ferguson, David F. Wright, and James I. Packer (Leicester: InterVarsity, 1988), 565-569.

[12] Colin E. Gunton, "Historical and Systematic Theology," in *The Cambridge Companion to Christian Doctrine*, ed. Colin E. Gunton (Cambridge: Cambridge University Press, 1997), 18.

The history of Christian doctrine and pastoral practice could well be written as a history on the interpretation of grace.[13]

In pointing out that the church is dependent on grace for its very being, Schwöbel emphatically declares: "The Church is *creatura verbi divini*: the creature of the divine Word. The Church is constituted by God's action and not by any human action."[14] What we are to learn from the ecclesiology of the Reformers, he asserts, "is the art of distinguishing and relating *opus Dei* and *opus hominum*."[15] In drawing attention to the ultimate task of Christian theology, John Webster likewise identifies the doctrine of grace as being a central feature: "Christian theology is rational speech about the Christian gospel."[16] Christian theology, conceived in this way, "takes its rise in an act done *to* the church rather than *by* the church." Describing the crucial nature of this task, which is directed to the person and work of Jesus Christ, and the order of reality declared in the gospel, he asserts: "It arises out of the devastatingly eloquent and gracious self-presence of God, by which it is endlessly astonished and to which it never ceases to turn in humility and hope."[17] As such, as Webster points out, "all Christian theology, whatever its tradition, is properly speaking evangelical in that it is determined by and responsible to the good news of Jesus Christ."[18]

Yet here we are presented with a dilemma: why is it that theology in the Reformation tradition, which is ostensibly driven by the doctrine of grace, has in its more recent history, contributed so ineffectively to socio-political debates? If it is the case that this doctrine is the driving force behind this theological tradition, then is this doctrine of grace deficient in addressing contemporary issues? Thus following from our exploration of our primary theological question, the associated question we will set out to express, which is concerned with specific practical considerations, is: *what are the implications of the church's distinctiveness for its socio-political mission in an age of globalization?* Accordingly, as this book sets out to explore a political theology in a distinctly ecclesial fashion, foremost in our analysis will be these three essential and interrelated facets of the life of the church: its global catholic nature; its grace-defined existence; and its vocation and mission in the contemporary world.

An intrinsic part of our study, therefore, will entail evaluating to what extent a theology of grace is evident in the theological projects of the three scholars

---

[13] Christoph Schwöbel, "Grace," in *The Oxford Companion to Christian Thought*, ed. Adrian Hastings, Alistair Mason, and Hugh Pyper (Oxford: Oxford University Press, 2000), 276.

[14] Christoph Schwöbel, "The Creature of the Word: Recovering the Ecclesiology of the Reformers," in *On Being the Church: Essays on the Christian Community*, ed. Colin E. Gunton and Daniel W. Hardy (Edinburgh: T&T Clark, 1989), 122.

[15] Ibid., 149.

[16] John Webster, *Word and Church: Essays in Christian Dogmatics* (Edinburgh: T&T Clark, 2001), 3.

[17] Ibid., 4.

[18] Ibid., 191.

mentioned above, and subsequently analyzing how this theology shapes our conception of (and directs our response to) globalization. In undertaking this investigation, although each scholar draws from the Reformation heritage, they are sufficiently diverse to exemplify the differences of approach in this tradition, as they each develop their political theologies from differing theological influences. Our intention in this book is to undertake critical dialogue with theologians representative of this tradition to contribute to the interdisciplinary debate in such a way as to encourage the most pressing needs of globalization to be approached from an informed theological perspective.

The Method of Investigation

Characteristic of our approach to theology will be the priority we place on biblical interpretation. It is the biblical writings, as Gunton notes, which "as the record of revelation, provide the source and criterion of Christian theology."[19] Such is the basic presupposition of our study and it is not part of our present purpose to argue it.[20] It is from this basis that we will seek to assess what the commitment of the church should be to the contemporary world.

We also recognize the importance of a theology, which is both descriptive and prescriptive in order to be faithful to its theological task of providing an enduring contribution to the self-understanding of God's people within the contemporary context. Carl Henry makes this point explicitly clear: "Evangelical theology is heretical if it is only creative and unworthy if it is only repetitious. That it can be freshly relevant for each new generation of persons and problems is a continuing asset."[21] In his discussion of Reformational theology, Gordon Spykman presents much the same claim in declaring: "No healthy theology ever arises *de novo*. By honouring sound tradition, theological continuity with the past is assured. At the same time tradition creates the possibility of opening new doors to the future."[22]

This requires theology to be practical and relate to living and not merely to belief. Thus as we seek to answer our theological questions, we will go further than setting forth a systematic reflection on the theological basis for the church's socio-political involvement. This is not our ultimate goal in theological practice. With construction must be added application, which recognizes that theological commitment is to be applied to life. Essential to this application, as Stanley Grenz notes, is the place of

---

[19] Gunton, "Historical and Systematic Theology," 6.

[20] For a robust defense of biblical authority, see "Authority and Scripture," in Richard J. Bauckham, *God and the Crisis of Freedom* (Louisville: Westminster John Knox Press, 2002), 50-77.

[21] Carl F.H. Henry, *God, Revelation, and Authority: The God Who Speaks and Shows*, vol. 1 (Waco, TX: Word, 1976), 9.

[22] Gordon J. Spykman, *Reformational Theology: A New Paradigm for Doing Dogmatics* (Grand Rapids, Eerdmans, 1992), 5.

ethics: "Theology must overflow into ethics."[23] In other words, Grenz declares: "Ethics is theology in action."[24] Gunton concurs and insists: "Christian theology is concerned with practice as well as theory...No systematic theology is complete unless ethics and ecclesiology are in some way integral to its articulation."[25]

In order to achieve this objective and due to the demands of our fundamental theological questions, this book is deliberately interdisciplinary. The study will involve assessing the specific implications a theology of grace brings, for how the church interprets its thoughts and policies in the context of a globalized world. Alister McGrath endorses this interdisciplinary requisite in theological scholarship: "Systematic theology does not operate in a water-tight compartment, isolated from other intellectual developments. It responds to developments in other disciplines."[26] In particular, behind the rapid social, political, and economic changes reshaping the contemporary world, as we will seek to demonstrate, globalization is to a large extent based on power and the transformation of power relations, which are transcending traditional national and geopolitical boundaries. As these changes have profound repercussions for nation-states, our focus will be to develop an understanding of the challenges for global justice found in this new global order, which will include a critical dialogue with leading international political theorists, such as Thomas Pogge and Onora O'Neill, due to their influence in contemporary socio-political debates.

Limitations to the Scope of Study

It is inevitable that a topic of such broad interest and scope as globalization has to be selective. Because power is an integral feature of globalization, our study will be concerned with focusing on the dynamics of transforming power relations and the associated implications for global justice and Christian involvement in the globalized socio-political arena. Therefore, while the issues indicated below are significant and may be mentioned in evaluating the phenomenon of globalization, the following limitations on the scope of this work should be noted:

1. Although we will assess the role of multinational corporations in our analysis of the forces driving globalization, this study is not concerned with arguments for and against economic efficiency that have arisen due to the global nature of business.

---

[23] Stanley J. Grenz, *Theology for the Community of God* (Grand Rapids: Eerdmans, 2000), 13.

[24] Stanley J. Grenz, *The Moral Quest: Foundations of Christian Ethics* (Downers Grove, Ill.: InterVarsity, 1997), 19.

[25] Gunton, "Historical and Systematic Theology," 12.

[26] Alister E. McGrath, *Christian Theology*, 2nd edn (Oxford: Blackwell, 1997), 147. Cf. Jonathan Chaplin, "Prospects for an 'Evangelical Political Philosophy,'" *Evangelical Review of Theology*, vol. 24/4 (October 2000), 354-373. As well as being grounded in a biblical-theological framework, Jonathan Chaplin argues evangelical political philosophy must also aspire to the formulation of a coherent and comprehensive conceptual apparatus addressed to the problems of political reality.

Nor will our focus be on the advances in technological innovation and the changes that have arisen across the globe through the use of the Internet.[27] Our concern in this study is with power transformations in the socio-political arena and the implications for global justice in the twenty-first century.

2. Within the socio-political arena itself, further limitation is necessary, due to the extent to which this phenomenon is leading to the transformation of virtually all aspects of human life. Thus, for example, no deliberate attempt has been made to analyze the impact of globalization on cultural regeneration and homogenization. Although claims of cultural uniformity are important issues, these concerns are not within the scope of our study.[28] Nor has there been an attempt to provide an analysis of the impact of globalization on the changing role of women in society.[29]

3. Due to living in an increasingly interconnected and interdependent world, this has brought risks of particular concern. These risks include the impact of globalization on the environment and claims of increased ecological degradation. Additionally, there have arisen increased security concerns, which were dramatically and tragically highlighted by the events on 11 September 2001. An analysis of these types of risks is not within the scope of our present work.[30]

To summarize, therefore, the primary aims of this book are to address the two key theological questions: *what does it mean for the Christian community to conceive of itself as a community defined by the covenant of grace* and *what are the implications of this distinctiveness for its socio-political mission in an age of globalization?* In exploring both questions, our study will investigate how the doctrine of grace, which is central to Reformational theology, directs the church's socio-political mission in the world.

---

[27] See the essay written by Viktor Mayer-Schönberger and Deborah Hurley, "Globalization of Communication," in *Governance in a Globalizing World*, ed. Joseph S. Nye and John D. Donahue (Washington D.C.: Brookings, 2000), 135-151.

[28] For research focusing on the impact of globalization on cultural identity, see Ted C. Lewellen, *The Anthropology of Globalization: Cultural Anthropology Enters the 21ˢᵗ Century* (Westport, Connecticut: Bergin and Garvey, 2002). Ted Lewellen describes how globalization has led to a cultural pluralism through opening new territory and challenging the bounded world of communities. Cf. Neal M. Rosendorf, "Social and Cultural Globalization," in *Governance in a Globalizing World*, 109-134.

[29] See two essays in *Global Tensions: Challenges and Opportunities in the World Economy*, ed. Lourdes Beneria and Savitri Bisnath (New York: Routledge, 2004): Nakila Kabeer, "Labour Standards, Women's Rights, Basic Needs: Challenges to Collective Action in a Globalizing World," 173-192; and Martha C. Nussbaum, "Promoting Women's Capabilities," 241-256.

[30] For an analysis of such risks, see Samuel P. Huntington, *The Clash of Civilizations and the Remaking of World Order* (London: Touchstone Books, 1998). Samuel Huntington examines the growing influence of civilizations, including Western, Eastern Orthodox, Latin American, Islamic, Japanese, Chinese, Hindu, and African, which he claims will comprise the battlegrounds of the future.

Survey of Theological Scholarship Pertaining to the Study

Introduction

The Christian church has been actively involved in addressing social and political issues throughout its long history. Oliver O'Donovan and Joan O'Donovan demonstrate this marked feature in their historical survey *From Irenaeus to Grotius: A Sourcebook in Christian Political Thought, 100-1625*.[31] This is also highlighted by Raymond Plant in his work *Politics, Theology and History*, in which he contributes to the ongoing debate about the relationship between liberalism and moral and religious pluralism. Drawing attention to the fact that key theologians throughout history have advocated an active political theology, Plant asserts that the Christian belief "has clear implications for the nature and organization of society and politics."[32]

Yet despite this historical emphasis on socio-political engagement, there remains disagreement amongst theologians as to the exact nature of the church's mission in the world. The extent of this polarization has widened due to the dynamic socio-political issues of our day. Some believe the church should be a radical voice in seeking to transform society. On the other hand, others believe the church should not get involved with the world's concerns. Philippe Maury comments on this dilemma, and claims that in its more recent history, due to this polarization, the church has become increasingly introverted.[33] The result of this lack of enthusiasm to be an informed contributor to critical socio-political debates is that the church has often lacked a credible voice in society. This has been particularly the case, asserts David Wright, within the evangelical movement. In engaging with the social, economic, and political realities of the world, "these are largely uncharted waters for evangelical mariners."[34] Agreeing with this analysis, Mark Greene states: "The primary reason Christianity has had little impact on the public sphere is not because the world has privatized the gospel, but because we have."[35] Significant challenges continue to confront the church, however, that have been highlighted by globalization.

---

[31] Oliver O'Donovan and Joan L. O'Donovan, *From Irenaeus to Grotius: A Sourcebook in Christian Political Thought, 100-1625* (Grand Rapids: Eerdmans, 1999).

[32] Raymond Plant, *Politics, Theology and History* (Cambridge: Cambridge University Press, 2001), xiii. See chapter 3 of this work for a survey of Augustine's, Calvin's, and Hegel's views about the nature of Christian political responsibility. For a further analysis of the history of political thought and the influence of religion, in particular the Protestant Reformation, see James H. Burns, *The Cambridge History of Political Thought 1450-1700* (Cambridge: Cambridge University Press, 1991), 159-218.

[33] Philippe Maury, *Evangelism and Politics* (London: Lutterworth, 1959), 7.

[34] David F. Wright (ed.), *Essays in Evangelical Social Ethics* (Exeter: Paternoster, 1978), 14.

[35] Mark Greene, "The Road to Irrelevance: The Great Divide," *Idea* (March 2003), 20.

Thus at the commencement of our study we will undertake a survey of Reformational theological scholarship, in its widest sense, pertaining to the study.[36] This will include engaging with scholars standing in the Anabaptist position, which was an integral feature of the Protestant Reformation in the sixteenth century. From the turn of the twentieth century in particular, there have been significant theological works published relating to the socio-political mission of the church. Because of these influential works, and also due to the events that have taken place since the turn of the twentieth century that have shaped how globalization has developed, this period will constitute the focus of our survey of theological scholarship.

Christian Pacifism and the Anabaptist Position

At one end of the theological debate is the position taken by scholars such as John Howard Yoder, one of the most influential Mennonite theologians of his time. In his seminal work *The Politics of Jesus*, Yoder restates the Anabaptist position that the Mennonites have traditionally held, calling the church to be separate from the world. Yoder's desire is to respond "to the ways in which mainstream Christian theology has set aside the pacifist implications of the New Testament message."[37] The core of his argument is that mainline ethicists have falsely assumed that Jesus Christ fails to present us with a normative social ethic.

In his study, focusing principally on the gospel of Luke, Yoder asserts that Jesus is "of direct significance for social ethics."[38] In reading the gospel narrative, the question he continually seeks to answer is: "Is there here a social ethic?"[39] What Yoder insists upon is that Jesus not only showed us a social ethic, but the early church accepted Jesus' ethic as normative. Jesus is therefore "not only relevant but also normative for a contemporary Christian social ethic."[40] In his life and teachings, Yoder declares, Jesus was the "bearer of a new possibility of human, social, and therefore political relationships. His baptism is the inauguration and his cross is the culmination of that new regime in which his disciples are called to share."[41] Thus Yoder argues that Jesus' deeds "show a coherent, conscious social-political character and direction, and that his words are inseparable therefrom."[42]

In locating ethics and theology in the person of Christ, Yoder highlights a key feature of the Reformation tradition. Significantly, however, the conclusions he draws from his analysis of the social ethics of Jesus is that Jesus believed in pacifism, which directs the church in rejecting any attempt to transform the world through social and political action where this involves the use of force. Rather,

---

[36] In subsequent sections of our study we will also engage with non-Reformational theology, in particular, the influence of liberation theology.

[37] John H. Yoder, *The Politics of Jesus* (Grand Rapids: Eerdmans, 1972), 5.

[38] Ibid., 23.

[39] Ibid., 22-23.

[40] Ibid., 23.

[41] Ibid., 62-63.

[42] Ibid., 115.

Yoder describes the impact on society "of the creation of an alternative social group," namely the church.[43] Refusing to accept this as a withdrawal from social issues, he states: "What can be called the 'otherness of the church' is an attitude rooted in her strength and not in her weakness."[44] For Yoder continues: "The primary social structure through which the gospel works to change other structures is that of the Christian community."[45] In holding such a position, he claims that it is "inappropriate and preposterous" to assume "that the fundamental responsibility of the church for society is to manage it."[46] Instead, we are called to follow a path of servanthood and subordination. Encapsulating this argument near the end of his work, Yoder states:

> The key to the obedience of God's people is not their effectiveness but their patience. The triumph of the right is assured not by the might that comes to the aid of the right, which is of course the justification of the use of violence and other kinds of power in every human conflict; the triumph of the right, although it is assured, is sure because of the power of the resurrection and not because of any calculation of causes and effects, nor because of the inherently greater strength of the good guys. The relationship between the obedience of God's people and the triumph of God's cause is not a relationship of cause and effect but one of cross and resurrection.[47]

Calvinism and Preserving God's Justice in Society

Offering a contrasting perspective from the Anabaptist position, scholars standing in the Calvinist tradition emphasize the need for Christians to seek to preserve God's justice in society, which means transforming all aspects of society through socio-political engagement. Commenting on the Reformed tradition derived from John Calvin, Robert Letham states: "Reformed theology has consistently sought to order the whole of life according to the requirements of God in Scripture."[48] At the turn of the twentieth century, Abraham Kuyper, a Dutch theologian and statesman, exemplifies this position.[49] Following a conversion during his first pastorate in Beesd, Kuyper began anew his study of theology, influenced by the work of Frederick Denison Maurice. Drawing inspiration from the Dutch Calvinist tradition,

---

[43] Ibid., 111.

[44] Ibid., 151.

[45] Ibid., 157.

[46] Ibid., 248.

[47] Ibid., 238.

[48] Robert W.A. Letham, "Reformed Theology," in *New Dictionary of Theology*, 570. Cf. Quentin Skinner, *The Foundations of Modern Political Thought, vol. 2: The Age of Reformation* (Cambridge: Cambridge University Press, 1978); and W. Fred Graham, *The Constructive Revolutionary: John Calvin & His Socio-Economic Impact* (Richmond: John Knox Press, 1971).

[49] For a critique of this Calvinist position, see Moltmann, *The Church in the Power of the Spirit*, 43-44.

this led to Kuyper actively engaging in church politics. In his inaugural address in 1880 at the founding of the Free University of Amsterdam, Kuyper's stance was unambiguously clear when he proclaimed: "There is not a square inch in the whole domain of our human existence over which Christ, who is sovereign over all, does not cry, 'Mine!'"[50] Subsequently, Kuyper led a secession movement from the state church to form the independent Reformed Church, and as leader of the Anti-Revolutionary Party, he served as Prime Minister of Netherlands from 1901 to 1905.

Kuyper is best remembered for the priority he attaches to the kingdom of God in Christian thinking, and his theological doctrine of common grace. Keenly aware of the dangers of totalitarianism, he espoused the value of liberty and despised the oppression of the weak. Hence as Irving Hexham states, "His [Kuyper's] social and political theory of sphere sovereignty is an attempt to give an intellectual justification to pluralism and create a structural means of limiting the power of the state."[51] Moreover, the function of the state was perceived as being that of preserving God's justice in society. This was reflected in the six lectures he delivered at Princeton University in 1898 under the auspices of the L.P. Stone Foundation. "The highest duty of the government remains," Kuyper declared, "unchangeably that of justice."[52]

In seeking to articulate how Christians should insert themselves into the modern social order, Calvinist scholar, Nicholas Wolterstorff, has produced two significant works of philosophical theology. These include *Until Justice and Peace Embrace*, which were his Kuyper Lectures for the Free University of Amsterdam, and *Religion in the Public Square*, in which he debates philosopher Robert Audi on the proper role of religious convictions within the political arena.[53] Championing the early Calvinist version of what he describes as "world-formative Christianity," which is where "the structure of the social world was held up to judgment, was pronounced guilty, and was sentenced to be reformed,"[54] Wolterstorff asserts that this form of Christian life is both biblically faithful and relevant to our modern world. Adherents of a world-formative Christianity attach significance to the kingdom of God, "when they wish to describe that ultimate state for which they work and hope."[55]

Close parallels are found between Wolterstorff's works and those of Richard Mouw. In *Politics and the Biblical Drama*, Mouw contends that to discuss theology is to raise political questions: "To submit to the lordship of Jesus Christ is to become

---

[50] Quoted in James D. Bratt (ed.), *Abraham Kuyper: A Centennial Reader* (Grand Rapids: Eerdmans, 1998), 488.

[51] Irving Hexham, "Kuyper, Abraham," in *Evangelical Dictionary of Theology*, ed. Walter A. Elwell, 2nd edn (Grand Rapids: Baker, 2001), 667.

[52] Abraham Kuyper, *Lectures on Calvinism* (Grand Rapids: Eerdmans, 1943), 93.

[53] Nicholas Wolterstorff, *Until Justice and Peace Embrace: The Kuyper Lectures for 1981 Delivered at The Free University of Amsterdam* (Grand Rapids: Eerdmans, 1983); and Robert Audi and Nicholas Wolterstorff, *Religion in the Public Square: The Place of Religious Convictions in Political Debate* (Lanham, Maryland: Rowman & Littlefield, 1997).

[54] Wolterstorff, *Until Justice and Peace Embrace*, 3.

[55] Ibid., 11.

committed to the political dimensions of his lordship."[56] Yet this commitment must be carried out with critical theological reflection. "Orthodoxy without orthopraxy may be dead," he proclaims, "but the latter without the former will quickly slip into mindlessness, a quality which at least matches dead orthodoxy as a corrupting influence among Christians."[57] Essential to Christian engagement with contemporary political and ethical thought and practice is the Bible. Mouw maintains: "The Bible is the locus and record of God's address to human beings in their 'wholeness,' including the entire network of relationships, institutions, and projects in which they participate. The biblical message, then, addresses our political lives."[58] Centering on Scripture will result in Christian theology being faithful to God's revelation of his will for his creation.[59] Indeed, it must be "the touchstone" for any political theology that might be developed.[60] From such a foundation we find a call to identify with the oppressed of society, which "is directly related to its mandate to promote a society characterized by justice."[61] Describing the "complex mission" of the people of God, Mouw asserts:

> Neither its internal life nor its external mission can be neglected. It cannot be a force for justice in the world unless it is also itself a community that has been shaped by the justice and mercy of God. But it cannot be the community God calls it to be unless it is also the agent of God's redemptive mission in the world.[62]

Duncan Forrester contributes to discussions of the church's socio-political mission and states that theology's role is to help people to identify the challenges of the contemporary world, "in the broad frame of God's purposes of love and justice, and his special care for the poor and the oppressed."[63] Forrester insists that a theology capable of addressing issues of public policy must of necessity be a church theology, which means "it is rooted not just in a community of scholars but in a believing fellowship."[64] Outlining how Christian theology may most appropriately contribute to debates about public policy, he claims the church must have a wider perspective than that of its own interests if it is "to show that it is other than one social institution among many, but the sign and foretaste of the kingdom of God."[65]

With his desire being that the Christian impacts society in an effective way, Forrester raises probing questions in *Christian Justice and Public Policy* concerning

---

[56] Richard J. Mouw, *Politics and the Biblical Drama* (Grand Rapids: Eerdmans, 1976), 7.

[57] Ibid., 8.

[58] Ibid., 11.

[59] Ibid., 13.

[60] Ibid., 15.

[61] Ibid., 77-78.

[62] Ibid., 81.

[63] Duncan B. Forrester, *Theology and Politics* (Oxford: Basil Blackwell, 1988), 171.

[64] Duncan B. Forrester, *Beliefs, Values and Policies: Conviction Politics in a Secular Age* (Oxford: Oxford University Press, 1989), 13-14.

[65] Ibid., 52.

the relationship of Christianity to political theory, law, and social policy. He seeks to achieve this goal through focusing on the central issue of justice.[66] Yet there is a lack of understanding about justice in the world resulting in a conception of justice that simply benefits a particular group's own interests.[67] It is a dilemma that has its roots in the individualistic rationalism, which is characteristic of post-Enlightenment social thought. Because of these varied understandings of justice, "attempting to frame and apply policies that are just become perplexing and systematically confusing operations."[68] Forrester points out that "what is unusual about the modern situation is the apparent breakdown of the belief in an objective grounding of justice."[69] This exposes the need to rectify the gulf that has opened up between theology and theories of justice.[70] We find that in the Bible, God is depicted as having a special care for the poor, who "stand as a test of the justice of any society."[71] Hence the church is to be "a community that affirms and expresses the equal worth of all human beings."[72]

It is thus evident that scholars standing in the Calvinist tradition present an understanding of ecclesial witness in the contemporary world, which stands in noticeable contrast to the Anabaptist position in its adherence to Christian pacifism.

The German Context and the Development of a Public Theology

A significant voice in advocating that theology must operate within the public realm is that of Karl Barth. The development of Barth's theological position for engaging with the challenges of the surrounding world was made all the more urgent in his leadership role against Nazism, and the attendant compromising of theology by the German Christians. Refusing to accept any system or ideology that was in conflict with the priorities of the kingdom of God, Barth's position is captured in *The Theological Declaration of Barmen*: "We reject the false teaching that the state has the right or the power to exceed its own particular remit and become the sole and total authority in human life thus fulfilling the task of the church as well."[73] In

---

[66] Duncan B. Forrester, *Christian Justice and Public Policy* (Cambridge: Cambridge University Press, 1997), 36.

[67] Ibid., 165.

[68] Ibid., 1.

[69] Ibid., 45.

[70] Ibid., 3.

[71] Ibid., 107.

[72] Duncan B. Forrester, *On Human Worth: A Christian Vindication of Equality* (London: SCM Press, 2001), 212.

[73] Karl Barth, *The Theological Declaration of Barmen*, 1934, para. 5. Quoted in Peter Matheson (ed.), *The Third Reich and the Christian Churches* (Edinburgh: T&T Clark, 1981), 47. The Barmen text was largely a personal Barth composition. This episode is detailed in Eberhard Busch, *Karl Barth: His Life from Letters and Autobiographical Texts*, trans. John Bowden (London: SCM Press, 1976), 235-248.

making this statement, Barth also repudiated Luther's doctrine of the two kingdoms.[74]

In three theological essays that address the issues of community, state and church, Barth stresses that the Christian community has a special task that the civil community can never relieve it of and which it can never pursue. This task, as displayed in his repudiation of Nazism, is to proclaim the rule of Jesus Christ and the hope of the kingdom of God.[75] Although the members of the church belong to the inner circle of the church, they also belong to the wider circle of the world. Thus, "Jesus Christ is still its centre: they, too, are therefore responsible for its stability."[76] In short, the church is to seek the glory of God in all aspects of his creation. With such a focus, Forrester notes that Barth's distinctive contribution is due to his thought coming to the public square as theology, and not simply and exclusively as ethics.[77]

Engaging with issues of social and political concern will result in the church concentrating first on the lowest levels of human society. In *Against the Stream*, Barth states: "He whom the Bible calls God is on the side of the poor. Therefore the Christian attitude to poverty can consist only of a corresponding allegiance."[78] Thus he claims: "The poor, the socially and economically weak and threatened, will always be the object of its primary and particular concern, and it will always insist on the State's special responsibility for these weaker members of society."[79] For the church is not an end in itself, but exists to serve God and thereby serves man.[80] Indeed, in *The Knowledge of God and the Service of God*, Barth refused to separate our knowledge of God from how we are to live if God is properly acknowledged. This is what it means for the church to be authentic: "The primary ground for the church service lies outside ourselves. It lies in the presence and the action of Jesus Christ. He wishes to rule in mercy and faithfulness." That is why, Barth contends, Christ creates and sustains the church.[81] Hence Christians are to be characterized by

---

[74] Luther's interpretation of government and Christian witness is outlined in Timothy F. Lull (ed.) *Martin Luther's Basic Theological Writings* (Minneapolis: Fortress, 1989), 655-703. For a further discussion of Luther's two kingdoms doctrine, see Helmut Thielicke, *Theological Ethics, 1. Foundations*, ed. William H. Lazarerth (London: Black, 1968), 359-382.

[75] Karl Barth, *Community, State, and Church* (Gloucester, Mass.: Peter Smith, 1968), 158. See also Karl Barth, "The Christian Community and the Civil Community," in *Against the Stream: Shorter Post-War Writings 1946-52*, ed. Ronald G. Smith, trans. E. M. Delacour and Stanley Godman (London: SCM Press, 1954), 13-50.

[76] Barth, *Community, State, and Church*, 159.

[77] Forrester, *Beliefs, Values and Policies*, 13.

[78] Karl Barth, "Poverty," in *Against the Stream*, 245.

[79] Barth, *Community, State, and Church*, 173.

[80] Ibid., 166.

[81] Karl Barth, *The Knowledge of God and the Service of God According to the Teaching of the Reformation: Recalling the Scottish Confession of 1560* (London: Hodder & Stoughton, 1938), 193-194.

servanthood: "In the political community, therefore, the church can only regard all ruling that is not primarily a form of service as a diseased and never as a normal condition." [82]

The extent of Barth's influence is evidenced not least in the life of the pastor and theologian Dietrich Bonhoeffer. Sparking responses in both conservative and liberal wings of Christianity, Bonhoeffer was acutely aware of the need to protect the powerless and engage with issues of social and political concern. Even though he was born to privilege, Bonhoeffer spoke of the incomparable value of learning to see the world with the "view from below," which is the perspective of the outcast of society. It was clear to Bonhoeffer that if love is to be responsible it must be manifested. As such he refused to accept the pacifist line. Writing of what he terms "the divine mandate," Bonhoeffer insists that this is "the conferment of divine authority on an earthly agent," which means, "there is established in the sphere of the mandate an unalterable relation of superiority and inferiority."[83] It is precisely this theocentric focus on the "divine commission" that directs the church in its social aspect.

Following his execution at the age of thirty-nine in a Nazi concentration camp, Bonhoeffer's *Letters and Papers from Prison* were first published. Integral to his thinking, Bonhoeffer asserts: "It is not the religious act that makes the Christian, but participation in the sufferings of God in the secular life."[84] In his own experience, this meant political involvement, and like Barth, the opposition to Nazism. For this reason, the life and works of Bonhoeffer have been a source of inspiration for those who suffer under oppressive political regimes, as was the case during the years of apartheid rule in South Africa. In post-apartheid South Africa his writings continue to influence both black and white leaders who seek to establish a just society.[85]

The influence of the German context in the development of a public theology is evidently significant. And foremost amongst these influences within the Christian community are the monumental works of Barth. We will therefore be returning to an analysis of his theology in chapter 2, in which we will seek to further outline the methodology and foundations that we will employ in this study.

Christian Realism and Socio-Political Engagement

The brothers Richard and Reinhold Niebuhr are two significant figures in the debates surrounding the socio-political mission of the church in the modern world.[86] They

---

[82] Barth, *Community, State, and Church*, 177.

[83] Dietrich Bonhoeffer, *Ethics*, ed. Eberhard Bethge, trans. Neville H. Smith (London: SCM Press, 1955), 254-255.

[84] Dietrich Bonhoeffer, *Letters and Papers from Prison*, ed. Eberhard Bethge, trans. Reginald Fuller (London: SCM Press, 1967), 198.

[85] Ruth Zerner, "Bonhoeffer, Dietrich," in *Evangelical Dictionary of Theology*, 181-182.

[86] There were also noticeable differences between these two brothers, as reflected in articles published in *Christian Century*, soon after Japan's invasion of Manchuria. See H. Richard Niebuhr, "The Grace of Doing Nothing," *Christian Century*, vol. 49 (March 1932),

were also the leaders of a new "Christian realism" that represented an American counterpart to European neo-orthodoxy.

In assessing Richard Niebuhr first, his most significant work *Christ and Culture*, Mark Noll states, "offered a classic schematization of the different ways in which believers over the centuries have interacted with their surrounding worlds."[87] In elaborating on what he describes as "the enduring problem," about the relationship between Christianity and civilization, Niebuhr argues that so many confident but diverse assertions about the Christian answer to the social problem are being made, that bewilderment and uncertainty beset many Christians.[88] Niebuhr argues that "the Christ and culture issue" has been with us since New Testament times and has continued right through until the present day.[89] In clarifying his analysis, Niebuhr defines the world of culture as, "the world so far as it is man-made and man-intended."[90] In seeking to make sense of these different voices, he identifies five categories for describing Christian approaches in political, economic and social affairs. These include "Christ against culture," "the Christ of culture," "Christ above culture," "Christ and culture in paradox," and "Christ the transformer of culture."

In providing a Christian philosophical critique of *Christ and Culture*, although Mouw identifies himself with those who long for the "transformation of culture," he points out the potential weaknesses of such an approach to questions of culture:

> We are complex people attempting to serve a complex Lord in a complex cultural environment. Because of these complexities, it is unlikely that any neat set of labels, such as the scheme set forth by Niebuhr, will accurately portray our actual views on cultural participation.[91]

Richard's brother, Reinhold Niebuhr served as a pastor in Detroit, which shaped his political thought as he encountered the harsh realities of industrial America. Fundamental to the development of solutions to the human crisis as he perceived it, Niebuhr advocated a new "Christian realism" for theology. It is an approach that begins with a pessimistic view of human nature standing in contrast to the confidence of a social gospel, Robin Lovin notes, which believed a new age of social Christianity was about to begin.[92] Lovin highlights an underlying component of this

---

378-380; and Reinhold Niebuhr, "Must We Do Nothing?" *Christian Century*, vol. 49 (March 1932), 415-417.

[87] Mark A. Noll, "Niebuhr, H. Richard," in *Evangelical Dictionary of Theology*, 841.

[88] H. Richard Niebuhr, *Christ and Culture* (London: Faber, 1952), 17. Niebuhr's desire is to build on Ernst Troeltsch's *The Social Teaching of the Christian Churches*.

[89] Ibid., 25-26.

[90] Ibid., 48.

[91] Richard J. Mouw, *When the Kings Come Marching In: Isaiah and the New Jerusalem* (Grand Rapids: Eerdmans, 2002), 3.

[92] Robin W. Lovin, *Reinhold Niebuhr and Christian Realism* (Cambridge: Cambridge University Press, 1995), 5. See also Forell, *Christian Social Teachings*, 361-379 for a critique of the social gospel, in which he notes that the Great Depression and World War II undermined its more utopian hopes.

approach: "Christian realism agrees with the broad and basic premise of natural law that the moral life is life lived in accordance with nature."[93] As an approach to the theory and practice of international relations, realism has indeed had an enormous influence in the modern world. And as Michael Smith points out, due to the range, depth and complexity of his thought, this makes Niebuhr the most profound thinker of the modern realist school.[94] Recognizing the impact of Niebuhr's thought, yet disagreeing markedly with his position, Hauerwas claims Niebuhr "began his long career as a social gospel advocate, became its most powerful critic, and was quite possibly the last publically accessible and influential theologian in America."[95]

Among Niebuhr's prolific writings, one of the most important was *Moral Man and Immoral Society*, which repudiated liberal optimism concerning humanity. Niebuhr's thesis is that whereas "individual men may be moral in the sense that they are able to consider interests other than their own in determining problems of conduct,"[96] we must recognize "the brutal character of the behavior of all human collectives, and the power of self-interest and collective egoism in all inter-group relations."[97] Social groups were selfish almost by their very definition, which has profound implications for how we approach the discipline of international relations.

Furthermore, in *Nature and Destiny of Man*, Niebuhr provided a discussion of what he called man's "most vexing problem: How shall he think of himself?"[98] Christianity, he taught, provided the best insights into reality in obtaining an account of the human condition, and for guiding action in the public realm. This led Niebuhr to famously warn against concentrating power in the hands of one person or a few people: "Man's capacity for justice makes democracy possible; but man's inclination to injustice makes democracy necessary."[99] Basic to the realist thesis is that due to the nature of human beings, the struggle for power is a permanent feature of social life, and is evident particularly in the relations between nation-states.[100] In the person

---

[93] Lovin, *Reinhold Niebuhr and Christian Realism*, 17. For a further discussion of natural law, see C.A. Hooker, "Laws, Natural," in *Routledge Encyclopedia of Philosophy*, vol. 5, ed. Edward Craig (London: Routledge, 1998), 470-475.

[94] Michael J. Smith, *Realist Thought from Weber to Kissinger* (Baton Rouge: Louisiana State University Press, 1986), 99.

[95] Stanley M. Hauerwas, "On Keeping Theological Ethics Theological," in *Revisions: Changing Perspectives in Moral Philosophy*, ed. Stanley M. Hauerwas and Alasdair MacIntyre (Notre Dame, Ind.: University of Notre Dame, 1983), 22. For a further critique of Niebuhr and Christian realism, see Stanley M. Hauerwas, *With the Grain of the Universe: The Church's Witness and Natural Theology: Being the Gifford Lectures Delivered at the University of St. Andrews in 2001* (Grand Rapids: Brazos Press, 2001), 87-140; and Stanley M. Hauerwas, *Wilderness Wanderings: Probing Twentieth-Century Theology and Philosophy* (London: SCM Press, 2001), 48-61.

[96] Reinhold Niebuhr, *Moral Man and Immoral Society* (New York: Scribner's, 1934), xi.

[97] Ibid., xx.

[98] Reinhold Niebuhr, *Nature and Destiny of Man*, vol. 1 (London: Nisbet, 1941), 1.

[99] Reinhold Niebuhr, *The Children of Light and the Children of Darkness* (London: Nisbet, 1945), vi.

[100] Smith, *Realist Thought from Weber to Kissinger*, 1.

of Christ, however, Niebuhr found a unique example of power used only for good. The cross of Christ was a core theme for Niebuhr since it revealed the paradox of powerlessness turned into power, of a love in justice that overcame the sinful world. Reflecting on this paradox, Niebuhr claimed: "The history of Christianity is the history of the truth of Christ contending constantly against the truth as men see it."[101]

Christian realism has indeed profoundly impacted debates vis-à-vis social and political issues, and not least in the area of international relations. Hence, this school of thought presents a further landmark in the ongoing debate as to what constitutes a theologically informed understanding of ecclesial witness in the contemporary world.

The Political Content of the Biblical Text

In recent years, several biblical scholars have produced significant works reexamining the biblical basis for the church's socio-political engagement. We will introduce two scholars in particular, first being the work of New Testament scholar Richard Bauckham. In *The Bible in Politics*, Bauckham emphasizes the political relevance of the Bible and provides insight in how to interpret the Bible politically. At the commencement of this work, he comments on the need for recovery of the temporarily mislaid social conscience of the church. In helping the church to recover an awareness of the political dimension of the Christian faith, Bauckham articulates the shape of a Christian political ethic, and describes the nature of this task:

> This is really a return to normality, since the notion that biblical Christianity has nothing to do with politics is little more than a modern Western Christian aberration, which would not have been entertained by the church in most periods and places of its history.[102]

Although there are differences between the Old Testament and the New Testament in their treatment of political matters, Bauckham claims: "The difference between the testaments might be better expressed in terms of a difference of political context." For whereas "much of the Old Testament is addressed to a people of God which was a political entity and for much of its history had at least some degree of political autonomy," he notes that "the New Testament is addressed to a politically powerless minority in the Roman Empire."[103] As such, the overtly political material in the New Testament largely concerns the responsibilities of citizens and subjects who had no ordinary means of political influence. Yet as Bauckham points out: "God and his purposes for human life remain the same in both testaments."[104]

Functions of government, Bauckham reminds us, are more extensive now than they were in biblical times, due to the sheer complexity of modern society. There is a

---

[101] Reinhold Niebuhr, *Nature and Destiny of Man*, vol. 2 (London: Nisbet, 1943), 49.
[102] Bauckham, *The Bible in Politics*, 1.
[103] Ibid., 3.
[104] Ibid., 6.

need therefore "to take a thoroughly historical attitude to this matter."[105] Because of these differences there is a danger of a simplistic application in relating the Bible to contemporary situations.[106] Two antidotes are provided to prevent this happening. The first is "careful study of the texts in their historical context, which will alert us to the real differences between that context and the modern one." Second, "the more we realize how biblical texts relate to the actual social structures and economic conditions of their time," Bauckham asserts, "the more we shall see the need to engage in serious analysis of our contemporary world if we are to specify the Bible's relevance to it."[107] Thus in discerning the Bible's meaning for today this cannot result automatically from the correct use of a set of hermeneutical principles. Rather, Bauckham notes:

> It requires in the interpreters qualities of insight, imagination, critical judgment, and expert knowledge of the contemporary world. It all requires the guidance of the Holy Spirit, who inspired not the mere text but the contextual meaning of the text, and therefore remains active at the interface between the text and its changing contexts.[108]

In *God and the Crisis of Freedom*, Bauckham argues convincingly for a vision of human freedom that is derived from being in relationship with the triune God of Christian faith. Importantly, in grasping an awareness of the different dimensions of freedom, Christians will be concerned to address society's multidimensional issues. For due to God being the creator, Lord, and savior of human life in all its dimensions, "to know God is to relate to God in all dimensions of life."[109] It is not simply that oppression occurs in many different dimensions of life, but most forms of oppression actually affect several dimensions and can be attacked by liberating activity in more than one dimension. This is exactly the challenge presented to the church by the multidimensional phenomenon of globalization. In this situation, the task for the biblical interpreter is to discern hermeneutical approaches to identify what would constitute an appropriate and relevant Christian perspective to their own context.[110]

The second biblical scholar we will introduce is Christopher Wright. In *Living as the People of God*, Wright reflects on the Old Testament text for developing an

---

[105] Ibid., 10.

[106] Cf. Richard B. Hays, *The Moral Vision of the New Testament: A Contemporary Introduction to New Testament Ethics* (New York: HarperCollins, 1996). As the biblical and modern worlds are so different, Richard Hays states, hermeneutical appropriation necessitates "an integrative act of the imagination": "Whenever we appeal to the authority of the New Testament, we are necessarily engaged in metaphor-making, placing our community's life imaginatively within the world articulated by the texts" (6).

[107] Bauckham, *The Bible in Politics*, 19.

[108] Ibid.

[109] Bauckham, *God and the Crisis of Freedom*, 22.

[110] Ibid., 75.

understanding of how to approach contemporary issues.[111] He states: "What we have to try to do is to put ourselves in Israel's position and understand how Israel perceived and experienced their relationship with God and how that experience affected their practical living as a community."[112] In developing our understanding of how to approach contemporary issues from a biblical perspective, Wright concurs with Bauckham and suggests that we are to appreciate the culturally specific situation of the biblical text, and then see it as a "paradigm" for our own time. Wright provides an explanation of this paradigm concept: "A paradigm is not so much imitated as applied. It is assumed that cases will differ but, when necessary adjustments have been made, they will conform to the observable pattern of the paradigm."[113] Thus it is Wright's aim to highlight the unique features of the Old Testament law. From these features insights can be derived as to how modern society can learn from the whole law of God. In doing so, Wright explains that the Bible provides models of God's desires in a particular historical and political situation, which provides guidance as to how we can implement God's purposes in the contemporary context.[114]

In his other major work, *God's People in God's Land*, Wright evaluates the economic structure of Israel's society concerning land, property, and dependent persons within the family. Assessing how Israel came to terms with socio-economic facts of life in the light of its distinctive historical traditions and theological self-understanding leads to the central claim of this work, which is that the interaction between Israel's life and faith is the foundation of biblical social ethics. This socio-economic dimension of the Old Testament provides insight in which to evaluate the nature of the mission of the church in the world in its social aspect, and is a reminder that the Bible in its entirety provides guidance for the mission of the church. Wright states: "Christianity has a social basis, which has transcended the land and kinship structure of Old Testament Israel – but not in such a way as to make that original structure irrelevant."[115] In conclusion, Wright challenges the reader to take the Old

---

[111] See also Christopher J.H. Wright, *Walking in the Ways of the Lord: The Ethical Authority of the Old Testament* (Leicester: Apollos, 1995). In this collection of essays, Wright claims that one of the biggest issues facing the church in the modern world is "how do we 'take account of the Bible' in working out our social ethics, in a way that is true to the nature and content of the Bible itself and also appropriate to the world we live in now" (13).

[112] Christopher J.H. Wright, *Living as the People of God: The Relevance of Old Testament Ethics* (Leicester: InterVarsity, 1983), 19.

[113] Ibid., 43.

[114] This is supported by Bauckham in *The Bible in Politics*, who declares in commenting on the Old Testament law and the prophets: "We cannot apply their teaching directly to ourselves, but from the way in which God expressed his character and purposes in the political life of Israel we may learn something of how they should be expressed in political life today" (6).

[115] Christopher J.H. Wright, *God's People in God's Land: Family, Land and Property in the Old Testament* (Carlisle: Paternoster, 1997), 114.

Testament text and compare it with their contemporary context and the issues they face, to determine what the Lord requires of them today.[116]

Accordingly, in drawing attention to the biblical basis for the involvement of the church in addressing critical public issues, Bauckham and Wright have demonstrated how both testaments provide guidance to the church in its approach to the challenges inherent in an increasingly interdependent twenty-first century world.

The Social Conscience of the Evangelical Churches

Examining the theological motivation for evangelical socio-political action, historian David Bebbington points out that in stressing the doctrine of the atonement as central to their worldview, the target of evangelical social campaigns "was consistently sin."[117] Yet the evangelical churches in their more recent history stand out as being reluctant in addressing contemporary issues. Describing recent images of evangelicalism as being "an escapist religious movement," John Wolffe declares:

> In some respects evangelicals themselves have relished that sense of apartness, feeling themselves chosen by the grace of God in the intensely personal and spiritual experience of conversion, and living under the authority of the Bible in a world self-evidently in thrall to very different standards and outlooks.[118]

In confronting this dilemma, John Stott, who is acknowledged as being one of the most influential evangelicals in modern times, has identified several reasons for the evangelicals' departure from socio-political action from around the 1920s. One of the primary reasons was the perception that the social gospel arose through the teachings of liberal theologians.[119] Christopher Sugden highlights a further objection raised that to be committed to social action leads to reductionism in christology, as it has a focus only on Jesus' example of a ministry of good works, and implies that humanity through its own efforts would bring in God's kingdom of justice and peace.[120] Timothy Smith, who described this major shift as "The Great Reversal,"

---

[116] Ibid., 265.

[117] David Bebbington, "Evangelicals, Theology and Social Transformation," in *Movement for Change: Evangelicals and Social Transformation*, ed. David Hilborn (Carlisle: Paternoster, 2004), 3-4.

[118] John Wolffe, "Introduction," in *Evangelical Faith and Public Zeal: Evangelicals and Society in Britain 1780-1980*, ed. John Wolffe (London: SPCK, 1995), 1. For a further historical analysis, see Boyd Hilton, *The Age of Atonement: The Influence of Evangelicalism on Social and Economic Thought, 1795-1865* (Oxford: Clarendon, 1988).

[119] John R.W. Stott, *Issues Facing Christians Today* (Basingstoke: Marshall, 1984), 6. Cf. David Bebbington, *Evangelicalism in Modern Britain* (London: Unwin Hyman, 1989), 214-217; and George Marsden, *Fundamentalism and American Culture* (New York: Oxford University Press, 1980), 85-93.

[120] Christopher M. Sugden, "Social Gospel," in *New Dictionary of Christian Ethics and Pastoral Theology*, ed. David J. Atkinson and David H. Field (Leicester: InterVarsity, 1995), 799.

has demonstrated, though, that the social gospel does not have its roots in religious skepticism, but rather in the Evangelical Revival. When the social gospel first appeared it was a serious evangelical effort to apply the compassion of Christ to the lives of men.[121] The result of this misconception, according to Sherwood Wirt, has been that "instead of religion serving the people, it so often turns out that the people are serving religion."[122] It is only in recent years that evangelicals have begun to return to the social concerns that had marked them until the eve of World War I.[123] Orlando Costas highlights the reasons for this movement in the 1970s toward a more holistic approach to mission and evangelism: "At the heart of this trend seemed to be a deep and sincere longing for the recovery of the wholeness of the gospel."[124]

In his works such as *The Uneasy Conscience of Modern Fundamentalism* and *Aspects of Christian Social Ethics*, Henry is of particular significance in calling the evangelical constituency to recognize its social responsibilities.[125] Such voices were strategic in leading evangelicals to adopting the *Wheaton Declaration* in 1966, which was one of the definitive steps that resulted in the Lausanne Movement.[126] The International Congress on World Evangelization held in July 1974 at Lausanne, Switzerland, saw 2,750 participants gathering from more than 150 nations, convened under the chairmanship of Billy Graham. It was to be a watershed for evangelicals, reflected in the endorsement of the *Lausanne Covenant*, which expressed a primary commitment to evangelism, and also significantly, a commitment to social justice in service in the world.[127] John Stackhouse describes the *Lausanne Covenant* as "perhaps the definitive statement of international evangelical commitment in the twentieth century."[128] Papers contributed by scholars such as René Padilla and Samuel Escobar were influential in stressing that God's concern for justice in society

---

[121] Timothy L. Smith, *Revivalism and Social Reform in Mid-Nineteenth Century America* (Nashville: Abingdon Press, 1957), 148-162.

[122] Sherwood E. Wirt, *The Social Conscience of the Evangelical* (New York: Harper, 1968), 26.

[123] See David Bebbington, "The Decline and Resurgence of Evangelical Social Concern 1918-1980," in *Evangelical Faith and Public Zeal*, 175-197.

[124] Orlando E. Costas, *Christ Outside the Gate: Mission Beyond Christendom* (Maryknoll, NY: Orbis, 1982), 162. Particular attention is given to mission in the Latin American context.

[125] Carl F.H. Henry, *The Uneasy Conscience of Modern Fundamentalism* (Grand Rapids: Eerdmans, 1947); and *Aspects of Christian Social Ethics* (Grand Rapids: Eerdmans, 1964).

[126] A. Scott Moreau, "Congress on the Church's Worldwide Mission," in *Evangelical Dictionary of World Missions*, ed. A. Scott Moreau (Grand Rapids: Baker, 2000), 222-223.

[127] Increasing political awareness in evangelical theology is reflected in works such as Ronald J. Sider, *Rich Christians in an Age of Hunger* (London: Hodder & Stoughton, 1990). Ronald Sider calls on Christians in the affluent North to live a simpler lifestyle, while giving to organizations that promote public policy and structural change for justice (194).

[128] John G. Stackhouse, "Evangelical Theology Should Be Evangelical," in *Evangelical Futures: A Conversation on Theological Method*, ed. John G. Stackhouse (Grand Rapids: Baker, 2000), 53.

extends to include all forms of oppression.[129] For example, Padilla insisted: "The New Testament knows nothing of a gospel that makes a divorce between soteriology and ethics, between communion with God and communion with one's neighbour."[130]

Speaking not only of social responsibility but also of "socio-political involvement" the *Lausanne Covenant* was pivotal in that political engagement looks beyond purely humanitarian work to the transformation of the structures in society itself. It is an engagement, as Vinay Samuel and Christopher Sugden indicate, that involves struggle: "Struggle arises out of Christian understanding of the world, which is in rebellion against God and is the arena of his activity, loved by him."[131] In seeking to overcome tensions that followed the Congress, the World Evangelical Fellowship and the Lausanne Committee for World Evangelization jointly sponsored a Consultation on the Relationship between Evangelism and Social Responsibility in June 1982. The result was the publication of *Evangelism and Social Responsibility*, which emphasized: "Social action not only follows evangelism as its consequence and aim, and precedes it as its bridge, but also accompanies it as its partner."[132]

Helping evangelicals to engage with the major issues of society is Stott's work *Issues Facing Christians Today*. Stott urges Christians to hold five key doctrines in their biblical fullness: the doctrines of God (creator, lawgiver, Lord and judge); of human beings (their unique worth due to being made in God's image); of Jesus Christ (who identified with us and calls us to identify with others); of salvation (a radical transformation); and of the church (distinct from the world as salt and light, yet penetrating it for Christ). These doctrines constitute the biblical basis for mission including both evangelistic and social responsibility.[133] At the heart of his argument, Stott exhorts evangelicals to catch a vision of a world that can be won for Christ by evangelism, and made more pleasing to Christ by social action. Accordingly, Stott calls upon Christians to be not only servants, but to be servant-leaders.[134] It is leadership not based on the authority of power but of love: "Leaders have power, but power is safe only in the hands of those who humble themselves to serve."[135]

---

[129] The Congress papers were published as *Let the Earth Hear His Voice*, ed. James D. Douglas (Minneapolis: World Wide Publications, 1975). See especially, Samuel Escobar, "Evangelization and Man's Search for Freedom, Justice and Fulfillment," and René Padilla, "Evangelism and the World."

[130] Padilla, "Evangelism and the World," 131.

[131] Vinay K. Samuel and Christopher M.N. Sugden, "Toward a Theology of Social Change," in *Evangelicals and Development*, ed. Ronald J. Sider (Exeter: Paternoster, 1981), 45.

[132] Consultation on the Relationship between Evangelism and Social Responsibility, *Evangelism and Social Responsibility: An Evangelical Commitment* (Grand Rapids: Reformed Bible College, 1982), 23.

[133] Stott, *Issues Facing Christians Today*, 15-26.

[134] Ibid., 327-340.

[135] Ibid., 335.

A Need for Further Study

As may be obvious from the above, the main reasons why there is a need for a study of this kind are primarily twofold. First, conflicting opinions remain within the church and the academy as to the church's involvement in addressing issues of social and political concern. Although "the Christian religion," states Charles Dodd, "is an ethical religion in the specific sense that it recognizes no ultimate separation between the service of God and social behaviour," there is a tension, "which appears always to be latent between religion and ethics."[136] Daniel Bell highlights this situation:

> In recent decades, the claim that the Christian faith is about justice and liberation has achieved the status of a veritable truism. And this is as it should be, for the Word rightly proclaimed is a word of justice and liberation. Yet how Christians are to respond to that Word, what doing justice and liberating the oppressed entails, is not self-evident. Rather, it is a matter of discernment.[137]

Furthermore, what is lacking in theological research is an investigation as to how an understanding of a theology of grace shapes the political theologies of leading contemporary thinkers standing in the Reformation tradition who hold differing positions as to the church's socio-political witness. Such a dialogue developed from the concepts and categories inherent in a biblical theology of grace, exposing how each theologian's position is rooted in their differing presuppositions, will provide additional insight into making sense of the various voices in Reformation theology.

Second, there is a need for further study due to the fact that there has not been undertaken as yet, in any adequate way, a theological investigation as to how a Christian is to insert him or herself in the globalized socio-political arena. William Storrar highlights this need in public theology for addressing the new world of globalization. In drawing attention to the term "glocalization," which is where the local and the global meet, Storrar declares: "Recognizing the *glocal* character of globalization has profound implications for rethinking the relationship between theology and public issues in the twenty-first century."[138] In addressing the public influence of religion, particularly in an age of globalization, Peter Beyer likewise raises a central theological question that has yet to be fully addressed in contemporary academic scholarship: "What are the abstract possibilities in today's

---

[136] Charles H. Dodd, *Gospel and Law: The Relation of Faith and Ethics in Early Christianity* (Cambridge: University Press, 1951), 3. For a further discussion of the role of religion in politics, see Jeff Haynes, *Religion in Global Politics* (Harlow: Longman, 1998); José Casanova, *Public Religions in the Modern World* (Chicago: University of Chicago Press, 1994); and Steve Bruce, *Politics and Religion* (Cambridge: Polity Press, 2003).

[137] Daniel M. Bell, "Deliberating: Justice and Liberation," in *The Blackwell Companion to Christian Ethics*, ed. Stanley Hauerwas and Samuel Wells (Malden, MA: Blackwell, 2004), 182.

[138] William F. Storrar, "Where the Local and the Global Meet," in *Public Theology for the 21st Century: Essays in Honour of Duncan B. Forrester*, ed. William F. Storrar and Andrew R. Morton (London: T&T Clark, 2004), 407.

world for religion...to be a determinative force in social structures and processes beyond the restricted sphere of voluntary and individual belief and practice?"[139]

There is, however, evidence of this contemporary issue being the focus of increasing research as demonstrated by the theological works produced by scholars such as Max Stackhouse and Peter Paris,[140] and Bob Goudzwaard.[141] Scholars that have begun to address this phenomenon from an ethical perspective include John Dunning,[142] David Hollenbach,[143] Timothy Gorringe,[144] and Peter Sedgwick.[145] A further contribution is David Smith's work *Against the Stream*, which focuses on the impact of globalization for the mission of the church, particularly in light of the global spread of Christianity and the growth of the church in the southern hemisphere.[146]

While these works have contributed in developing a greater understanding of globalization and exposed some of the attendant challenges facing the church, there still remains a dearth of scholarly literature specifically in relation to the articulation of a Christian vision of global justice in this contemporary context. For although there is a growing awareness in the church that Christians must be at the forefront of seeking to transform society, answers in determining what a Christian response should be to some of the world's pressing needs are still required.[147] Alan Storkey notes that for the evangelical movement in particular, due to the years of neglect, this

---

[139] Peter Beyer, *Religion and Globalization* (London: SAGE, 1994), 12.

[140] Max L. Stackhouse and Peter Paris (ed.), *God and Globalization*, 3 vols. (Harrisburg, Pa.: Trinity Press International, 2000-2002); Max L. Stackhouse, "Public Theology and Civil Society in a Globalizing Era," *Bangalore Theological Forum*, vol. 32/1 (June 2000), 46-72; and "Public Theology and Political Economy in a Globalizing Era," in *Public Theology for the 21st Century*, 179-194.

[141] Bob Goudzwaard, *Globalization and the Kingdom of God* (Washington D.C.: Baker, 2001).

[142] John H. Dunning (ed.), *Making Globalization Good: The Moral Challenges of Global Capitalism* (Oxford: Oxford University Press, 2003).

[143] David Hollenbach, S.J., *The Common Good and Christian Ethics* (Cambridge: Cambridge University Press, 2002), 212-244.

[144] Timothy J. Gorringe, "Invoking: Globalization and Power," in *The Blackwell Companion to Christian Ethics*, 346-359.

[145] Peter Sedgwick, "Globalization," in *The Blackwell Companion to Political Theology*, 486-500.

[146] David W. Smith, *Against the Stream: Christianity and Mission in an Age of Globalization* (Leicester: InterVarsity, 2003).

[147] This was evident in the Evangelical Alliance, *Uniting for Change: An Evangelical Vision for Transforming Society* (London: Evangelical Alliance, 2002). The forces associated with globalization were identified as being "probably the most controversial change of all." The question is asked for which an answer cannot yet be given: "What is a proper Christian response to this kind of change?" (3).

"is a vision and tradition that needs to mature and grow in coherence."[148] It is a need that must be met through interdisciplinary engagement. For only in an interdisciplinary approach can theologians make an informed contribution to the debates as to how we address the global social and political challenges of the twenty-first century.

Concluding Remarks

The primary objective in this study is to relate theological critique and analysis to some of the most pressing challenges of the contemporary world. Our theological survey that we have carried out in this chapter has sought to provide the background and context that will help us to assess the specific challenges globalization brings for how the church interprets its thoughts and policies in response to this phenomenon. Globalization is indeed rapidly leading to a distinctly different world order. The interconnected nature of this internationalized world system transcends traditional concepts of international relations, and has impacted upon all spheres of human life. The challenge brought to the church is in articulating a coherent and informed theology as to a Christian vision of global justice in this historical and cultural context. Consequently, globalization warrants theological analysis and brings to the fore the perennial question vis-à-vis the mission of the church in the socio-political arena. In analyzing issues of social and political concern in light of the biblical text, the purpose of this book is to contribute in meeting this need in contemporary theological scholarship.

---

[148] Alan Storkey, "The Bible's Politics," in *Witness to the World: Papers from the Second Oak Hill College Annual School of Theology*, ed. David Peterson (Carlisle: Paternoster, 1999), 78.

CHAPTER 2

The Church as a Grace-Defined Community

Religious communities are widely defined by a complex of moral, social, political, ethical, cultic/ liturgical, philosophical, and other convictions. Common to the Christian community stemming from the Reformation tradition would be a concern to see itself as governed by the theology of grace. The concern of this chapter is to consider what this might mean and how this might look. Our particular focus will be to consider the implications of this doctrine for the socio-political involvement of the church in the world. It is not our goal, however, to develop a theological political theory at this stage. Our aim is to articulate the key theological concepts and categories pertinent for critical dialogue with the positions of Jürgen Moltmann, Stanley Hauerwas, and Oliver O'Donovan in subsequent chapters of this study. In chapter 7, we will apply these theological insights in our evaluation of the mission of the community of grace in the context of a globalized socio-political arena.

Introduction

The need for responsible theological engagement has been demonstrated by the increasing pluralism in contemporary society. In particular, there is a requirement in theological scholarship to examine the theological grounds for the socio-political engagement of the church with contemporary issues. Alan Torrance elaborates on this dilemma: "Too often political theology, even when advocated in the name of the church, has been theologically superficial. Though it may reflect admirable sentiments and concerns, it can lack theological consistency and coherence and thus theological warrant."[1] What we will seek to do, therefore, in this chapter, is give serious theological consideration as to how we can determine God's will for his world, and to assess the associated implications for the mission of the church.[2]

---

[1] Alan J. Torrance, "Introductory Essay," in Eberhard Jüngel, *Christ, Justice and Peace: Toward a Theology of the State*, trans. D. Bruce Hamill and Alan J. Torrance (Edinburgh: T&T Clark, 1992), ix.

[2] For a further discussion of the primary theological questions facing the Christian, see Joseph H. Oldham, "The Function of the Church in Society," in *The Church and its Function in Society*, ed. Willem A. Visser't Hooft and Joseph H. Oldham (London: George Allen & Unwin, 1937), 242.

In articulating our theological method,[3] we will formulate and defend a primary interpretive motif in our approach to the task of systematic theology. It is an approach that enables the demonstration of unity and coherence, which Colin Gunton points out is core to Christian theology: "Being systematic in theology involves, first, responsibility for the overall consistency of what one says."[4] Commenting on the integrative motif of *community* around which his whole discussion revolves, Stanley Grenz asserts: "This concept serves as a systematic theology's central organizational feature, the theme around which it is structured."[5] Specifically, the central motif around which our theological analysis will be developed in this study is *the grace of God*, which is indeed central to the Reformation tradition. We find that in the New Testament, grace is inextricably linked with each person of the Trinity: the Father (1 Peter 5:10); Son (Acts 15:11); and Holy Spirit (Hebrews 10:29).

In considering this theological motif we can offer an approximate working definition of the grace of God as: *the out-flowing of the eternal triune love of God in and through his free, reconciling self-disclosure and self gift to his creatures, supremely demonstrated in the incarnation of Jesus Christ and through the presence of the Holy Spirit, bringing them into communion both with himself and with each other, such that they are given to share in his mission to the world.*[6]

Yet although the doctrine of grace defines the Christian gospel, confused assumptions that have become prevalent within our Western culture have undermined the message of this doctrine and our perception of its significance. When we come to consider this central Christian doctrine we find there are two key identifiable challenges in particular for grasping the implications of God's grace for the socio-political mission of the church in the contemporary world.

First, is the challenge presented by the influence of the Renaissance and the Enlightenment. For one of the inclinations in the Enlightenment era is its desire to

---

[3] See Stackhouse (ed.), *Evangelical Futures* for a discussion of methodology in a postmodern context.

[4] Gunton, "Historical and Systematic Theology," 12. Cf. Robert W. Jenson, "The Church and the Sacraments," in *The Cambridge Companion to Christian Doctrine*, 207. Robert Jenson states: "All loci of theology are interconnected as nodes of an intricate web."

[5] Grenz, *Theology for the Community of God*, 20. Thus Grenz takes the concept of a theological motif a step further and argues for a single motif method. This is supported in Millard Erickson, *Christian Theology*, 2nd edn (Grand Rapids: Baker, 2001), 80-82. For a contrasting perspective, see Conrad Cherry, *The Theology of Jonathan Edwards: A Reappraisal* (Bloomington: Indiana University Press, 1990), 7. In commenting on the theology of Jonathan Edwards, he states: "In a theologian of Edwards' stature...there are a number of fundamental and distinctive motifs operative, and his outlook cannot be reduced to any one of them." Quoted in Stephen R. Holmes, *God of Grace and God of Glory: An Account of the Theology of Jonathan Edwards* (Edinburgh: T&T Clark, 2000), 243-244.

[6] The grace of God provides a more integral motif than that of community as it encapsulates both this relational dimension of God's reign, yet also significantly, the means by which we can know God and his will for his all-encompassing reign in the world.

place humanity at the centre and not God. Gunton calls our attention to this tendency:

> Enlightenment is essentially an eschatological concept, referring to the state of those who have achieved complete vision. To arrogate to a person or era the claim of being enlightened is to assert that the present era is, or contains the seeds of, a perfect knowledge and understanding...To put it crudely, to claim for ourselves enlightenment is to claim to be 'like God.'[7]

Second, is the subtle and yet profound misunderstanding of the nature of the covenant relationship established by God. Significantly, as James Torrance points out, the Reformers recognized that it was from an understanding of the covenant of grace that the church was informed and motivated to engage with issues of social and political concern.[8] Both of these challenges in theological scholarship must be confronted if we are to derive a theologically coherent and valid methodological approach for assessing how the church is to respond to the social and political concerns presented in the context of an increasingly interdependent world.

As we explore in this chapter the implications of the grace of God for the mission of the church, what we will seek to demonstrate is that a biblically grounded theological method, which recognizes this central Christian doctrine, is foundational if there is to be theologically responsible and integrative engagement with contemporary socio-political issues. Furthermore, in articulating our theological method, we will give particular attention to the considerably influential works of the twentieth century Reformed theologian Karl Barth, in which he placed an unprecedented emphasis on divine grace.[9] No single figure in modern time has more effectively articulated the theological basis for the socio-political mission of the Christian community.

---

[7] Colin E. Gunton, *Enlightenment and Alienation: An Essay towards a Trinitarian Theology* (Basingstoke, Hants: Marshall, Morgan and Scott, 1985), 150.

[8] James B. Torrance, "The Covenant Concept in Scottish Theology and Politics and its Legacy," in *Scottish Journal of Theology*, vol. 34/3 (June 1981), 225-243.

[9] For a discussion of this controlling motif in Barth's work, see Herbert Hartwell, *The Theology of Karl Barth: An Introduction* (London: Duckworth, 1964), 167-177. Herbert Hartwell declares: "The grace of God is the light in which we have to understand Barth's theology as a whole as well as every individual part of it, and for that reason must be regarded as the key to the true understanding of his theology." For an example of his stress on grace, see Karl Barth, *Church Dogmatics*, vol. 2/1, ed. Geoffrey W. Bromiley and Thomas F. Torrance, trans. Geoffrey W. Bromiley (Edinburgh, T&T Clark, 1956-1975), 351-368. Barth states at the outset of this chapter on 'the perfections of the divine being': "The divinity of the love of God consists and confirms itself in the fact that in himself and in all his works God is gracious, merciful and patient, and at the same time holy, righteous and wise" (351). Cf. Karl Barth, "Gospel and Law," in *God, Grace and Gospel: Scottish Journal of Theology Occasional Papers*, No. 8, trans. James S. McNab (Edinburgh: Oliver & Boyd, 1959), 3-27. How Reformed theologians and confessional writings of this period, particularly John Calvin, shaped Barth's theology, is outlined in Webster, *Word and Church*, 91-98.

Characteristic of Barth's approach is the priority he places on biblical interpretation. Francis Watson highlights this ubiquitous feature of his work: "From beginning to end, Barth's *Church Dogmatics* is nothing other than a sustained meditation on the texts of Holy Scripture."[10] This will also be characteristic of our approach to theology. Our aim will be to develop what Millard Erickson describes as a "systematic biblical theology." It is a theology, which "draws on the product of the biblical theologian's work."[11] And as the development of theological concepts and the exegesis of Scripture complement each other, we will return to scriptural exegesis throughout this book. This will enable the development of a systematic theology that strives to incorporate the diversity of biblical writings within the unity of its theology.

Grace as the Context of Knowledge of God

The Anthropocentric Culture of the West

The first challenge to be overcome in assessing the implications of the doctrine of grace for the socio-political involvement of the church is the worldview dominating throughout modernity.[12] To begin with God as the creator and ultimate reference point is to stand in diametrical opposition to this anthropologically centred understanding of reality. At its root, the difference between the modern and Reformational positions derives from the divergent methodological approaches employed. Modernity starts with the self; Reformation theology starts with God. Exemplifying this contrast in approach is the fifteenth century Florentine philosopher Pico della Mirandola, who imagined God addressing the newly created Adam:

> The nature of other creatures, which has been determined, is confined within the bounds prescribed by us. You, who are confined by no limits, shall determine for yourself your own nature, in accordance with your own free will, in whose hands I have placed you.[13]

This vision of humans as sovereign subjects, Richard Bauckham points out, is a freedom conceived "as radical independence." In short, it is the vision of human beings aspiring to be their own creators.[14]

---

[10] Francis Watson, "The Bible," in *The Cambridge Companion to Karl Barth*, ed. John Webster (Cambridge: Cambridge University Press, 2000), 57.

[11] Erickson, *Christian Theology*, 26.

[12] In seeking to spell out the content of a biblical worldview, Albert Wolters defines a worldview as "the comprehensive framework of one's basic beliefs about things" (2). The Reformational worldview, he claims is based on the three categories of creation, fall, and redemption. See Albert M. Wolters, *Creation Regained: Biblical Basics for a Reformational Worldview* (Grand Rapids: Eerdmans, 1985).

[13] Quoted in Delwin Brown, *To Set at Liberty: Christian Faith and Human Freedom* (Maryknoll, NY: Orbis, 1981), 16.

[14] Bauckham, *God and the Crisis of Freedom*, 32.

A profound influence in the development of the modern worldview is of course René Descartes, often called the father of modern philosophy.[15] With the foundation of his philosophy being the identity of the self with thought, as Grenz enunciates, "Descartes shifted the focus of rationality to the inner self of the autonomous individual."[16] Helmut Thielicke reacts against such an approach and declares that Cartesian theology "inevitably focuses on the difference in form between the pre-modern or mythical proclamation of the Bible and the type of proclamation demanded by modern science and self-awareness."[17] Thus by placing the identity of the self at the very heart of existence and analyzing God and everything else from this supreme centre, Descartes succeeded in creating a momentous gulf from how truth about God and truth about all other reality was traditionally perceived.

Building on this shift in the understanding of reality, an increasing number of scholars have insisted on making self-transcendence the very basis of their worldview. In a more recent work, Karl Rahner is one example of a theologian who has employed this methodological approach in seeking to reconcile a theological framework with anthropocentricism.[18] Fundamental to his project was the desire to offer an account of the Christian faith that would appeal to the modern mind.[19] Accordingly, Rahner's vision of the whole of theology opens with the human person, rather than beginning with God or Scripture.[20] With this anthropocentric basis, every act of knowledge is predicated on an implicit knowledge of being, disclosed in the process of questioning, particularly as the questioner asks for the ground of his own existence. In declaring that all our knowing can be rooted in sensation, Rahner follows Immanuel Kant's transcendental approach and advocates a priori conditions of subjectivity for knowing. Along with this interpretation of Kant, Rahner sought to demonstrate that Thomas Aquinas' epistemology and description of human freedom requires that the subject possess an openness to a universal horizon of being, which is essentially an openness to God.[21] Due to this "pure openness for absolutely everything," universal being and hence the being of God himself stands behind all

---

[15] For a review of Descartes' position, see Daniel Garber, "Descartes, René," in *Routledge Encyclopedia of Philosophy*, vol. 3, 1-19.

[16] Stanley J. Grenz, *The Social God and the Relational Self: A Trinitarian Theology of the Imago Dei* (London: Westminster John Knox Press, 2001), 70.

[17] Helmut Thielicke, *The Evangelical Faith*, vol. 1, trans. Geoffrey W. Bromiley (Edinburgh: T&T Clark, 1978), 107.

[18] Karl-Heinz Weger, *Karl Rahner: An Introduction to His Theology*, trans. David Smith (London: Burns & Oates, 1980), 18-22.

[19] Herbert Vorgrimler, *Karl Rahner: His Life, Thought and Works*, trans. Edward Quinn (London: Burns & Oates, 1965), 52.

[20] Anne E. Carr, "Starting with the Human," in *A World of Grace: An Introduction to the Themes and Foundations of Karl Rahner's Theology*, ed. Leo J. O'Donovan (New York: Seabury Press, 1980), 17.

[21] Jack A. Bonsor, "Rahner, Karl," in *Routledge Encyclopedia of Philosophy*, vol. 8, 35-39.

human knowledge. This underlies Rahner's notion of the *Vorgriff*.[22] The effect of this openness is that in essence, the human person is, by the nature of their intellect, disposed to the knowledge of God.

Consequently, an inherent weakness deriving from the Enlightenment worldview was the tendency of establishing a priori prolegomena to theological perception. Indeed it was Rahner's desire to go behind the church in endorsing presuppositions of God, which led to a break from the biblical portrayal of the self-manifestation of God. The inevitable result, however, in seeking to come to an understanding of God through our own self-awareness, is that God simply becomes a subjective condition of our own understanding. As his doctrine means that we get in touch with God internally, it also begs the question how human finitude can grasp an infinite creator God. Thus, in summary, due to his a priori determinations of the human ability to know God and transcend the self, Rahner represents a theology that tends to undermine the significance of the gospel of grace for the knowledge of God.

Modernity and its Influence on Socio-Political Engagement

In claiming that the Christian cannot be neutral in the socio-political sphere, Eberhard Jüngel describes this as "the political existence of the Christian."[23] Yet characteristic of much recent scholarship is that theologians who engage with issues of social and political concern have often displayed the anthropocentric influences of modernity in drawing their theological conclusions.[24] The effect of this shift from a theocentric worldview is that the assertions of the gospel are not identified as being the foundation for engaging with contemporary issues. This was evident in a dramatic fashion in the social context from which *The Theological Declaration of Barmen* emerged in Germany in 1934. Embracing the ideology of German National Socialism led to the German state church, as Bruce Demarest notes, adhering to a religion "founded not on the Word of God but on the divine will allegedly embedded in the natural order."[25] Reflecting on this period in world history, Jüngel points out "how very much the Christian church depends on solid theology and of how little value there is in a theology, which evades its concrete responsibility to the church."[26]

---

[22] Karl Rahner, *Foundations of Christian Faith: An Introduction to the Idea of Christianity*, trans. William V. Dych (London: Darton, Longman & Todd, 1984), 20.

[23] Jüngel, *Christ, Justice and Peace*, 3, 54.

[24] Alan J. Torrance, *Persons in Communion: An Essay on Trinitarian Description and Human Participation* (Edinburgh: T&T Clark, 1996), 203. Torrance assesses this anthropocentric theological method and claims, "the desire for an anthropocentric *Umkehrung* is the most fundamental temptation with which Western theology has had to struggle and with which it must still continue to wrestle."

[25] Bruce A. Demarest, *General Revelation: Historical Views and Contemporary Issues* (Grand Rapids: Zondervan, 1982), 15. Demarest records how the primacy of conscience and the flow of history were seen as the chief modalities of revelation that provided theoretical justification for the Nazi ideology.

[26] Jüngel, *Christ, Justice and Peace*, 5.

Two widespread tendencies in theological scholarship that highlight the influence of modernity for socio-political engagement have been exposed by Torrance. One is the "fundamentalism of culture," which is "where the demands of a culture, defined in terms of its own prior self-understanding, are accepted uncritically as defining theological conclusions." The other is "cultural foundationalism," where it is believed "that culture defines the necessary form of theological questioning, even though those who advocate this may wish to deny (problematically) that they are conditioning in advance the actual content of their conclusions."[27]

Perhaps traces of modernity's influence can be similarly found in liberation theology. The distinguishing hermeneutical key emerging out of the Latin American context is summarized by Hugo Assmann, who is one of the first to talk about the epistemological privilege of the poor.[28] Liberation theology, which has made noteworthy achievements in bringing to the fore the plight of the oppressed, has been defined by Phillip Berryman as "an attempt to read the Bible and key Christian doctrines with the eyes of the poor."[29] For all practical purposes, it equates loving one's neighbour with loving God, which results in God and our neighbour becoming virtually indistinguishable, as emphasized by Gustavo Gutiérrez: "The encounter with God takes place in the encounter with our neighbour; it is in the encounters with human beings that I encounter God."[30] Moreover, this encounter occurs "with those whose human features have been disfigured by oppression, despoliation, and alienation."[31] Gerald West notes this key distinction from Reformation theology: "It is not just that liberation theologies have a different content, they are more profoundly different in that they have a different methodology."[32] In particular, as liberation theology asserts that the revelation of God is to be found in the matrix of human interaction with history,[33] from the perspective of classical Reformational theology, some of the concerns of liberation theology would perhaps be overcome by a fuller recognition of the significance of divine grace for knowing God and his will.

---

[27] Alan J. Torrance, "Introduction," in *Christ and Context: The Confrontation between Gospel and Culture*, ed. Hilary Regan and Alan J. Torrance (Edinburgh: T&T Clark, 1992), 2.

[28] Hugo Assmann, *Theology for a Nomad Church*, trans. Paul Burns (Maryknoll, NY: Orbis, 1976).

[29] Phillip Berryman, *Liberation Theology: Essential Facts about the Revolutionary Religious Movement in Latin America and Beyond* (London: Tauris, 1987), 4.

[30] Gustavo Gutiérrez, "Toward a Theology of Liberation," in *Liberation Theology: A Documentary History*, ed. Alfred T. Hennelly (Maryknoll, NY: Orbis, 1992), 74.

[31] Gustavo Gutiérrez, *A Theology of Liberation*, trans. Sister Caridad Inda and John Eagleson (London: SCM Press, 1974), 202. For a discussion of theology in Latin America, see Mario I. Aguilar, *Current Issues on Theology and Religion in Latin America and Africa* (Lewiston, NY: Edwin Mellen, 2002).

[32] Gerald West, "The Bible and the Poor: A New Way of Doing Theology," in *The Cambridge Companion to Liberation Theology*, ed. Christopher Rowland (Cambridge: Cambridge University Press, 1999), 129.

[33] Gutiérrez, *A Theology of Liberation*, see especially 3-19, 189-212.

In contrast to the approach advocated by modernity, the Reformers affirmed that because Christ is Lord, the contemporary world cannot be allowed to set the agenda for theological practice. Rather, the agenda is rooted firmly in divine grace as revealed in Scripture. Torrance comments on this integral aspect of Reformational theology: "Culture, therefore, may neither determine the sphere of the gospel nor relativise its imperatives but, conversely, culture and society require to be perceived, interpreted, and evaluated critically in the light of the gospel."[34] It is this recognition of divine grace that is intrinsic to the gospel, which is foundational if we are to know God's intentions for his world. Howard Marshall shares this approach, and declares that in using the Bible in ethics, we must inquire into the underlying theological and ethical principles that are expressed in it, in order to identify how we can apply these truths today.[35] Therefore in identifying the grounds upon which we will base our theological conclusions in this book, we will move beyond "political theologies" to "theological politics," which Torrance declares is "a theologically driven approach to the state rather than a politically driven approach to God."[36]

The Being of God as Prior to All Theological Questioning

Unparalleled in helping the church to recover the imperative of divine grace for knowing God and his will is Karl Barth. Having an academic training that placed him in the audience of some of the leading nineteenth and early twentieth century European scholars, Barth's methodological approach to theological inquiry was further shaped when he served as a pastor in Safenwil in the Aargau from 1911 to 1921. Of significance to discussions pertaining to the witness of the church in the socio-political arena, is the fact that ethical interests were an integral part of Barth's theology throughout his career. John Webster remarks on this pervasive feature: "Barth always maintained that one of the distinctives of the Reformed tradition of theology and Christian practice was the high place it accorded to morals."[37]

Significantly, in this position in Safenwil, Barth came to a new conception of the greatness and supremacy of God through reading the Bible.[38] This "moment of conversion" was crucial because subsequently he effectively took the greater part of European theology with him.[39] In coming to this new conception of God, he refused

---

[34] Torrance, *Christ, Justice and Peace*, xii.

[35] I. Howard Marshall, "Using the Bible in Ethics," in *Essays in Evangelical Social Ethics*, 50.

[36] Torrance, *Christ, Justice and Peace*, xx.

[37] John Webster, *Barth 'Outstanding Christian Thinkers Series'* (London: Continuum, 2003), 141.

[38] Reflecting on how reading the Bible projected him into a fundamental theological revision, Barth asks rhetorically: "More fundamental than all...was it the discovery (of) the theme of the Bible?" See Karl Barth, "The Humanity of God," in *God, Grace and Gospel*, 34.

[39] I am indebted to Bruce Milne for commenting upon Barth's change in thought, and the basis for why he took this new direction: "Socio-ethical concerns were part of it, but it was not so much his need to address socio-ethical issues (he was doing that already), but rather

to accept that knowledge of God is to be found within us. Rather, as reflected in his *The Epistle to the Romans* (*Der Römerbrief*), Barth highlighted the mystery of God, and stressed that God is the Lord (*Gott der Herr*) and the wholly other (*totaliter aliter*).[40] There is an essential discontinuity between creator and creature.[41] It is here we find a distinguishing strength of Barth's theology in that he categorically refuses to accept the anthropocentric worldview dominating since the Enlightenment. In rejecting this approach, as John Bowden declares, "Karl Barth's greatness was that he brought to twentieth century Christian thinking a towering conception of God."[42]

The consequence of this fundamental difference between God and humanity is that humankind is entirely dependent upon God graciously making himself known. Barth states: "The knowledge of God occurs in the fulfillment of the revelation of his Word by the Holy Spirit, and therefore in the reality and with the necessity of faith and its obedience."[43] Due to our finite, sinful condition, as Barth claimed, all our attempts at understanding God, who is uncompromisingly transcendent, will end in failure. The only way to God must reside with God himself.[44] Without this as our starting point, "there is only the descending way in the opposite direction."[45] This essential feature of Barthian theology, as Bruce McCormack notes, is that "human beings do not 'have' God; at best, they are 'had' by him."[46] For as Barth is at pains to stress: "He has seen to it that he is to be found by those who seek him where he himself has given himself to be found."[47] Justification by God's grace alone, which Barth contrasted so radically to human theologizing, means that we can never look for the truth in ourselves, but we must always look for it beyond ourselves in God.[48]

---

the failure of the ethics of liberal Protestantism in face of the Kaiser's war policy, which meant that their theology was wrongly based."

[40] Karl Barth, *The Epistle to the Romans*, trans. Edwyn C. Hoskyns (London: Oxford University Press, 1933). Barth later qualifies this position with his christological emphasis.

[41] For example in "The Humanity of God," he refers "to God's sovereign togetherness with man, based on himself, and determined, delimited, arranged only by himself" (37).

[42] John Bowden, *Karl Barth: Theologian* (London: SCM Press, 1983), 15.

[43] See Barth, *Church Dogmatics*, vol. 2/1, 3. Barth is at pains to stress that questions of possibility can only be raised in the context of questions of actuality: "Where the actuality exists there is also the corresponding possibility" (5). Barth works this epistemology out in full in *Anselm: Fides Quaerens Intellectum: Anselm's Proof of the Existence of God in the Context of his Theological Scheme*, trans. Ian W. Robertson (London: SCM Press, 1960).

[44] Barth, *Church Dogmatics*, vol. 1/2, 1; *The Göttingen Dogmatics: Instruction in the Christian Religion*, vol. 1, ed. Hannelotte Reiffen, trans. Geoffrey W. Bromiley (Grand Rapids: Eerdmans, 1991), 11,57; *Evangelical Theology: An Introduction*, trans. Grover Foley (Edinburgh: T&T Clark, 1963), 16.

[45] Barth, *Church Dogmatics*, vol. 2/1, 63.

[46] Bruce L. McCormack, *Karl Barth's Critically Realistic Dialectical Theology* (Oxford: Oxford University Press, 1997), 182.

[47] Barth, *Church Dogmatics*, vol. 2/1, 197.

[48] See this critique of Barth's theology in Thomas F. Torrance, *God and Rationality* (London: Oxford University Press, 1971), 68. Cf. Alan J. Torrance, "The Trinity," in *The Cambridge Companion to Karl Barth*, 72.

It is precisely from this awareness that we derive a core facet of Christian theology: the being of God is prior to all theological questioning. To put it slightly differently, the pressure of interpretation must always come from God himself. It is why theological ethics is necessarily a sub-category of the doctrine of God.[49]

Acknowledging the greatness of God as revealed in Scripture was pivotal for Barth in advocating a radically different methodological approach from the liberalism that dominated European theology.[50] Chief among Barth's methodological concerns was his desire to reverse any prior set of preconditions as constituting the vestibule to theological knowledge. God's self-disclosure constitutes its own vestibule. T.F. Torrance comments on this sense of beyond and argues that if God really is God then even to consider that we can know him in any way except out of himself would be a form of irrationality.[51] The nature of this knowledge must derive from our knowledge of the divine self-communication, which is grounded solely in God's freedom and grace to make himself known to humanity.[52] As God cannot be controlled by our a priori presuppositions, Barth insisted: "There is total sovereignty and grace on the part of God, but total dependence and need on that of man."[53] Wolfhart Pannenberg echoes this starting point for theology, as is core to the doctrine of grace: "Human knowledge of God can be a true knowledge that corresponds to the divine reality only if it originates in the deity itself...The loftiness of the divine reality makes it inaccessible to us unless it makes itself known."[54] In short, God is the supreme reality and God's self-revelation is where our theological enterprise must begin.

Grace and General Revelation

The question of revelation is central to Christian theology, not least in the articulation of a public theology, as was evident in the German state church's tragic embrace of Nazi ideology. Arthur Headlam emphasizes the importance of this question by declaring: "The primary question in theology must be, what is the source

---

[49] See also Erickson, *Christian Theology*, 24. Erickson states: "The practical effect or application of a doctrine is a consequence of the truth of the doctrine, not the reverse."

[50] For example, see Karl Barth, "Barth's Reply to Wurm, 29 May 1947," in *Karl Barth/ Rudolf Bultmann Letters 1922-1966*, ed. Geoffrey W. Bromiley and Bernd Jaspert (Grand Rapids: Eerdmans, 1982), 142. In a letter to Bishop Theophil Wurm, Barth refuses to base theology on a philosophical ontology, as this "pre-understanding" will sooner or later lead to the overthrow of theology.

[51] Thomas F. Torrance, *Theological Science* (London: Oxford University Press, 1969), 54. Cf. Christoph Schwöbel, "Theology," in *The Cambridge Companion to Karl Barth*, 32.

[52] See Barth, *Church Dogmatics*, vol. 1/1, 42.

[53] Barth, *Church Dogmatics*, vol. 3/2, 219.

[54] Wolfhart Pannenberg, *Systematic Theology*, vol. 1, trans. Geoffrey W. Bromiley (Edinburgh: T&T Clark, 1991), 189.

of our knowledge of God?"[55] Making much the same claim, G.C. Berkouwer puts it slightly more forcefully in stating: "There is no more significant question in the whole of theology and in the whole of human life than that of the nature and reality of revelation."[56] This question was thus at the heart of Barth's theological project. Indeed, the central theme that resonates throughout the *Church Dogmatics* is the need to take seriously the self-revelation of God in Christ through Scripture.

In postulating an infinite distinction between God and sinful humankind, Barth rejected the analogy of being (*analogia entis*) as the ground for revelation. Utter dependency on God's grace meant that the analogy of faith (*analogia fidei*) was the only possible means of understanding the task of Christian theology. The idea of a "scientific theology" was rejected, where it is perceived that science is restricted to the objects of sense experience, which employs experimentation and follows strict procedures of inductive logic. Instead, a method of theology was proposed, which starts from the object itself, the beyond.[57] This is what is meant by a genuinely scientific theology. In espousing this theocentric worldview, Barth inverted the approach to theology that had become dominant since Descartes, which advocated the viability of a natural theology based on a point of contact between God and humankind. In contrast, as Barth stressed, we are wholly dependent on God's gracious self-revelation for our knowledge of God and his will.

In repudiating the form of 'scientific theology' advocated by modernity, this led Barth to reject both natural theology and general revelation.[58] His rejection of the latter is bound up with his theological pilgrimage, in which he rejected the assumption of a fundamental continuity between God and "the Christian man."[59] Berkouwer stresses the vigour of Barth's offensive against a natural theology: "Barth has centred his attack more and more upon natural theology as the great enemy of faith, and general revelation was always involved in his attack as well."[60] For Barth

---

[55] Arthur C. Headlam, *Christian Theology* (Oxford: Clarendon, 1934), 7. Cf. Trevor A. Hart, "Revelation," in *The Cambridge Companion to Karl Barth*, 37.

[56] Gerrit C. Berkouwer, *General Revelation* (Grand Rapids: Eerdmans, 1968), 17.

[57] Jean-Loup Sebam, "Barth, Karl," in *Routledge Encyclopedia of Philosophy*, vol. 1, 653.

[58] Thomas Aquinas was particularly influential in developing a natural theology. His assumption that God can be known by natural reason apart from transcendent divine revelation can be seen as an unwitting preparation for the revolt of early modern philosophy against special revelation. See Carl F.H. Henry, "Revelation, Special," in *Evangelical Dictionary of Theology*, 1021 for a further review.

[59] In particular, Barth rejected the notion that the Christian consciousness, as advocated by Friedrich Schleiermacher, had become an authentic sphere of divine revelation alongside Scripture and Christ. On Barth's justification of this position theologically, see Barth, "Gospel and Law," 3-27.

[60] Berkouwer, *General Revelation*, 21. For a further discussion, see Alvin Plantinga, "Religious Belief as 'Properly Basic,'" in *Philosophy of Religion: A Guide and Anthology*, ed. Brian Davies (Oxford: Oxford University Press, 2000), 42-94. Alvin Plantinga states: "The twentieth-century theologian Karl Barth is particularly scathing in his disapproval of

considers both "to be on the same plane."[61] Moreover, Barth discarded any discussion of God's relationship to the world that is not christologically derived, and hence refused to acknowledge the possibility of any revelation outside the Word of God.[62] Revelation is always and only the revelation of God in Jesus Christ.[63] Webster describes Barth's distinctively christocentric understanding of revelation as "his insistence on the radically interceptive character of God's revelation in Christ."[64] Reflecting on this distinguishing trait, Louis Berkhof summarizes Barth's doctrine of revelation:

> Revelation never exists on any horizontal line, but always comes down perpendicularly from above. Revelation is always God in action, God speaking, bringing something entirely new to man, something of which he could have no previous knowledge, and which becomes a real revelation only for him who accepts the object of revelation by a God-given faith.[65]

As knowledge of God is an impossibility for humans, Barth perceived revelation as nothing less than a miracle: "The Word of God is God's miraculous act."[66] Consequently, for Barth, revelation and reconciliation are inextricably related. Trevor Hart elaborates on this central feature of Barth's understanding of divine grace, which has the implication "that there can be no question of human beings strategizing or devising systematic methods for acquiring such knowledge which, when it arises within the human sphere, does so necessarily as a result of God's own particular choosing and activity."[67] Revelation, according to Barth, is hence dynamic rather than static, in which God speaks in his uncreated sovereign freedom.[68] And because God is the creator who transcends the world, his self-revelation is always particular rather than general. Barth explains this effect of God's particular choosing:

> God always has something specific to say to each man, something that applies to him and to him alone. The real content of God's speech or the real will of the speaking

---

natural theology. *That* he disapproves is overwhelming clear. His *reasons* for thus disapproving, however, are much less clear." (78).

[61] Berkouwer, *General Revelation*, 33.

[62] For example, in *Church Dogmatics*, vol. 2/1, 119, Barth comments on Romans 1 and declares: "There can be no doubt that Paul meant by this the revelation of the grace of God in Jesus Christ."

[63] Karl Barth, *Revelation*, ed. John Baillie and Hugh Martin (New York: Macmillan, 1937), 49.

[64] Webster, *Barth*, 38.

[65] Louis Berkhof, *Systematic Theology* (Edinburgh: The Banner of Truth Trust, 1958), 39.

[66] Barth, *Church Dogmatics*, vol. 1/1, 182.

[67] Hart, "Revelation," 42-43.

[68] Ibid., 45.

person of God is not in any sense, then, to be construed and reproduced by us as a general truth.[69]

In God's sovereignty, God chooses to reveal himself to some, and yet remains hidden from others. Barth states: "Concretely this means that the hearing and receiving of the Word of God by a man can be known by him and others only in faith."[70] For it is by the Holy Spirit that we are enlightened to a revelation of God's Word.[71] Where this revelation occurs is within the context of the body of Christ, the ecclesia, which is the sphere of the Spirit's witness to Christ.[72] As such, the place of the discernment of God is itself a God-given context of the recognition of God through the Spirit. Here again we are dependent on divine grace for appropriating and realizing God's self-communication. The implication of this dynamic, as Hart points out, is that "to whom the gift of faith is not yet granted, the media or vehicles of God's self-objectifying remain opaque, veiling God rather than disclosing him."[73]

Reformational theology has as a central tenet this understanding of the necessity of divine grace for our knowledge of God. For example, Berkhof claims: "Theology would be utterly impossible without a self-revelation of God." Additionally, Berkhof emphasizes that revelation is not something in which God is passive, but is something in which God is actively making himself known. In contrast to the thinking of modernity, revelation is not a deepened spiritual insight that culminates in the discovery of God on the part of man. Rather, it is "a supernatural act of self-communication, a purposeful act on the part of the living God."[74]

Where disagreements arise with Barth, however, is in the understanding of general revelation.[75] Whereas Barth stands against the whole concept of general revelation, emphasizing that every act of revelation is specific and particular, Berkhof compellingly asserts that the Bible testifies to a twofold revelation of God. This includes, "a revelation in nature round about us, in human consciousness, and in the providential government of the world; and in a revelation embodied in the Bible as the Word of God."[76] Similarly, Erickson argues that in order to know God, this must come about by God's manifestation of himself, of which there are two basic forms. First, through general revelation, God communicates something of himself to all persons at all times and in all places. Second, through special revelation, God communicates and manifests himself to particular persons at particular times.[77] Benjamin Warfield distinguishes between these two forms of revelation as follows:

---

[69] Barth, *Church Dogmatics*, vol. 1/1, 140.

[70] Ibid., 183.

[71] Barth, *Church Dogmatics*, vol. 1/2, 203.

[72] Barth, *Church Dogmatics*, vol. 2/1, 3.

[73] Hart, "Revelation," 47.

[74] Berkhof, *Systematic Theology*, 34.

[75] For a comprehensive survey of how general revelation has been understood in the history of the church, see Demarest, *General Revelation*.

[76] Berkhof, *Systematic Theology*, 36.

[77] Erickson, *Christian Theology*, 178.

The one is addressed generally to all intelligent creatures, and is therefore accessible to all men; the other is addressed to a special class of sinners, to whom God would make known his salvation. The one has in view to meet and supply the natural need of creatures for knowledge of their God; the other to rescue broken and deformed sinners from their sin and its consequences.[78]

A concept of general revelation is supported by Charles Hodge, who claims that although our knowledge of God is both partial and imperfect, God is what we believe him to be, "so far as our idea of him is determined by the revelation which he has made of himself in his works, in the constitution of our nature, in his Word, and in the person of his Son."[79] It is this recognition of the revelation of God in the created order, however limited this might be for mediating elemental knowledge of God's existence and character (Psalms 19; Romans 1:18-32), which is lacking in Barth's doctrine of revelation. Commenting on the opening chapter of Romans, Douglas Moo provides a further clarification and concludes: "The text teaches that all people have, by reason of God's revelation in creation, access to some degree of knowledge about God." Moo supports this assertion by a detailed exegesis of Romans 1, which reveals that the aorist tenses of vv.19b-28 "do not allow us to conclude that only a past generation is in view."[80] Yet as Moo continues, "it is vitally important...to see that the knowledge of God that people possess outside special revelation is woefully inadequate, of itself, to save." For "without grace," sinful human beings "are unable to respond appropriately to whatever knowledge of God they may possess."[81] What is necessary, as John Calvin captures in his *Institutes of the Christian Religion*, is "that another and better help be added to direct us aright to the very creator of the universe." Expressly, it is through the Scriptures, as we read with the "spectacles" of faith that we are able to come to a genuine knowledge of our creator.[82]

In acknowledging the existence of a general revelation, which nonetheless is severely limited in what it reveals, Carl Henry points out that God's revelation is a unity, which "invariably correlates general revelation with special redemptive revelation." For general revelation is introduced alongside special revelation, culminating in the incarnation of the living Word in order to emphasize humanity's predicament as a finite creature, made for fellowship with God, but now separated

---

[78] Benjamin B. Warfield, *Revelation and Inspiration* (London: Oxford University Press, 1927), 6.

[79] Charles Hodge, *Systematic Theology*, vol. 1 (London: Thomas Nelson, 1871-1873), 338.

[80] Douglas J. Moo, *The Epistle to the Romans* (Grand Rapids: Eerdmans, 1996), 123.

[81] Moo, *The Epistle to the Romans*, 123-124. For Paul's statements about general revelation in Romans 1 and 2 must be viewed in the light of what is said about sinful humanity in Romans 3.

[82] John Calvin, *Institutes of the Christian Religion*, vol. 1/6, ed. John T. McNeill, trans. Ford L. Battles (Philadelphia: Westminster Press, 1960), 69-70.

from God by sin.[83] This highlights the failure that arose in Protestant theology during the Middle Ages when it sought to make a distinction between natural revelation (*revelatio realis*) and supernatural revelation (*revelatio verbalis*). As Berkhof points out, this distinction is ambiguous, "since all revelation is supernatural in origin and, as revelation of God, also in content."[84] Therefore in conclusion, although there is a general revelation without natural theology, this is inextricably linked to special revelation and the necessity of divine grace for our knowledge of God and his will.

Divine Self-Revelation and the Incarnate Word of God

Despite man's inability to know God by his own means, at the heart of the universe, as Barth claimed, is the person of a speaking God who seeks fellowship with his creatures. This message, which is at the centre of the gospel, reveals that the way God has supremely made himself known is in the history of Israel, culminating in the incarnate Word of God, Jesus Christ (John 1:1-18).[85] "Divine revelation," Kevin Vanhoozer therefore contends, "is God in communicative action."[86] As was affirmed at the Council of Nicea in 325AD, in the incarnation, God, whose being and nature is self-giving, has decided in his grace to come into our midst (the *homoousios*). Although God is *totaliter aliter*, as Barth stated, God is also with us. To be true to the otherness of God is to be true to the freedom of God. Yet, "this grace," asserts Torrance "is infinitely costly to God because it is grace through the blood of Christ."[87] It is here we also find a primary theological insight that was integral to the theology of Calvin. Calvin, as with Barth, identified an inseparable relationship between revelation and reconciliation.[88] Both are made possible by the grace of God. God is truly known only as he graciously reconciles our alienated minds to himself.

Central to Barth's doctrine of the Word of God is the authority and norm of Scripture as the revelation of God that witnesses to Jesus Christ, the Word that became flesh.[89] In short, as Barth emphasized, the divine Word is the source of

---

[83] Henry, "Special Revelation," 1021-1022.

[84] Berkhof, *Systematic Theology*, 36-37.

[85] For example, Barth highlights his distinctive christocentrism in *Church Dogmatics*, vol. 1/2, 883: "God is active in his Word...And God's Word is his Son Jesus Christ." See also Karl Barth, *Dogmatics in Outline*, trans. George T. Thomson (London: SCM Press, 1949), 66. Barth declares: "Tell me how it stands with your christology and I will tell you who you are." Cf. Hartwell, *The Theology of Karl Barth*, 96-153.

[86] Kevin J. Vanhoozer, "The Voice and the Actor," in *Evangelical Futures*, 72.

[87] Torrance, *God and Rationality*, 56. See also Thomas F. Torrance, *The Doctrine of Grace in the Apostolic Fathers* (Edinburgh: Oliver & Boyd, 1948). In examining the early Christian understanding of grace, Torrance claims that in certain periods "the great mistake has been to detach the thought of grace from the person of Jesus Christ" (v).

[88] Thomas H.L. Parker, *The Doctrine of the Knowledge of God: A Study in the Theology of John Calvin* (Edinburgh: Oliver and Boyd, 1952), 81.

[89] Karl Barth, *The Word of God and the Word of Man*, trans. Douglas Horton (London: Hodder & Stoughton, 1928), 43.

theological knowledge and the foundation of Christian dogmatics.[90] As Christ reveals who God is and his purposes for creation a correct christology is essential for the life and witness of the church. It is in Christ that we come into contact with God's grace and God's love in person. In the Son of God becoming flesh this is the action by which God is moulding the world for his own glory.[91] It is God's glory, as John Bright states, "reached through the doorway of the cross of the Servant."[92]

This brings us to our second point in relation to divine self-revelation, in that not only does witness take place in the context of those to whom God has graciously revealed himself, but also the church follows Christ by way of the servant. Indeed the concept of servanthood is intrinsic to the mission of the incarnate Word as reflected in his threefold office (*triplex munus*) as Prophet, Priest, and King. Attention is drawn to this feature of Christ's mission by means of a significant theme running throughout Scripture, which is the title the "Servant of the Lord," deriving from the Servant Songs in Second Isaiah.[93] Thus in the Book of Isaiah we are able to grasp something of the character and mission of the incarnate Word, and its relevance for the witness of the church in the world. In order to grasp the importance of Christ's servanthood, we will now examine more closely the Servant of the Lord title as it appears in Isaiah.

Isaiah was one of the major prophets, who in the midst of prophecies of judgment delivered to Judah for their rebellion against God, writes prophetically about the Messiah. The dominant figure in Isaiah 40-53 is the Servant of the Lord, who would execute judgment and establish justice on the earth. The prophet introduces the special relationship that the Servant has to the Father; he is God's Servant par excellence (Isaiah 42:1). In Isaiah 49:1-6, the Servant assumes the prophetic office and returns Israel to the Lord. The Servant will come to realize everything that the nation can become, with the ultimate task being the deliverance of Jacob's offspring and their restoration to Yahweh (Isaiah 49:5). In Isaiah 50:4-9, the Servant is a faithful teacher and is determined to be faithful to the call of God upon his life. Yet God will vindicate his Servant (Isaiah 50:9). In Isaiah 52:13-53:12, the Servant

---

[90] In *Church Dogmatics*, vol. 2/2, 4, Barth states categorically: "Theology must begin with Jesus Christ…Theology must also end with him." This is not only a Reformed emphasis, the Lutheran pastor Dietrich Bonhoeffer shares this christocentric focus: "The church's silence is silence before the Word." See Dietrich Bonhoeffer, *Christology*, trans. John Bowden (London: Collins, 1966), 27.

[91] See Walter A. Whitehouse, *The Authority of Grace: Essays in Response to Karl Barth*, ed. Ann Loades (Edinburgh: T&T Clark, 1981), 7.

[92] John Bright, *The Kingdom of God in Bible and Church* (London: Lutterworth, 1955), 217.

[93] For a further discussion, see Gerrit C. Berkouwer, *The Work of Christ*, trans. Cornelius Lambregtse (Grand Rapids: Eerdmans, 1965), 66. Berkouwer notes that when Christian theology speaks of Christ's threefold office it does so to differentiate and not separate, for Christ viewed his revelatory role as inextricably linked with his reconciling and ruling roles.

becomes the priest who intercedes for Israel and offers himself as a sacrifice. Finally, the Servant of the Lord is rightfully exalted (Isaiah 53:10-12).[94]

In the time of Christ's life on earth, however, different groups among the Jews had an enormous range of expectations of the prophesied Messiah (Luke 9:19). Walter Kasper asserts: "The title 'Messiah' was undefined, even unclear."[95] Opinions ranged from believing John the Baptist was the Messiah, to the nationalistic political hopes of the Zealots, and the rabbinic expectation of a new teacher of the law. Priestly groups such as those found among the desert community of Qumran looked for a priestly Messiah. The popular opinion favoured the view that the Messiah would deliver the Jewish people from the oppressive yoke of Roman rule.[96] In sharp contrast to these false expectations, Jesus went to Nazareth and read in the synagogue Isaiah 61, claiming he was the Messiah promised of old who was to establish justice, provide salvation, be a light to the Gentiles, and dispense God's Spirit (Luke 4:14-30). Significantly, therefore, Jesus revealed his identity both as Messiah (John 4:25-26) and as Suffering Servant (Luke 22:37), which was dramatically represented in the scene of his baptism in the River Jordan.[97] What this demonstrates, as Thomas Manson points out, is that in the execution of his mission, Jesus lived for the kingdom of God, which was to live a life of service.[98]

Although the disciples were never comfortable with Jesus' servanthood (John 13:3-17), as Christ's body, the church continues the ministry of Christ as a servant.[99] Barth captured this characteristic of servanthood and argued that a christological investigation reveals that man is created to serve God.[100] Thus as Christ became incarnate "taking the very nature of a servant" (Philippians 2:7), if the church is to be true to its founder, she is to give herself to serve others (Matthew 20:26-28). It is this aspect of servanthood that has significant relevance for the socio-political mission of the church. For a church that is willing to serve will not seek to dominate society for its own purposes. In contrast, as Erickson states: "It will seek to follow its Lord's example of service. It will be willing to go to the undesirables and helpless, those who cannot give anything in return to the church."[101] Thus Torrance highlights that

---

[94] See J. Alec Motyer, *The Prophecy of Isaiah* (Leicester: InterVarsity, 1993), 287-458; Carl F. Keil and Franz Delitzsch, *Commentary on the Old Testament: Isaiah*, vol. 7, trans. James Martin (Grand Rapids: Eerdmans, 1983), 139-342; and Bright, *The Kingdom of God in Bible and Church*, 138-157.

[95] Walter Kasper, *Jesus the Christ*, trans. Verdont Green (London: Burns & Oates, 1976), 104.

[96] See Richard J. Bauckham, et al. *Jesus 2000* (Oxford: Lion, 1989), 57.

[97] See Charles H. Dodd, *The Founder of Christianity* (New York: MacMillan, 1970), 105.

[98] Thomas W. Manson, *The Servant Messiah: A Study of the Public Ministry of Jesus* (Cambridge: Cambridge University Press, 1977), 76-77. Cf. Bright, *The Kingdom of God in Bible and Church*, 219.

[99] Lawrence O. Richards and Gib Martin, *A Theology of Personal Ministry* (Grand Rapids: Zondervan, 1981), 82.

[100] Barth, *Church Dogmatics*, vol. 3/2, 74.

[101] Erickson, *Christian Theology*, 1077.

the self-revelation of God in Christ leads to a distinctive motivation of the church's service.[102] It is service which has as its goal the furthering of God's kingdom through displaying the servanthood of Christ.

In summary, therefore, in seeking to address the first challenge presented in assessing the implications of the doctrine of grace for the socio-political involvement of the church, we have discovered that the gospel of grace is necessarily the starting point for our whole theological project. In contrast to the anthropocentric worldview dominating throughout modernity, we have found that it is only in the gracious self-revelation of the triune God, which was supremely exhibited in the person and work of Jesus Christ, that we can come to a true understanding of the nature and being of God and his purposes for how humankind is to live in his created world.

Grace and Covenant Relationship with God

The Covenant of Grace and the Kingdom of God

The second challenge to be overcome in assessing the implications of the doctrine of grace for the socio-political involvement of the church is the nature of the covenant relationship established by God with his chosen people. Unquestionably the covenant provides a major theological motif in Scripture.[103] F.F. Bruce highlights the central importance of the covenant in the canonical Scriptures of the Old and New Testaments and points out that the unity of the Bible is found in that it "tells the story of salvation - the story of God's covenant-mercy."[104] If we were to think of the Bible as comprising 'The Books of the Old Covenant,' and 'The Books of the New Covenant,' Bruce claims, "we shall be well on our way to understanding what the Bible is and what it contains."[105] Furthermore, as the covenant is the means by which

---

[102] Thomas F. Torrance, "Service in Jesus Christ," in *Service in Christ: Essays Presented to Karl Barth on his 80th Birthday*, ed. James I. McCord and Thomas H.L. Parker (London: Epworth Press, 1966), 2.

[103] See for example, Ernest W. Nicholson, *God and His People: Covenant and Theology in the Old Testament* (Oxford: Clarendon Press, 1986), 83-117.

[104] Frederick F. Bruce, *The Books and the Parchments* (London: Marshall Pickering, 1991), 73. Cf. Gary A. Herion, "Covenant," in *Eerdmans Dictionary of the Bible*, ed. David N. Freedom (Grand Rapid: Eerdmans, 2000), 292. Although the covenant is the organizing principle that provides coherence to Scripture, and is mentioned in patristic and late medieval writings, it was not developed as a doctrine until the Reformation, of which particular influence was Heinrich Bullinger's *One and Eternal Testament or Covenant* (1534).

[105] Bruce, *The Books and the Parchments*, 67. Cf. F. Charles Fensham, "Covenant, Alliance," in *New Bible Dictionary*, ed. James D. Douglas and Norman Hillyer, 2nd edn (Leicester: InterVarsity, 1982), 243. Charles Fensham points out that the Davidic covenant with the promise of an eternal throne led to the expectation of the coming Messiah, which provides an important link between both testaments.

God establishes a relationship with his people, it is intrinsic to soteriology, because it expresses the fact that God wishes humankind to live in communion with himself.[106]

The word *covenant* is the normal English translation of the Hebrew word *berit*.[107] The first biblical mention of the covenant is seen in the relationship confirmed by God with Noah (Genesis 6:17-18). William Dumbrell emphasizes that this first mention of the covenant in Scripture is of significance, since here we find a definite link between the Noahic covenant and creation itself.[108] Also, it provides the biblical-theological framework within which all subsequent divine-human covenants operate. Paul Williamson comments on the importance of the "universal scope" of this covenant, as it encompasses not just one people or nation, but the entire earth.[109] Dumbrell develops this further, though, by postulating a unity for biblical theology in covenant and persuasively argues that there can be only one divine covenant. Foundational to his thesis, he asserts that there is a unity between the testaments that is derived from the unfolding of God's purpose.[110] Arthur Thompson supports this claim, and declares that although God confirmed his covenant with different people on different occasions, and differing promises were given according to the particular circumstances, there is still essentially only one covenant of grace.[111]

Where Dumbrell goes yet further is in presenting an exegetical case for a "covenant with creation." Arguing that the "fact of creation itself" involved God's entering into relationships with the world in the form of a covenant, Dumbrell proclaims that this is an all-embracing covenant between God and creation. Any theology of covenant, he subsequently asserts, must thus begin with Genesis 1. Later biblical covenants, such as the covenant confirmed with Noah, are to be seen as subsets and a renewal of an already existing covenant.[112] For the presupposition behind covenant, Dumbrell argues, is the present kingship of God. And God will not allow his divine purposes to be frustrated, either in regard to man himself or his

---

[106] See George E. Mendenhall and Gary A. Herion, "Covenant," in *The Anchor Bible Dictionary*, vol. 1, ed. David N. Freedman (New York: Doubleday, 1992), 1179; Jean Giblet and Pierre Grelot, "Covenant," in *Dictionary of Biblical Theology*, ed. Xavier León-Dufour (London: Geoffrey Chapman, 1967), 75; and Robert Davidson, "Covenant," in *The Oxford Companion to Christian Thought*, ed. Adrian Hastings, Alistair Mason, and Hugh Pyper (Oxford: Oxford University Press, 2000), 141-142.

[107] Moshe Weinfeld, "berit," in *Theological Dictionary of the Old Testament*, vol. 2, ed. G. Johannes Botterweck and Helmer Ringgren, trans. John T. Willis (Grand Rapids: Eerdmans, 1975), 253-279.

[108] William J. Dumbrell, *Covenant and Creation: A Theology of the Old Testament Covenants* (Carlisle: Paternoster, 1997), 11-46.

[109] Paul R. Williamson, "Covenant," in *Dictionary of the Old Testament: Pentateuch*, ed. T. Desmond Alexander and David W. Baker (Downers Grove, Ill.: InterVarsity, 2003), 141. Cf. Robert S.J. Murray, *The Cosmic Covenant: Biblical Themes of Justice, Peace, and the Integrity of Creation* (London: Sheed and Ward, 1992).

[110] Dumbrell, *Covenant and Creation*, 42.

[111] J. Arthur Thomson, "Covenant (OT)," in *The International Standard Bible Encyclopedia*, ed. Geoffrey W. Bromiley (Grand Rapids: Eerdmans, 1979-1988), 792.

[112] Dumbrell, *Covenant and Creation*, 43.

world.[113] This all-embracing covenant, Dumbrell insists, means "we cannot entertain the salvation of man in isolation from the world, which he has affected."[114]

It is unclear, however, whether God actually entered into a covenant relationship with creation itself, as Dumbrell claims. Just because two things are related to one another in some way does not necessitate a covenant.[115] Despite this uncertainty, due to the sovereign reign of God over his created world, as Dumbrell highlights, this unified kingly rule indicates that the world and man should be viewed as "part of one total divine construct." This is supported by the fact that in Genesis 9:8-17, the covenant God makes with Noah after the flood is with all living creatures, and not only with Noah and his descendents. Consequently, as Dumbrell notes, a biblical doctrine of covenant "cannot be merely anthropologically related."[116] Rather, the biblical metanarrative is the story about the whole of God's creation.

So why is it significant to recognize the unity and continuity of the divine covenants for the church's mission? And what is its bearing to this central integrative motif of theology, namely, the grace of God? In recognizing there can be essentially only one covenant of grace, this highlights a principal feature of the covenant in that it demonstrates a progression of purpose and promise in which God's purposes for his kingdom will prevail. Indeed the theme of the kingdom, which is inherently holistic in character, ties the covenant time lie together. Meredith Kline explains the nature and significance of this elemental link: "To follow the course of the kingdom is to trace the series of covenants by which the Lord administers his kingdom."[117]

---

[113] Cf. John H. Stek, "What Says the Scripture?" in *Portraits of Creation: Biblical and Scientific Perspectives on the World's Formation*, ed. Howard J. Van Til (Grand Rapids, Eerdmans, 1990), 203-265. John Stek explains that Genesis 1 is full of imagery presenting God as "the Great King" in creating his visible kingdom: "God's creative words are presented in form and function as royal decrees" (232).

[114] Dumbrell, *Covenant and Creation*, 41. For a biblical survey of the creation account, see Bauckham, *God and the Crisis of Freedom*, 128-177; and Richard J. Bauckham, "Joining Creation's Praise of God," in *Ecotheology*, vol. 7/1 (July 2002), 45-59. Richard Bauckham points out the Bible places humanity among the creatures in creation's worship of God. Thus he refutes Lynn White's claims that "Christianity is the most anthropocentric religion the world has seen," in Lynn White, "The Historical Roots of our Ecological Crisis," in *Western Man and Environmental Ethics: Attitudes Toward Nature and Technology*, ed. Ian G. Barbour (Reading, Mass.: Addison-Wesley, 1973), 25.

[115] Williamson notes that Dumbrell's argument leans heavily on his exegesis of Genesis 6:18. It is from this position he infers that the Noahic covenant is simply the confirmation of the covenant God had previously brought into existence, which uses a possessive pronoun "my covenant." Yet, Williamson asserts, prior to this there is no mention of any covenant being established – at least between God and humans. See Williamson, "Covenant," 141.

[116] Dumbrell, *Covenant and Creation*, 41. Cf. Michael S. Northcott, *The Environment and Christian Ethics* (New York: Cambridge University Press, 1996), 164-198. In modernity, the word *dominion* has been misinterpreted to mean *domination* rather than *stewardship*.

[117] Meredith G. Kline, *Kingdom Prologue: Genesis Foundations for a Covenantal Worldview* (Overland Park, Kansas: Two Age Press, 2000), 1.

Entering into a covenant with God, therefore, determines the goal of God's people which is to further the rule of God over his creation in opposition to all that alienates, disrupts and damages. If the church is to recognize this kingly reign, then this provides firm theological warrant for directing the church's mission in addressing issues of social and political concern. This theocentric foundational priority to God's kingdom, which is at the core of the doctrine of grace, is precisely the reason why the grace of God is a key interpretive motif for approaching the task of systematic theology, and around which theology will be developed in this work.

The Nature of the Covenant

We have established that the covenant of grace is intrinsic to the kingdom of God, due to its intrinsic unity and continuity in which God's purposes for his kingly reign will always prevail; but what exactly is the nature of this covenant? In Scripture we find that the term *berit* is used to describe both interpersonal (Genesis 14:13; 21:27; 26:28; 31:44; Exodus 23:32: 34:12; Deuteronomy 7:2) and also divine-human covenants. In concluding a covenant the most common Hebrew expression used is "he cut a covenant" (*karat berit*), which is the term used of God's covenant with humankind. It points to the ancient rite of cutting an animal with the forming of a treaty or covenant. For in order to communicate in a meaningful way with his people living in the ancient Near East (ANE), there were elements in God's revelation, which had similarities with concepts found in that particular historical and cultural period.[118] Indeed the idea of making a treaty, as Charles Fensham points out, pervades almost the whole history of the ANE.[119]

Several studies have identified both similarities and polemics between the biblical covenants and these ANE covenants and treaties.[120] Yet the key difference between

---

[118] See John Bright, *Covenant and Promise* (London: SCM Press, 1977), 15-48.

[119] Fensham, "Covenant, Alliance," 240.

[120] For example, in the ratification of God's covenant with Abraham in Genesis 15 several similarities have been found with ANE practice. Dennis J. McCarthy in *Treaty and Covenant: A Study in Form in the Ancient Oriental Documents and in the Old Testament* (Rome: Biblical Institute, 1978), 86-94, describes how the animals that were involved in the covenant ceremony with Abraham, have parallels to what is recorded in Hittite texts dating to the second millennium BC. Comparative studies have also analysed the Old Babylonian texts of both Mari and Alalakh, which include the killing of animals as part of the ritual involved in the making of treaties. Moshe Weinfeld in "The Covenant of Grant in the Ancient Near East," in *Essential Papers on Israel and the Ancient Near East*, ed. Frederick E. Greenspahn (New York: New York University Press, 1991), 70, has suggested that the covenant God made with Abraham was based on the form used in Assyrian grants. In particular, Weinfeld claims that the terminology used in the context of God's covenant with Abraham is very similar to the grant of Ashurbanipal to his servant Bulta. Additionally, Piotr Michalowski in "The Torch and the Censer," in *The Tablet and The Scroll*, ed. William W. Hallo (Maryland: CDL Press, 1993), 152-160, states that the smoking firepot with a blazing torch are of conceptual significance and have close parallels with that used in Mesopotamia, as these items were usually included in the initiation of purification rites.

the biblical covenants and the treaties found in the ANE is that the covenants demonstrate a commitment made by God, and accordingly differed sharply in function through being a means to a more comprehensive end rather than being an end in themselves.[121] In contrast with covenants and treaties made between humans, stress is placed on the initiative of God in the covenant he makes with mankind, by the use of the verbs "establish" (Genesis 6:18; 9:11; 17:7), "grant" (Genesis 9:12; 17:2; Numbers 25:12), "set down" (2 Samuel 23:5), and "command" (Joshua 7:11, 23:16; 1 Kings 11:11). This cannot be said about a mutual agreement.[122] Thus the covenant made by God differs crucially from these other covenants and treaties.[123]

Confusion has arisen, however, in the exact nature of this relationship between God and his creation. Its root cause can be traced to the translation of the Hebrew word *berit*.[124] The word *berit* was subsequently translated into the Greek Septuagint as *diatheke*. Gleason Archer asserts that *diatheke* signifies "an arrangement made by one party with plenary power, which the other party may accept or reject but cannot alter."[125] Oswald Becker states that this term, which occurs from Democritus and Aristoph onwards in the sense of a will or testament, denotes an irrevocable decision that cannot be cancelled by anyone. Therefore *diatheke* must be clearly distinguished from *suntheke*, which is the classical and Hellenistic word for an agreement.[126] Bruce declares that the word *diatheke* is better suited to the biblical idea of covenant, "which God initiates by his saving grace and freely bestows upon his people."[127]

Misunderstandings were to follow when *diatheke* was translated into the Latin New Testament as *foedus* bringing with it not only the understanding of covenant, but also the notions of contract and agreement.[128] As Latin was the dominant influence of government and intellectuals, Timothy Gorringe observes: "The New Testament was inevitably read through the interpretive lens of the Latin genius, which was law."[129] Subsequently, there arose the idea that God's relation to

---

[121] See John Walton, *Covenant: God's Purpose; God's Plan* (Grand Rapids: Zondervan, 1994).

[122] See Weinfeld, "berit," 255.

[123] Ibid., 278. Weinfeld claims: "The covenantal idea was a special feature of the religion of Israel, the only one to demand exclusive loyalty and to preclude the possibility of dual or multiple loyalties such as were permitted in other religions…The stipulation in political treaties demanding exclusive fealty to one king corresponds strikingly with the religious belief in one single, exclusive deity."

[124] I am indebted to Christopher R. Seitz who points out the need to recognize that words also function in specific literary contexts. See James Barr, *The Semantics of Biblical Language* (London: Oxford University Press, 1961). In this case, however, the problem would appear to be chiefly translational.

[125] Gleason L. Archer, "Covenant," in *Evangelical Dictionary of Theology*, 300.

[126] Oswald Becker, "Covenant," in *The New International Dictionary of New Testament Theology*, vol. 1, ed. Colin Brown (Exeter: Paternoster, 1975-1986), 365.

[127] Bruce, *The Books and the Parchments*, 65-66.

[128] See Leonard R. Palmer, *The Latin Language* (London: Faber, 1954), 217.

[129] Timothy J. Gorringe, *God's Just Vengeance: Crime, Violence and the Rhetoric of Salvation* (Cambridge: Cambridge University Press, 1996), 224.

humanity is contractual rather than covenantal, a subtle, yet key misunderstanding of this relationship. Whereas a covenant "is a promise binding two people or two parties to love one another unconditionally," as Torrance points out, a contract "is a legal relationship in which two people or two parties bind themselves together on mutual conditions to effect some future result."[130] Inherent in this misinterpretation is the danger of legalism due to turning the covenant of grace into a legal contract.

Differing from contractualism the gospel declares that out of his love God made a covenant with humankind. What this demonstrates, as Torrance emphasizes, is that "the God of the Bible is a covenant-God and not a contract-God."[131] Although this covenant involved two parties, it was only made by one of them. It is a covenant of grace bringing with it promises and obligations. Yet these obligations are not conditions of grace, which was the heart of the Reformation rediscovery. The Pauline teaching about justification was crucial to the Reformers in that God accepts us through his grace received by faith (Ephesians 2:8-9). This is also evident in the characteristic statement of God's relationship with his people: "They will be my people, and I will be their God" (Jeremiah 11:4; 24:7; 30:22; 32:38; Ezekiel 11:20; 14:11; 36:28; 37:23; Zechariah 8:8). It indicates that God unreservedly gives himself to his people, and they in turn give themselves to him and belong to him. Kline thus observes: "The *berit* arrangement is no mere secular contract but rather belongs to the sacred sphere of divine witness and enforcement."[132] That is why it is mistaken to perceive God's relation to humanity as being contractual rather than covenantal.

Frequently misconstrued is the nature of the Sinai covenant as reflected in the work of Walther Eichrodt in *Theology of the Old Testament*, which proceeds from a strong covenant base. Before the parallels between the Israelite covenant and the ANE treaty had been brought to light, Eichrodt's work highlighted the importance of the covenant idea in the religion of Israel. Eichrodt stressed that basic phenomena in Israelite religion, such as the kingship of God, revelation, liberation from myth and personal attitudes to God are to be explained against the background of the covenant. Yet it would appear that Eichrodt may be mistaken in his analysis of the nature of the covenant made by God in his reference to "two contracting parties." Eichrodt states:

> The use of the covenant concept in secular life argues that the religious *berit* too was always regarded as a bilateral relationship; for even though the burden is most unequally distributed between the two contracting parties, this makes no difference to the fact that the relationship is still essentially two-sided.[133]

As Dumbrell points out, however, in focusing on the Sinai covenant almost to the exclusion of other Old Testament divine covenant material, Eichrodt has taken too

---

[130] Torrance, "The Covenant Concept in Scottish Theology," 228. Torrance notes that society at large builds upon a network of such contractual arrangements (229).

[131] Ibid., 229-230, 239.

[132] Kline, *Kingdom Prologue*, 1.

[133] Walther Eichrodt, *Theology of the Old Testament*, vol. 1, trans. John A. Baker (London: SCM Press, 1961), 37.

little account of the entire biblical presentation that identifies a sequence in which there can be no question of two parties being involved.[134] Moreover, the Ten Commandments do not set out contractual conditions, nor do they indicate the establishment of a bilateral covenant. Rather, the giving of the Torah emphasized Yahweh's faithfulness and the unilateral covenant commitment of Yahweh. For before the Decalogue commences, there is the vital preface: "I am the Lord your God, who brought you out of Egypt, out of the land of slavery" (Exodus 20:2). Discussing the laws given in the Sinaitic covenant which are set in the context of a gracious, divine initiative, Gordon Wenham states: "Obedience to the law is not the source of blessing, but it augments a blessing already given." With the promise to be God's own possession among all peoples if they obey his covenant (Exodus 19:5), he notes, "Israel thus finds herself in a virtuous circle. Obedience to the law issues in further experience of the initial grace of God, who brought them to himself."[135]

The relationship between God's commands and his previous acts on behalf of Israel in bringing them out of Egypt is highlighted in Deuteronomy where the whole historical prologue (Deuteronomy 1-4), precedes the Decalogue (Deuteronomy 5). It is from this demonstration of divine grace that the obligations to the covenant stem. Israel's keeping of God's law was simply to be a response to what God had already done. It is this foundation, claims Christopher Wright, which runs through the moral teaching of the whole Bible.[136] It is a motivation that derives "from the facts of our redemption and our membership of God's people, consciously living under his kingship."[137] Dumbrell gives a summary of this essential nature of the covenant:

> The initiative has lain entirely with God. Responses of course have been and would have been demanded, but they are responses, which would have brought with them the blessings, which attached to the covenant on the one hand, or the curses, which the rejection of the covenant would have invoked on the other. They are no part of the covenant itself, but rather results of attitudes taken to the covenant.[138]

What this underlines is that the obligations to the unilateral covenant commitment made by God are a response to God's prior grace and are not a condition of God's grace. It is sheer gratitude to God's grace that compels obedience.[139] The warrant for this is that the indicatives of grace, as revealed in Scripture, are always prior to the

---

[134] Dumbrell, *Covenant and Creation*, 32.

[135] Gordon Wenham, "Grace and Law in the Old Testament," in *Law, Morality and the Bible: A Symposium*, ed. Bruce Kaye and Gordon Wenham (Leicester: InterVarsity, 1978), 5. Cf. Bruce, *The Books and the Parchments*, 76. Bruce highlights the unilateral nature of this covenant: "The covenant at Sinai might be a covenant of works so far as Israel's undertaking was concerned; but it was a covenant of grace so far as God's fulfilling it was concerned, for he continued to treat Israel as his people even when Israel forgot that he was their God."

[136] Wright, *Living as the People of God*, 23.

[137] Ibid., 141.

[138] Dumbrell, *Covenant and Creation*, 31.

[139] See Torrance, "The Covenant Concept in Scottish Theology," 239.

imperatives of law and human obligation. Consequences arise whether one chooses to obey these obligations, which results either in blessing or disaster, the so-called descriptive ifs (Deuteronomy 8:19-20; John 15:9-10).[140]

God's grace is seen supremely in how he deals with his people leading up to the coming of Christ.[141] Despite the rebellion of the Israelites and their disobedience to his laws, the plan of the covenant remains unchanged. Since, as we have seen, the covenant of grace is inextricably linked with the sovereign rule of God over creation. In his monumental work on creation and covenant, Barth underlines this relationship:

> Creation comes first in the series of works of the triune God, and is thus the beginning of all the things distinct from God himself. Since it contains in itself the beginning of time, its historical reality eludes all historical observation and account, and can be expressed in the biblical creation narratives only in the form of pure saga. But according to this witness the purpose and therefore the meaning of creation is to make possible the history of God's covenant with man which has its beginning, its centre and its culmination in Jesus Christ. The history of this covenant is as much the goal of creation as creation itself is the beginning of this history.[142]

There will be a "New Covenant" (*kaine diatheke*) established with God's people in the messianic era (Jeremiah 31:31-34; 32:40; 50:5; Ezekiel 16:60; 37:26; Hosea 2:18). It is a New Covenant realized in Christ (1 Corinthians 11:25; Hebrews 8:1-13).[143] As it was God alone who determined that he should be Israel's God and that Israel should be his people, it is God alone who can restore the covenant when it is broken. Tom Smail declares that this is what God does in Christ in representing the Israelites in keeping of the covenant on their behalf, dealing with the consequences of their unfaithfulness.[144] Hence the righteous requirements and obligations (*dikaiomata tou nomou*) of the covenant communion with God, as these are outlined in the Torah, are realized in Christ. Torrance comments on this supreme act of grace:

---

[140] For a further discussion, see Kline, *Kingdom Prologue*, 2. Kline points out that the two possible ways of treating a *berit*, by observing or violating it, are the most conspicuous and pervasive ideas found in immediate association with that term in the Bible.

[141] Whereas in the Hebrew Bible the concept of grace is expressed mainly by three groups of words: the noun *hesed* focusing on the faithful maintenance of a covenantal relationship; *hanan* expressing the gratuitous gift of affection; and *raham* denoting mercy and compassion, in the New Testament the definitive manifestation of grace is the revelation of God in Christ.

[142] Barth, *Church Dogmatics*, vol. 3/1, 42. Section 1 of this part of *Church Dogmatics* is headed: "Creation, History and Creation History;" section 2: "Creation as the External Basis of the Covenant;" and section 3: "The Covenant as the Internal Basis of Creation." Cf. Gerrit C. Berkouwer, *The Triumph of Grace in the Theology of Karl Barth* (London: Paternoster, 1956), 53. Berkouwer notes that for Barth, creation is seen as indissolubly related to the covenant of grace in Jesus Christ.

[143] For a further discussion of the church being a covenant people, see Grenz, *Theology for the Community of God*, 464-467.

[144] Tom Smail, *Once and For All: A Confession of the Cross* (London: Darton, Longmann & Todd, 1998), 37.

Grace in the New Testament is the basic and the most characteristic element of the Christian gospel. It is the breaking into the world of the ineffable love of God in a deed of absolutely decisive significance, which cuts across the whole of human life and sets it on a new basis. That is actualized in the person of Jesus Christ, with which grace is inseparably associated, and supremely exhibited on the cross by which the believer is once and for all put in the right with God.[145]

Because of this supreme act of grace, the worship owed to God in response to God's unconditional covenant commitment to us is itself realized for us and on our behalf in the New Covenant.[146] This implies that the covenant theme is the background for the whole New Testament even where it is not explicitly noted.[147] Although the first covenant was defective, it was God who prepared the way for another covenant that would replace the first and succeed where it had failed. Bruce points out that this means both the Old and the New Covenant alike speak of Christ: "It is he who gives unity to each and to both together. The former collection looks forward with hope to his appearance and work; the latter tells how that hope was fulfilled."[148] Yet because God's promises cannot fail, this New Covenant is not new in essence. Rather, it is new in fulfillment.[149] God's law would be written on hearts of flesh, which allows his people to keep the covenant in a more effective way.

Grace and the Dynamics of Community

That God has graciously established a covenant with those he has created has profound implications for our perception of human existence and personal relations. What it reveals is that humankind was created to be in covenant relationship with God. This is captured by St. Augustine of Hippo, who became known as 'the doctor of grace' (*doctor gratiae*), at the start of his *Confessions*: "You have made us for yourself, and our hearts are restless until they rest in you."[150] Pannenberg relates this internal yearning after God with not being bound to a particular environment.[151] Man's unlimited openness to the world results only from his destiny beyond the

---

[145] Torrance, *The Doctrine of Grace in the Apostolic Fathers*, 34.

[146] James B. Torrance, "The Vicarious Humanity of Christ," in *The Incarnation: Ecumenical Studies in the Nicene-Constantinopolitan Creed AD381*, ed. Thomas F. Torrance (Edinburgh: Handsel, 1981), 128-129. Cf. Nicholas T. Wright, *Jesus and the Victory of God*, vol. 2 (London: SPCK, 1996), 275. N.T. Wright comments on the human response to this supreme act of grace: "Precisely because it concerned the renewal of the covenant, the restoration of Israel, the fulfillment of the promises, and the realization of the hope, Jesus' retelling of Israel's story included the call and challenge to his hearers to live as the renewed Israel, the people of the New Covenant."

[147] See Giblet and Grelot, "Covenant," 78-79.

[148] Bruce, *The Books and the Parchments*, 68-69.

[149] See Thomson, "Covenant (OT)," 792.

[150] St. Augustine of Hippo, *Confessions*, vol. 1/1. (Oxford: Clarendon Press, 1992), 3.

[151] Wolfhart Pannenberg, *What is Man?: Contemporary Anthropology in Theological Perspective*, trans. Duane A. Priebe (Philadelphia: Fortress, 1970), 1-13.

world. This unending movement into the open is directed toward God, who is beyond everything that confronts man in the world. It is a path towards man's destiny to be in "community with God."[152] Indeed the biblical theme of creation, as Alistair McFadyen notes, "is not ultimately concerned with cosmogony or cosmology but with the relationship between God and God's creatures."[153]

As we are created to be in relationship with God, Barth describes this as being created to be God's covenant-partner.[154] A genuine knowledge of humanity comes from realizing that to be a man is to be with God.[155] In this covenantal relationship we see a unique feature, which is that among all God's creatures, it is the human being who has been chosen, fundamentally and ontologically, to be the object of God's personal election. Yet true selfhood is not something we can take for granted. On the contrary, it is a gift of divine grace.[156] Here again we see the inextricable relationship between revelation and reconciliation. Our real humanity to be in covenantal relationship with God has only become visible and made possible in Jesus Christ. Starting from this point, which Barth calls the "Archimedean point," enables us to discover the ontological determination of man.[157] For Christ does not merely show our true humanity, he enables the fulfillment of our destiny to be in fellowship with God (Romans 8:29). This priestly ministry of Christ, Gunton notes, means "the representative bearer of the image becomes, as the channel of the Spirit, the vehicle of the renewal of the image in those who enter into relation with him."[158]

If the church is to operate from this basis of divine grace for becoming God's covenant-partners, then it is important to understand the nature of the being of God as triune.[159] Before the world was made, the Trinity planned humankind's redemption. The Father purposed that the Lamb would be "slain from the creation of the world" (Revelation 13:8). The Son entered the world as the Servant to fulfill this plan. The Spirit, who is the facilitator of the covenant community, would indwell

---

[152] Ibid., 54-55. In contrast with Rahner's anthropocentric understanding of humankind's "pure openness" to God, we find here that humankind is still entirely dependent upon divine grace for knowing God and in coming into community with God.

[153] Alistair I. McFadyen, *The Call to Personhood: A Christian Theory of the Individual in Social Relationships* (Cambridge: Cambridge University Press, 1990), 18.

[154] Barth, *Church Dogmatics*, vol. 3/2, 204.

[155] Ibid., 135.

[156] For a further discussion, see Hans Urs von Balthasar, *The Theology of Karl Barth: Exposition and Interpretation,* trans. Edward T. Oakes (San Francisco: Ignatius Press, 1992), 127, and William S. Johnson, *The Mystery of God: Karl Barth and the Postmodern Foundations of Theology* (Louisville, Kentucky: Westminster John Knox Press, 1997), 79.

[157] Barth, *Church Dogmatics*, vol. 3/2, 132. This does raise the issue, however, of Barth's repeated insistence on the ontological determination of all people in God's covenant with humanity in Jesus Christ. It is this aspect of universal divine determination in Christ that is a controversial feature of Barth's view of humankind's covenant relationship with God.

[158] Colin E. Gunton, *Christ and Creation* (Carlisle: Paternoster, 1992), 101.

[159] See Vladimir Lossky, *In the Image and Likeness of God* (London: Mowbrays, 1975), for a prime example of this recognition.

those who accepted the Messiah as their Lord. In deriving significance from the doctrine of the Trinity for how we act, Grenz claims, the ethical life is "the life-in-relationship."[160] For when the Spirit indwells Christians we share in the love found at the heart of the triune God himself.[161] Thus, as we have argued, the theocentric and trinitarian nature of the covenant of grace not only reveals that we were created to be in relationship with God, but it also reveals that we were created to be in relationship with other people and with all of creation. We are rescued from our sin to enable us to participate in the new humanity in a redeemed world in the presence of the triune God (Ephesians 2:14-19). This is in turn a foretaste, asserts Grenz, of the full fellowship God will bring to pass at the culmination of history:

> The corporate-cosmic dimension of God's program arises from a wider soteriology related to the fuller biblical picture of the nature of guilt and estrangement...The divine program leads not only toward establishing individual peace with God in isolation; it extends as well to the healing of all relationships – to ourselves, to one another, and to nature.[162]

This relational dimension of the covenant of grace exposes another weakness of Descartes' philosophy. Descartes advocated a conception of humanity that isolated the self from the world beyond the self. Catherine LaCugna notes that Descartes "presupposed that the self can be a self by itself, apart from relationship with anything or anyone else."[163] Therefore in contrast with this individualistic philosophy, the covenant of grace declares that we were created to be part of a community, the church. This is what is meant by *ecclesial koinonia* (1 Corinthians 1:9; 1 John 1:3).

We see this being for others supremely in the person of Jesus Christ. As well as being for God, as Barth states, Jesus is for men and is committed to meeting their needs.[164] It verifies the inextricable connection between being for others and being for God.[165] Stressing this juxtaposition and its attending ethical implications, Barth firmly refused to accept that true humanity can live in isolation.[166] In taking this stance, Barth's understanding of the relational self presents a strong parallel with the

---

[160] Grenz, *Theology for the Community of God*, 76.

[161] Ibid., 484. Cf. James B. Torrance, *Worship, Community and the Triune God of Grace* (Carlisle: Paternoster, 1996), 40.

[162] Grenz, *Theology for the Community of God*, 482. Cf. Kevin J. Vanhoozer, "Human Being, Individual and Social," in *The Cambridge Companion to Christian Doctrine*, 184. Kevin Vanhoozer states: "To know oneself, as one whose individual and social being has been decisively shaped by Jesus Christ, is to accept gratefully one's vocation as a responsive and responsible communicative agent who exists in covenantal relation with oneself, with others and with God."

[163] Catherine M. LaCugna, *God for Us: The Trinity and Christian Life* (San Francisco: Harper, 1992), 251.

[164] Barth, *Church Dogmatics*, vol. 3/2, 223.

[165] Ibid., 211-212.

[166] Ibid., 229.

communal ontology espoused by John Zizioulas, who offers a theological dimension of the self as person. "The highest form of capacity for man," Zizioulas claims, "is to be found in the notion of the imago Dei."[167] It is this relational aspect of the imago Dei, which "is a condition for an ontology of personhood."[168] Ontological identity, it follows, "is to be found ultimately not in every 'substance' as such, but only in a being which is free from the boundaries of the 'self.'"[169] Freedom of this kind derives as the Spirit through Christ forms human beings in community.

Contributing to our understanding of what it means to live as a community is the work of John Macmurray, who describes the self as existing only in dynamic relation with the Other.[170] To be part of a community, Macmurray explains, is fundamentally different from being part of an impersonal society. A society is based on self-interested relationships that are contractual. In contrast, to be part of a community is to be part of a covenant, which constitutes a fellowship. Yet although Macmurray emphasizes the importance of community for human relationships, there is tension with the full implications of the covenant of grace. For Macmurray, a community is constituted and maintained by mutual affection. It is within the family, where a child experiences dependence on a personal Other, which is "the basis as well as the origin of all subsequent communities."[171] In its full development, "the idea of a universal personal Other is the idea of God."[172] This suggests a failure to recognize that we are to live in community due to being created by a covenant-keeping God.

Divine Affirmation of Human Value

Finding our true personhood through being in communion with God and with others has significance for our conception of human nature on which so much depends. Leslie Stevenson and David Haberman claim that for individuals, this will relate to the meaning and purpose of their lives. For societies, this will relate to our vision of community.[173] Our answers to these basic questions of life will depend on the value we place on a human being. Yet, in recent years, the belief that the self is purely material has increased impacting upon our conception of human dignity.[174]

---

[167] John D. Zizioulas, "Human Capacity and Human Incapacity: A Theological Exploration of Personhood," in *Scottish Journal of Theology*, vol. 28/5 (October 1975), 446.

[168] John D. Zizioulas, "On Being a Person: Towards an Ontology of Personhood," in *Persons, Divine and Human*, ed. Christoph Schwöbel and Colin E. Gunton (Edinburgh: T&T Clark, 1999), 41.

[169] Zizioulas, "Human Capacity and Human Incapacity," 409.

[170] John Macmurray, *Persons in Relation: Being the Gifford Lectures Delivered in the University of Glasgow in 1954* (London: Faber, 1961), 17.

[171] Ibid., 154-155.

[172] Ibid., 164.

[173] Leslie Stevenson and David L. Haberman, *Ten Theories of Human Nature* (Oxford: Oxford University Press, 1998), 3.

[174] For a further analysis, see Dallas Willard, *The Divine Conspiracy: Rediscovering Our Hidden Life in God* (San Francisco: Harper, 1998), 82.

In contrast to physicalist accounts, in entering into a covenant of grace with humankind, this indicates that God affirms the value of every person. We were created in God's image, which demonstrates that out of all creation humanity was made to be in a special relationship with God (Genesis 1:26; 9:5-6). This leads to the conclusion that man's life is sacred as the image marks man as God's possession. It denotes that humanity's nature and destiny are tightly interwoven.[175] Calvin captured this when he claimed there is something intrinsic about the way God is that is like the way we are also: "No one can look upon himself without immediately turning his thoughts to the contemplation of God, in whom he 'lives and moves.'"[176] Hence, Calvin argues "we are not to consider that men merit of themselves but to look upon the image of God in all men, to which we owe all honour and love."[177]

This understanding of our true nature and destiny highlights the differentiating feature that sets human beings apart from animals. We have been created to resemble God in certain important, though limited, ways. This includes the capacity to reason, to relate deeply on an interpersonal level, to be morally responsible, to make free choices, to be self-conscious, rationally reflective, and to be creative. Summarizing these features of what it is to be human, James Moreland declares: "We have been made in the likeness of a supremely valuable, self-aware, good, creative, free being."[178] Here we find the source of our personal identity. It is due to being created by God in his image, to be in a covenant relationship with God and with all creation, which gives persons tremendous intrinsic dignity and worth. In his examination of the imago Dei, Webster highlights its inextricable relationship with the theocentric nature of the covenant of grace and God's plans for his creation:

> Theological teaching about the divine image…is a central motif in ensuring the co-inherence of creation and redemption; it offers a means of emphasizing that salvation concerns the restoration of human fellowship; it roots a Christian understanding of human nature in language about God's relation to his creation; and it serves to underline that the saving work of God includes within it a moral and cultural imperative.[179]

Thus by highlighting the concept of the imago Dei through emphasizing the relational dimensions of human existence and life in community, the covenant of

---

[175] See David Cairns, *The Image of God in Man* (London: Collins, 1973), 29.

[176] Calvin, *Institutes of the Christian Religion*, vol. 1/1, 35.

[177] Calvin, *Institutes of the Christian Religion*, vol. 3/7, 696. The parable of the Good Samaritan, Calvin claimed, taught the word neighbour extends to every man, "because the whole human race is united by a sacred bond of fellowship." See John Calvin, *Commentary on a Harmony of the Evangelists, Matthew, Mark, and Luke*, vol. 3, trans. William Pringle (Grand Rapids: Eerdmans, 1956), 61.

[178] James P. Moreland, *What is the Soul?: Recovering Human Personhood in a Scientific Age* (Norcross, Georgia: RZIM, 2002), 41.

[179] John Webster, "What's Evangelical about Evangelical Soteriology?" in *What Does it Mean to be Saved?: Broadening Evangelical Horizons of Salvation*, ed. John G. Stackhouse (Grand Rapids: Baker, 2002), 180.

grace presents a concept of human value that stands in sharp contrast with a post-Enlightenment understanding of human worth based on principles of natural reason.

The Will of God and the Mission of the Church

As the covenant of grace affirms the intrinsic worth of every person, this informs the church in how it responds to issues of social and political concern. Not only will our understanding of the self be changed when we recognize that human beings are made in God's image to be in relationship with God; our sense of morality will change also. Charles Taylor argues convincingly in *Sources of the Self* that selfhood and morality turn out to be inextricably intertwined themes. Here again Descartes has been influential in the way we think about morality. In analyzing Cartesian philosophy, Taylor claims that by situating the moral sources within us, the result is that we no longer see ourselves as related to moral sources outside of us.[180] Contrary to Descartes' understanding of morality, through the covenant of grace, we discover the will of God and his desire for justice to be manifest in the world. This reflects the divine attributes of God who is the ultimate standard of righteousness and justice. No idea, Wright points out, is more all-pervasive in the Old Testament.[181] Hence, Wright maintains: "Knowledge of God is prior to the practice of justice."[182]

With the goal being to reflect God's divine attributes, God calls his covenant people to righteousness, which means to live in accordance with his will and character (Deuteronomy 32:4; Psalm 89:14; Isaiah 61:8). The Hebrew word for righteousness is *tsedaqah*, which refers to the way things are supposed to be.[183] The way things are supposed to be is based on the inherent value God places on his creation. This is translated into Greek as *dikaiosune* and into Latin as *iustitia*, which means justice, fairness and equity. What we find in Scripture is that any form of injustice is in direct opposition to God's will. Biblical justice is a comprehensive term denoting God's desire for right relationships among all creation. For example, following the exodus from Egypt, God gave the Israelites laws of justice in order to protect the powerless of society (Exodus 23:1-9). Justice is to extend to the land itself and with all of creation (Exodus 23:10-12). We are to act justly and love mercy (Proverbs 31:9; Isaiah 10:1-2; Ezekiel 16:49; Hosea 12:6; Micah 6:8; Zechariah 7:9-10). God's complaint against Israel is a warning to those who exploit the powerless: "They trample on the heads of the poor as upon the dust of the ground and deny justice to the oppressed" (Amos 2:7). Likewise, the New Testament teaches that God chooses the poor to correct the injustice done to them by the rich (James 2:5).[184]

---

[180] Charles Taylor, *Sources of the Self: The Making of the Modern Identity* (Cambridge: Cambridge University Press, 1989), 143.

[181] Wright, *Living as the People of God*, 133.

[182] Ibid., 146.

[183] The root meaning of *tsedaqah* is rightness and that which matches up to a standard (Leviticus 19:36; Deuteronomy 25:15; Psalm 23:3).

[184] See Richard J. Bauckham, *James: Wisdom of James, Disciple of Jesus the Sage* (London: Routledge, 1999), 185-203.

The poor receive God's special attention not because they are of greater value than the rich, but rather because God desires justice to be displayed for all humankind, which includes this group in society who are on the "wronged" side of a situation of injustice. For God's righteous will to be done, Wright notes, this requires the execution of justice to have this situation redressed.[185] Jesus' desire to affirm the dignity of the marginalized of society was therefore not a neglect of others. Rather, as Bauckham highlights, it was Jesus' mission to reach all with God's loving solidarity. In order to achieve this aim, Jesus placed a particular emphasis on serving those who were excluded from human solidarity. Bauckham asserts:

> Jesus' vision of the kingdom of God, provisionally present in a fragmentary way through his ministry, was of a society without the privilege and status, which favour some and exclude others. Thus those who had no status in society as it was then constituted were given a conspicuous place in society as God's rule was reconstituting it through Jesus.[186]

If the Christian community is to see itself charged with continuing Christ's mission on earth, then to be true to the founder, God's desire for universal justice has profound implications for the socio-political mission of the church. This is a hallmark of Reformational theology in that the indicatives of grace carry the imperatives of obligation. Central throughout Scripture is the conviction that the divine initiative in redeeming the world calls forth a response of faith from God's people commensurate with his revealed will.[187] Indeed as God's covenant people, whether this is Israel in the Old Testament or the New Testament church, it follows that the ethical life is a dimension of the response to God's grace. Elaborating on the nature of these imperatives, David Field claims: "If knowledge of right and wrong is not so much an object of philosophical enquiry as an acceptance of divine revelation, it is only to be expected that imperatives will be prominent among the indicatives in the Bible."[188]

In his discussion of social morality, Richard Longenecker draws attention to this human response to God's grace arguing that the final measure for human conduct "stems from the nature of God, from the quality of his love for mankind, and from

---

[185] Wright, *Living as the People of God*, 147.

[186] Bauckham, *The Bible in Politics*, 146.

[187] For example, see Brevard S. Childs, *Biblical Theology of the Old and New Testaments: Theological Reflection on the Christian Bible* (London: SCM Press, 1992), 658; J. Andrew Kirk, "Christian Mission and the Epistemological Crisis of the West," in *To Stake a Claim: Mission and the Western Crisis of Knowledge*, ed. J. Andrew Kirk and Kevin J. Vanhoozer (Maryknoll, NY: Orbis, 1999), 164; and Dodd, *Gospel and Law*, 8-12. Charles Dodd notes that the *kerygma* (proclamation) always came before *didaché* (ethical instructions).

[188] David H. Field, "Ethics," in *New Dictionary of Theology*, 233. Cf. Grenz, *The Moral Quest*, 97-98. Elaborating on how the doctrine of grace underpins Christian ethics, Grenz argues: "What we might call the ethical life is the theme of covenant."

the character of his redemptive activity."[189] Thus Longenecker notes that obligation stems not only from the covenant in isolation, but due to God's graciously revealed nature in its entirety. Moreover, due to the moral teaching of the Bible always being presented in closest relation to the Bible's message as a whole, ethics for a Christian can never be considered as a trivial matter.

In summary we can say that due to God's desire for universal justice, in response to the divine work, the church is not to be passive. As Barth explains, the effect of grace is that it becomes the altered world-context into which our lives are inserted: "Grace is knowledge of the will of God, and as such it is the willing of the will of God."[190] Describing heaven as "the ultimate reality of God's sovereign rule," Howard Peskett and Vinoth Ramachandra illustrate how this vision of God's future embraces and informs human actions in the present.[191] The church, in being a sign of this eschatological kingdom, undertakes its mission through the empowering of the Spirit and is motivated and free to do so in response to God's grace. It is a response that has arisen from a life-changing encounter with the triune God, which leads to living in accordance with God's design and will for human existence.

Conclusion

As we have sought to demonstrate in this chapter, a central interpretive motif in approaching systematic theology as a whole is the grace of God. Few doctrines more effectively sum up the Reformation position as this doctrine. An appreciation of the covenant of grace will therefore shape our theological critique throughout this book. Specifically, that in his grace God has spoken is the starting point for the theological enterprise. It is here that we derive knowledge of God and his purposes for the world. Inextricably linked with the self-communication of God is the redemption of his chosen people, which derives from the unilateral covenant of grace. It is the indicatives of grace that provide the impetus for the church to respond to the imperatives of law. If the church is to operate from this theological basis, then in responding to the divine work, the church as an eschatological community of grace will seek to further the kingdom of God on earth, of which God's righteousness and justice are such essential constituents of his unified kingdom reign. Hence the grace of God is a central Christian doctrine for the witness of the Christian community in addressing contemporary issues of social and political concern.

---

[189] Richard N. Longenecker, *New Testament Social Ethics for Today* (Grand Rapids: Eerdmans, 1984), 9. In a paper delivered by Christopher J.H. Wright at the University of St. Andrews in August 2003 entitled "Mission as a Matrix for Hermeneutics and Biblical Theology," he argues that a holistic understanding of mission necessarily follows a holistic reading of Scripture: "The Bible renders to us the story of God's mission through God's people in their engagement with God's world for the sake of the whole of God's creation."

[190] Barth, *The Epistle to the Romans*, 207.

[191] Howard Peskett and Vinoth Ramachandra, *The Message of Mission: The Glory of Christ in All Time and Space* (Leicester: InterVarsity, 2003), 276.

PART 2

The Comparison

CHAPTER 3

Grace and Jürgen Moltmann's Political Theology

In our previous chapter, we considered the implications of the doctrine of grace for the socio-political mission of the church. We will now offer a theological exposition and comparative analysis of three influential contemporary theologians evaluating the extent to which this central Christian doctrine is evident in their theological enterprise, and particularly their conception of ecclesial witness. We will commence this task by engaging with Jürgen Moltmann's political theology, and structure this chapter around the key concepts and controlling motifs in his works. First, Moltmann's theology of the eschatological kingdom of God will be assessed and the implications for the church's socio-political involvement. Second, his emphasis on the inescapable link between christology and christopraxis will be analyzed to identify how this relationship provides direction for the church's mission. Finally, we will undertake a critical reflection on Moltmann's theological conclusions and determine to what extent this is consistent with a biblical theology of grace.

Introduction

In the midst of the debate as to the involvement of the church in the socio-political arena, one of the leading contemporary scholars who has called upon the church to be more involved in meeting the full range of society's needs is the German Protestant theologian Jürgen Moltmann. A distinctive characteristic throughout Moltmann's theological works is his desire to relate Christian faith to political goals in the contemporary world. It is Moltmann's conviction that theology must not only be deeply informed by the Bible and the Christian tradition; theology must also be able to relate critically to its particular historical and cultural context.[1] Practice is therefore at the core of Moltmann's theological method. Richard Bauckham notes the significance of Moltmann's theology in that it has opened up hermeneutical structures for relating biblical Christian faith to the realities of the contemporary world.[2] Commenting on Moltmann's comprehensive work, Gary Dorrien declares that in his opinion Moltmann has "offered the most generative, socially valuable, and suggestive theological work of the past generation. More than any other

---

[1] Jürgen Moltmann, *Theology Today* (London: SCM Press, 1988), 94.

[2] Richard J. Bauckham, *Moltmann: Messianic Theology in the Making* (Basingstoke, Hants: Marshall Pickering, 1987), 140.

contemporary theologian, he has revealed the enduring power of the biblical witness."[3]

With Moltmann's desire being to relate theology to the issues and political goals of the contemporary world, he decries the growing gap between theology and Christian life in the churches: "Theologians are regarded as dwelling in an ivory tower, while congregations are regarded as living in a theological backwater. A regrettable situation indeed!"[4] Reaffirming the purpose of theology is his passionate desire, which entails capturing the vision of God in Christ and having a concern for the Christian community in the world. Indeed Christian identity is inseparable from public relevance: "It thinks about what is of general concern in the light of hope in Christ for the kingdom of God. It becomes political in the name of the poor and the marginalized in a given society."[5] Thus Moltmann developed his political theology in the sense of a politically critical theology aiming at radical change in modern society.[6] It is a theology that is political in the broadest sense of the word.[7]

In undertaking their theological project, Moltmann is adamant that theologians must be members of the Christian community. For theology is in the service of the church's mission to the world. "Theology comes into its own when it responds to the needs of the church," states Moltmann, and "the church rediscovers her certainty as the church of Christ when she takes theology seriously and makes use of it in her daily life."[8] It is also central to his theological enterprise that it derives from biblical origins.[9] "Without biblical theology," Moltmann claims, "theology cannot be Christian theology."[10] This emphasis on rooting theology in biblical scholarship points to the methodological convictions which link Moltmann's work with that of Karl Barth.[11] Foundational to the theology of both theologians is the role of Scripture in revealing knowledge of God and his plans for the world.

---

[3] Gary J. Dorrien, *Reconstructing the Common Good: Theology and the Social Order* (Maryknoll, NY: Orbis, 1990), 99.

[4] Jürgen Moltmann, *Hope for the Church: Moltmann in Dialogue with Practical Theology* (Nashville, Tennessee: Abingdon, 1979), 128.

[5] Jürgen Moltmann, *God for a Secular Society: The Public Relevance of Theology* (Minneapolis: Fortress, 1999), 1.

[6] Richard J. Bauckham, "Jürgen Moltmann," in *The Modern Theologians: An Introduction to Christian Theology in the Twentieth Century*, ed. David F. Ford, 2nd edn (Cambridge, MA: Blackwell, 1997), 219.

[7] Jürgen Moltmann, *The Experiment Hope* (London: SCM Press, 1975), 11-12.

[8] Moltmann, *Hope for the Church*, 129.

[9] Although Moltmann's earlier work is characterized by its emphasis on biblical scholarship, in his later work he adheres to some questionable hermeneutical principles. See Richard J. Bauckham, "Time and Eternity," in *God Will Be All In All: The Eschatology of Jürgen Moltmann*, ed. Richard J. Bauckham (Edinburgh: T&T Clark, 1999), 155-226.

[10] Moltmann, *The Experiment Hope*, 7.

[11] Bauckham, *Moltmann*, 5. Yet Moltmann breaks from Barth's theological convictions in several key areas due to the eschatological perspective he employs to his entire theology.

Supremely, knowledge of God is centred on the death and resurrection of Jesus Christ. This dialectical interpretation of the cross and resurrection of Christ, which provides the hope of the eschatological transformation of the world, is the most significant controlling theological idea in Moltmann's early work and shapes his understanding of political theology.[12] It is not simply that the eschatological is one element of Christianity. Rather, "it is the medium of Christian faith as such, the key in which everything in it is set."[13] In short, Christian theology is eschatologically orientated theology.[14] With Moltmann's uncompromising focus on this eschatological horizon of theology, his theology is immediately distinguishable from the tendency in recent theology to reduce the significance of the resurrection.[15] Consequently, Moltmann's biblically based theological engagement ignites debate as to the socio-political involvement of the church in the twenty-first century.

The Eschatological Kingdom of God and a Vision of Transformation

The Resurrection of Christ and Christian Hope

Characteristic of Moltmann's theology is a strong christological centre, which is evident in the work by which he first became widely known, *Theology of Hope*.[16] In this highly acclaimed work, Moltmann is adamant that the resurrection of Christ, which is an event of dialectical promise, has profound significance for the world and the universal mission of the church.[17] Christ's resurrection is a history-making event. All other history is transformed in the light of this event. Moltmann states:

> The eschaton of the parousia of Christ, as a result of its eschatological promise, causes the present that can be experienced at any given moment to become historic by breaking away from the past and breaking out towards the things that are to come.[18]

Of supreme importance, the resurrection of Christ initiated the movement towards the eschatological kingdom of God, which includes God's eschatological promise of

---

[12] Bauckham, "Jürgen Moltmann," 210. Moltmann outlines his systematic eschatology in *The Coming of God: Christian Eschatology* (London: SCM Press, 1996). Its title is taken from 1 Corinthians 15:28, which encapsulates his understanding of the new creation that God will indwell.

[13] Moltmann, *Theology of Hope*, 16.

[14] Ibid., 325-326.

[15] Richard J. Bauckham, *The Theology of Jürgen Moltmann* (Edinburgh: T&T Clark, 1995), 39.

[16] In *Theology of Hope* every aspect of Christian theology was considered from the eschatological perspective of God's future, which provided the eschatological direction for Moltmann's later works.

[17] George Wilhelm Friedrich Hegel and Hans Joachim Iwand were of significance to the development of Moltmann's dialectical interpretation of Christ's death and resurrection. See M. Douglas Meeks, *Origins of the Theology of Hope* (Philadelphia: Fortress, 1974), 19-53.

[18] Moltmann, *Theology of Hope*, 227.

the world's future transformation.[19] Geiko Müller-Fahrenholz claims that for Moltmann, "'kingdom of God' is the basic symbol for the eschatological dimension which shapes his theology."[20] With this promise of the future transformation of the world, Moltmann asserts: "Christian hope is resurrection hope."[21] Trevor Hart notes that Moltmann's theology of hope is an assured hope "in the sense that it is invested in the capacities of the one who raised Christ from the dead."[22] It is this central integrative motif grounded in the resurrection of Christ, Bauckham points out, which "gives to Moltmann's theology at the same time a christological centre and a universal eschatological horizon."[23]

In grasping an understanding of Christian hope in the resurrection, this motivates Christians to revolutionary political praxis. For the things that are not yet, that are future, "become 'thinkable' because they can be hoped for."[24] Thus Moltmann's ethic of hope became a political theology: "The theologian is not concerned merely to supply a different interpretation of the world, of history and of human nature, but to transform them in expectation of a divine transformation."[25] With the world being seen as transformable, the task of the church is to be an agent of transformation in the world in keeping society moving towards the eschatological kingdom of God. The sphere of obedience to God's laws therefore categorically includes the socio-political arena. It is to live in active obedience to God's command, which is the reverse side of his promise. Moltmann states: "Politics is the wider context of all Christian theology. It must be critical with respect to political religion and religious politics and affirmative with respect to the concrete involvement of Christians for 'justice, peace and the integrity of creation.'"[26]

It is important to recognize that the key concept here for Moltmann is *anticipation*.[27] Rather than human activity in the present building the future kingdom of God, the hope of a new reality arouses activity in the present, which anticipates the eschatological kingdom: "These anticipations are not yet the kingdom of God itself. But they are real mediations of the kingdom of God within the limited

---

[19] Moltmann, *The Experiment Hope*, 45. For an overview of the context in which Moltmann developed his theology, see Christopher Morse, *The Logic of Promise in Moltmann's Theology* (Philadelphia: Fortress, 1979), 3. Morse notes that Moltmann's work is to be found amidst the resurgence of interest in eschatological themes, which became prominent in German theology in the 1960s.

[20] Geiko Müller-Fahrenholz, *The Kingdom and the Power: The Theology of Jürgen Moltmann*, trans. John Bowden (London: SCM Press, 2000), 221.

[21] Moltmann, *Theology of Hope*, 18.

[22] Trevor A. Hart, "Imagination for the Kingdom of God?" in *God Will Be All In All*, 69.

[23] Bauckham, *The Theology of Jürgen Moltmann*, 35.

[24] Moltmann, *Theology of Hope*, 30.

[25] Ibid., 84.

[26] Jürgen Moltmann, "Covenant or Leviathan? Political Theology for Modern Times," in *Scottish Journal of Theology*, vol. 47/1 (February 1994), 40.

[27] Moltmann, *The Church in the Power of the Spirit*, 24-26, 191-194.

possibilities of history."[28] In anticipating the future transformation of the world the universal mission of the church includes political activity bringing with it resistance, suffering, and struggle.[29] It is a mission characterized by its goal of seeking justice in the world in all its dimensions. Inextricably linked with the notion of anticipation, therefore, involves the church being critically against the status quo. This is the first political effect of Christian hope. It is a vision for the manifestation of God's righteousness in a world characterized by suffering and injustice. Moltmann states: "To live in anticipation means letting one's own present be determined by the expected future of God's kingdom and his righteousness and justice."[30]

This vision of transformation and hope for the world arises through the Christian himself being transformed by the gospel.[31] Yet personal transformation, Moltmann claims, is not an end in itself: "Not to be conformed to this world does not mean merely to be transformed in oneself, but to transform in opposition and creative expectation the face of the world in the midst of which one believes, hopes and loves."[32] Consequently, the church's mission includes two key imperatives: proclamation of the gospel and social action. Despite the need for the church to be an agent of transformation in the world, however, Moltmann claims that many in the church "have become so blind that they no longer see that the need to free the oppressed has a Christian justification."[33] Elaborating on this tension, Moltmann declares: "Nearly every denomination of Christianity is becoming polarized between those calling for old-fashioned soul-winning and those advocating new styles of social action that shock and startle the faithful."[34] Yet there is a growing inequality between the rich North and the ever-poorer South, which the world cannot ignore. Moltmann describes this crisis "as a congenital defect of the civilization itself."[35] Faced with these contemporary issues of social and political concern the church is to be a critical agent of transformation in the world. The church undertakes this holistic mission guided by a Christian hope as revealed in the resurrection, and in anticipation of the all-encompassing eschatological kingdom of God.

Human Rights and a Theology of Liberation

Human rights have come to occupy a prominent place in the development of Moltmann's political theology, and have enabled the formulation of specific political

---

[28] Jürgen Moltmann, *On Human Dignity* (London: SCM Press, 1984), 109.

[29] Moltmann, *The Church in the Power of the Spirit*, 191.

[30] Jürgen Moltmann, "The Liberation of the Future and its Anticipations in History," in *God Will Be All In All*, 286.

[31] Moltmann, *Theology of Hope*, 328-329.

[32] Ibid., 330.

[33] Jürgen Moltmann, *The Future of Creation* (London: SCM Press, 1979), 106.

[34] Moltmann, *The Experiment Hope*, 4-5.

[35] Jürgen Moltmann, *The Way of Jesus Christ: Christology in Messianic Dimensions* (London: SCM Press, 1990), 64-65. The plight of those living in the developing world has particular prominence in this theological work.

goals in his theological project.[36] Moltmann declares: "Church guidelines on political and social matters gain their universal significance only through reference to human rights. Through its relationship to human rights the church becomes the church of the world."[37] Central to his theological position on human rights, Moltmann identifies the dignity of every person due to being created in the image of God. For although "the doctrine of creation sees all things as a creation of God," states Moltmann, "man as the image of God…indicates the special position of man in the world."[38] Yet the image of God is not simply the given constitution of human nature. Rather, Moltmann insists it is a destiny to be realized: "The human rights to life, freedom, community, and self-determination mirror God's right to the human being because the human being is destined to be God's image in all conditions and relationships of life."[39] This created destiny to be in a relationship with God affirms the irreducible dignity of all members of society: "Of all creatures it is man alone that has been created and destined as the image of God upon earth."[40]

To deny persons their rights is therefore to deny them their humanity. Christians have a duty to prevent such abuse, asserts Moltmann, "to stand for the dignity of human beings in their life with God and for God."[41] Due to being created by God to have a relationship with God, God has a claim upon human beings whom he has created in his image. Furthermore, in highlighting the worth of all humankind, Moltmann calls on all Christians to recognize the holistic nature of the salvation that Christ brings: "Christian theology is theology of liberation, for it understands Christ in the comprehensive sense as liberator."[42] A holistic concern for the human person demonstrated by Christ should correspondingly be characteristic of the church. In short, holistic christology requires holistic soteriology.[43] It is this multidimensional understanding of human oppression and liberation that is such a distinctive and pervasive feature of Moltmann's political theology. This includes liberating activity in the economic, political, cultural, and industrial dimensions of human existence.

In his engagement with contemporary issues, Moltmann highlights the challenges of the world's economic systems working in a spiral making the rich nations richer and the poor nations poorer. Because of the vicious circle of poverty produced through these relationships between powerful and weaker nations, the church is to work for liberation in the political sphere.[44] Moltmann describes these unjust systems

---

[36] We will be analyzing the concept of human rights more fully in chapter 7.

[37] Moltmann, *On Human Dignity*, 7.

[38] Jürgen Moltmann, *Man: Christian Anthropology in the Conflicts of the Present* (London: SPCK, 1974), 109.

[39] Moltmann, *On Human Dignity*, 17.

[40] Moltmann, *Man*, 108.

[41] Moltmann, *On Human Dignity*, 20.

[42] Moltmann, *The Experiment Hope*, 154.

[43] Bauckham, "Jürgen Moltmann," 220.

[44] Moltmann, *The Crucified God*, 329-332.

and the worldwide economic order as "structural sins."[45] These systems of exploitation and their impact on poverty can only be overcome by a redistribution of economic power to achieve greater social justice in the world. Liberation from the circle of oppression in the political dimension of life also requires democracy to be established for the world's citizens, which recognizes the human rights of all people. Moltmann declares: "Democracy is the symbol for the liberation of men from the vicious circle of force."[46] The effect of these changes will result in life returning to this world "when God's justice restores their rights to the people who have none, and makes the unjust just, and makes both righteous."[47]

Although Moltmann notes that progress has been made with the establishment of the 'Universal Declaration of Human Rights' of 1948 and the 'International Covenants' of 1966, "the social utopias of human equality" have found themselves left behind. Moltmann states: "The globalization of the economy and the total marketing of everything is producing ever-greater social inequalities, and is endangering political democracy in the process." The implication of these changes is that they are "reducing the dignity of human beings to their market value; they are making an increasing number of men and women 'surplus people.'"[48] In a world of increasing individualism the unspoken belief is that the worth of people is perceived to be equivalent to what they are able to buy.[49] Hence it is people living in the developing world, claims Moltmann, "who through their struggle for freedom and self-determination have impressed upon all human beings and states the urgent necessity of recognizing and realizing fundamental human rights."[50] Direction is here given to the church in its mission to the world to strive for the realization of human rights for all people across the globe "to develop new social utopias which envisage a society deserving of the name 'humane.'"[51] For our horizontal relationship with the rest of humanity means that we share with others the inescapable fact that God has created all of us. This egalitarian understanding of the common humanity of all people "precedes every society and every established system of rule."[52]

The Glory of God in Creation

A theocentric worldview dominates Moltmann's political theology. It is a worldview focused on the expectation of the kingdom and lordship of the triune God. Moltmann

---

[45] Jürgen Moltmann, *The Spirit of Life: A Universal Affirmation* (London: SCM Press, 1992), 138.

[46] Moltmann, *The Crucified God*, 332-333.

[47] Moltmann, *The Spirit of Life*, 123.

[48] Jürgen Moltmann, "What Has Happened to Our Utopias?" in *God Will Be All In All*, 121.

[49] Jürgen Moltmann, *Experiences in Theology: Ways and Forms of Christian Theology* (London: SCM Press, 2000), 153.

[50] Moltmann, *On Human Dignity*, 19.

[51] Moltmann, "What Has Happened to Our Utopias?" 121.

[52] Moltmann, *The Church in the Power of the Spirit*, 179.

declares: "It is plain that even in the early days of Israel, the hope which has its ground in the promise is directed towards the lordship of Yahweh."[53] Thus although humans are made in God's image they are not the centre of creation. Humans exist with the rest of creation in having its goal in God. Creation is to be further understood in the light of the gospel of Christ, which gives it an eschatological orientation.[54] For the kingdom of God is "a future in which God is finally and completely present, in which men receive their freedom in God, and in which all the misery of the creation is overcome."[55] The kingdom represents the eschatological goal of the whole material cosmos. It is not a promise of another world. Instead, it is the promise of the transformation of this present world where all things will be made anew. It is a world in which God's glory will indwell his perfected creation. God will be honoured and there will be justice on earth. Moltmann states:

> The subject of eschatology is the future, and more than the future. Eschatology talks about God's future... In his future, God comes to his creation and, through the power of his righteousness and justice, frees it for his kingdom, and makes it the dwelling place of his glory.[56]

An integral feature of Moltmann's theology of the glory of God in creation is the concept of the trinitarian history. This is the history of God's involvement in the world in the history of Jesus Christ and the Holy Spirit, which together accomplish the world's eschatological goal. In characterizing the Spirit as the "the divine subject of the history of Jesus," Moltmann declares that the mission of the Spirit derives from the key historical event of the cross and resurrection.[57] Pneumatology thus brings christology and eschatology together.[58] This mission of both the Spirit and the Son are directed to God's all-encompassing eschatological kingdom, which will climax "in the glorifying of God and the liberation of the world."[59] Moltmann makes this explicitly clear in *The Coming of God*: "The glorification of God is the ultimate purpose of creation."[60] In doing so, Moltmann exposes his disagreement with Barth's doctrine of creation and refuses to accept that creation is merely "a stage for God's history with men and women." Instead, "the goal of this history is the consummation of creation in its glorification."[61] With this dimension to Christian eschatology, he

---

[53] Moltmann, *Theology of Hope*, 216.

[54] Jürgen Moltmann, *God in Creation: An Ecological Doctrine of Creation: The Gifford Lectures 1984-1985* (London: SCM Press, 1985), 4-5.

[55] Moltmann, *The Experiment Hope*, 53.

[56] Moltmann, "The Liberation of the Future," 265.

[57] Moltmann, *The Church in the Power of the Spirit*, 36.

[58] Moltmann, *The Spirit of Life*, 69.

[59] Moltmann, *The Church in the Power of the Spirit*, 60.

[60] Moltmann, *The Coming of God*, 323.

[61] Moltmann, *God in Creation*, 56.

states: "Out of the resurrection of Christ, joy throws open cosmic and eschatological perspectives that reach forward to the redemption of the whole cosmos."[62]

Recognizing the priority of God's glory will cause Christians to grasp the nature of the church's mission in anticipation of God's eschatological kingdom. It is a mission of multidimensional liberation to seek the glory of God in all aspects of his creation: "Wherever on the way to this goal the gospel is preached to the poor, sins are forgiven, the sick are healed, the oppressed are freed and outcasts are accepted, God is glorified and creation is in part perfected."[63] This relentless theocentricity conspicuously demonstrates that Moltmann's theological project is diametrically opposed to the anthropocentricism dominating since the Enlightenment. On the contrary, for Moltmann, the rule of God is primary, which is reflected in how he views the task of theology: "Theology is never concerned with the actual existence of a God. It is interested solely in the rule of this God in heaven and on earth."[64]

The Lordship of Christ Over His Church

Fundamental to Moltmann's ecclesiology as outlined in *The Church in the Power of the Spirit* is the fact that the church is subject to the lordship of Jesus Christ alone.[65] Because Christ is "the eschatological person" who is the founder of the church, "the church does not live from the past; it exists as a factor of present liberation, between remembrance of his history and hope of his kingdom."[66] This messianic ecclesiology has its basis in Moltmann's eschatological christology, which "requires us to see Christ as the subject of his church and to bring the church's life into alignment with him."[67] Consequently, the mission of the church is directed towards the messianic kingdom, which the church serves.[68] For the kingdom of God and Christ "belong inseparably together."[69] With this theocentric focus on God's kingdom, Moltmann states: "The church's first word is not 'church' but Christ. The church's final word is not 'church' but the glory of the Father and the Son in the Spirit of liberty."[70] Its mission is participation in the mission of Jesus.[71] Moreover, it is a mission undertaken with joy: "In the remembered and hoped-for liberty of Christ the church serves the liberation of men by demonstrating human freedom in its own life and by

---

[62] Moltmann, *The Coming of God*, 338.

[63] Moltmann, *The Church in the Power of the Spirit*, 60.

[64] Jürgen Moltmann, *The Trinity and the Kingdom of God: The Doctrine of God* (London: SCM Press, 1981), 191.

[65] *Theology of Hope*, *The Crucified God*, and *The Church in the Power of the Spirit* comprise Moltmann's early trilogy.

[66] Moltmann, *The Church in the Power of the Spirit*, 73-75.

[67] Ibid., 66.

[68] Ibid., 6.

[69] Jürgen Moltmann, *Jesus Christ for Today's World* (London: SCM Press, 1994), 7.

[70] Moltmann, *The Church in the Power of the Spirit*, 19.

[71] Jürgen Moltmann, *The Power of the Powerless* (London: SCM Press, 1983), 71.

manifesting its rejoicing in that freedom."[72] It is here that we see Moltmann's political theology is based on obedience to Christ's lordship in all dimensions of life.

In being under the lordship of Christ the kingdom of God is not there for the sake of the church. Quite the reverse; the church exists for the sake of God's coming kingdom and its righteousness and justice.[73] Moltmann insists: "All the church's own concerns and interests must be subordinated to Jesus' concern for God's kingdom."[74] The church lives for the kingdom in two distinct senses. One is the missionary proclamation of the gospel with the goal being that the entire world would know of God's promise of new creation through the power of the resurrection. Yet a true holistic understanding of salvation must derive from "shalom" in the Old Testament sense. This does not mean merely salvation of the soul, but includes "the realization of the eschatological hope of justice, the humanizing of man, the socializing of humanity, peace for all creation." It is this "other side" of reconciliation with God, claims Moltmann, which has often been ignored in the history of Christianity. But it is only in the light of this "other side" of reconciliation that Christians "can gain new impulses for the shaping of man's public, social, and political life."[75]

Seeking a holistic salvation for the world brings to the fore what it means to be the "messianic fellowship," which is a "christologically founded and eschatologically directed doctrine of the church."[76] What this means is that the church is always a provisional reality. For when God's eschatological kingdom comes the church will have fulfilled its role. Indeed when its mission is accomplished the Christian community will find its own fulfillment in the eschatological kingdom of God.[77] Thus here again we see a distinctive mark of Moltmann's thought. Moltmann consistently maintains an eschatological orientation to the whole of his theological enterprise. For as Moltmann famously claimed in *Theology of Hope*: "From first to last, and not merely in the epilogue, Christianity is eschatology, is hope."[78]

The Servanthood of Christ and the Universal Mission of the Church

The Implications of Christology for Christopraxis

Throughout his theological works Moltmann has stressed the necessity of relating systematic theology and social ethics. A core methodological principle of his theology is that good theology is practical theology. Theology is to be orientated

---

[72] Jürgen Moltmann, *Theology and Joy* (London: SCM Press, 1971), 87.

[73] Moltmann, *The Church in the Power of the Spirit*, 164; and *Jesus Christ for Today's World*, 147; "What Has Happened to Our Utopias?" 121.

[74] Moltmann, *Jesus Christ for Today's World*, 147.

[75] Moltmann, *Theology of Hope*, 328-329.

[76] Moltmann, *The Church in the Power of the Spirit*, 13.

[77] Ibid., 358.

[78] Moltmann, *Theology of Hope*, 16

both to praxis and to doxology.[79] As such, Moltmann insists: "Theory and practice cannot be separated."[80] For what we *know* and what we *do* belong together. In particular, a correct christology is essential for the life and witness of the church. Yet not only do the ethical teachings of Christ give direction to the church in addressing issues of social and political concern, but they also give unity and coherence to the whole theological project.[81] Christology is therefore not a remote theory unrelated to the modern world. To confess faith in Christ is inseparable from discipleship.

Although every christology is related to christopraxis, Moltmann declares that this relationship is "so complex that they resist the imposition of any simple pattern."[82] Precisely because Christ is the foundation for salvation and new life, christology and Christian ethics cannot be separated.[83] To know Christ does not simply mean learning the facts of christological dogma. Knowing Christ involves "learning to know him in the praxis of discipleship." A mere theoretical knowledge of Christ is therefore rejected as being insufficient. Rather than simply holding onto certain beliefs about the Christian faith, this knowledge must translate into action in confronting the social and political issues of the contemporary world. Christological theory has to point beyond itself, Moltmann states, "to the doing of God's will, in which 'knowing Jesus' as the Lord really becomes whole and entire."[84]

In *The Church in the Power of the Spirit* Moltmann presents the holistic nature of Christian praxis by evaluating the church's participation in Christ's messianic mission in terms of the doctrine of Christ's threefold office (*munus triplex*): Prophet, Priest, and King. In each of these three offices he emphasizes the church's activity as having an outward and forward direction. First, Jesus' all-embracing mission of proclaiming the gospel in word and deed follows the church's mission of liberation. Second, from Jesus' priestly office, the church participates in his passion as "the church under the cross" through solidarity with the godforsaken and marginalized of society. Third, from Jesus' exaltation, who changes the meaning of lordship into

---

[79] Scholars are recognizing the need for academic theology to provide Christians with guidance in relating their faith to contemporary issues. For example, see Oldham, "The Function of the Church in Society," 223; and McGrath, *Christian Theology*, 80-81. Criticizing this lack of theological engagement, Alister McGrath claims that as orthodoxy became prominent following the Reformation, it became "an academic preoccupation with logical niceties, rather than a concern for relating theology to the issues of everyday life."

[80] Moltmann, *The Way of Jesus Christ*, 41.

[81] Ibid., 41-43. In *The Theology of Jürgen Moltmann*, Bauckham claims Moltmann's work is "one of the few recent christologies which is capable of reinvigorating christological thinking, expanding its horizons and realigning it with the church's task of witness to the contemporary world" (199). Additionally, in "Jürgen Moltmann," in *The Dictionary of Historical Theology*, ed. Trevor A. Hart (Grand Rapids: Eerdmans, 2000) Bauckham declares that this work highlights the three prominent elements of Moltmann's theology: the biblical sources of Christian faith; traditional Christian doctrine; and the contemporary world (376).

[82] Moltmann, *The Way of Jesus Christ*, 41.

[83] Ibid., 42.

[84] Ibid., 43.

servanthood follows the church as the fellowship of freedom in which the power of the Spirit results in the acceptance of the other.[85] Two further forms of the church's participation in the mission of Christ are added. Christ in his transfiguration focuses on the life of the church in the risen life of Christ as a festival of freedom. The other is the friendship of Jesus, where this fellowship in freedom with Christ is the source of the church's own fellowship as open friendship.[86] In each of these roles the church is to emulate the self-giving example set by Christ in his messianic mission. A characteristic mark of the church is therefore to be one of servanthood in which the church shares Christ's compassion for the oppressed and marginalized of society.

The Cross of Christ and Solidarity with the Powerless

Standing in solidarity with the powerless of society was the dominant theme of Moltmann's work on the crucifixion in *The Crucified God*. Whereas *Theology of Hope* focused on the resurrection of Christ and the implications for how the church witnesses in light of the kingdom of God, in *The Crucified God* Moltmann focuses back on the cross of the risen Christ. Moltmann states: "The theology of the cross is none other than the reverse side of the Christian theology of hope."[87] The cross is the criterion of Christian praxis in the sense of Luther's epigram, *Crux probat omnia* ("The cross is the criterion of all things").[88] It is here that Christian theology finds both its identity and its relevance.[89] Moltmann thus emphatically declares: "Christian faith stands and falls with the knowledge of the crucified Christ."[90] With such a pronounced focus on this event in world history many scholars have acknowledged the significance of Moltmann's theology of the cross. For example, Miroslav Volf unequivocally announces: "The most significant contributions in recent years on the implications of the cross for the life in the world come from Jürgen Moltmann."[91]

The cross is God's solidarity with the world in all its negativity, which Moltmann calls its godlessness, godforsakenness, and transitoriness.[92] It is a divine love that identifies with and suffers alongside those who suffer in this world. This was achieved in the incarnation where God in Christ shares the fate of the godforsaken in loving solidarity. Moltmann declares: "Through his death the risen Christ introduces the coming reign of God into the godless present by means of representative

---

[85] Moltmann, *The Church in the Power of the Spirit*, 76-108.

[86] Ibid., 108-121.

[87] Moltmann, *The Crucified God*, 5.

[88] Ibid., 7.

[89] Moltmann, *The Experiment Hope*, 4.

[90] Moltmann, *The Crucified God*, 65.

[91] Miroslav Volf, *Exclusion and Embrace: A Theological Exploration of Identity, Otherness, and Reconciliation* (Nashville: Abingdon Press, 1996), 22.

[92] The cross meets the problem of suffering with the voluntary fellow suffering of love. Yet as Moltmann states in *The Trinity and the Kingdom of God*: "No one can answer the theodicy question in this world, and no one can get rid of it" (49).

suffering."[93] Not only did Christ experience his own sufferings on the cross, his sufferings include "the sufferings of the poor and weak, which Jesus shares in his own body and his own soul, in solidarity with them."[94] On the cross we find that Christ both "identifies God with the victims of violence" and identifies "the victims with God, so that they are put under God's protection and with him are given the rights of which they have been deprived by human beings."[95]

Thus the primary shape of Christ "is ultimately one of suffering. He lives among beggars and lepers."[96] Yet this solidarity does not mean assimilation. Rather it involves voluntary identifying with those who suffer.[97] This was accomplished through God suffering in love and protesting against this suffering, which always takes the side of the victims of injustice.[98] As such, God suffers with those he has created: "In the passion of the Son, the Father himself suffers the pains of abandonment. In the death of the Son, death comes upon God himself, and the Father suffers the death of his Son in his love for forsaken man."[99] It is from the event, which took place at the cross that we must seek to understand the being of God.[100]

The implication for the church of Christ's identification with the marginalized is that the praxis deriving from the hope of the resurrection is complemented by the praxis deriving from the solidarity of the cross. The cross will cause us to overcome our individualism and lack of commitment, Moltmann declares, "if we find ourselves and the meaning of our lives in the community which confesses Christ, liberates the men and women who have been debased and humiliated, and makes itself one with people all over the world."[101] Hence the mission of the church is deepened to include solidarity with those who suffer most acutely the injustices in the world. The aim of this altruistic mission is conquering an inhuman world in which not God but man reigns.[102] In pursuing this goal Moltmann perceives it as being entirely consistent with Jesus' focus on the kingdom of God: "For the sake of Christ, every Christian theology of the kingdom of God will become a theology of liberation for the poor, the sick, the sad, and the outcast."[103] It becomes evident therefore that Moltmann uses the word "poor" in a broad sense describing the dehumanization of humankind in a variety of ways. This dehumanization includes economic, social, physical,

---

[93] Moltmann, *The Crucified God*, 185.

[94] Moltmann, *The Spirit of Life*, 130. Moltmann supports this claim with reference to Hebrews 2:16-18; 11:26; 13:13.

[95] Ibid., 131.

[96] Johann-Baptist Metz and Jürgen Moltmann, *Faith and the Future* (Maryknoll, NY: Orbis, 1995), 111.

[97] Moltmann, *The Crucified God*, 25-6, 28, 50-51.

[98] Ibid., 52-53; *The Future of Creation*, 57; *The Church in the Power of the Spirit*, 97-98.

[99] Moltmann, *The Crucified God*, 192.

[100] Ibid., 215.

[101] Moltmann, *The Power of the Powerless*, 166.

[102] Jürgen Moltmann, *The Gospel of Liberation* (Waco, TX: Word, 1973), 119.

[103] Jürgen Moltmann, *A Passion for God's Reign: Theology, Christian Learning and the Christian Self*, ed. Miroslav Volf (Grand Rapids: Eerdmans 1998), 53.

psychological, moral, and religious poverty. Essentially, the poor consist of all those who endure acts of injustice without being able to defend themselves.[104]

God's solidarity with the world in the cross of Christ gives direction to the church in terms of its holistic ministry of service in the contemporary world. For in standing in solidarity with the poor, the church will demonstrate a radical counter-culture in the wider society. Moltmann declares that it is to "be present where Christ awaits it, amid the downtrodden, the sick and the captives."[105] The community of Christ that lives and acts in this way "practices the great alternative to the world's present system." Such a community is a "contrast-society" and through its existence it calls in question the present systems of injustice.[106] It is a contrast-society grounded in the divine loving solidarity found in the cross of Jesus Christ.

Distinctive to Moltmann's interpretation of the cross is that it is a trinitarian event between the Father and the Son, which led to an understanding of the trinitarian history of God with the world. The history of God's own trinitarian relationship as a community of divine persons allows the world to be included within their love. Moltmann states: "The history of salvation is the history of the eternally living, triune God who draws us into and includes us in his eternal triune life with all the fullness of its relationships."[107] In the unity of this relationship, "the triune God himself is an open, inviting fellowship in which the whole creation finds room."[108] Moltmann therefore perceives a mutual involvement of God and the world, in which God affects and is affected by the world. It is a love where one is vulnerable to suffering. Yet in making this claim, Moltmann rejects the traditional doctrine of divine impassibility. Instead his doctrine of divine passibility means that God could be affected by his creation. Bauckham notes that what we find here, according to Moltmann, is God's changing experience of the world is seen as a changing experience of himself.[109]

Freedom to Serve and Socio-Political Involvement

The distinguishing mark of a true church, insists Moltmann, is that it is a free church.[110] Characteristic of the true church, therefore, is that it is a voluntary fellowship of committed disciples. The way of committed living comes into being "whenever people experience and hold on to the meaning of human life."[111] Specifically, the life that committed disciples are called to share is Christ's messianic

---

[104] Moltmann, *The Church in the Power of the Spirit*, 79.

[105] Ibid., 129.

[106] Moltmann, *The Way of Jesus Christ*, 122.

[107] Moltmann, *The Trinity and the Kingdom of God*, 157.

[108] Moltmann, *The Spirit of Life*, 218.

[109] Bauckham, "Jürgen Moltmann," 217.

[110] Jürgen Moltmann, "The Challenge of Religion in the 1980s," in *Theologians in Transition: The Christian Century 'How My Mind Has Changed Series*,' ed. James M. Wall (New York: Crossroad, 1981), 110.

[111] Moltmann, *The Church in the Power of the Spirit*, 275.

mission within the setting in which God has placed them. It is a mission embracing "all activities that serve to liberate man from his slavery in the presence of the coming God, slavery which extends from economic necessity to godforsakeness."[112] This all-embracing messianic mission corresponds to Christ's messianic mission on earth.[113] Becoming agents of Christ's ministry is thus in sharp contrast with a form of religion deriving from the state church that seeks to control the status quo of society. A church characterized by non-committal religion leads to a church without any critical effect on society. Moltmann describes this institutionalized absence of commitment as "the product of organized religion."[114] Instead it is the free church that is committed to fulfilling its holistic missionary service to the world.[115]

At the heart of Moltmann's theological enterprise, which is highlighted by the description he makes of the church as being free, is his insistence that a missionary church cannot be apolitical. On the contrary, a true understanding of Christian discipleship always has political consequences: "A consistent theological doctrine of the church is by its very nature an eminently political and social doctrine of the church as well."[116] Following from this awareness of the political dimension of the church, Moltmann broke decisively with the German Protestant church's post-war commitment to political neutrality. Criticizing this institutionalized partnership between the established churches and the state, Moltmann claimed it simply led to the churches fulfilling "stabilizing and ideological functions of civil religion desired by the state and society."[117] In contrast, a church political theology "must begin with a critical awareness of its own political existence and its actual social functions."[118]

In describing the church as a messianic fellowship, Moltmann claims that Christians are free to identify with the victims of society.[119] It is a fellowship based on the nature of friendship combining affection with respect and loyalty.[120] This open friendship emulates Jesus' solidarity and fellowship with the poor: "We find the kingdom of God with Jesus when we enter into community with the poor, the sick, the sorrowing, and the guilty."[121] Essential to the mission of the church, therefore, is that it lives in the presence of society's victims. In taking such a position, this will increase the right of the church to challenge prophetically the consciences of that society.[122] Thus significant for Moltmann's ecclesiology is the linking of the nature of the free church as a voluntary fellowship as a key requirement for a socially critical church. Yet he recognizes the dangers of losing

---

[112] Ibid., 10.

[113] Ibid., 11.

[114] Moltmann, *The Power of the Powerless*, 159.

[115] Moltmann, *The Church in the Power of the Spirit*, 329-330.

[116] Ibid., 6.

[117] Moltmann, *On Human Dignity*, 97.

[118] Ibid., 99.

[119] Moltmann, *The Church in the Power of the Spirit*, 225-226.

[120] Ibid., 115, 316; *The Spirit of Life*, 217, 255.

[121] Moltmann, *Hope for the Church*, 25.

[122] Moltmann, "The Liberation of the Future," 288.

focus on God in serving the poor, and affirms that political theology is unwilling to reduce Christian beliefs to politics or to substitute humanism for Christianity.[123]

Integral to Moltmann's thought is his emphasis that political hermeneutics is basically a theology for all members of the church: "Its subject is not the hierarchy but the people of God who live in the world with the poor, the blind, the oppressed, and the apathetic and cry out for liberation."[124] As such, "the *Sitz im Leben* of political theology today is the life of Christians in the world."[125] Moltmann points out that this awareness was indeed core to the Protestant Reformation: "The Reformers' rediscovery of the 'universal priesthood of all believers' made it plain that the call of the gospel is issued to every man."[126] Christian theology must be a practical theology for the laity in their callings in the world. This will be directed not only toward service in the church, but also toward service in the everyday life of the world, which involves equipping Christians to "think independently and act in a Christian way in their own vocations in the world."[127] It is this aspect of service that gives meaning to our lives and is our mark of distinction.[128]

In emphasizing the holistic mission of the church, Moltmann argues that although the church has a special relationship to the kingdom of God, it has this relationship only in relation to others in God's creation: "The church cannot understand itself simply from itself alone. It can only truly comprehend its mission and its meaning, its roles and its functions in relation to others."[129] Therefore as well as describing the church in terms of a messianic ecclesiology, Moltmann describes the church in terms of relational ecclesiology.[130] It is an approach that "leads to an understanding of the living nature of the church."[131]

In developing his theology of how the church relates to the world, Moltmann bases this on his fully social doctrine of the Trinity in which God is three divine subjects in interpersonal relationship with each other: "The unity of the divine tri-unity lies in the union of the Father, the Son and the Spirit, not in their numerical unity. It lies in their fellowship, not in the identity of a single subject."[132] This divine relationship is a fellowship based on love and intense empathy, which causes the Father, Son and Spirit to live and dwell together to such an extent that they are

---

[123] Jürgen Moltmann, et al., *Religion and Political Society* (New York: Harper and Row, 1974), 45.

[124] Moltmann, *On Human Dignity*, 108.

[125] Moltmann, *The Experiment Hope*, 101.

[126] Moltmann, *Theology of Hope*, 330.

[127] Moltmann, *The Experiment Hope*, 11.

[128] Moltmann, *The Trinity and the Kingdom of God*, 219.

[129] Moltmann, *The Church in the Power of the Spirit*, 19.

[130] In describing his ecclesiology alternatively as "messianic ecclesiology" or "relational ecclesiology," both terms used by Moltmann situate the church within God's trinitarian history with the world.

[131] Moltmann, *The Church in the Power of the Spirit*, 20.

[132] Moltmann, *The Trinity and the Kingdom of God*, 95.

one.[133] The significance of this relationship, claims Moltmann, is that not only do Christians participate in the life of the Trinity by God's grace, but it provides a model in which people are mutually free for one another and find freedom in relation with one another.[134] Hence for Moltmann, the Trinity is the foundational reason for why the church exists as a community of freedom in relationship with others.

Critical Reflection

Christ as the Foundation for Social and Political Action

Moltmann is a theologian deeply aware of the contemporary world. Yet an integral strength of Moltmann's works is that he does not start from this point in his theological engagement. The starting point begins by relating Jesus Christ, who is the central figure of world history, to the challenges of the contemporary context. It is from this determining centre focused on God's grace shown in the person and work of Christ that Moltmann develops his political theology. As a result, from a Reformational theological position, Moltmann's political theology has considerable merit in that it is grounded firmly in biblical origins and is deeply theological. Bauckham comments upon this core feature of Christian theology: "Jesus Christ is the centre of the canon of Scripture. All the themes of Scripture converge on him and find their final and fullest significance with reference to him."[135]

Moltmann's theology also has particular relevance for the church's socio-political engagement in the twenty-first century faced with the multidimensional phenomenon of globalization, as it is in the full extent of a biblically based christology that the church is able to begin meeting the full range of society's multidimensional needs. Alan Torrance highlights this essential nature of Moltmann's theology, which involves "rethinking our interpretations of God and of Christ in such a way that our reality is addressed by Christ's reality in its cosmic dimension and significance."[136]

By demonstrating in his theology the implications of the universal mission of Christ, Moltmann further challenges the escapist mentality of Christians who have sought to withdraw from socio-political action. But although Moltmann exposes the weaknesses of such positions, he does not go to the other extreme and ignore the priority of Christian faith. Bauckham comments on this distinguishing trait: "For Moltmann Christian political engagement is no substitute for Christian faith, but one of the forms which faith must take in action; and political theology is no substitute for dogmatic theology, but theology's critical reflection on its own political functions."[137] Thus the starting point for Moltmann's theological project, of which his political theology is so prevalent, is consistent with a theology of grace as it has its primary focus on the self-revelation of God in the person and work of Christ.

---

[133] Ibid., 175.

[134] Ibid., 157-158.

[135] Bauckham, *The Bible in Politics*, 142.

[136] Torrance, *Christ and Context*, 192.

[137] Bauckham, *The Theology of Jürgen Moltmann*, 99.

The Concept of Servanthood for the Social Witness of the Church

In presenting Jesus Christ as the foundation for the socio-political involvement of the church, Moltmann is justified in calling upon the church to recognize the holistic nature of its mission of service to the world. For in balancing a correct christology with christopraxis the church will be characterized by the solidarity and compassion of Christ as he manifested during his physical incarnation on earth. In so doing, the church will demonstrate a visible counter-culture to the quest for power in contemporary society. Walter Kasper echoes Moltmann's call for the church to be a contrast-society, and claims that in following the example of Christ's servanthood, the church has the opportunity of displaying a radical departure from common practice and strengthening its claim to care for the whole of man as Christ did.[138]

George Hunsinger emphasizes this requirement for the church to be a servant community in his insightful work *Social Witness in Generous Orthodoxy*. Hunsinger claims that the chief criterion of social witness "is conformity to the enacted patterns of the divine compassion as revealed and embodied in Jesus Christ."[139] Accordingly, Hunsinger, as with Moltmann, highlights the need for the church to reflect not merely the social disorders of the surrounding world, but also social witness requires the church to be a countercultural community with its own distinctive profile. For "the church does not have a social ethic," claims Hunsinger, "so much as it is a social ethic." In displaying this social witness, the church will "stand over against the larger culture when that culture's values are incompatible with the gospel."[140]

Yet despite drawing significant theological conclusions for the mission of the church from his biblical vision of servanthood, Moltmann appears to disregard all forms of power and authority equating these with domination. Moltmann states: "True dominion does not consist of enslaving others but in becoming a servant of others; not in the exercise of power, but in the exercise of love; not in being served but in freely serving."[141] This indicates that Moltmann does not develop in his theology the possibility of power and authority being used positively in society as a response to the covenant of grace. Perhaps this is reflected in that although he has been influential in challenging the church as to its socio-political responsibility, his political theology is relatively lacking in concrete proposals.[142] Consequently, what is absent in Moltmann's political theology is the recognition that power, which has

---

[138] Kasper, *Jesus the Christ*, 245.

[139] George Hunsinger, "Social Witness in Generous Orthodoxy," *Princeton Seminary Bulletin*, vol. 21/1 (2000), 62. In this paper, Hunsinger is echoing the argument Stanley Hauerwas made, as we will discover in chapter 4.

[140] Hunsinger, "Social Witness in Generous Orthodoxy," 44.

[141] Moltmann, *The Church in the Power of the Spirit*, 103.

[142] See Arne Rasmusson, *The Church as Polis: From Political Theology to Theological Politics as Exemplified by Jürgen Moltmann and Stanley Hauerwas* (Notre Dame, Ind.: University of Notre Dame, 1995), 175. Arne Rasmusson claims that although Moltmann's theology has a practical dimension, most of his writings do not deal with specific ethical questions.

as its goal the furthering of the kingdom of God and his rule on earth, can increase human freedom rather than suppress human freedom and liberty on earth.[143]

A further questionable conclusion Moltmann draws in relation to the servant nature of the church is that not only does God allow us to participate in the life of the Trinity, but the Trinity also provides the model for people to live in community. Bauckham, however, identifies problems with this attempt at holding together these two ideas. This view of the Trinity as an external model that human relationships are to reflect has no clear biblical basis. The danger of holding to the idea of the Trinity as a model for human community, Bauckham points out, is that it comes close to suggesting that the trinitarian relationships are "no more significant than the differences in human relationships within the kind of community Moltmann envisages." Instead, Bauckham declares: "Human community comes about, not as an image of the trinitarian fellowship, but as the Spirit makes us like Jesus in his community with the Father and with others."[144] In short, the basis from which the church lives in relationship with other people throughout the world and is free to serve others is due to being in Christ and continuing the ministry of Christ on earth.

Eschatology and Universal Justice

Moltmann's emphasis on the universal dimension of eschatology is effective in overcoming the weaknesses of an anthropocentric theology of the kingdom of God. It is a theology which recognizes that God's righteousness and justice will extend to the whole world. "In Christian ethics earthly justice," he states, should "prepare the way for God's coming kingdom." Consequently, "what we do now for people in need we do filled with the power of hope, and lit by the expectation of God's coming day."[145] Douglas Meeks succinctly articulates the ramifications of this dimension for Moltmann's conception of Christian ethics: "By claiming that eschatology suffuses the whole of Christian theology, Moltmann is simultaneously claiming that ethics is part and parcel of all Christian theological reflection."[146] Close parallels are found here with Helmut Thielicke's understanding of Christian ethics: "Christian ethics is an impossible enterprise inasmuch as it lies under the disruptive fire of the coming world. Yet it is also a necessary enterprise inasmuch as we live in that field of tension between the two aeons and must find a *modus vivendi*."[147] And even more

---

[143] The concept of servant-leadership in the globalized socio-political arena and its significance for the holistic mission of the church will be discussed in chapter 7.

[144] Bauckham, *The Theology of Jürgen Moltmann*, 177-178. Similarities can also be found here with the theology of Karl Barth. For in showing our true humanity, Barth stresses that the person of Jesus Christ has supreme ontological significance for every human being.

[145] Moltmann, "The Liberation of the Future," 289.

[146] Meeks, *Origins of the Theology of Hope*, 43.

[147] Thielicke, *Theological Ethics*, 45. Cf. Gerrit C. Berkouwer, *The Return of Christ*, trans. James Van Oosterom (Grand Rapids: Eerdmans, 1972). G.C. Berkouwer declares: "Eschatology is not a projection into the distant future; it bursts forth into our present existence, and structures life today in the light of the last days" (19).

explicitly, Thielicke affirms: "Theological ethics is eschatological or it is nothing."[148] With this profoundly ethical dimension, John Webster highlights what is a distinguishing trait of Moltmann's works: "Christian eschatology is practical rather than speculative."[149]

His bringing a theocentric eschatological perspective to the whole of theology gives a renewed emphasis to the intrinsic value of all human beings throughout the world. Central to this universal concept of justice is Moltmann's understanding of human rights.[150] Nicholas Wolterstorff provides a degree of assent with Moltmann's focus on the intrinsic worth of all humankind, which is grounded in their God-given dignity, and claims: "An act of injury to my fellow human being is an act of injury to God."[151] To deny people their human rights, as Moltmann and Wolterstorff argue is therefore ultimately an affront against God. Indeed as Proverbs 14:31 states: "He who oppresses the poor shows contempt for their Maker."

This theocentric worldview is foundational to a theology of grace as revealed in Scripture. A biblically based political theology recognizes the centrality of God and has as its over-riding goal the glorifying of God in the world. With Moltmann's focus being this anticipation of the world's eschatological transformation by God and for the glory of God, he exposes additional weaknesses in the arguments of those who object as to the church's socio-political involvement. For the gospel is primarily about the lordship of Christ and God's kingdom. The proclamation of the gospel awakens hope to God's plan of salvation, while social action seeks to transform life in the here and now in anticipation of the promised kingdom. Richard Hays concurs and describes the church as embodying "the power of the resurrection in the midst of a not-yet-redeemed world." As such, "the eschatological framework of life in Christ imparts to Christian existence its strange temporal sensibility, its odd capacity for simultaneous joy amidst suffering and impatience with things as they are."[152] This eschatological focus is also a primary feature of Richard Mouw's political theology:

> Christian political involvement must take place before the cross, and it must be a means of sharing in the agonies of the cross. But it must also be carried on in the hope that God will allow our present activities to count as preparatory signs of his coming kingdom.[153]

It is interesting to note here the parallels with leading evangelicals such as John Stott, who echoes Moltmann's vision of universal justice, and claims that a vision of transformation is an imaginative perception of things, combining insight and foresight. Stott declares: "It is compounded of a deep dissatisfaction with what is and

---

[148] Thielicke, *Theological Ethics*, 47.

[149] Webster, *Word and Church*, 284.

[150] Yet as we will see in chapter 7, the concept of human rights also has some weaknesses.

[151] Wolterstorff, *Until Justice and Peace Embrace*, 78.

[152] Hays, *The Moral Vision of the New Testament*, 198.

[153] Mouw, *Politics and the Biblical Drama*, 139.

a clear grasp of what could be."[154] Hence rather than negating the power of the gospel, as Vinay Samuel and Christopher Sugden also point out, socio-political action leads to the glory of God, due to parts of his creation being objects of his redeeming activity.[155] For in Christian mission, "it is necessary that the rule of the one true God be proclaimed in all areas and levels of life."[156]

Influenced by the theology of Moltmann, Bauckham and Hart in *Hope Against Hope* elaborate on the significance of a hope derived from a fully cosmic scope of Christian eschatology for the role of the church in the world. In being true to the universal scope of God's redemptive purpose the church cannot be content with being preoccupied with seemingly irrelevant activities. Instead the church will be:

> A place in the world, which is not properly of the world, the people who live up to the hilt in this life but with their sights set firmly on a horizon lying beyond it, and who therefore model for society how this life may be lived in hope even when hope seems hopeless.[157]

This unyielding theocentric foundation, which is distinctive to Moltmann's political theology, leads to a degree of differentiation from Latin American liberation theology, which was nevertheless deeply influenced by Moltmann. Leading liberation theologian José Míguez Bonino highlights this contribution and refers to Moltmann as "the theologian to whom the theology of liberation is most indebted and with whom it shows the closest affinity."[158] Yet although Moltmann claims that in the present we are able to experience God's presence, which anticipates the eschatological kingdom, the eschatological kingdom itself remains transcendent beyond history. A further distinguishing feature is that whereas the origins of liberation theology emphasized the Exodus as the basis for directing efforts at liberation, Moltmann grounds his theology in a christological basis, primarily in the resurrection of the crucified Christ.[159] Consequently, although liberation theology has been a powerful force in highlighting the political responsibility of Christians to seek the liberation of the oppressed, Moltmann's theology could be perceived as having a possibly wider significance than liberation theology. This is due to the Exodus having a subordinate place as part of the Old Testament history of promise.

---

[154] Stott, *Issues Facing Christians Today*, 328.

[155] Vinay K. Samuel and Christopher M.N. Sugden, "God's Intention for the World," in *The Church in Response to Human Need*, ed. Vinay K. Samuel and Christopher M.N. Sugden (Grand Rapids: Eerdmans, 1987), 153-155.

[156] Ibid., 143.

[157] Richard J. Bauckham and Trevor A. Hart, *Hope Against Hope* (London: Darton, Longman & Todd, 1999), 209-210.

[158] José Míguez Bonino, *Doing Theology in a Revolutionary Situation* (Philadelphia: Fortress, 1975), 144. This influence between Moltmann and liberation theology may indeed go both ways.

[159] For a description of liberation theology's theological interpretation see Douglas D. Webster, "Liberation Theology," in *Evangelical Dictionary of Theology*, 686-688.

As Bauckham notes, the Exodus is taken up into the culminating event of promise in the resurrection of Jesus Christ.[160] The promise of the resurrection does include the hopes of political and economic liberation as found in the Exodus. Yet significantly, it also includes the renewal of God's creation in which God's glory will indwell it.

There are potential exposures, however, in having too pronounced a focus on eschatology in Christian theology. Richard Niebuhr argues that one of the risks in overly emphasizing the eschatological dimension is what he describes as "wishful thinking." Niebuhr claims that the concentration on the eschatological kingdom of God can easily lead to a denial that God reigns in the here and now. There is a danger that "the desire for what is not present may easily bring with it the affirmation that what is presented comes from a devil rather than from God."[161] Making eschatology the universal horizon of all theology, therefore, can bring intrinsic weaknesses. In particular, there is a risk of seeking to interpret God and all other reality from this presupposed theological framework. Hence despite the benefits that Moltmann has brought with his distinctive focus on the eschatological dimension of theology, the extent to which he seeks to employ this eschatological horizon appears to have brought with it specific failings. These weaknesses become increasingly pronounced in relation to his theology of divine passibility and the freedom of God.

Grace and the Freedom of God

As we have discovered, for Moltmann, eschatology is the framework by which everything is interpreted, including God. This framework includes introducing the eschatological perspective into statements on divine revelation and the knowledge of God, which he claims are to be understood within the horizon of history as the sphere of promise.[162] What this distinctive feature of Moltmann's theology demonstrates is that the history of the world is perceived as being an inescapable means of God's self-revelation. God does not make himself known without history or future. Moltmann elaborates on this theological conclusion in *Theology of Hope*:

> God reveals himself in the form of promise and in the history that is marked by promise. This confronts systematic theology with the question whether the understanding of divine revelation by which it is governed must not be dominated by the nature and trend of the promise.[163]

Noticeably, it is here that Moltmann broke with the methodological convictions linking his work with that of Barth. In contrast to dialectical theology, which conceives of God as the wholly other who enters the world graciously in his Word, according to Moltmann, God is no longer perceived as being a transcendental self beyond history. Instead, God is one who pledges himself to act in the context of

---

[160] Bauckham, *The Theology of Jürgen Moltmann*, 104-105.

[161] Niebuhr, *Christ and Culture*, 148.

[162] Moltmann, *Theology of Hope*, 19, 116.

[163] Ibid., 42.

history. Yet differing sharply from this thought, although Barth recognized that God has acted within history, Barth was also concerned with the absolute independence of God's self-revelation. God was not dragged into history. He is involved in history freely. This is indeed an integral difference between Barth and Moltmann's doctrine of God, and exposes a primary weakness of Moltmann's attempt at employing an eschatological dimension to the whole of his theological project. But it is apparent, though, that in bringing a renewed emphasis to eschatology, Moltmann is able to open his theology to the world and to the future, more so indeed than that of Barth.

A critical question that Moltmann's insistence on employing an eschatological framework to all aspects of theology raises is, does this mean that world history is the necessary process by which God realizes himself? The answer, according to Moltmann, would appear to be yes. In criticizing the conviction that God cannot be affected by the world, Moltmann's doctrine of God required a doctrine of possibility in the broad sense that God can be affected by his creation.[164] Moltmann captures the essence of this theology in *The Crucified God*: "If one conceives of the Trinity as an event of love in the suffering and the death of Jesus...then the Trinity is no self-contained group in heaven, but an eschatological process open for men on earth, which stems from the cross of Christ."[165] The freedom of God is neither simply the absence of interference nor self-control but "vulnerable love."[166] Yet despite our agreeing with Moltmann's vision of history being the eschatological kingdom of God, in rejecting the traditional doctrine of divine impassibility Moltmann fails to avoid this "Hegelian mistake."[167] Since if history is the process by which God realizes himself, then this inevitably compromises the freedom of God. It also leaves precariously exposed the conclusion that God simply dissolves into history.

In contrast to Moltmann's understanding of divine possibility, Barth emphatically affirmed that God is absolutely free in himself. Barth states: "He could have remained satisfied with himself and with the impassible glory and blessedness of his own inner life. But he did not do so. He elected man as a covenant-partner."[168] God is supreme in all creation, and he is not dependent in anyway on anyone or anything at any time. That is precisely why the being of God is prior to all theological questioning, which is an essential component of deriving a theologically valid understanding of the grace of God for the church's socio-political mission. Yet this aspect of God's character is distinctly absent in Moltmann's theological enterprise.

---

[164] Bauckham, "Jürgen Moltmann," 217.

[165] Moltmann, *The Crucified God*, 249.

[166] Moltmann, *The Trinity and the Kingdom of God*, 56.

[167] For a further discussion of "a suffering God," see Thomas G. Weinandy, *Does God Suffer?* (Edinburgh: T&T Clark, 2000).

[168] Barth, *Church Dogmatics*, vol. 2/2, 166.

A Victim-Orientated Soteriology and the Covenant of Grace

In presenting the eschatological hope of the transformation of the world as a key motivation for the socio-political mission of the church, Moltmann is surely correct. The question arises, however, whether this is the primary or overarching motivation for the church's socio-political involvement. From our analysis of the doctrine of grace in the previous chapter, it would appear that the supreme motivation for the church in addressing contemporary issues is in response to the covenant of grace, which has resulted in our redemption by a redeeming God. This is highlighted by Hart who declares that the logic of the Christian gospel of grace, where the priority of indicatives over imperatives is everywhere apparent, "sets us utterly free from the burden of having to become the condition for the realization of the kingdom."[169] It is to be set free by a covenant-keeping God, from which stem the obligations to his covenant of grace as the direct human response to divine grace already shown.

Likewise, P.T. Forsyth, who has demonstrated more forcefully than any other theologian in the Reformation tradition the absolute necessity of the doctrine of the atonement for Christian life and witness, appealed to what he believed was the pivotal centre of Scripture, which is the gospel of redeeming grace.[170] Forsyth highlights the central biblical truth of God's grace in Christ in his work *The Church and the Sacraments* in which he stressed: "A theology and a church stand or fall together."[171] Commenting upon this core Christian doctrine, Forsyth writes:

> The church rests on the grace of God, the judging, atoning, regenerating grace of God, which is his holy love in the form it must take with human sin. Wherever that is heartily confessed, and goes on to rule, we have the true church.[172]

Forsyth thus perceived the heart of the Christian faith to lie in the message of the atoning death of Christ. The cross is the crisis of God's righteous judgment and as such, "it was required by his holiness and given by his love."[173] What this means, as Forsyth points out is that "the church's one foundation is not simply Jesus Christ, but him as crucified and atoning."[174] In recognizing the central importance of the atoning death of Christ for Christian theology, Forsyth was especially critical of a theology that portrayed God exclusively as love, while neglecting his holiness.[175] Hart elaborates on the significance of God's holy grace in the thought of Forsyth:

---

[169] Hart, "Imagination for the Kingdom of God?" 70-71.

[170] Donald G. Bloesch, "Forsyth, Peter Taylor," in *Evangelical Dictionary of Theology*, 462-463.

[171] Peter T. Forsyth, *The Church and the Sacraments* (London: Independent Press, 1953), 57.

[172] Ibid., 34. Cf. Barth, *Church Dogmatics*, vol. 2/1, 363. Barth likewise stresses that God's holiness and grace are integrally related: "God is holy because his grace judges and his judgment is gracious."

[173] Ibid., 5.

[174] Ibid., 51.

[175] Peter T. Forsyth, *The Work of Christ* (London: Independent Press, 1952), 26.

The way from love to grace lay across a deep chasm of natural human resentment and theological repentance, a chasm bridged only at one point, across which Forsyth himself had stumbled, and to which he henceforth sought to lead his readers and fellow travellers – namely the cross of Christ and all that it signified.[176]

Yet this aspect of God's saving activity is relatively lacking in Moltmann's work. Instead Moltmann concentrates his understanding of the cross on solidarity with the most marginalized of society. Although Moltmann states in later works such as *The Spirit of Life* that in the cross "there is more in this than Christ's solidarity with 'the accursed of the earth,'" solidarity with the victims of society dominates Moltmann's theology.[177] This focus also permeates how he suggests we should read the Bible. In declaring that the Bible is the book of the poor, Moltmann asserts: "We must read it with the eyes, and in the community, of the poor, the godless, and the unjust."[178] Hence for Moltmann, solidarity and redemption from suffering are the leading thoughts; atonement and the justification of sinners would appear to be carried along with these other over-riding theological considerations. Tom Smail is therefore justified in claiming that Moltmann's theology of the cross speaks in terms of theodicy rather than of atonement.[179] Yet Smail also notes: "We cannot be true to the gospel unless we also give full weight to its claim that the primary meaning of the death of Jesus is that through it we are delivered from our sins."[180]

Hunsinger discusses the recurring phenomenon in the history of Christian theology of the displacement of central truths by lesser truths, which is perhaps a key failing of Moltmann's understanding of the cross. Hunsinger notes that contemporary theology has increasingly witnessed the emergence of victim-orientated soteriologies. The plight of victims has been pushed to the fore and urged by prominent theologians "as the central soteriological problem."[181] Although victim-orientated soteriologies have contributed to a better understanding of the church's social responsibility, the plight of victims has to a large extent displaced the soteriological plight of sinners. The ramification of a victim-orientated soteriology is that it tends to define the meaning of sin entirely in terms of victimization. When this happens, the true meaning of the cross is lost. The cross is deemed to be simply the demonstration of divine solidarity with victims, and is no longer the supreme divine intervention of grace for the forgiveness of sins. In contrast, although Hunsinger notes that no reason exists why the cross as atonement for sin should be viewed as

---

[176] Trevor A. Hart, "Morality, Atonement and the Death of Jesus: The Crucial Focus of Forsyth's Theology," in *Justice the True and Only Mercy: Essays on the Life and Theology of Peter Taylor Forsyth*, ed. Trevor A. Hart (Edinburgh: T&T Clark, 1995), 17-18.

[177] Moltmann, *The Spirit of Life*, 136.

[178] Moltmann, *The Experiment Hope*, 7.

[179] Tom Smail writes in a personal correspondence: "A deep question that haunts the whole Moltmann opus is the relationship between liberation and reconciliation." It is this theology of the cross, which can lead to "a utopian sentimentality" in Moltmann's theology.

[180] Smail, *Once and For All*, 49.

[181] Hunsinger, "Social Witness in Generous Orthodoxy," 55.

logically incompatible with the cross as divine solidarity with the oppressed, he insists: "The central significance of the cross, as attested by Holy Scripture, is the forgiveness of sins."[182]

Furthermore, when the primary soteriological problem of sin is recognized, this actually leads to a greater appreciation of liberating grace and motivation for the church's socio-political involvement. This point is expressed by Keith Clements, who in critiquing the work of Forsyth, declares that there is a "positive and substantive connection between the cross and social justice."[183] That is the primary reason why Forsyth criticises the contentment of Christians resting on individual salvation while ignoring the plight of the world. Forsyth proclaims forthrightly:

> We must have a social gospel. And this you cannot get upon the basis of mere individual or sectional salvation. You can only have a social gospel upon one basis, namely, that Christ saved, reconciled the whole world as a unity, the whole of society and history.[184]

Additionally, Hunsinger explains this effect of God's redeeming grace upon the Christian community in its service to the world:

> When recognition is accorded to the universality of divine grace, moreover, I am freed from moralistic forms of obligation. For when grounded in the reception of grace, social obligation is not an externally imposed duty, but a response to the needs of others in gratitude to the God who has already responded so graciously to me. My response to others is based on solidarity in sin and grace.[185]

Social witness and the forgiveness of sins stand in inseparable unity. It is this solidarity, claims Hunsinger, which is "the open secret of generous orthodoxy, which knows that there is always more grace in God than sin in us."[186] Yet as Hunsinger reminds us, the fundamental plight of all human beings is that they are sinners before God, rather than being victims before oppressors. What this highlights is that victim-orientated soteriologies require a properly sin-orientated soteriology in order to be theologically adequate. Balanced with this recognition, a sin-orientated soteriology requires victim-orientated soteriologies to be socially responsible.[187] It is thus interesting to note that as Moltmann lacks a sin-orientated soteriology there is less emphasis in his theology on responding to the covenant of grace in gratitude as a consequence of the grace already shown by God. Instead Moltmann places the

---

[182] Ibid., 55-56.

[183] Keith W. Clements, "P.T. Forsyth: A Political Theologian?" in *Justice the True and Only Mercy*, 167.

[184] Forsyth, *The Work of Christ*, 171-172.

[185] Hunsinger, "Social Witness in Generous Orthodoxy," 57-58.

[186] Ibid., 44.

[187] George Hunsinger, "Baptism and the Soteriology of Forgiveness," *International Journal of Systematic Theology*, vol. 2/3 (November 2000), 251.

emphasis on eschatological hope as being the primary motivation for the mission of the church in its social aspect in the contemporary world.

In seeking to overcome these weaknesses in Moltmann's theology of divine grace, Volf speaks of "divine self-donation" rather than "divine solidarity" in the cross. In doing so, Volf assesses the social significance of the theme of self-giving: "God does not abandon the godless to their evil but gives the divine self for them in order to receive them into divine communion through atonement."[188] Sharing Hunsinger's criticism of victim-orientated soteriologies, Volf argues that if the claim that "Christ died for the ungodly" (Romans 5:6) is the New Testament's fundamental affirmation, then the theme of solidarity, though indispensable, "must be a sub-theme of the overarching theme of self-giving love." For as Volf asserts: "To claim the comfort of the crucified while rejecting his way is to advocate not only cheap grace but a deceitful ideology."[189] Thus Volf rightly affirms that a theology of Christian witness in the socio-political arena must necessarily be rooted in the self-giving love of God as manifested in the cross of Christ. It is here that God's grace is supremely shown to sinful humanity. It is therefore in light of God's atoning grace that the church becomes involved in the contemporary issues of the world.

Conclusion

In this chapter we have sought to provide a critique of Moltmann's political theology analyzing to what extent a theology of grace is evident in his theological project. From a Reformational theological position, Moltmann's engagement with socio-political issues is of significance in that he holds to a firmly theocentric and trinitarian worldview. This results in Moltmann's emphasis that the study of theology has vital practical consequences. But in adopting an eschatological perspective to the whole of his theology, and in emphasizing the solidarity of Christ to the neglect of the atonement, he appears not to acknowledge fully the implications of a theology of grace for the holistic mission of the church. Despite these areas of weakness, however, due to his success in integrating some of the fundamental beliefs of the Christian faith with the social and political challenges of the contemporary world, the Christian community has much to learn from Moltmann's theological works.

---

[188] Volf, *Exclusion and Embrace*, 23.
[189] Ibid., 24.

CHAPTER 4

Grace and Stanley Hauerwas' Political Theology

Few have grasped the significance of socio-political discussions for ecclesial witness in the world as Stanley Hauerwas. Therefore in this chapter we will continue our analysis of three leading contemporary Reformational theologians by focusing on Hauerwas' political theology, evaluating the extent to which a theology of grace is evident. First, we will undertake an evaluation of the three controlling motifs of his theological enterprise: narrative, vision, and character. Second, following from this analysis, we will explore how Hauerwas engages with issues of social and political concern and the theological rationale he employs for the nature of this engagement. Third, we will undertake a critical evaluation of Hauerwas' theological approach in the context of dialogue with Jürgen Moltmann's political theology.

Introduction

One of the foremost ethicists and theologians in the contemporary world is Stanley Hauerwas. *Time* magazine reveals the extent of Hauerwas' influence by describing this Mennonite scholar as "America's best theologian," and "contemporary theology's foremost intellectual provocateur."[1] John Berkman claims that Hauerwas is "certainly the most prolific and comprehensive theological ethicist alive."[2] Pervasive throughout Hauerwas' theological works are his severe criticism of traditional liberalism, which he perceives to be the dominant moral ethos in American society, and his insistence in maintaining the significance of narrative for Christian ethics.[3] What constitutes public theology is a focal question Hauerwas resolutely seeks to address in his theological project, as he insists: "I simply do not believe that theology can be done as if our social and political considerations are an afterthought."[4]

---

[1] Jean B. Elshtain, "Christian Contrarian," *Time*, vol. 158/11 (17 September 2001), 76.

[2] John Berkman, "An Introduction to the Hauerwas Reader," in *The Hauerwas Reader*, ed. John Berkman and Michael G. Cartwright (Durham: Duke University Press, 2001), 3.

[3] Yet as William T. Cavanaugh humorously points out in "Stan the Man: A Thoroughly Biased Account of a Completely Unobjective Person," in *The Hauerwas Reader*, "For all his critiques of liberal individualism...Hauerwas blends into a crowd like a bull blends into a china shop!" (17).

[4] Stanley M. Hauerwas, *After Christendom?: How the Church is to Behave if Freedom, Justice, and a Christian Nation are Bad Ideas* (Nashville: Abingdon Press, 1991), 19.

Having been trained at Yale University, Hauerwas is steeped in the tradition of the Niebuhrs. Reflecting on this educational journey, Hauerwas quips: "At Yale I was taught to engage in theology as a tradition-determined practice that is not determined by any one tradition – other than Yale's."[5] Yet he perceives concerns that have arisen from this particular tradition: "The recent history of Christian ethics has largely been the story of the attempt to work out the set of problems bequeathed to us by the social gospel and the Niebuhrs."[6] Despite this educational background, it is the Mennonite theologian and ethicist John Howard Yoder who has been most prominent in shaping Hauerwas' theology.[7] The appeal of Yoder is that he is perceived as representing "a fundamental challenge" to the tradition of the Niebuhrs.[8] In particular, he challenges "the dominance of Reinhold Niebuhr's understanding of the Christian's relation to liberal democracies."[9] When Christians look back on theology in twentieth century America, Hauerwas predicts, Yoder's *The Politics of Jesus* "will be seen as a new beginning."[10] Reflecting this influence, Yoder's emphasis on the notion of a separated Christian community, which is characteristic of the Anabaptist tradition, is found throughout Hauerwas' works.[11]

Additionally, the reading of the Christian philosopher Alasdair MacIntyre and his emphasis on the place of virtues in Christian living was of significance in shaping Hauerwas' thought.[12] This led Hauerwas to break decisively from the influence of the Enlightenment and its desire to ground morality in terms of individuals, reason, and isolated facts. Instead, he argues that virtues are rooted in a particular narrative. Challenging the Enlightenment assumption that theological and ethical claims require to be founded on universally accepted categories of reason and experience, Hauerwas maintains that truth claims emerge out of specific worship communities: "For in truth there can be no 'method' for theology in a world without foundation."[13] Dismissing these anthropocentric presuppositions, Hauerwas explicitly declares he

[5] Stanley M. Hauerwas, "The Testament of Friends," *The Christian Century*, vol. 107/7 (February 1990), 214.

[6] Hauerwas, "On Keeping Theological Ethics Theological," 27.

[7] Hauerwas, "The Testament of Friends," 214; Stanley M. Hauerwas, *Dispatches from the Front: Theological Engagements with the Secular* (Durham: Duke University Press, 1994), 21-22. These theological influences are discussed in Samuel Wells, *Transforming Fate into Destiny: The Theological Ethics of Stanley Hauerwas* (Carlisle: Paternoster, 1998), 1-12.

[8] Hauerwas, *The Peaceable Kingdom*, xxiv.

[9] Hauerwas, *Dispatches from the Front*, 23.

[10] Stanley M. Hauerwas, *A Better Hope: Resources for a Church Confronting Capitalism, Democracy, and Postmodernity* (Grand Rapids: Brazos Press, 2000), 129.

[11] See Rasmusson, *The Church as Polis*, 25. Rasmusson claims that Yoder helped Hauerwas "to develop an ecclesiology that was the necessary concomitant to his ethics of character and virtue and made his whole approach less abstract."

[12] William C. Placher, "Postliberal Theology," in *The Modern Theologians*, 349.

[13] Stanley M. Hauerwas, "The Church's One Foundation is Jesus Christ Her Lord; Or, In a World Without Foundations: All We Have is the Church," in *Theology Without Foundations: Religious Practice and the Future of Theological Truth*, ed. Stanley M. Hauerwas, Nancey C. Murphy, and Mark T. Nation (Nashville: Abingdon Press, 1994), 162.

has "no use for moral or political liberalism in any of their guises."[14] This vigorous engagement with Enlightenment thought highlights the priority Hauerwas places on Christian ethics, which he insists is at the heart of the theological enterprise.[15]

Foundational to Christian ethics is the message of Jesus Christ, which was a radical one. Yet many Christians, claims Hauerwas, ignore this teaching today - resulting in Christians becoming indistinguishable from the world at large: "I am angry at Christians, including myself, for allowing ourselves to be so compromised that the world can no longer tell what difference it makes to worship the Trinity."[16] In seeking to overcome this dilemma, Hauerwas appeals for contemporary theology to be accessible to those within the church, and not just other theologians. For he adamantly insists: "Theology should be a form of discourse that is meant to help us live more faithfully as Christians who are part of that community called church."[17] In presenting a church-orientated social ethics, Hauerwas declares: "If theology is a servant ministry in and for the church, I do not think the alienation of theology from the church's common life, which is so prevalent today, can be a matter of indifference."[18] Addressing this challenge, and urging for a renewal of the centrality of ecclesiology, is the basic concern of Hauerwas' theological project.[19]

Narrative as a Mode of Moral Reflection

Postliberal Theology and the Particularity of Christian Faith

The emergence of postliberalism, asserts Alister McGrath, is one of the most important aspects of western theology in recent years.[20] It is a theological movement commonly linked with Yale Divinity School.[21] Postliberal trends, though, have now become more widely established within North American and British academic theology. What is distinctive about postliberalism, McGrath points out is that it "reintroduces a strong emphasis on the particularity of the Christian faith, in reaction

---

[14] Hauerwas, *A Better Hope*, 23.

[15] Hauerwas, *The Peaceable Kingdom*, xvii.

[16] Hauerwas, *Dispatches from the Front*, 25.

[17] Stanley M. Hauerwas, *Unleashing the Scriptures: Freeing the Bible from Captivity to America* (Nashville: Abingdon Press, 1993), 8.

[18] Stanley M. Hauerwas, *Sanctify Them in the Truth: Holiness Exemplified* (Nashville: Abingdon Press, 1998), 6.

[19] I am indebted to Samuel Wells for summarizing, in a personal communication, Hauerwas' approach to theology and the vital role of the church in this task: "Hauerwas regards himself as a theologian and should be treated as one who believes one can't understand, embody, or express theology without the practices of the church."

[20] Alister E. McGrath, *A Passion for Truth: The Intellectual Coherence of Evangelicalism* (Leicester: InterVarsity, 1996), 120.

[21] Timothy R. Phillips and Dennis L. Okholm, "The Nature of Confession: Evangelicals and Postliberals," in *The Nature of Confession: Evangelicals and Postliberals in Conversation*, ed. Timothy R. Phillips and Dennis L. Okholm (Downers Grove, Ill.: InterVarsity, 1996), 11.

against the strongly homogenizing tendencies of liberalism."[22] And it is Hauerwas whom William Placher singles out as being "the most widely read advocate of postliberal theology in church circles and among ethicists."[23]

Placher has identified three features of postliberal thought clarifying the boundaries and direction of this theological method, and thus of Hauerwas' theology. The first is the primacy of narrative as an interpretive category for the Bible. The second is the hermeneutical primacy of the world created by the biblical narratives over the world of human experience. The third is the primacy of language over experience.[24] Celebrating the distinctiveness of the Christian tradition has indeed enabled postliberalism to represent a decisive move away from the liberal strategy of an earlier generation grounded on the foundational role of experience.[25] Yet although these positions describe the main elements of postliberalism and help identify the core features of Hauerwas' theology, it is also to be noted that Hauerwas does not hold to one grand theological position. Thus his work can be described as "antisystematic."[26] Robert Jenson points out this distinguishing characteristic: "Linear exposition of a system has not to date been Hauerwas' greatest contribution."[27] It is this fact, claims Emmanuel Katongole, which is responsible for much of the misunderstandings and in some cases frustrations with Hauerwas' otherwise provocative work.[28]

Commenting on the liberalism so prevalent in modern society, Hauerwas perceives most contemporary Christian ethics to presuppose George Lindbeck's experiential-expressivist model.[29] In presenting a summary of Lindbeck's analysis, Hauerwas states this model assumes "there is some universal experience that all people have that can be characterized as religious."[30] Therefore in breaking from the liberalism that has dominated theological engagement since the Enlightenment era, Hauerwas is adamant that our understanding of how we are to live in the world does not lie in some generic human or natural law ethic.[31] For "there is no such thing as universal 'ethics' but…every ethic requires a qualifier." Yet he points out, "such a

---

[22] McGrath, *A Passion for Truth*, 121.

[23] Placher, "Postliberal Theology," 348.

[24] William C. Placher, "Paul Ricoeur and Postliberal Theology: A Conflict of Interpretations," *Modern Theology*, vol. 4/1 (October 1987), 35-52.

[25] McGrath, *A Passion for Truth*, 120-121.

[26] Berkman, "An Introduction to the Hauerwas Reader," 11.

[27] Robert W. Jenson, "The Hauerwas Project," *Modern Theology*, vol. 8/3 (July 1992), 285.

[28] Emmanuel Katongole, *Beyond Universal Reason: The Relation between Religion and Ethics in the Work of Stanley Hauerwas* (Notre Dame, Ind.: University of Notre Dame, 2000), ix.

[29] See George A. Lindbeck, *The Nature of Doctrine: Religion and Theology in a Postliberal Age* (Philadelphia: Westminster Press, 1984).

[30] Stanley M. Hauerwas, *Against the Nations: War and Survival in a Liberal Society* (Minneapolis: Winston Press, 1985), 2.

[31] Hauerwas, *The Peaceable Kingdom*, 63.

suggestion is deeply at odds with the main direction of modern ethical theory, which seeks a foundation for morality that will free moral judgments from their dependence on historically contingent communities."[32] Indeed the tendency in liberalism is to regard the self as being detached from the entanglements of society and history, while correspondingly according pride of place to rationality.

In contrast to liberalism and its celebration of pluralism, for Hauerwas, the church is devoted to a particular God and a particular way of life that follows Jesus Christ. This is reflected in how he describes the subject of theology, which is "the truthful worship of God."[33] William Werpehowski asserts that this understanding of the church is that "its members know themselves not in the first instance as autonomous individuals but as bound to God, to their tradition, and to one another."[34] For as Hauerwas explains: "By our becoming members of a particular community formed by Christian convictions, an experience not otherwise available is made possible." A true understanding of Christian ethics will not simply conform to our preconceptions of right living. Rather, it "requires a transformation both personally and socially if we are to be true to the nature of our convictions."[35] And it is Christian convictions that are the starting point for Christian ethics shaping our understanding of moral existence.[36] Timothy Phillips therefore highlights that at the core of the postliberal theological method is the desire "to reverse modern Christianity's accommodation to culture by cultivating the distinctive language of the Christian community."[37] It is this emphasis on particularity and the articulation of the distinctive grammar of the Christian faith that is foundational to Hauerwas' theology.

Theological Ethics and the Narrative of Scripture

Christian ethics has always been central in Reformational theology. So maintains Hauerwas who declares: "Neither Luther nor Calvin distinguished between theology and ethics."[38] Despite this inextricable link, however, he draws attention to how Christians have mistakenly assumed that a distinction can be drawn between doctrine and ethics.[39] Specifically, the reason why ethics "has been artificially separated from the central theological task" is due to "the abstract way in which the relation between creation and redemption, nature and grace, has been understood."[40] Yet this division

---

[32] Ibid., 17.

[33] Hauerwas, *Dispatches from the Front*, 1.

[34] William Werpehowski, "Theological Ethics," in *The Modern Theologians*, 320.

[35] Hauerwas, *Against the Nations*, 2.

[36] Stanley M. Hauerwas, *Truthfulness and Tragedy: Further Investigations in Christian Ethics* (Notre Dame, Ind.: University of Notre Dame, 1977), 9.

[37] Timothy R. Phillips, "Postliberal Theology," in *Evangelical Dictionary of Theology*, 937.

[38] Stanley M. Hauerwas, "On Doctrine and Ethics," in *The Cambridge Companion to Christian Doctrine*, 28.

[39] Hauerwas, *Unleashing the Scriptures*, 7.

[40] Hauerwas, *The Peaceable Kingdom*, 55.

cannot be justified theologically. As such, the task of theologians, he claims, is "to refuse their supposed ontological and practical independence."[41] Hauerwas supports this position by making reference to Karl Barth, whom he praises as being "undisputedly the greatest Protestant theologian of this century." It is Barth who has shown "there can be no ethics that is not from beginning to end theological."[42] Agreeing with this stance, Hauerwas is at pains to stress that "the persuasive power of Christian discourse rests upon the indissociable unity of the theological and the ethical aspects of Christian faith, not their separation."[43]

Integral to Hauerwas' understanding of theological ethics is that the self and personal character develops through one's personal history.[44] To describe how this takes effect and thus integrate convictions with the moral life, he introduced three interconnected concepts.[45] This includes narrative, character, and vision.[46]

First, narrative features extensively as "theology cannot be construed by one overarching doctrine or principle."[47] Paul Nelson remarks on this underlying idea: "The moralities into which we are socialized are not so much sets of rules or principles as they are collections of stories about human possibilities and paradigms for action."[48] This identification of a parallel between stories and human living in the world is characteristic of Hauerwas' theology, as it is the narrative that gives moral guidance and binds together these contingent events and agents in an intelligible pattern. Hauerwas highlights the nature of such connections: "Stories seem to be the glue that binds together such diverse literary enterprises as history, autobiography, biography, novels, folktales and myths."[49] Every community and polity thus involves and requires a narrative.[50] Narrative describes not only the world in the present but indicates how it ought to be changed.[51] It makes us face the reality of our situation "and provide us with the skills to yank us out of our self-deceptions."[52]

---

[41] Hauerwas, "On Doctrine and Ethics," 22.

[42] Ibid., 32.

[43] Ibid., 36. Hauerwas comments on the interrelatedness of theology and ethics in Stanley M. Hauerwas, *A Community of Character: Toward a Constructive Christian Social Ethic* (Notre Dame, Ind.: University of Notre Dame Press, 1981): "I have accepted the current academic designation of 'ethics' only because as a theologian I am convinced that the intelligibility and truthfulness of Christian convictions reside in their practical force" (1).

[44] Stanley M. Hauerwas, *Vision and Virtue* (Notre Dame, Ind.: Fides, 1974), 67. For a philosophical critique of Hauerwas' contribution toward a socially constituted and historically embodied account of the moral life, see Katongole, *Beyond Universal Reason.*

[45] In *Sanctify Them in the Truth*, Hauerwas accentuates the importance of maintaining a balance in theology, and "not to be distorted by overemphasis on one aspect of the faith" (2).

[46] Hauerwas, *The Peaceable Kingdom*, 16.

[47] Hauerwas, *The Peaceable Kingdom*, xvi.

[48] Paul Nelson, *Narrative and Morality: A Theological Inquiry* (University Park: Pennsylvanian State University Press, 1987), 9.

[49] Hauerwas, *Truthfulness and Tragedy*, 75.

[50] Hauerwas, *A Community of Character*, 4.

[51] Hauerwas, *Vision and Virtue*, 73.

[52] Hauerwas, *Truthfulness and Tragedy*, 80.

In conjunction with narrative, Hauerwas focuses on the concept of character for linking convictions with the moral life. "Character," he asserts, is "the name we give to the cumulative source of human actions."[53] It is "our deliberate disposition to use a certain range of reasons for our actions rather than others."[54] In developing the full dimension of a classical Aristotelian conception of ethics, he claims: "To emphasize the importance of character is not only a way of re-emphasizing the agent's perspective, but also an attempt to rethink what moral objectivity involves."[55]

And along with character, life entails "vision."[56] Vision is required for how we view the world and ourselves, and is formed and given content by "the stories through which we have learned to form the story of our lives."[57] Here again we see the importance of narrative for Hauerwas' project. Hauerwas states: "I am convinced that narrative is a perennial category for understanding better how the grammar of religious convictions is displayed and how the self is formed by those convictions."[58] By introducing such concepts to questions of Christians ethics, as Samuel Wells points out, "Hauerwas has redirected Christian ethics away from what is always right for everyone to what is currently faithful for the church."[59]

What is clearly apparent from Hauerwas' theological enterprise is that the role of narrative is intrinsic in grounding the particularity of Christian faith and in shaping our understanding of Christian ethics. Described by Nelson as "the most significant and influential exponent of narrative among contemporary Christian ethicists,"[60] Hauerwas provides additional explanation: "Narrative is but a concept that helps clarify the interrelation between the various themes I have sought to develop in the attempt to give a constructive account of the Christian moral life."[61] Similarities can also be seen between Hauerwas and Hans Frei who is widely recognized as being the seminal figure in the formulation of modern narrative theology.[62] Yet whereas Frei talks about "narratives," Hauerwas tends to talk about "stories."[63] The idea remains the same, however, and is indeed central to the thought of both theologians.

---

[53] Ibid., 29.

[54] Hauerwas, *Vision and Virtue*, 59.

[55] Hauerwas, *Truthfulness and Tragedy*, 1-2.

[56] Hauerwas, *Vision and Virtue*, 29,36.

[57] Ibid., 74.

[58] Hauerwas, *Truthfulness and Tragedy*, 8.

[59] Samuel Wells, "Introduction to the Essays," in *Faithfulness and Fortitude: In Conversation with the Theological Ethics of Stanley Hauerwas*, ed. Mark Thiessen Nation and Samuel Wells (Edinburgh: T&T Clark, 2000), 5.

[60] Nelson, *Narrative and Morality*, 109.

[61] Hauerwas, *The Peaceable Kingdom*, xxv.

[62] For an account of the leading narrative theologians, see Edward L. Nanno, "Narrative Theology," in *The Dictionary of Historical Theology*, 385-386.

[63] See Hans W. Frei, *The Eclipse of Biblical Narrative: A Study in Eighteenth and Nineteenth Century Hermeneutics* (New Haven: Yale University Press, 1974).

Narrative and Divine Self-Communication

The primary reason why narrative features so prominently in Hauerwas' works is that narrative is perceived to be God's chosen means of self-disclosure: "God has entrusted his presence to a historic and contingent community...Therefore the existence of Israel and the church are not accidentally related to the story but are necessary for our knowledge of God."[64] Accordingly, as we learn about God in the form of a story, a primary task of theological reflection is reminding us of a story.[65] Exposing the failings of contemporary theology in neglecting this means of divine self-communication, Hauerwas declares:

> The basis of any Christian social ethic should be the affirmation that God has decisively called and formed a people to serve him through Israel and the work of Christ. The appropriation of the critical significance of the latter depends on the recognition of narrative as a basic category for social ethics.[66]

Drawing out the implications of God's chosen means of revelation, Hauerwas states: "Narrative is not secondary for our knowledge of God; there is no 'point' that can be separated from the story. The narratives through which we learn of God are the point."[67] That is why it is inappropriate to single out specific issues of religious truth, for the prior question is how such affirmations "fit into the story of the kind of God we have come to know in the story of Israel and Jesus."[68] It follows that narrative is central to Christian character as it is the medium through which God has chosen to reveal himself. Hauerwas elaborates on this means of divine self-communication: "Christian ethics does not begin by emphasizing rules or principles, but by calling our attention to a narrative that tells of God's dealing with creation."[69]

Narrative is thus vital for how we interpret the self. Hauerwas insists: "Not only is knowledge of self tied to knowledge of God, but we know ourselves truthfully only when we know ourselves in relation to God." Locating our own life stories within God's story, we are to recognize, is the basis by which "we participate morally in God's life."[70] For central to divine grace, Hauerwas explains, is the journey of the self with God: "Grace...is God's choice to be a Lord whose kingdom is furthered by our concrete obedience through which we acquire a history befitting our nature as God's creatures."[71] What this indicates is that the Bible is essentially a story of a people's journey with God: "In Scripture, we see that God is taking the disconnected elements of our lives and pulling them together into a coherent story that means

---

[64] Hauerwas, *The Peaceable Kingdom*, 97-98.

[65] Hauerwas, *Truthfulness and Tragedy*, 71.

[66] Hauerwas, *A Community of Character*, 9.

[67] Hauerwas, *The Peaceable Kingdom*, 26.

[68] Hauerwas, *Truthfulness and Tragedy*, 73.

[69] Hauerwas, *The Peaceable Kingdom*, 24-25.

[70] Ibid., 27.

[71] Ibid.

something."[72] Fundamental here is the church's existence for embodying the narrative of God at work in history for the sake of the world. The task of Christian ethics is therefore to assist the church in being the people in whom "the narrative of God is lived in a way that makes the kingdom visible."[73] Indeed our goal, Hauerwas proclaims, is to be found in the community of faith as it witnesses to God's kingdom.[74] And basic to this witness is learning to find our role in God's story.[75]

Virtues and the Communal Nature of the Christian Life

Recognizing the importance of character and virtues, which is inextricably related to narrative as a mode of moral reflection, is a key priority for Hauerwas. Berkman notes Hauerwas' influence in describing the nature of the Christian life, and declares that Hauerwas "is clearly a seminal figure in the 'recovery of virtue' in theological ethics."[76] Colin Gunton praises this rediscovery of the centrality of virtues for human beings, which he claims "is one of the gifts of inestimable value that Stanley Hauerwas has given to the world."[77] Yet the idea of character, Hauerwas claims, has not been prominent in recent theological ethics.[78] Supporting this claim, he points to the conclusion MacIntyre draws in that we live in a world of "moral fragments." Such a world "is always on the edge of violence, since there are no means to ensure that moral argument in itself can resolve our moral conflicts."[79] As a result, the metaphors of virtue and character in Hauerwas' theology stand in sharp contrast to this recent tendency in theological scholarship where there is seemingly intractable disagreement on matters of paramount importance. Haurerwas highlights this distinction and notes that Christian thinkers have tended to assume:

> That questions of 'right' were more primary than questions of good, that principles were more fundamental than virtues, that for morality to be coherent required some one principle from which all others could be derived or tested, that the central task of moral reflection was to help us think straight about quandaries, and that we had to see the world as neatly divided into facts and values, rather than an existence filled with many valuational possibilities, some of which may well be in conflict.[80]

---

[72] Hauerwas and Willimon, *Resident Aliens*, 53.

[73] Hauerwas, *The Peaceable Kingdom*, 97.

[74] Ibid., 102.

[75] Ibid., 44.

[76] Berkman, "An Introduction to the Hauerwas Reader," 3.

[77] Colin E. Gunton, "The Church as a School of Virtue? Human Formation in Trinitarian Framework," in *Faithfulness and Fortitude*, 211. This is in contrast, Gunton notes, with "the rootless I of existentialism and consumerism."

[78] Stanley M. Hauerwas, *Character and the Christian Life: A Study in Theological Ethics* (Notre Dame, Ind.: University of Notre Dame Press, 1994), 1.

[79] Hauerwas, *The Peaceable Kingdom*, 5.

[80] Hauerwas, *Against the Nations*, 41.

In espousing the primacy of the virtues for the shape of the Christian life, Hauerwas reminds us that virtues are to be found in Thomas Aquinas' understanding of the moral life.[81] It is an account of the virtues, which "remains unmatched in Christian theology."[82] Along with Aquinas, Hauerwas emphasizes that Aristotle presents a powerful account of the virtues: "For Aristotle, the virtues are acquired over a lifetime – or, even more forcefully put, we only know what a proper lifetime looks like as we come to see it as we acquire the virtues."[83] Summarizing the influence of both scholars, Hauerwas claims: "Aristotle and Aquinas, more than any other philosophers, were concerned with how the self, through its activity, acquires character."[84] Here we also see the influence of MacIntyre upon the theology of Hauerwas in that they both share a commitment to virtue ethics.[85] With this focus, Hauerwas' desire is "to remind Christians what kind of life they are committed to living if they believe that their lives are not their own but God's."[86] And it is stories, which are central for pointing us to the importance of virtue and character in ethics.[87]

Where this committed living is most adequately displayed is within the church, which "for Christians…is the most significant ethical unit."[88] The church is uniquely God's story, wherein ethical character finds its appropriate setting, rather than in the individual or dominant culture. Indeed, "knowing the commandments requires a lifetime embodiment of a set of practices peculiar to the church."[89] As such, Hauerwas contends, if theologians are "to contribute to reflection on the moral life in our particular situation, they will do so exactly to the extent they can capture the significance of the church for determining the nature and content of Christian ethical reflection."[90] In *Sanctify Them in the Truth*, Hauerwas elaborates on this communal nature of the Christian life, and argues that there is no such thing as truth that is not embodied truth. Thus "one of the most important questions you can ask theologians is where they go to church." For to be truthful, theology must be, "embedded in the practices of actual lived communities."[91] Whenever theology is divorced from the

---

[81] Hauerwas, "On Doctrine and Ethics," 28.

[82] Stanley, M. Hauerwas and Charles R. Pinches, *Christians Among the Virtues: Theological Conversations with Ancient and Modern Ethics* (Notre Dame, Ind.: University of Notre Dame Press, 1997), xiii. For a further account of Aquinas' works in understanding moral behaviour, see Charles R. Pinches, *Theology and Action: After Theory in Christian Ethics* (Grand Rapids: Eerdmans, 2002).

[83] Hauerwas and Pinches, *Christians Among the Virtues*, x.

[84] Hauerwas, *A Community of Character*, 135.

[85] See Alasdair MacIntyre, *After Virtue: A Study in Moral Theory*, 2nd edn (London: Duckworth, 1985).

[86] Hauerwas, *Truthfulness and Tragedy*, 12.

[87] Hauerwas, *A Community of Character*, 134.

[88] Hauerwas and Willimon, *Resident Aliens*, 81.

[89] Stanley M. Hauerwas and William H. Willimon, *The Truth About God: The Ten Commandments in Christian Life* (Nashville: Abingdon Press, 1999), 13.

[90] Hauerwas, "On Keeping Theological Ethics Theological," 33-34.

[91] Hauerwas, *Sanctify Them in the Truth*, 157.

practices of the church, theology cannot help but be ideology. That is why "all theology must begin and end with ecclesiology."[92] To be a theologian is therefore to occupy an office in the church of Jesus Christ.[93]

The concept of virtues is developed in *The Peaceable Kingdom* where Hauerwas describes ethics as learning God's story of our sinfulness. As such, "Christian ethics reflects a particular people's history, the appropriation of which requires the recognition that we are sinners."[94] Christian ethics is unique to its story, and there cannot be a continuity between Christian and non-Christian morality. Here again we see the influence of Barth upon Hauerwas. Hauerwas notes that for Barth, "ethics can be done only in the context of dogmatics, for it is only within the circle of the being and activity of God that the ethical question of man's determination can be raised with proper seriousness."[95] Hauerwas exposes this essential difference from liberalism: "The story that liberalism teaches us is that we have no story."[96] Yet he maintains that we can make thoughtful moral decisions only in the context of the traditions of some community, which are shaped by communal narratives. The Bible is thus indispensable to the Christian community.[97] It is concerned with "whether or not we shall be faithful to the gospel."[98] And central to being faithful to the gospel is the place of virtues: "To be like Jesus requires that I become part of a community that practices virtues, not that I copy his life point by point."[99]

Placher draws a parallel here between this core aspect of Hauerwas' theology with that of Lindbeck's theology: "Just as Lindbeck insisted that a religious language creates possibilities of religious life and experience, so Hauerwas says that stories create possibilities for different forms of virtuous life."[100] Limiting oneself to external conformity to moral rules or ideals is therefore clearly not how Hauerwas understands the moral good. In contrast, it is the dynamic of the story that is intrinsic to a correct understanding of the virtuous life. Rather than conforming to a set of principles, Hauerwas contends: "Goodness is a way of being that which brings unity to the variety of our activities."[101] Specifically, it is the gospel that gives direction as to how we are to live. As such, the gospel is to be worked out in and through every aspect of our life. To ignore the ethical implications of the gospel as revealed in the biblical narrative will result in the Christian simply being "shaped by the forces of his environment rather than by his determination in Christ."[102]

---

[92] Stanley M. Hauerwas, *In Good Company: The Church as Polis* (Notre Dame, Ind.: University of Notre Dame, 1995), 58.

[93] Hauerwas, *Dispatches from the Front*, 19.

[94] Hauerwas, *The Peaceable Kingdom*, 17.

[95] Hauerwas, *Character and the Christian Life*, 137.

[96] Hauerwas, *A Community of Character*, 84.

[97] Ibid., 66.

[98] Hauerwas and Willimon, *Resident Aliens*, 22.

[99] Hauerwas, *The Peaceable Kingdom*, 76.

[100] Placher, "Postliberal Theology," 349.

[101] Hauerwas, *Character and the Christian Life*, 179.

[102] Ibid., 183.

Christian Distinctiveness and Socio-Political Involvement

Contemporary Culture and a Separated Christian Community

In his most popular work *Resident Aliens*, Hauerwas and co-author William Willimon revisit an Anabaptist form of the church as an alternative to the influential work undertaken by Richard Niebuhr in *Christ and Culture*.[103] They describe a contemporary society in which Christians find themselves outsiders to the dominant cultural values, and argue that this is a positive outcome for the church's integrity. Calling for the church to be faithful as the church, the authors claim that this means living a way of life that is at odds with an unchristian world.[104] It means refocusing on its Jesus-centered tradition, which has been frequently ignored to accommodate to the world in order to make the Christian beliefs acceptable. Although culture cannot be escaped, the church must live a dislocated or "alien" existence: "The church is a colony, an island of one culture in the middle of another. In baptism our citizenship is transferred from one dominion to another, and we become, in whatever culture we find ourselves, resident aliens."[105] Yet rather than being a colony, the church is too often a "gathering of strangers who see the church as yet another 'helping institution' to gratify further their individual desires."[106] Because of this failure, "church thought and life need to change direction."[107] The church must recover its mission, the authors argue, to build community that exemplifies God's kingdom and its values.

As Christians are to be a pilgrim people the church is to be distinctive and stand as a contrast to liberal society. It is a community of a particular kind, Hauerwas argues, "capable of being faithful to a way of life, even when that way of life may be in conflict with what passes as 'morality' in the larger society."[108] It is the faithful church that demonstrates the truthfulness of Christian convictions.[109] For if the world is basically Christian then the church is not required. In such a scenario, "all that is needed is a slight change of mind, an inner change of heart, a few new insights."[110] Yet the world is not Christian. Consequently, theologians are charged not with making the gospel credible to the modern world, but with making the world credible to the gospel. Rather than being "under the spell of Christendom," those working in Christian ethics should not disguise the fact that they write and speak out of and to a distinctive community. In fulfilling this task theologians will stress the importance of the church as "a community faithful to our belief that we are creatures of a graceful

---

[103] In their criticism of *Christ and Culture*, they state: "'Culture' became a blanket term to underwrite Christian involvement with the world without providing any discriminating modes for discerning how Christians should see the good or the bad in 'culture'" (40).

[104] Likewise, in *The Nature of Doctrine*, Lindbeck speaks about the need to develop "close-knit groups…to sustain an alien faith" (78).

[105] Hauerwas and Willimon, *Resident Aliens*, 12.

[106] Ibid., 138.

[107] Ibid., 12.

[108] Hauerwas, "On Keeping Theological Ethics Theological," 35.

[109] Hauerwas, "The Testament of Friends," 214.

[110] Hauerwas and Willimon, *Resident Aliens*, 29.

God."[111] Hence with this focus, Hauerwas' goal is "to reassert the social significance of the church as a distinct society with an integrity peculiar to itself."[112] Accentuating the key features of this counter-cultural community, Hauerwas notes:

> The church's social ethic is not first of all to be found in the statements by which it tries to influence the ethos of those in power, but rather the church's social ethic is first and foremost found in its ability to sustain a people who are not at home in the liberal presumptions of our civilization and society.[113]

Aware of criticisms that he is calling for Christians to withdraw from social and political engagements, Hauerwas denies this, and claims the image of withdrawal is wrong: "I am not trying to force Christians to withdraw but to recognize that they are surrounded. There is no question of withdrawing, as all lines of retreat have been cut off." What Hauerwas is intent on addressing is how Christians will "survive when surrounded by a culture we helped create but which now threatens to destroy us."[114] In short, he asserts: "I simply want them to be there as Christians and as church."[115]

One of the effects of the increasingly secular nature of contemporary culture, coupled with the loss of social power held by Christians, will result in fewer being attracted to the ministry and the work of theology. Yet Hauerwas takes heart at this expected change in society:

> Since no-one expects Christians to make the world safe, since Christians are no longer required to supply the ideologies necessary 'to govern,' since Christians are not expected to be able to provide philosophical justifications to insure the way things are or the way things should be, we are free to be Christians.[116]

What this means for the true church is that it will be a "confessing church," which is "a radical alternative" to other approaches to church. Hauerwas and Willimon describe the confessing church as one that "seeks the visible church," and is thus "a place, clearly visible to the world, in which people are faithful to their promises, love their enemies, tell the truth, honour the poor, suffer for righteousness, and thereby testify to the amazing community-creating power of God."[117] It is a church in which people "are bound together in loyalty to a story." When this story includes "something as strange as the Sermon on the Mount," this results in a life, which is at odds with the world.[118] In living in such a fashion the church exists as resident aliens, "an adventurous colony in a society of unbelief."[119]

---

[111] Hauerwas, "On Keeping Theological Ethics Theological," 35-36.

[112] Hauerwas, *A Community of Character*, 1.

[113] Hauerwas, *Against the Nations*, 11-12.

[114] Hauerwas, *Dispatches from the Front*, 18.

[115] Hauerwas, *Against the Nations*, 1.

[116] Hauerwas, *Dispatches from the Front*, 17.

[117] Hauerwas and Willimon, *Resident Aliens*, 45-46.

[118] Ibid., 94.

[119] Ibid., 49.

Power, Politics, and the Witness of the Church

In *With the Grain of the Universe,* which were originally delivered as the 2001 Gifford Lectures at the University of St. Andrews, Hauerwas seeks to demonstrate that Christian thought should not begin with our abilities to grasp rational claims. Rather, it begins by bearing witness to God's life among us. Through telling "the theological story," Hauerwas outlines what went wrong with theology in the twentieth century with an examination of William James, Reinhold Niebuhr, and Karl Barth. Hauerwas holds that Barth, whom he "has been profoundly influenced by," is the hero of Christian theological argument.[120] The *Church Dogmatics* were Barth's significant attempt at outlining the conceptual and moral skills that we must have for such witness to God.[121] Barth showed "what it might mean not only to think but to live when God is acknowledged as the beginning and end of our existence."[122] Disparities are thus identified with James' theological approach who was bothered by the fact that "Christianity challenged the moral and political arrangements necessary to sustain the human project without God."[123] Sharing James' failure to understand the nature of the witness of the church, Hauerwas argues that Niebuhr "regarded the church as a sociological necessity for Christianity to exist across time, but he did not regard it as an ethical or epistemological necessity."[124] As such, Hauerwas concludes his work with a meditation on the "necessity of witness." Complementing his earlier works where he appropriated terms from moral philosophy such as character and virtue, the term witness introduces a new theme in his theological project. Yet he confirms that witness is now central to his understanding of the life of the church:

> When Christianity is tempted to become a civilizational religion in a manner that makes witness secondary to knowing the truth about God, Christians lose the skills necessary to make known to themselves and others how what we believe is true to the way things are.[125]

Denouncing the "epistemological overcoming of theology," where the temptation is to cast Christianity as a truth separable from truthful witness, Hauerwas describes this as "Constantinianism."[126] In contrast, Hauerwas is emphatic that we cannot

---

[120] Hauerwas, *With the Grain of the Universe*, 20.

[121] Ibid., 175-176.

[122] Ibid., 204.

[123] Ibid., 78-79.

[124] Ibid., 137. Hauerwas explains where Niebuhr went wrong: "In spite of Niebuhr's early identification as a 'neo-orthodox' theologian, he always worked within the 'givens' of Protestant liberalism, which means, at the very least, that Niebuhr, like James, assumed that Christianity must be tested by standards generally accepted by the intellectual elites of the day" (87).

[125] Ibid., 32.

[126] Ibid., 36. For a further critique of 'Constantinianism' see *Resident Aliens*, 15-29.

know God abstracted from how God makes himself known.[127] Inseparably associated with how God makes himself known is Christian witness. It is a witness that presents an alternative mode of existence in the world. Significantly, Hauerwas claims this form of witness involves the political existence of the Christian. For "any attempt to provide an account of how Christian theological claims can tell us the way things are requires a correlative politics. In theological terms, such a politics is called 'church.'"[128] Political engagement for Hauerwas therefore consists in faithful witness as the church. It is "politics as defined by the gospel," which means joining "a counter-cultural phenomenon."[129] Describing the nature of this witness, he asserts: "For the church to be a social ethic, rather than to have a social ethic, means the church must be (is) a body polity."[130] Shaping the nature of this political existence is the life and teachings of Jesus, who shows how "God's kingship and power consists not in coercion but in God's willingness to forgive and have mercy on us."[131]

Power in Hauerwas' thought is therefore to be rejected, which he perceives to be exemplified in the person of Jesus Christ. With this christology, when he speaks about a polis called church, this is markedly different from a politically active church. Quick to point out that the relation between church and state over the years has been marked by conflict, Hauerwas declares: "Christian theologians make a profound mistake when they posit some kind of harmony between the two by means of a so-called church-state theory."[132] Advocating an alternative perspective of political existence that rejects the use of power and coercion, Hauerwas contends: "The main political task of the church is the formation of people who see clearly the cost of discipleship and are willing to pay the price."[133] For a faithful witness that does not compromise with the world "leads to worldly hostility."[134] Political loyalty is thus to be with the church: "The more interesting political question for me is what is required of the church in such a society to produce congregations who require that a ministry exists which has the courage to preach truthfully."[135]

The implication of this concept of witness is that the Christian is not charged with seeking to transform the world through socio-political involvement. Hauerwas makes this unambiguously clear: "The political task of Christians is to be the church rather than to transform the world."[136] Instead, "the gospel represents an elaborate training in the appropriation of skills to live joyously in the face of the tragic." In living in

---

[127] Hauerwas, *With the Grain of the Universe*, 16.

[128] Ibid., 39.

[129] Hauerwas and Willimon, *Resident Aliens*, 30.

[130] Stanley M. Hauerwas, "What Could it Mean for the Church to be Christ's Body?: A Question Without a Clear Answer," in *Scottish Journal of Theology*, vol. 48/1 (February 1995), 13.

[131] Hauerwas, *The Peaceable Kingdom*, 85.

[132] Hauerwas, *In Good Company*, 199.

[133] Hauerwas and Willimon, *Resident Aliens*, 48.

[134] Ibid., 47.

[135] Hauerwas, *Dispatches from the Front*, 11.

[136] Hauerwas and Willimon, *Resident Aliens*, 38.

the face of the tragic, "our task is not to bring God's kingdom, but rather to witness to it by being the earnest of his kingdom of peace."[137] It is thus Hauerwas' aim "to convince everyone who calls himself or herself a Christian that being Christian means that one must be non-violent."[138] And non-violence involves the rejection of all forms of power in addressing issues of social and political concern. Werpehowski points out this distinctive feature of Christian witness: "Hauerwas believes that pacifism is the normative mode of witness to God's reign in history."[139] The key features of this alternative to the use of power are found in *Resident Aliens*:

> We want to assert, for the church, politics that is both truthful and hopeful. Our politics is hopeful because we really believe that, as Christians, we are given the resources to speak the truth to one another...Our politics is truthful because it refuses to base itself on the false gods that make us so prone to violence. Here is power politics, not as the world usually defines it, but power derived from ordinary people who are trying to base their lives on what is true.[140]

In contrast to the clamour for power in contemporary society, Hauerwas challenges Christians "to recapture the posture of the peasant. The peasant does not seek to become the master, but rather she wants to know how to survive under the power of the master."[141] This is the social ethic of the church. Whereas the world depends on the power of the sword, "the church is that community that trusts the power of truth and charity and thus does not depend on any further power."[142] The church is therefore political in the sense that "her first political act, is to be herself." In doing so, the church will "establish the boundaries between the world and the people called Christian," which are necessary for the world to understand what it means to be the world.[143] This challenges the assumption "that the church is judged politically by how well or ill the church's presence in the world works to the advantage of the world."[144] Hence Hauerwas attacks the political theologies that "want to maintain Christendom, wherein the church justifies itself as a helpful, if sometimes complaining, prop for the state."[145] And it is precisely this rejection of all forms of power that is significant for Hauerwas' understanding of social justice.

---

[137] Hauerwas, *Truthfulness and Tragedy*, 12.
[138] Hauerwas, *Dispatches from the Front*, 5.
[139] Werpehowski, "Theological Ethics," 321.
[140] Hauerwas and Willimon, *Resident Aliens*, 156-157.
[141] Hauerwas, *Dispatches from the Front*, 105.
[142] Hauerwas, *Truthfulness and Tragedy*, 141.
[143] Ibid., 139-140.
[144] Hauerwas and Willimon, *Resident Aliens*, 30.
[145] Ibid., 38.

Understanding Justice in a Secular Society

Deriving from his distinctive political theology is Hauerwas' conceptuality of justice in a secular society. What Hauerwas is intent on stressing is that charity and justice go together, "for justice involves those basic obligations we owe others and ourselves that charity presupposes."[146] Moreover, what is rejected is a notion of justice that does not begin with God. Dismissing the notion that society understands the true meaning of justice in *After Christendom*, Hauerwas attacks the emphasis on an understanding of justice linked with the fulfillment of rights.[147] As Christians, he declares, "we will speak more truthfully to our society and be of greater service by refusing to continue the illusion that the larger social order knows what it is talking about when it calls for justice."[148] The influential work of John Rawls suffers sustained attacks by Hauerwas as it "stands as a testimony to the moral limits of the liberal tradition."[149] Shortcomings are identified in this leading political theorist and his presuppositions about society being a collection of individuals:

> Missing entirely from Rawls' position is any suggestion that a theory of justice is ultimately dependent on a view of the good; or that justice is as much a category for individuals as for societies...As a result he represents the ultimate liberal irony: individualism, in an effort to secure societal cooperation and justice, must deny individual preferences.[150]

Along with the purported deficiencies of Rawls' position,[151] Hauerwas claims that on the whole, much of our talk about justice does not have its foundation in God: "Most of our social activism is formed on the presumption that God is superfluous to the formation of a world of peace with justice."[152] Making this more pertinent to the church, Hauerwas criticizes activist Christians who talk about justice and claim that what is being promoted is "a notion of justice that envisions a society in which faith in God is rendered quite unnecessary, since everybody already believes in peace and justice even when everybody does not believe in God."[153] Frequently what happens is that the church's call for justice "unwittingly reinforces liberal assumptions about freedom in the name of the gospel."[154] Hauerwas' chief concern is thus not with secular political liberals, but rather with Christians who assume that political liberalism ought to shape the agenda of the church. For although we can learn from

---

[146] Hauerwas, *Truthfulness and Tragedy*, 142.

[147] Hauerwas, *After Christendom?* 45-68.

[148] Ibid., 68.

[149] Hauerwas, *A Community of Character*, 82. For a further critique of Rawls' position, see Hauerwas, *After Christendom?* 47-48, 61-62.

[150] Hauerwas, *A Community of Character*, 83.

[151] We will be assessing Rawls' position in greater depth in chapter 7.

[152] Hauerwas and Willimon, *Resident Aliens*, 36.

[153] Ibid., 37.

[154] Hauerwas, *A Community of Character*, 12.

its "various mutations," liberalism "can become a distraction for Christians just to the extent that our agenda is first and foremost set by the church."[155]

Disagreeing with recent political philosophy in making justice the dominant criterion or virtue of social and moral life, Hauerwas urges for fellowship, friendship, loyalty and truthfulness to be seen as equally important marks for society. Hauerwas claims: "It may be necessary even to qualify the demands of justice in order to have a society that wishes to let friendship flourish as one of its central virtues."[156] Taking this contrasting position also leads Hauerwas to be critical of Christian justifications of democracy.[157] Challenging commonly held conceptions about how the church should interact with a liberal democratic social system, he argues that although democratic social orders may have some advantages, "the Christian fascination with democracy as 'our' form of government has rendered us defenseless when, for example, that state goes to war."[158] An alternative paradigm is offered involving the discipline of a Christian community helping people learn to worship God.[159] Indeed, it is claimed, there is no service more important.[160] Hauerwas declares:

> The church does not exist to provide an ethos for democracy or any other form of social organization, but stands as a political alternative to every nation, witnessing to the kind of social life possible for those that have been formed by the story of Christ.[161]

Not only does Hauerwas criticize popular notions of justice and democracy, he challenges, as we have seen, "the very idea that Christian social ethics is primarily an attempt to make the world more peaceable or just."[162] For when theories of justice are treated as the fundamental questions of social ethics, the church's contribution is easily lost. Rather than justice being the driving concern of the church, "the first social ethical task of the church is to be the church – the servant community."[163] Hauerwas encapsulates this thought in *Truthfulness and Tragedy*:

> The church does not have a social ethic, but rather is a social ethic. That is, she is a social ethic inasmuch as she functions as a criteriological institution – that is, an institution that has learned to embody the form of truth that is charity as revealed in the person and work of Christ. Such a charity some may find ineffective, but it is the kind

---

[155] Hauerwas, *A Better Hope*, 9-10.

[156] Hauerwas, *Truthfulness and Tragedy*, 142.

[157] Hauerwas, *Dispatches from the Front*, 25.

[158] Ibid., 91-106.

[159] This is emphasized in Hauerwas and Wells (ed.) *The Blackwell Companion to Christian Ethics*, where the first section is entitled "Studying Ethics through Worship."

[160] Hauerwas, *A Better Hope*, 25.

[161] Hauerwas, *A Community of Character*, 12.

[162] Ibid., 3.

[163] Hauerwas, *The Peaceable Kingdom*, 99.

of character required of those of us who are pledged to serve the kingdom of God as he has revealed it in the cross.[164]

In short, to live an alien existence as a member of the Christian community is to resign oneself to the fact of one's inability to make a tangible difference to the social and political concerns of this world. Yet this should not lead Christians to despair. Why? Because the church is offered in Christ "a story that helps us sustain the task of charity in a world where it can never be successful. That is why charity for Christians is not something we wish to do, it is an obligation." Hence we are "freed from the compulsion to combine power with charity, effectiveness as the criterion and form of charitable actions...For we are commanded not to be revolutionaries, or to be world-changers, but simply to be perfect." The charge of the church "is not the removing of all injustice in the world, but rather meeting the need of the neighbour where we find him."[165] It is a vision of discipleship standing in marked contrast to the world's concept of seeking social justice through the use of power and coercion.

Critical Reflection

Grace, Revelation, and the Self-Manifestation of God

In order to capture the essential features of Hauerwas' theology of grace and how this doctrine shapes his political theology, it is necessary to analyze first his concept of revelation. For Hauerwas it is Scripture, which as a narrative or story, is the source of Christian ideas and values. In affirming the centrality of Scripture, Hauerwas follows Barth's concern in preventing ideas from outside the church to assume a controlling influence within it. Recapturing the importance of Scripture's grand narrative is indeed a noteworthy achievement of his theological method, as McGrath points out: "Hauerwas presents an important and persuasive account of the manner in which Scripture is used within the church, which is particularly welcome because of the close connection he establishes between the Bible and the church."[166]

This integral feature of Hauerwas' theology is summarized by Timothy Phillips and Dennis Okholm in their analysis of postliberalism: "Postliberalism includes a theory that explains the loss of Scripture's formative authority and the church's correlative accommodation to culture as well as a strategy for cultivating Christian identity."[167] Therefore, in redirecting attention toward Scripture and the distinctive

---

[164] Hauerwas, *Truthfulness and Tragedy*, 143. For a striking critique of Hauerwas' claim that the church does not have, but is a social ethic, see Duncan B. Forrester, "The Church and the Concentration Camp: Some Reflections of Moral Community," in *Faithfulness and Fortitude*, 189-207. Forrester claims that the Christians in Dachau went to church in the morning and gassed Jews in the afternoon: "Dachau and the other camps not only had, but exemplified and embodied a social ethic, albeit an ethic of almost unbelievable evil" (198).

[165] Hauerwas, *Truthfulness and Tragedy*, 138.

[166] Alister E. McGrath, "An Evangelical Evaluation of Postliberalism," in *The Nature of Confession*, 39.

[167] Phillips and Okholm, "The Nature of Confession," 11.

features of the Christian moral life, there are core features of postliberalism and thus Hauerwas' approach to theological engagement, which others can learn from.[168]

Yet although Hauerwas emphasizes the priority of Scripture, his work, and postliberalism as a whole, does raise a question as to precisely why Scripture possesses this authority. There is a suggestion that in some way the community of faith simply imposes this authority on the text, while being free to acknowledge alternative authorities.[169] In short, it is not altogether clear on what basis we are able to choose among the various stories that compete for our attention. This question of scriptural authority is brought into focus by Nigel Biggar who distinguishes between Barth's narrative approach and that of Hauerwas:

> Whereas for Barth the biblical story is significant in its reference to the reality of the living God, for Hauerwas its importance lies immediately in its sociological function in forming the identity of the Christian community and thereby providing the rationale of its morality.[170]

It is this form of relativism that appears to lack the acknowledgement of the truth of Christian faith, and instead just report the stories told within a particular community, which is the most common criticism of postliberalism. Hence the question that immediately comes to the fore not only has to do with what the Christian community chooses to make of Scripture, but, moreover, is it right? McGrath echoes these criticisms and notes that postliberalism "appears to represent a purely intratextual affair, with little concern for its possible relation to an external objective reality."[171] A key concern therefore with postliberalism and thus with Hauerwas' work is that "the prioritization of Scripture is not adequately grounded at the theological level." Rather, it would appear to be defended on cultural, historical, or contractual grounds.[172] Hauerwas' discussion of Scripture and the church exposes the extent to which there is a question over this aspect of his theology:

> Authority is that reflection initiated by a community's traditions through which a common goal can be pursued. Authority is, therefore, the means through which a community is able to journey from where it is to where it ought to be. It is set on its

---

[168] See McGrath, "An Evangelical Evaluation of Postliberalism," 35. McGrath claims postliberalism's sense of community "stands in sharp contrast to evangelicalism's tendency toward social atomism."

[169] Here we see the influence of John Milbank upon Hauerwas' theology.

[170] Nigel Biggar, *The Hastening that Waits: Karl Barth's Ethics* (Oxford: Clarendon Press, 1993), 118.

[171] McGrath, "An Evangelical Evaluation of Postliberalism," 28. In *With the Grain of the Universe*, however, Hauerwas' treatment of truth does appear to offer more than intratextuality, which has tended to be the case in some of his previous theological works. In a personal communication, Wells defends Hauerwas' understanding of the role of community vis-à-vis questions of authority: "He [Hauerwas] just sees how easy it is to fall into self-deception if you read the Bible without the community."

[172] McGrath, *A Passion for Truth*, 155.

way by the language and practices of the tradition, but while on its way it must often subtly reform those practices and language in accordance with its new perception of truth.[173]

In contrast, as is inherent to the doctrine of grace, theology is grounded upon and evaluated on the basis of the self-revelation of God, and is not reliant upon a community for recognizing its authority. It has this authority simply because of what it is and what it conveys. However the concept of truth may be stated, as McGrath compellingly argues, it is to be understood as being located outside the language of Christianity, as well as within it.[174] George Hunsinger shares McGrath's unease and claims: "The account of scriptural unity, authority and inspiration among the postliberals is, to say the least, fairly thin and unsatisfying so far."[175] Elaborating on the inherent authority of the scriptural text, and the problems presented by the theological method advocated by Hauerwas, McGrath declares:

> Postliberalism reduces the concept of truth to internal consistency. There can be no doubt that intrasystemic consistency is a quality that is to be admired. However, it is perfectly possible to have an entirely coherent system that has no meaningful relation to the real world. Christianity is not simply about interpreting the narrated identity of Jesus or giving a coherent account of the grammar of faith. It is about recognizing the truth of Jesus Christ as Saviour and Lord.[176]

David Fergusson highlights a related feature of Hauerwas' concept of revelation in that he repeatedly insists on calling for a distinctive church.[177] Yet Fergusson differs from Hauerwas on account of his over-concentration upon this distinctiveness of the church. Fergusson comments: "He insists upon the close relationship between christology and ecclesiology to the extent that the truth about Jesus can only be perceived from within a life of discipleship in the community of the church."[178] Indeed as Hauerwas unequivocally asserts: "Outside the church there is no saving knowledge of God."[179] Here we see again the question over biblical authority in Hauerwas' theological project and whether God is dependent on the Christian community for his self-revelation. For as Fergusson points out, resonating

---

[173] Hauerwas, *A Community of Character*, 63.

[174] McGrath, "An Evangelical Evaluation of Postliberalism," 39. For an analysis of the role of language in the Christian faith, see Lesslie Newbigin, *Foolishness to the Greeks: The Gospel and Western Culture* (London: SPCK, 1986), 3. Newbigin states: "The language of a people provides the means by which they express their way of perceiving things and of coping with them."

[175] George Hunsinger, "What Can Evangelicals and Postliberals Learn From Each Other? The Carl Henry-Hans Frei Exchange Reconsidered," in *The Nature of Confession*, 136.

[176] McGrath, "An Evangelical Evaluation of Postliberalism," 38.

[177] David Fergusson, "Another Way of Reading Stanley Hauerwas?" in *Scottish Journal of Theology*, vol. 50/2 (May 1997), 242.

[178] Ibid., 244.

[179] Hauerwas, *After Christendom?* 16, 26, 35.

throughout Hauerwas' writings is the assertion that "the life of discipleship within the church is the indispensable epistemological condition for confessing Christ."[180]

In providing an analysis of Hauerwas' understanding of Scripture, John Sykes argues that Hauerwas' account of biblical authority suffers due to his attempt at circumventing the issue of revelation.[181] Sykes notes that for Hauerwas, "Scripture has authority for the simple reason that Christian communities regard it as authoritative." Although the community and Scripture "are mutually implicating entities which are logically dependent upon each other," it is the community which, "as the source of the stories and the traditions that interpret them, is logically prior."[182] In contrast to a conception of revelation relying on a community for its authority, Sykes, echoing Barth, argues for a clearer rationale for declaring Scripture has God's authority: "The Christian community's interpretation of the Bible should be seen as a sacrament whereby God graciously makes himself present."[183] In making much the same argument as McGrath, Sykes concludes: "The authority of Scripture derives from its speaker, God, who is free to make himself known in it, and who has chosen faithfully to do so."[184] Such is the nature of grace in God's self-revelation.

Christology and the Political Existence of the Christian

An integral strength of Hauerwas' thought is that at its core it is theocentric. This characteristic feature of the Reformation tradition is reflected in that Hauerwas concurs with Barth's position that theology can have no other subject but God.[185] In flatly rejecting the anthropocentrism of the Enlightenment, he declares: "How wonderful it is to be creatures of a gracious God who is capable of beckoning us from our self-fascination."[186] For being a Christian implicitly involves recognizing that we are "to look upon ourselves as creatures rather than as creators."[187] What this means is that "each age must come, fresh and new, to the realization that God, not nations, rules the world."[188] Wells summarizes Hauerwas' theocentric focus and the human response to divine revelation: "Christians are called to be a holy people, the communion of saints, imitating the character of the one, sovereign, holy God...Christian ethics is about forming the human response to God's revelation."[189]

---

[180] Fergusson, "Another Way of Reading Stanley Hauerwas?" 244.

[181] John Sykes, "Narrative Accounts of Biblical Authority: The Need for a Doctrine of Revelation," *Modern Theology*, vol. 5/4 (July 1989), 327.

[182] Ibid., 331-332.

[183] Ibid., 339.

[184] Ibid., 340.

[185] Hauerwas, *With the Grain of the Universe*, 144.

[186] Hauerwas, *Dispatches from the Front*, 2.

[187] Hauerwas, "On Keeping Theological Ethics Theological," 35.

[188] Hauerwas and Willimon, *Resident Aliens*, 28.

[189] Wells, *Transforming Fate into Destiny*, 127.

Retaining a theocentric worldview is indeed central to a biblical doctrine of grace, and thus to determining the church's socio-political engagement in the world.

At the heart of this theocentric worldview, as Hauerwas insists, is the person of Jesus Christ: "The heart of my work is to think christologically in a manner Yoder taught me."[190] It is the story of Jesus, especially his passion, death and resurrection, and the Sermon on the Mount, that Hauerwas constantly turns.[191] As the story of Jesus is crucial to becoming a people marked by Christian ethics, Hauerwas asserts: "By learning to imitate Jesus, to follow in his way, the early Christians believed they were learning to imitate God."[192] Indeed, the Son of God is declared in Scripture to be "the image of the invisible God," thus revealing who God is and his purposes for humankind as to how they live (Colossians 1:15-20). Mark Nelson concurs and affirms that Christianity is an ethical religion: "It means that one cannot characterize the Christian view of God, the world, and the relation between them, without reference to ethical ideas, such as good and bad, right and wrong, virtue and vice."[193] Similarly, David Field recognizes the theocentric basis to the Bible's ethical teaching and claims that doctrine is inseparable from ethics: "The special concern of Christian ethics is to relate an understanding of God to the conduct of men and women and, more specifically, to explore the response to God which Jesus Christ requires and makes possible."[194] This highlights a key strength of Hauerwas' project in affirming the centrality of Christ for the life and thought of the church.

Yet in following in Christ's way, Hauerwas concludes that the church is to resist engagement in the world's political activities. Holding to a wide and somewhat questionable interpretation of non-violence and its ramifications for the use of power in contemporary society, including that of the political arena, Hauerwas asserts: "The Sermon on the Mount presupposes the existence of a community constituted by the practice of non-violence, and it is unintelligible divorced from such a community."[195]

In critiquing the contributions of Hauerwas' christology for the political existence of the Christian, it is helpful to compare and contrast his theology with that of Jürgen Moltmann. In doing so, it is immediately noticeable that Moltmann shares Hauerwas' christocentric approach to theology and Christian living. Both theologians recognize that Christ is central to the orthodox Christian faith. What is also apparent is that Moltmann shares Hauerwas' concept of power, and rejects the use of power by the church, which is instead called to be a servant community. Such a position is in fact problematic, as has already been argued, and as we will seek to

---

[190] Stanley M. Hauerwas and Chris K. Huebner, "History, Theory, and Anabaptism: A Conversation on Theology after John Howard Yoder," in *The Wisdom of the Cross: Essays in Honour of John Howard Yoder*, ed. Stanley M. Hauerwas, et al (Grand Rapids: Eerdmans, 1999), 394.

[191] For a further discussion, see Wells, *Transforming Fate into Destiny*, 63-65.

[192] Hauerwas, *The Peaceable Kingdom*, 78.

[193] Mark Nelson, "Ethics," in *The Oxford Companion to Christian Thought*, 212.

[194] Field, "Ethics," 232.

[195] Hauerwas, *Unleashing the Scriptures*, 64.

demonstrate further in chapter 7. Although the church is to be characterized by servanthood, it is also to be a servant-leader necessitating the use of power.

Where Moltmann differs from Hauerwas, however, is in the conclusions he draws as to the implications of Christ's life and work for the church's socio-political involvement. For in contrast with Hauerwas, Moltmann has convincingly shown the far-reaching implications of the universal mission of Christ for the life and witness of the church. Drawing out the eschatological dimension of the resurrection, this leads to a degree of differentiation between Moltmann and Hauerwas' interpretation of the Christian's political existence. Whereas Hauerwas perceives the life and teachings of Jesus calling the church to be a separate community, Moltmann argues that the cosmic dimensions of christology results in the church being called to seek the transformation of the world as it anticipates the eschatological kingdom of God. Miroslav Volf, who advocates a vision of a public theology for a public gospel, captures this holistic imperative: "Looking through the spectacles of its own culture, it sees the city whose builder and architect is God...Dwelling on the margins, it seeks to bring the reign of the triune God to bear on all domains of life."[196]

This recognition of the glorification of God in all aspects of creation is at the centre of a biblical theology of grace, due to the holistic nature of the kingdom of God tying the covenant time line together, and is thus elementary to the mission of the church in continuing the holistic ministry of Christ on earth. Yet this essential feature is conspicuously downplayed in Hauerwas' theology. For example, in his rejection of liberation theology, he appears to not give sufficient attention to the imperative of socio-political action: "I am sure that the poor have a special place in God's kingdom, but I am equally sure that the Christian life involves more than being oppressed or identifying with the oppressed."[197] Discussing Gustavo Gutiérrez's use of the word "liberation," Hauerwas insists: "Christians' most important contribution to such struggles is to be a community of the liberated who can witness to paradigmatic forms of service."[198] As such, his focus is on the experience of a people, namely the church, which as a society of the liberated, give concrete expression to liberty in how they live. With this critique of liberation theology, Hauerwas highlights how his own work, which is indeed significant for recapturing the imperative of the church to be a faithful community, may have been strengthened had he given greater recognition to the priority of God's universal reign in his creation, as made manifest in a theology of grace, for the socio-political witness of the church in the contemporary world.

---

[196] Miroslav Volf, "Theology, Meaning and Power," in *The Nature of Confession*, 66.

[197] Hauerwas, *Truthfulness and Tragedy*, 134.

[198] Stanley M. Hauerwas, "Some Theological Reflections on Gutierrez's Use of 'Liberation' as a Theological Concept," *Modern Theology*, vol. 3/1 (October 1986), 75.

The Use of Narrative as a Hermeneutical Tool

As we have seen, a noteworthy contribution of Hauerwas' theological project is the priority he places on the role of Scripture in the life of the Christian community. Yet, the question arises as to how we interpret the biblical text. The divergence of opinion between Hauerwas and Moltmann exposes the risk of leaning too heavily on narrative as a hermeneutical tool for such a task. For due to Hauerwas placing a primary emphasis on narrative, there is a danger of adopting too selective a reading of the text when a particular narrative is chosen to the neglect of its canonical context. In discussing Hauerwas' hermeneutical strategy, which could also incidentally be said of some aspects of Moltmann's later theology, Richard Hays states: "Hauerwas' interpretations of biblical texts rarely depend upon detailed exegesis or sustained close reading."[199] Wrestling with sustained close reading of the text, however, "is likely to produce more compelling and sophisticated results than one who reads the texts casually or superficially. Serious exegesis is a *sine qua non* for New Testament ethics."[200] Brevard Childs supports this critique. Although Hauerwas is "one of the most exciting and illuminating ethicists in recent times,"[201] his use of narrative "increasingly turns out to be an abstraction without specific biblical content."[202]

Richard Bauckham stresses the necessity of responsible interpretation of biblical texts, which recognizes the meaning of a text is dependent on its context. And central to a responsible hermeneutic is to read a text "in the context of the whole biblical story of God's dealings with his people and the overriding theological and moral themes of the Bible."[203] Nelson comments upon this danger of failing to employ a responsible hermeneutic, which is a slight tendency of the postliberal method, and concludes that narrative is necessary but insufficient for Christian ethics:

> "Narrative" is not a universal solvent for all theological disagreements. In the first place, attention to different narratives within Scripture may yield discrepant conclusions. Second, the same narrative or biblical narrative as a whole can be construed in different ways and used to warrant a variety of substantive theological proposals.[204]

Thus although Hauerwas holds to a theocentric worldview, due to relying on a selective mode of biblical interpretation, his theological works run the risk of failing to recognize the church's over-riding goal being the glorifying of God in the world. It is this aspect of the lordship of Christ over his church and the resulting implications for its socio-political mission, which is a more noticeable feature of Moltmann's theology. Indeed a holistic understanding of mission necessarily follows

---

[199] Hays, *The Moral Vision of the New Testament*, 258.

[200] Ibid., 291.

[201] Childs, *Biblical Theology of the Old and New Testaments*, 663.

[202] Ibid., 665.

[203] Bauckham, *The Bible in Politics*, 17.

[204] Nelson, *Narrative and Morality*, 83-84.

from a holistic reading of Scripture. Bauckham argues for this political aspect of Christ's life and mission, and claims: "Because the kingdom of God he served embraces the whole of human life...his mission impinged on the political along with other dimensions of life."[205] Consequently, in employing a holistic reading of the biblical text and in acknowledging the attendant imperatives inherent in a theology of grace, we are able to gain a greater appreciation of the political dimension of Christ's mission and its ramifications for ecclesial witness in the modern world.

The Politics of the World and the Politics of the Church

Following from Hauerwas' rejection of all forms of power and his call for a separate Christian community, there is a sense of inevitability in his project of the church withdrawing from active participation in the socio-political arena.[206] This is the charge James Gustafson makes, who provokingly describes his former student as a "sectarian, fideistic tribalist."[207] Hauerwas seeks to refute these suggestions of "sectarianism" in his theology due to "giving up on the church as a public political actor."[208] In countering this charge, he claims: "Christians are engaged in politics, but it is a politics of the kingdom that reveals the insufficiency of all politics based on coercion and falsehood and finds the true source of power in servanthood rather than dominion."[209] Supporting the dismissal of these charges put to Hauerwas, Biggar argues that in Hauerwas' thought, although "the church's primary task is to be faithful to its own theological norms of practice and speech...this does not amount to irresponsible indifference to the fate of the world."[210] It is a vision, Biggar claims, of the church shaping society-at-large in fashion that is true to its own norms.

Yet despite this defense, and although it has evidently been over-stated by some commentators, there is a recurring tendency for Hauerwas to move in a sectarian direction albeit he is at pains to avoid being labeled in such a fashion. The reason for this withdrawal from active socio-political engagement, which derives at its core from how Hauerwas interprets the biblical text, is that he has made a deliberate distinction between the politics of the world and the politics of the church. In comparing Hauerwas and Moltmann, Arne Rasmusson notes that both theologians stress the importance of the practical ecclesial context for the work of theology. Yet Rasmusson reveals the major difference between Hauerwas' understanding of a

---

[205] Bauckham, *The Bible in Politics*, 142. This message of the kingdom was at the heart of Jesus' own proclamations, as we will discover in our analysis of Oliver O'Donovan's work.

[206] For a further discussion of Christian witness in the world, see Michael G. Cartwright, "Being Sent: Witness," in *The Blackwell Companion to Christian Ethics*, 481-494.

[207] James M. Gustafson, "The Sectarian Temptation: Reflections on Theology, the Church, and the University," *Proceedings of the Catholic Theological Society*, vol. 40 (1985), 83-94.

[208] Hauerwas, *In Good Company*, 58.

[209] Hauerwas, *The Peaceable Kingdom*, 102.

[210] Nigel Biggar, "Is Stanley Hauerwas Sectarian?" in *Faithfulness and Fortitude*, 142-143.

political church, which he calls "Radical Reformation theology," with what has been traditionally described as the contexts and roots of political theology. While both theologies stress the political nature of Christianity, they do this in markedly different ways: "Radical Reformation theology gives primacy not to politics understood as the struggle for control over the processes of social change (the politics of the world), but to the politics of the church as an alternative polis."[211] As such, it can be seen that there are different interpretations of what constitutes politics, whether this is the politics of the church or the politics of a secular global community. Rasmusson seeks to offer a defense and explanation of this distinction:

> A basic reason for their difference is their divergent understanding of politics. Moltmann's political theology makes the politics of the world primary. The consequence is that the political issues he discusses are already given by the social and political conflicts of the contemporary world...In contrast, Hauerwas' theological politics makes the church the primary locus for its politics. As a contrast society the church has its own agenda that challenges the way the world's politics is understood and therefore does not fit current divisions.[212]

In providing this defense of Hauerwas' work, Rasmusson rightly emphasizes the gospel sets the agenda for approaching contemporary issues. In Reformational theology the gospel is always primary. Yet is it the case that Hauerwas does not fully acknowledge that it is this same gospel, which informs and motivates the church to engage with social and political concerns? Fergusson comments upon this absence due to Hauerwas' over-determination of the distinctiveness of the church: "It becomes difficult to understand both how the will of God may be done outwith the church and how Christians may make common cause with other agencies and individuals."[213] In his work *Community, Liberalism and Christian Ethics*, Fergusson disputes Hauerwas' thesis: "Within pluralist societies, the church can recognize common moral ground – thus making common cause with other forces, agencies, and movements – even in the absence of common moral theory."[214] There is thus a question whether Hauerwas can deliver a constructive political ethic. Jenson shares such concerns about the relationship of the church to the world in Hauerwas' thought: "It does seem I must somehow disagree with Hauerwas at some deep level...I could not myself say, for example, that Christianity and democracy are simply not 'integrally related.'"[215]

Lesslie Newbigin highlights this aspect of the gospel of grace for the nature of the church's holistic mission, and is critical of those insisting that the church is not to be actively concerned with matters of politics and economics. From its beginning and

---

[211] Rasmusson, *The Church as Polis*, 17.

[212] Ibid., 331.

[213] Fergusson, "Another Way of Reading Stanley Hauerwas?" 246.

[214] David Fergusson, *Community, Liberalism and Christian Ethics* (Cambridge: Cambridge University Press, 1998), xi.

[215] Jenson, "The Hauerwas Project," 292.

throughout, the Bible views the person as involved in relationships with other human beings and with the world of nature.[216] We find this in Torah, which concerns God's guidance for his people for the whole of life, including that which we would describe as jurisprudence, public health, education, and economic policy.[217] Moreover, it is not only in the Old Testament that we find a clear biblical mandate for such activity. Jesus' teaching on the kingdom of God is inextricably bound with the social and political issues of the world: "Truth has been manifested once for all in Jesus Christ. It is the business of the church to bear witness in the public realm to that truth."[218] Rather than calling men and women out of the world into "a safe religious enclave," Newbigin pronounces, the gospel calls them out in order to send them back into it as "agents of God's kingship."[219] It is precisely this aspect of holistic witness to God's kingdom that is relatively lacking in Hauerwas' theological works, and is the primary reason why his theology may lack the full implications of a doctrine of grace.

Conclusion

In this chapter we have sought to provide a critique of Hauerwas' political theology analyzing to what extent a theology of grace is evident in his theological project. Hauerwas' prolific theological works have been of significance in exposing the weaknesses of liberalism and in capturing the importance of narrative for biblical interpretation. Yet, due to his tendency in adopting a selective reading of the biblical text, coupled with his insistence on separating the politics of the church from the politics of the world, there are aspects of his theology that does not do full justice to the holistic nature of a theology of grace for ecclesial witness. Despite these potential deficiencies, however, as a result of his vigorous theological engagement with a variety of socio-political issues, combined with his articulation of the distinctive lifestyle to be displayed by a community shaped by the gospel, Hauerwas has been a positive influence in the ongoing debate as to what constitutes the church's mission in the contemporary world.

---

[216] Newbigin, *Foolishness to the Greeks*, 95-97.
[217] Ibid., 97-98.
[218] Ibid., 122.
[219] Ibid., 124.

CHAPTER 5

Grace and Oliver O'Donovan's Political Theology

Evangelicals, in recent years, have begun to address contemporary social and political concerns, not least in part due to the influence of Oliver O'Donovan. In this chapter we will engage with O'Donovan's political thought evaluating to what extent a doctrine of grace is evident in his theological project. This chapter will be divided into three sections, and is structured consistently with his two main works relating to the church's socio-political involvement. First, we will undertake an evaluation of O'Donovan's thought in *Resurrection and Moral Order*, focusing initially on the role Scripture plays in his theological enterprise, and the recognition given to the primacy of the gospel. Second, we will assess the arguments espoused in *The Desire of the Nations*, and the implications for the holistic mission of the church. Third, we will undertake a critique of O'Donovan's theological conclusions, which will include a dialogue with Jürgen Moltmann and Stanley Hauerwas' political theology.

Introduction

Described by William Schweiker as "one of the most astute contemporary Christian ethicists,"[1] Oliver O'Donovan considers himself to be "a pastoral theologian, seeking to help my contemporaries in their tasks." With this theological aim in sight, primary attention is devoted to assisting his contemporaries in undertaking "the task of envisaging political action."[2] Pervasive throughout his work, therefore, is the awareness that theology must be both descriptive and prescriptive. O'Donovan asserts: "In teaching Christian ethics I am teaching how to think from truths of Christian faith to conclusions in Christian action."[3] Defending the need to teach a form of political ethics, O'Donovan contends: "Since decisions of different kinds interlock with one another, even those who do not face them directly as decision-makers or advisors may face them indirectly in the context of other decisions."[4] In particular, the biblical concept of the kingdom of God, which embodies the analogy

---

[1] William Schweiker, "Freedom and Authority in Political Theology: A Response to Oliver O'Donovan's *The Desire of the Nations*," in *Scottish Journal of Theology*, vol. 54/1 (February 2001), 110.

[2] Oliver O'Donovan, "Deliberation, History and Reading: A Response to Schweiker and Wolterstorff," in *Scottish Journal of Theology*, vol. 54/1, 128.

[3] Oliver O'Donovan, *Common Objects of Love: Moral Reflection and the Shaping of Community – The 2001 Stob Lectures* (Grand Rapids: Eerdmans, 2002), 3.

[4] Ibid., 4.

between God's rule and human rule, is perceived as being the foundation for developing a political conceptuality as derived from Scripture.

Foremost amongst O'Donovan's scholarly works are *Resurrection and Moral Order* and *The Desire of the Nations*. Nicholas Wolterstorff underscores the significance of these theological contributions: "*The Desire of the Nations* is, in my judgment, the most important contribution to political theology in our century."[5] Richard Neuhaus echoes this commendation: "*The Desire of the Nations* is an astonishing *tour de force* that nobody writing on political theology or the public nature of the gospel can responsibly ignore."[6] Consistently emphasized in both works is that theology is inherently political if it is to be true to the gospel of Jesus Christ.

In the shaping of O'Donovan's theological position, he has been greatly influenced by his reading and critique of St. Augustine of Hippo.[7] Explicating the political thought of Book 19 of Augustine's *City of God*, in which Augustine seeks to offer "a general theory of society from the point of view of a Christian theology of history," O'Donovan remarks: "For nearly two decades it has shaped my mind, and I regard it as one of the unchallengeable masterpieces of Western writing."[8] It was an attempt, he claims, "at Christian political thinking, working towards a conception of the earthly political community which would comport adequately with the self-understanding of the City of God." Specifically, O'Donovan points out that Augustine replaced Cicero's definition of a community, by defining a community as "the assembly of a rational multitude associated by a harmonious sharing in the objects of its love."[9] The significance of Augustine's definition is explained:

> The great difference between ancient and modern political theory is that the modern has severed the ancient's connexion between society and virtue. If that is so, then Augustine has, to all appearances, set up the first standard of modern political thought against ancient, casting the political community off from its moorings in justice to drift on the tide of popular consensus.[10]

---

[5] Nicholas Wolterstorff, "A Discussion of Oliver O'Donovan's *The Desire of the Nations*," in *Scottish Journal of Theology*, vol. 54/1, 100.

[6] Richard J. Neuhaus, "Commentary on *The Desire of the Nations*," *Studies in Christian Ethics*, vol. 11/2 (August 1998), 61.

[7] As reflected in the work that formed the matter of his Ph.D thesis: Oliver O'Donovan, *The Problem of Self-Love in St. Augustine* (New Haven: Yale University Press, 1980).

[8] Oliver O'Donovan, "Augustine's City of God XIX and Western Political Thought," *Dionysius*, vol. 11 (December 1987), 89. This essay can also be found in Oliver O'Donovan and Joan L. O'Donovan, *Bonds of Imperfection: Christian Politics, Past and Present* (Grand Rapids: Eerdmans, 2004), 48-72.

[9] In contrast, Cicero defined a community as: "The assembly of a multitude associated by agreement about right and by a shared utility," as quoted in "Augustine's City of God XIX," 96. A further distinctive feature of Augustine's political thought, in contrast with modern assumptions, is that "it lacks a theory of progress" (103).

[10] Ibid., 96.

In drawing a comparison between O'Donovan and Augustine's theology of the role of the church in God's work, Gerrit de Kruijf states: "We might even conclude that O'Donovan, in *The Desire of the Nations*, has presented us with a contemporary version of *The City of God*!"[11] Additionally, O'Donovan acknowledges the part Paul Ramsey has played in his theological project, "whose kindnesses and intellectual stimulus leave me with a debt that defies account."[12] Yet it is the pre-eminent Reformed theologian Karl Barth whom O'Donovan identifies as being "the greatest of twentieth-century theologians."[13] What will become immediately apparent is that both O'Donovan and Barth share an unwavering conviction that Scripture is the basis from which we derive a theologically coherent political theology. As such, the exegetical detail of O'Donovan's interdisciplinary work, Craig Bartholomew concludes, causes it to hold great hope for breaking down the divide between biblical studies and theology.[14] And moreover, as Brian Blount notes, the distinctive contribution O'Donovan makes in this biblically informed theological endeavor is "demonstrating how Scripture not only warrants but demands a political theology."[15]

The Gospel of Jesus Christ and Ethical Directions

Scripture as the Source of Socio-Political Debate

A Christian ethic must arise from the gospel itself. Such is the unequivocal position of O'Donovan, who maintains that basic moral categories are to be read in their biblical context.[16] As political theology is concerned with opening up politics to divine activity, O'Donovan states: "Scripture contextualizes these categories into their history, which is the history of God's saving act, and therefore enables our activity to be a formed reference to that act of God."[17] Affirming the priority of Scripture as a whole in his ethic, O'Donovan insists "our decisions must arise out of long reflection on the biblical ethic understood in the light of biblical theology."[18] The importance of maintaining this theological stance is made unambiguously clear:

---

[11] Gerrit de Kruijf, "The Function of Romans 13 in Christian Ethics," in *A Royal Priesthood?: The Use of the Bible Ethically and Politically. A Dialogue with Oliver O'Donovan*, ed. Craig G. Bartholomew, et al. (Grand Rapids: Zondervan, 2002), 232.

[12] Oliver O'Donovan, "Karl Barth and Ramsey's 'Uses of Power,'" *The Journal of Religious Ethics*, vol. 19/2 (Fall 1991), 2.

[13] O'Donovan, *The Desire of the Nations*, 213.

[14] Craig G. Bartholomew, "A Time for War, and a Time for Peace: Old Testament Wisdom, Creation and O'Donovan's Theological Ethics," in *A Royal Priesthood?* 91.

[15] Brian K. Blount, "Response to *The Desire of the Nations*," *Studies in Christian Ethics*, vol. 11/2, 11.

[16] For a discussion of O'Donovan's theological method, see Victor L. Austin, "Method in Oliver O'Donovan's Political Theology," in *Anglican Theological Review*, vol. 79/4 (Fall 1997), 583-594.

[17] Oliver O'Donovan, *Liturgy and Ethics* (Bramcote: Grove, 1993), 12.

[18] Oliver O'Donovan, "The Possibility of a Biblical Ethic," *Theological Student Fellowship Bulletin*, vol. 67 (Autumn 1973), 22.

To treat the books of the Old and New Testaments, and perhaps the deutero-canonical books, as Scripture, is to suppose that these historically diverse corpora, Hebrew, Jewish-Christian and Hellenistic-Jewish, cohere as a narrative; and that their narrative coherence, however it may be elaborated, constitutes a decisive testimony for faith.[19]

Bartholomew identifies the key ingredients of O'Donovan's methodological approach as being biblical exegesis, theology, philosophy, and history.[20] It is an approach that enables the authority of Scripture to be brought in its entirety into constructing a Christian ethic. Although he respects historical criticism, Bartholomew observes that O'Donovan's work is driven by the possibility of a unified, biblical ethic.[21] Comparing O'Donovan with Barth in that their work never leaves Scripture behind as theological concepts take hold, Bartholomew notes that "not only do the concepts come from Scripture, but they are set in motion in tandem with a willingness to return to scriptural exegesis at myriad points."[22] Indeed even a cursory glance reveals O'Donovan's works contains a significant amount of biblical exegesis, which is grounded in the conviction of the need for a coherent biblical ethic. In providing a defense of exegesis in his "theoretical preoccupations," he states: "They do not mean that the exegesis is subservient to theory, any more than the theory is subservient to exegesis. It means simply that theory undertakes to justify itself in the sphere of exegesis."[23] In other words, political theology must be responsible to Scripture:

The thematic theologian thinks through ideas, the exegetical theologian through texts; yet neither is capable of doing his own work without the other, for where are the ideas to come from if not from the texts, and how are the texts to speak to us, if not through ideas?[24]

There is therefore a requirement for engagement to be not only biblical but also theological due to the necessity for concepts and models to mediate between Scripture and ethical issues. O'Donovan elaborates on this need:

If we are to form and justify opinions on specific questions in ethics, we must do so theologically; which means bringing the formal questions of ethics to theological interpretation and criticism. This by no means implies, of course, that we shall accept the current understanding of these questions unhesitatingly from the lips of

---

[19] O'Donovan, "Deliberation, History and Reading," 140.

[20] Craig G. Bartholomew, "Introduction," in *A Royal Priesthood?* 22.

[21] Ibid., 20.

[22] Ibid., 21.

[23] Oliver O'Donovan, "Response to Respondents: Behold, the Lamb!" *Studies in Christian Ethics*, vol. 11/2, 98.

[24] Oliver O'Donovan, "Response to Andrew Lincoln," in *A Royal Priesthood?* 170.

philosophers, for theology has something to say also about how the questions are formulated as well as about how they are answered.[25]

Submitting a paper to the Commission of Inquiry on Faith and Nation, O'Donovan underlines how the Bible informs his entire theological project. In proclaiming that the theological context for reflection about church, state and society is the mission of the church, O'Donovan insists: "The agenda is quite simply set by the practical and theological question of missionary obedience, *how may our society be addressed with the word of the gospel?*"[26] Thus O'Donovan refutes criticisms that he is leaving political theology and political ethics too distinct, as they are not to be seen as separate. In response, O'Donovan summarizes his hermeneutical approach:

> They are two moments in one train of theological thought, which leads us from the proclamation of the gospel to the conceiving of political action. But they are different moments: the one poses the reflective question, 'what have we been shown of our political good?,' and the other the deliberative question, 'how, then, shall we pursue it?'[27]

It is addressing this theological task that occupies the attention of this evangelical theologian, and the depth of exegesis he employs in undertaking such a scholarly endeavour is a distinctive and ubiquitous feature of his academic works.

The Ethical Implications of the Resurrection and the Created Order

In his vigorous engagement with Scripture, O'Donovan insists that a proper appreciation of the God-given natural order is intrinsic for Christian ethics. Defending a natural ethic, where the natural is held in the ontological sense, that being the created order, O'Donovan claims: "Revelation in history is certainly the lynchpin of Christian epistemology."[28] Although man's blindness is itself part of a disruption within nature due to the fall, "the very fact that nature can be called disrupted and disordered shows that it cannot be inherently meaningless." Warning against partial or selective positions, O'Donovan states: "Creation and redemption are not in hostile antithesis, but in complementarity, each providing the context in which we understand the other."[29] Neither the kingdom of God nor creation can therefore be known independently of each other. For "he who is called the King of kings is also called the Second Adam: nature and history in him are not divided."[30]

---

[25] O'Donovan, *Resurrection and Moral Order*, 182.

[26] Oliver O'Donovan, "Establishment," *Paper Submitted to the Commission of Inquiry on Faith and Nation* (2003), 3.

[27] O'Donovan, "Behold, the Lamb!" 92-93.

[28] Oliver O'Donovan, "The Natural Ethic," in *Essays in Evangelical Social Ethics*, 26.

[29] Ibid., 26-27.

[30] Ibid., 30.

This inextricable link between resurrection and the created order, and the ethical implications pertaining to this God-ordained relationship, is the thrust of O'Donovan's argument in *Resurrection and Moral Order*. Criticizing the presentation of "the unacceptably polarized choice between an ethic that is revealed and has no ontological grounding and an ethic that is based on creation and so is naturally known," he claims: "This polarization deprives redemption and revelation of their proper theological meaning as the divine reaffirmation of created order."[31] It is a vision of multidimensional redemption: "Redemption is what God has done for the whole, and not just for a part of that which he once made."[32] Setting out his overarching thesis at the commencement of this work, he declares: "The foundations of Christian ethics must be evangelical foundations; or, to put it more simply, Christian ethics must arise from the gospel of Jesus Christ. Otherwise it could not be Christian ethics."[33] A theological proposition is presented "that Christian ethics depends upon the resurrection of Jesus Christ from the dead."[34] Resulting from this decisive event in world history is the vindication of the entire created order:

> We are not attempting to deny the richness of the New Testament's ethical appeal; but it is the task of theology to uncover the hidden relation of things that gives the appeal force. We are driven to concentrate on the resurrection as our starting-point because it tells us of God's vindication of his creation, and so of our created life.[35]

God demonstrates that man's life on earth is important as he has given it its order. As such, "it matters that it should conform to the order he has given it." In grasping this priority, O'Donovan argues: "We can understand too how this order requires of us both a denial of all that threatens to become disordered and a progress towards a life which goes beyond this order without negating it."[36] Eschatological hope for mankind and the created order is consequently an inextricable feature of the relationship between the resurrection and creation: "The sign that God has stood by his created order implies that this order, with mankind in its proper place within it, is to be totally restored at the last."[37] How is this order to be fulfilled then? Through the eschatological transformation of the world: "It is the historical telos of the origin, that which creation is intended for, and that which it points and strives towards."[38] Christ's resurrection vindicates the created order in the double sense in that "it redeems it and it transforms it."[39] Thus "Christian ethics," O'Donovan notes, "looks both backwards and forwards, to the origin and to the end of the created order. It

---

[31] O'Donovan, *Resurrection and Moral Order*, 19.
[32] Ibid., 55.
[33] Ibid., 11.
[34] Ibid., 13.
[35] Ibid.
[36] Ibid., 14-15.
[37] Ibid., 15.
[38] Ibid., 55.
[39] Ibid., 56.

respects the natural structures of life in the world, while looking forward to their transformation."[40] In describing the Christian view of history as "eschatological" and not merely as "teleological," O'Donovan differentiates between the two as follows:

> The destined end is not immanently present in the beginning or in the course of movement through time, but is a "higher grace" which, though it comes from the same God as the first and makes a true whole with the first as its fulfillment, nevertheless has its own integrity and distinctness as an act of divine freedom.[41]

Opposing the debate between the so-called "ethics of the kingdom" and the "ethics of creation" O'Donovan contends that presenting the alternatives in such a way is simply not acceptable, "for the very act of God which ushers in his kingdom is the resurrection of Christ from the dead, the reaffirmation of creation."[42] It is the resurrection that restores creation and in which the kingdom of God dawns. Creation is to be understood "not merely as the raw material out of which the world as we know it is composed, but as the order and coherence in which it is composed."[43] This understanding of the created order leads O'Donovan to reject the idea that Christian ethics is esoteric. The way the universe is determines how man ought to behave: "The order of things that God has made is there. It is objective, and mankind has a place within it. Christian ethics, therefore, has an objective reference because it is concerned with man's life in accordance with this order."[44] Although man's rebellion has failed to destroy the natural order to which he belongs, however, "that is something which we could not say with theological authority except on the basis of God's revelation in the resurrection of Jesus Christ," claims O'Donovan.[45]

With this insistence on the necessity of the revelation of Christ, Bartholomew distinguishes O'Donovan's approach from natural law ethics: "We must distinguish ontology from epistemology – the creation order is real and holds for all, but in a fallen world it cannot be grasped outside of Christ."[46] Likewise, Victor Austin emphasizes this feature of O'Donovan's theology: "Oliver O'Donovan finds the natural law tradition wanting because of his methodological convictions. These are ultimately based in faith, faith in the Messiah of Israel."[47] Yet Jesus is not only a witness to the restored moral order, O'Donovan declares, "he is the one in whom that order has come to be. God has willed that the restored creation should take form in, and in relation to, one man."[48] Acknowledging the essentiality of divine revelation, and the epistemological priority of Jesus Christ, is precisely why his

---

[40] Ibid., 58.

[41] Ibid., 64-65.

[42] Ibid., 15.

[43] Ibid., 31.

[44] Ibid., 17.

[45] Ibid., 19.

[46] Bartholomew, "Introduction," 22.

[47] Austin, "Method in Oliver O'Donovan's Political Theology," 593.

[48] O'Donovan, *Resurrection and Moral Order*, 150.

ethics can be appropriately described as evangelical ethics. O'Donovan makes unmistakably clear the centrality of Christ, and his death and resurrection for Christian ethics: "Jesus' moral authority is evangelical in the fullest sense, since the moral order which he proclaims is the kingdom of God, the theme of his message of salvation."[49]

Love as the Human Response to Divine Act

The resurrection of Christ not only vindicates the creation order and is hence intrinsic to Christian ethics; the resurrection provides the impetus to the church in its mission in the world. From this event flows the human response to divine act, in which "we look not only back to the created order which is vindicated, but forwards to our eschatological participation in that order."[50] Motivation for mission is thus an integral outworking of the Christ-event: "Man is given the freedom to respond as a moral agent to what God has done for him."[51] It is a pattern of free response to objective reality that is formed and brought to expression by the Spirit.[52] O'Donovan points out the attendant implications of the resurrection of Christ for the life of the church: "Christian ethics, then, is distinguished from obedience to the law of the Old Covenant not only by its subjective moral power but by its content, because the believer shares in the authority realized in history by Christ himself."[53] Summarizing this understanding of human response to divine act, O'Donovan states:

> The dynamic of the Christian faith, calling us to respond appropriately to the deeds of God on our behalf, supposes that there is an appropriate conformity of human response to divine act. It supposes that divine initiative and human obedience are two movements, distinct though not independent, both of them free; that free human response is not overwhelmed by the necessity of the divine deed on the one hand, and that the divine deed is not reducible to the exercise of human decision on the other.[54]

Responding to what God has done involves man's participation in the created order. O'Donovan declares: "Christian morality is his glad response to the deed of God which has restored, proved and fulfilled that order, making man free to conform to it."[55] It is to act in direct response to the event of the death and resurrection of Christ. For it is not in social movements that hope is to be found, "but in the revelation of divine justice at Calvary. Only under the criticism of Christ's cross can the destructive dialectic of unrighteous order and disordered anger be exposed, and

---

[49] Ibid., 155.
[50] Ibid., 22.
[51] Ibid., 23.
[52] Ibid., 25.
[53] Ibid., 24.
[54] Ibid., 36.
[55] Ibid., 76.

the provisional and humble service of justice be maintained."[56] Hence, O'Donovan declares: "True knowledge of the moral order is knowledge 'in Christ.'"[57] With this christocentric focus, O'Donovan insists that Christian moral thought must respond to the objective reality of a world-order restored in Christ.[58] It is a response that has profound implications for the church in seeking justice in the world in all its forms. Explicating the ramifications of the human response to divine act, O'Donovan contends that political authority, at its simplest, is:

> A concurrence of the natural authorities of might and tradition with that other 'relatively natural' authority, the authority of injured right. When these three authorities are exercised together by one subject, then they are endorsed by a moral authority which requires that we defer to them. They are exercised together when the first two are put at the disposal of the third; that is, when one whose possession of might is in accord with the established order of a society takes responsibility for the righting of wrongs within that society.[59]

From this comprehension of political authority, justice can be defined as "public right action." It is a form of action where might is required. For might is "the power to coerce," and is "the guarantee that action can be effective."[60] Moreover, demonstrating the influence of Augustine in his theology, the form of the moral life, he contends, is love: "Love is the principle which confers unifying order both upon the moral field and upon the character of the moral subject."[61] Love is the fulfillment of the moral law, and involves the participation of the Christian community in the divine life of love. We love our neighbour because "the neighbour is ordered to the love of God. Self and neighbour are equal partners within a universe which has its origin and end in God." Thus, O'Donovan continues, "to recognize the neighbour as my equal is to recognize the generic ordering, prior to both of us, which relates us to one another as members of a common kind, as man alongside man."[62] For all human beings share "one common human nature, one common human experience and one common human destiny."[63] Love is indeed crucial in understanding the moral life:

> Many times in the history of thought respect for fellow-men, divorced from its theological context of love for the highest good, has collapsed into one of two corruptions: the attempt to tyrannize over the fellow-man by taking the responsibility

---

[56] Ibid., 74.

[57] Ibid., 85.

[58] Ibid., 101.

[59] Ibid., 128.

[60] Ibid., 129.

[61] Ibid., 226.

[62] Ibid., 228.

[63] Oliver O'Donovan, *Begotten or Made?* (Oxford: Clarendon Press, 1984), 1.

for his welfare out of his hands, and the enslavement of the self to the fellow-man who becomes an object of desire and need.[64]

Love of Christ is our primary obligation, as it is "the acceptance of him as the one whom the Father has sent." From this basis, O'Donovan argues, "we are given to love the whole of reality."[65] It is to live a life that points forward to the resurrection, in which "we must die with Christ so that at the last we may rise with him."[66] In doing so, we are never set free of our dependence upon God's prior kindness, as it is God's final judgment of grace upon man's life that is our hope of righteousness:

> It is not a question of man's doing what he can to please God, and of God's saying 'Yes' or 'No' in response to it; it is a question of man's being able to please God only because God will most definitely say 'Yes.' From that 'Yes' are derived both the possibility and the conditions of human morality.[67]

Even though our moral decisions "are never unambiguous or translucent," at the heart of evangelical ethics as declared in the gospel, O'Donovan points out, "it is given to them by God's grace in Christ to add up to a final and unambiguous Yes, a work of love which will abide for eternity."[68]

The Unfolding of God's Reign and Political Activity in the World

Christian Tradition and the Notion of Authority

The long and rich Christian tradition of political theology is accentuated in *The Desire of the Nations*, which provides the historical backdrop for challenging the modern separation of theology and politics. A biblically based political theology, O'Donovan asserts, "tries to recover for faith in God, Christ and salvation what scepticism surrendered to mechanistic necessity." Indeed, as O'Donovan summarizes his main thesis: "Theology must be political if it is to be evangelical. Rule out the political questions and you cut short the proclamation of God's saving power."[69] Yet despite the many centuries of politico-theological discourse during the patristic, medieval, and Reformation periods, "the relation of the contemporary political theology to the tradition can be summed up in a single bleak word: ignorance."[70] "Modernity," O'Donovan notes, "is characterized by a twofold tradition of radical suspicion directed against the classical political theology."[71] The first is voiced by

---

[64] O'Donovan, *Resurrection and Moral Order*, 229.

[65] Ibid., 243.

[66] Ibid., 249.

[67] Ibid., 253-254.

[68] Ibid., 264.

[69] O'Donovan, *The Desire of the Nations*, 3.

[70] Ibid., 4.

[71] Oliver O'Donovan, "Political Theology, Tradition and Modernity," in *The Cambridge Companion to Liberation Theology*, 236.

Immanuel Kant, in which he perceives the corruption of morality or theology by politicians.[72] The second is the apparent opposite, the corruption of politics by theology, as voiced by the imperialist theologians of the fourteenth century.[73]

Due to the modern liberal consensus of a separation between theology and politics, combined with the Enlightenment's attempt to establish a pure ethics, whether this be theological or rational, O'Donovan states: "With this move the two strands of suspicion in the liberal tradition are safeguarded; but they are woven back into a greater harmony in which ethics and politics are one again." Yet this matrix is political, not ethical, "for it is the social dynamisms of history that provide a context in which moral commitments become intelligible."[74] This reflects late liberalism's commitment to the primacy of the individual, which has as its consequence the misgiving of an enduring social ordering. In making such an attempt to reintegrate politics and ethics, O'Donovan proclaims, modern idealism has paid a high price:

> The historical processes of society, offered as the matrix which would unify them, do not, apparently, leave either of them intact. Ethics, on the one hand, is deprived of authority when it is made to serve merely a reactive critical function...On the other hand, social process, which is supposed to fill the place assigned to politics by Aristotle, is not the same thing as politics at all...There is no room for direction in a society ruled by the imperative of universal suspicion.[75]

Although O'Donovan praises the success of the Southern school, namely liberation theology, in challenging the late-modern liberal consensus on the separation of theology and politics, it has its own weaknesses, he claims. For "in framing its challenge, it drew help from secondary currents within late-modernity itself."[76] Criticizing a key aspect of this movement, O'Donovan argues that its flaw "lies not in taking up the cause of the poor in a preferential manner, but in partially concealing the theological warrants for doing so in order to conform to the historical dialectic of idealism."[77] In contrast, a theocentric methodological approach, which is intrinsic to the Reformation tradition, is foundational to his claims for deriving a biblically based political theology: "Political theology – as a theoretic discipline, though not detached from experience and engagement – must precede political ethics."[78]

---

[72] Kant famously declared: "I can indeed imagine a moral politician, i.e. someone who conceives of the principles of political expediency in such a way that they can co-exist with morality, but I cannot imagine a political moralist, i.e. one who fashions his morality to suit his own advantage as a statesman." See Immanuel Kant, "Perpetual Peace," in *Kant's Political Writings*, ed. Hans Reiss, trans. Hugh B. Nisbet (London: Cambridge University Press, 1970), 118.

[73] O'Donovan, "Political Theology, Tradition and Modernity," 236-238.

[74] O'Donovan, *The Desire of the Nations*, 9.

[75] Ibid., 9-10.

[76] O'Donovan, "Political Theology, Tradition and Modernity," 239.

[77] O'Donovan, *The Desire of the Nations*, 11.

[78] Ibid., 15.

As is typical throughout O'Donovan's work, the role of Scripture is vital in the search for true political concepts: "But if the notion of a 'political theology' is not to be a chimera, they must be authorized, as any datum of theology must be, from Holy Scripture." In doing so, "theory has to respond to the concepts found in Scripture, and its adequacy as theology will be measured by how well it has responded to them."[79] Identifying concepts is hence an exegetical task. Expressly, it is the biblical concept of authority that is imperative for political theology, and yet which is deficient in liberation theology. O'Donovan states: "Building itself on an acephalous idea of society, dissolving government in deconstructive scepticism, lacking a point of view which can transcend given matrices of social engagement, liberation theology has lacked a concept of authority."[80] It is a concept that is nonetheless irreplaceable to theology: "Authority is the nuclear core, the all-present if unclarified source of rational energy that motivates the democratic bureaucratic organizations of the Northern hemisphere." Central to pre-modern political theology, the theme of authority "sought to find criteria from the apostolic proclamation to test every claim to authority made by those who possessed, or wished to possess, power."[81] Noting the far-reaching implications of O'Donovan's explication of this concept, Blount declares: "Authority is the core principle which gives structure to any political entity in history."[82] For authority, O'Donovan maintains, is "the objective correlate of freedom," which "evokes free action, and makes free action intelligible."[83]

A core thesis of *The Desire of the Nations* then, "is that theology, by developing its account of the reign of God, may recover the ground traditionally held by the notion of authority." It is a notion that has been discounted in modernity, O'Donovan claims, "and with it the idea of political activity as kingly."[84] In placing political history within the history of God's reign, three elements are added, which overcome the arbitrariness of modern historicism. First, "the history of divine rule safeguards and redeems the goods of creation...When we speak of divine rule, we speak of the fulfillment promised to all things worldly and human." In the light of the divine rule politics is judged as to its "world-affirming and humane character."[85] Second, "when the divine rule forms the ground for speaking of human political authority, we are forced to strip away the institutional fashions with which the Western (or Northern) tradition has clothed the idea of authority." Thus instead of recognizing first of all the authority of institutions, we are to recognize the human or the 'political act,' that is performed on behalf of many, which "witnesses faithfully to the presence and future of what God has undertaken for all. The political act is the divinely authorized act." How and why God's rule confers authority upon such acts is the task of

---

[79] Ibid., 15-16.

[80] O'Donovan, "Political Theology, Tradition and Modernity," 245.

[81] O'Donovan, *The Desire of the Nations*, 16-17.

[82] Blount, "Response to *The Desire of the Nations*," 8.

[83] O'Donovan, *The Desire of the Nations*, 30.

[84] Ibid., 19.

[85] Ibid.

political authority.[86] Third, "the history of divine rule is presented to us as a revealed history which takes form quite particularly as the history of Israel."[87]

The Promised Unity of God's All-Sovereign Rule

Engaging with Scripture as a whole and not only certain texts within them, O'Donovan contends, is a priority, and reveals the kingly rule of God. This approach to the biblical text means "the moment of resurrection does not appear like an isolated meteor from the sky but as the climax of a history of the divine rule."[88] Indeed the Bible's all-pervasive message is that "the gospel is one gospel, which has manifold implications for us as we believe and obey it."[89] For "if the Scriptures are to be read as a proclamation, not merely as a mine for random sociological analogies dug out from the ancient world," O'Donovan claims, "then a unifying conceptual structure is necessary that will connect political themes with the history of salvation as a whole."[90] Recent theological enterprises have gained success precisely in part from its willingness to discover the political hermeneutic in a range of biblical texts.

Failure in reading Scripture as whole, O'Donovan claims, is a core weakness of liberation theology, and thus "what was needed was an architectonic hermeneutic which would locate political reflection on the Exodus within an undertaking that had its centre of gravity in the gospels." Such an endeavour would not be problematic, as "almost the whole vocabulary of salvation in the New Testament has a political pre-history of some kind."[91] From beginning to end Israel's knowledge of God's blessings was a political knowledge, "and it was out of that knowledge that the evangelists and apostles spoke about Jesus."[92] Accordingly, the story of Israel is to be read as a history of redemption. The hermeneutic principle governing a Christian appeal to political categories within the Hebrew Scriptures is Israel itself, and through this unique political entity the purposes of God were made known in the world. O'Donovan describes the underlying concepts deriving from this realization: "The governing principle is the kingly rule of God, expressed in Israel's corporate existence and brought to final effect in the life, death and resurrection of Jesus."[93]

It is from this insight that O'Donovan adds four more comments about the right and wrong ways of using the Old Testament in political theology. First, "if political theologians are to treat ancient Israel's political tradition as normative, they must observe the discipline of treating it as history."[94] Second, "nor can theologians do justice to it as a history by constructing a subversive counter-history, a history

---

[86] Ibid., 20.

[87] Ibid., 21.

[88] Ibid., 20.

[89] Ibid., 21.

[90] Ibid., 22.

[91] Ibid.

[92] Ibid., 23.

[93] Ibid., 27.

[94] Ibid.

beneath the surface which defies and challenges the official history of Israel."[95] Third, "nor may they rewrite Israel's history as a 'Whig' history of progressive undeception, in which the normative principle is simply the emergence of rationality from barbarism."[96] Fourth, "yet Israel's history must be read as a history of redemption...as the story of how certain principles of social and political life were vindicated by the action of God in the judgment and restoration of the people."[97]

When the Jews of the First Temple period sang the refrain *Yhwh malak*, "Yhwh is king," O'Donovan argues, this was "a liturgical act in which political and religious meanings were totally fused."[98] In particular, it carried with it three kinds of association. First, it offered a geophysical reassurance about the stability of the natural order. Second, it offered a reassurance about the international political order that God was in control of the turbulence of the nations. Third, it was associated with the ordering of Israel's own social existence by justice and law, which ensured the protection of the oppressed and vulnerable.[99]

Exploring the idea of Yhwh's kingship further still by referring to three common Hebrew words: *yshuah* (salvation), *mishpat* (judgment) and *nahlah* (possession), O'Donovan states: "Yhwh's authority as king is established by the accomplishment of victorious deliverance, by the presence of judicial discrimination and by the continuity of a community-possession."[100] As Israel perceived God's kingship to have these three components, this shaped Israel's sense of political identity and defined what is meant by saying that Yhwh rules as king: "He gives Israel victory; he gives judgment; he gives Israel its possession."[101] These terms are indeed central to O'Donovan's understanding of the kingdom of God, and constitute the exegetical framework of his political theology. Added to these terms is praise, which is Israel's response to the acts of God. O'Donovan declares:

> The threefold analysis of divine rule as salvation, judgment and possession will provide a framework for exploring the major questions about authority posed by the Western tradition. The unique covenant of Yhwh and Israel can be seen as a point of disclosure from which the nature of all political authority comes into view.[102]

Deriving from this conceptuality, O'Donovan presents six theorems outlining the nature of authority. First, "political authority arises where power, the execution of right and the perpetuation of tradition are assured together in one coordinated

---

[95] Ibid., 28.
[96] Ibid.
[97] Ibid., 29.
[98] Ibid., 32.
[99] Ibid.
[100] Ibid., 36.
[101] Ibid., 45. This is reflected in the acclamation of Isaiah 33:22: "For the Lord is our judge, the Lord is our lawgiver, the Lord is our king; it is he who will save us."
[102] Ibid.

agency."[103] Second, "that any regime should actually come to hold authority, and should continue to hold it, is a work of divine providence in history, not a mere accomplishment of the human task of political service."[104] Third, "in acknowledging political authority, society proves its political identity."[105] Fourth, "the authority of a human regime mediates divine authority in a unitary structure, but is subject to the authority of law within the community, which bears independent witness to the divine command."[106] Fifth, "the appropriate unifying element in international order is law rather than government."[107] Sixth, "the conscience of the individual members of a community is a repository of the moral understanding which shaped it, and may serve to perpetuate it in a crisis of collapsing morale or institution."[108] These six theorems drawn from Israel's political experience present "an outline of what theology may need to put in the place traditionally held by a notion of political authority."[109]

Clearly, therefore, what O'Donovan is at pains to stress is that the Old Testament discloses Yhwh's kingship. Yet despite God's kingly reign over the world through Israel, God's sovereignty is not universally acknowledged. The reason being that for authority to function, this requires an element of freedom:

> Political authority or kingly rule, including God's own, belongs to the category of act. It is something that is done, not something that simply is…A universe of pure regularity without the risks of history and freedom would be a universe without space for human action and so without space for kingly rule.[110]

This leads O'Donovan to incorporate an Augustinian framework, in which he develops the concept of a dual authority of God's reign within history. History can be perceived as dividing into two eras: Israel and Babylon followed by the church and Rome. Notwithstanding this duality, it is here that we come to an intrinsic feature of O'Donovan's conception of the kingly rule of God, namely, its unity. "Unity is proper to the creator," he notes, and "because the world is created, it has its own way of reflecting the creator's unity."[111] This is seen strikingly in the case of Israel. The story of Israel reaches its fulfillment in Jesus Christ, who discloses the rule of God, and thus challenges any concept of two kingdoms.[112] In doing so, Jesus unsettled the two kingdoms conception, which had shaped Israel's understanding of

---

[103] Ibid., 46.
[104] Ibid.
[105] Ibid., 47.
[106] Ibid., 65.
[107] Ibid., 72.
[108] Ibid., 80.
[109] Ibid., 80-81.
[110] Oliver O'Donovan, "Response to Craig Bartholomew," in *A Royal Priesthood?* 115.
[111] O'Donovan, *The Desire of the Nations*, 177.
[112] Ibid., 82-119.

its political position since the exile.[113] O'Donovan states: "Jesus' teaching-ministry, then, is taken by the evangelists to be something more than instruction. It is a disclosure of the reign of God, through which the authority of God asserts itself."[114] As the proclamation of God's kingdom spans both the 'political' and 'spiritual' we have "to rediscover politics not as a self-enclosed field of human endeavour but as the theatre of the divine self-disclosure; to rediscover God as the one who exercises rule."[115] Hence those who speak of two kingdoms as being fundamental to Christian political thought have spoken truly, yet at risk of distorting the truth if left here:

> The unity of the kingdoms, we may say, is the heart of the gospel, their duality is the pericardium. Proclaiming the unity of God's rule in Christ is the task of Christian witness; understanding the duality is the chief assistance rendered by Christian reflection.[116]

The exact point at which the sphere of the old authority is challenged with the assertion of the new is the death and resurrection of Jesus Christ.[117] In short, O'Donovan declares: "The kingly rule of Christ is God's own rule exercised over the whole world."[118] Christian political theorist Jonathan Chaplin notes the sweeping repercussions of this understanding of God's rule in the political sphere. It is not as though rulers are simply responsible in a general way to God as origin of all authority. Rather, rulers are responsible "to the kingdom of Christ, the historical inauguration of which two millennia ago established an entirely new providential dispensation under which political authority is now required to acknowledge the authority of Christ."[119]

The Church as a Political Society

Following from an understanding of God's all-sovereign rule, the mission of the church, argues O'Donovan, occupies a crucial role in its unfolding. Although the resurrection is an event already accomplished, it "is still an event for the future, and our faith in it must still be marked by a hope, and not a hope for our own private futures only but for the future of the world subject to God's reign."[120] Eschatological hope of this kind includes an ordered world peace.[121] With this holistic vision of the world's future transformation, Christian theology is to assume the prophet's task.

---

[113] Ibid., 137.

[114] Ibid., 89.

[115] Ibid., 82.

[116] Ibid.

[117] Ibid., 128.

[118] Ibid., 146.

[119] Jonathan Chaplin, "Political Eschatology and Responsible Government: Oliver O'Donovan's 'Christian Liberalism,'" in *A Royal Priesthood?* 276.

[120] O'Donovan, *The Desire of the Nations*, 144.

[121] Ibid., 267.

"God has no spies. He has prophets," O'Donovan states, and "their judgment consists precisely in what they have to say of God's purposes of renewal, his mercy towards even such weak and frangible societies as Israel and Judah, unstable communities on which the fate of souls depends."[122] Moreover, as the church is a political society, it is primarily "brought into being and held in being, not by a special function it has to fulfill, but by a government that it obeys in everything. It is ruled and authorized by the ascended Christ alone and supremely." As such, the church "has its own authority; and it is not answerable to any other authority that may attempt to subsume it."[123] The rule of Christ determines the loyalty of the church, O'Donovan claims. For although Christians are subject to the authority of the state in which they reside, their ultimate loyalty is to Jesus Christ, which directs the church in its mission to the world:

> The theological impulse behind the conception of international law is altogether superior to the theology of empire. It acknowledges the claim of Christ to be the sole ruler of the nations, and avoids erecting an icon of world-government in his place; yet his rule is not left as an empty ideal, but is given a clear institutional witness.[124]

Where the church received its authorization was at Pentecost in the moment of Christ's exaltation, by being united with the authorization of Christ.[125] Participating in the Christ-event, which is the structuring principle for all ecclesiology, is made possible by the work of the Spirit. The effect of the Spirit upon the church, claims O'Donovan, means that it "places it under and in authority, giving legitimacy to its existence, effect to its mission, right to the various relations it comprises. The church represents God's kingdom by living under its rule, and by welcoming the world under its rule."[126] Yet although church morality is an evangelical morality springing from the vindication of God's rule in Christ's resurrection, the gospel is not to be seen as being "apart from" God's law. Rather, the Mosaic Law "contained the promise of an active life, awaiting fulfillment in an Israel with the law written on its heart. That fulfillment is now offered. In Christ we may live and act acceptably to God."[127] A response is therefore called for in delight at what God has done. Delight is not only a matter of contemplation and reflection, O'Donovan states, but of active celebration: "When we care for our neighbour's welfare, it is because we are delighted by our neighbour: by the sheer facticity of this other human that God has made."[128]

In obeying Christ in every facet of life, "one of the tasks of the political theologian in any age is to discern the Antichrist," O'Donovan argues, which is "to

---

[122] Ibid., 11-12.
[123] Ibid., 159.
[124] Ibid., 267-268.
[125] Ibid., 161.
[126] Ibid., 174.
[127] Ibid., 183.
[128] Ibid.

trace within the movements of his own time the heaving shape of the titanic aspiration, which challenges the throne of God."[129] This necessitates a politically active church. How the church undertakes this task will depend upon the historical and cultural situation she finds herself in. Drawing attention to how the martyr church in the early Christian centuries had few public commitments to the Roman state of their day because of their particular circumstances, O'Donovan asserts:

> The political and social circumstances in which the church at any time and in any place has to fulfill its mission are not for it to choose. They are the historical vocation given by God to his saints in that place and time. It is those circumstances in which Christians in that time have to learn to be faithful – and they may not be exchanged at will for other circumstances.[130]

Controversially defended is the era of Christendom, which O'Donovan dates from the Edict of Milan (AD 313) to the first amendment of the US Constitution (AD 1791).[131] As the church's one project is to witness to God's kingdom, O'Donovan contends: "Christendom is response to mission, and as such a sign that God has blessed it."[132] In this era the truth of Christianity was accepted to be a truth of secular politics, which left a legacy of "the triumph of Christ in liberal institutions."[133] Characteristic of the political doctrine that emerged from this era is a notion that government is responsible. Indeed, society requires government to function as a moral agency in order to conduct its affairs under moral direction.[134] Hence O'Donovan declares: "Rulers, overcome by Christ's victory, exist provisionally and on sufferance for specific purposes. In the church they have to confront a society which witnesses to the kingdom under which they stand and before which they must disappear."[135] For the state exists "under the authority of Christ's rule," O'Donovan claims, and "it gives judgment under law, never as its own law."[136]

A distinctive feature then, of O'Donovan's conception of Christendom and ecclesial authority, is that rulers are to submit to the gospel, and it is the church that is mandated to declare this gospel. O'Donovan claims: "The Gentile mission had two

---

[129] Oliver O'Donovan, *Peace and Certainty: A Theological Essay on Deterrence* (Oxford: Clarendon Press, 1989), 28.

[130] O'Donovan, "Establishment," 4-5.

[131] O'Donovan, *The Desire of the Nations*, 244. Commenting on the doctrine of "separation of church and state," O'Donovan makes the following assertion: "The First Amendment to the United States Constitution, prohibiting the 'establishment' and protecting the 'free exercise' of religion, is the paradigm assertion of this doctrine, and so can usefully be taken as the symbolic end of Christendom."

[132] Ibid., 195. I am indebted to Jonathan Chaplin for pointing out that in defending Christendom, O' Donovan is seeking to retrieve the missiological thrust which gave rise to the best in Christendom, and is not arguing for a return to an established church.

[133] Ibid., 228.

[134] Ibid., 16.

[135] Ibid., 231.

[136] Ibid., 233.

frontiers, social and political. The church demanded the obedience of society, and it demanded the obedience of society's rulers."[137] Arne Rasmusson points out that O'Donovan stresses that "Christendom should not be understood as a direct and conscious political project of the church. Christendom rather should be viewed as the response of rulers and societies to the mission of the church."[138] O'Donovan seeks to provide support for his position by making reference to John of Patmos' vision in the book of Revelation, which is identified as being prominent in deploying such a broad array of political categories "to depict the eschatological triumph of the church."[139]

Chaplin articulates what the end of Christendom meant for O'Donovan: "If the beginning of Christendom occurred when secular authorities bowed before the rule of Christ, its end was heralded when they formally declined to pay such homage."[140] With the end of Christendom, however, this has not resulted in a more independent-minded church. Rather, O'Donovan claims, "much Christian enthusiasm for 'pluralism' has less to do with a relation to the state than with the church's yearning to sound in harmony with the commonplaces of the stock exchange, the law-courts and the public schools." Withstanding this pressure of social conformity will be achieved "to the extent that the Christian community is possessed by its gospel."[141]

Excluding governments "from evangelical obedience" has had repercussions for the way society is conceived. O'Donovan states: "Since the political formation of society lies in its conscious self-ordering under God's judgment, a society conceived in abstraction is unformed by moral self-awareness, driven by internal dynamics rather than led by moral purposes."[142] This nexus of ideas about society has the effect upon a conception of justice in that "it dissolves its unity and coherence by replacing it with a plurality of 'rights.'"[143] Particularly deplored by O'Donovan, Rasmusson notes, is the emergence of the modern state's claim to absolute sovereignty, which means that "regional identities, kinship, estates, and above all, church, must be subordinate to national identity and loyalty."[144]

This is dramatically portrayed in Revelation 17-18, O'Donovan claims, which provides a vision as to the extent to which wealth and power are pursued by nations: "Trade as much as conquest violates the integrity of communities which become dominated by the influence of the stronger trading partner...It is a cultural promiscuity by which one power exploits and drains the resources from many others."[145] Such issues the church is to confront in existing as a political society.

---

[137] Ibid., 243.

[138] Arne Rasmusson, "Not All Justifications of Christendom are Created Equal: A Response to Oliver O'Donovan," *Studies in Christian Ethics*, vol. 11/2, 69.

[139] O'Donovan, *The Desire of the Nations*, 155.

[140] Chaplin, "Political Eschatology and Responsible Government," 286.

[141] O'Donovan, *The Desire of the Nations*, 226.

[142] Ibid., 246.

[143] Ibid., 247.

[144] Rasmusson, "Not All Justifications of Christendom are Created Equal," 74.

[145] Oliver O'Donovan, "The Political Thought of the Book of Revelation," *Tyndale Bulletin* vol. 37 (1986), 85.

Critical Reflection

The Reign of God and Political Authority

From a Reformational position, O'Donovan's project has the appeal of being rooted in Scripture. Stanley Hauerwas highlights this feature, as although he stands in marked contrast to O'Donovan's conceptuality of the political existence of the church, he has much to applaud in O'Donovan's work, not least in refusing the framework set by modern political theory and the false dualisms that it fosters.[146] Describing his work as "a historical theology," which recognizes that Israel is God's promised people, Hauerwas and co-author James Fodor express admiration at O'Donovan in plumbing the depths of the biblical texts, which they compare with John Howard Yoder's theological approach: "Because he refuses the sequestering of the theological into the transcendental offered by modern political arrangements, his political theology is unreservedly scriptural in its content and orientation."[147] It is this attribute of O'Donovan's hermeneutic, "confident and unapologetic, avowedly guided by the resources of Scripture and the Christian tradition," which is to be esteemed. O'Donovan's intention, Hauerwas and Fodor continue is "to provide the reader not simply with a theology of politics but a bona fide political theology."[148]

Affirming a theocentric worldview is certainly omnipresent throughout O'Donovan's theological works, and it is from this primary basis that the concept of authority is deemed to be fundamental in constructing a biblically based political theology. Wolterstorff summarizes O'Donovan's approach to the concept of authority in political theology: "The political act is an authorized act of ruling over someone; and the authorizer is God."[149] It is a political authority that ardently affirms the centrality of God in his creation. This methodological approach to theological inquiry, which is a distinguishing hallmark of the Reformation heritage, is therefore strikingly at odds with the anthropocentric worldview dominating in modernity.

Yet our appreciation of O'Donovan's political theology must be qualified by several reservations. Occasionally, O'Donovan will make conclusions that appear to lack theological justification. In commenting on O'Donovan's understanding of Yhwh's kingship in Israel as being a model or paradigm of political authority, as presented in *The Desire of the Nations*, Wolterstorff highlights this tendency and claims O'Donovan offers no such argument: "It's not just obvious that Yhwh's rule of Israel was to be taken by Israel to be, and is to be taken by us to be, paradigmatic for political authority generally."[150] Blount agrees and claims that the political theology O'Donovan wants to become normative universally, "remains true for ancient Israel, but need not necessarily always be true for every other generation."[151]

---

[146] Stanley M. Hauerwas and James Fodor, "Remaining in Babylon: Oliver O'Donovan's Defense of Christendom," *Studies in Christian Ethics*, vol. 11/2, 30.

[147] Hauerwas and Fodor, "Remaining in Babylon," 31.

[148] Ibid., 35.

[149] Wolterstorff, "A Discussion of Oliver O'Donovan's *The Desire of the Nations*," 87.

[150] Ibid., 101.

[151] Blount, "Response to *The Desire of the Nations*," 17.

Furthermore, Wolterstorff disagrees with O'Donovan's argument vis-à-vis the governments' desire to secure the existence and identity of nations. Claiming that "membership in Christ replaced all other political identities,"[152] O'Donovan claims that "existing collective identities have to be set aside and replaced with this new collective identity."[153] But Wolterstorff fails to ascertain scriptural warrant "that there was a re-authorization of governmental authority corresponding to the inauguration of the church, so that now the state is authorized to do only what is needed to insure justice." Instead,

> Ever since God's call to Abraham to leave Chaldea, God's kingly rule of humanity has come in two forms: a providential form in 'secular' governmental authority, and a redemptive form in Israel and the church. Neither of these is to be assimilated to the other.[154]

While Wolterstorff agrees with O'Donovan that we now live in the time of two eras, he differs with O'Donovan in how to conceive this time. In giving up on O'Donovan's re-authorization thesis, however, this has consequences which impact upon the rest of his account. This includes a different understanding of Jesus' proclamation of the coming of the kingdom of God. Wolterstorff declares:

> O'Donovan understands it as the proclamation of the end of the people of God living under dual political rule and authority: not only does Christ alone now have full-fledged political authority over the people of God; slowly Christ is also bringing it about that he alone has full-fledged political rule over them. States are confining themselves to establishing justice. But if the authorization of the state is now no different from what it has always been, and if it is the permanent situation of the people of God ever since Abraham to live under dual rule, then that cannot be the significance of Jesus' proclamation.[155]

Differing from Wolterstorff's position in many respects, yet echoing similar critiques of O'Donovan's theological conclusions, Hauerwas and Fodor claim that "it is not clear…in what ways his hermeneutical theory actually guides his readings of and commentary on biblical texts. Nor is it readily apparent how his exegesis informs his theoretical claims, that is to say, his hermeneutic architectonic."[156] Expressing reservations about the centrality of the reign of God in O'Donovan's work, they argue for other scriptural images such as the shepherd.[157] Yet it is surely doubtful whether such images are as of significance, due to the royal rule of God being a pervasive and central theme throughout Scripture. Indeed, it is intrinsic to a theology of grace.

---

[152] O'Donovan, *The Desire of the Nations*, 148.

[153] Ibid., 178.

[154] Wolterstorff, "A Discussion of Oliver O'Donovan's *The Desire of the Nations*," 108.

[155] Ibid.

[156] Hauerwas and Fodor, "Remaining in Babylon," 39.

[157] Ibid., 47.

In response to Wolterstorff, O'Donovan seeks to clarify his position and claims that his intention is not to limit governmental interest in flourishing, except where the flourishing of a particular community is over against universal flourishing. O'Donovan states: "The force of my claim is not that governments are authorized only to perform justice and never to represent their community's identities; but that governments are required to subordinate considerations of community identity to the performing of justice."[158] This clarification does assist in grasping O'Donovan's intent. Nonetheless there is still a question as to the actual extent to which the sovereign state is recognized as being a legitimate entity in O'Donovan's theological enterprise. And yet Barth highlights convincingly the need for this recognition:

> The state is not a product of sin but one of the constants of the divine providence and government of the world in its action against human sin: it is therefore an instrument of divine grace...Its existence is not separate from the kingdom of Jesus Christ...it is an exponent of his kingdom.[159]

In summary, therefore, we can say that although O'Donovan recognizes the priority of Scripture in revealing knowledge of God and his will, he also appears to fail occasionally to adhere strictly to the declared basis of his own theological project.

The Servanthood of Christ and the Church's Socio-Political Witness

Political authority is a central concept for O'Donovan in ascertaining the mission of the church in the world. This has a potent influence in his work not least in relation to the church and secular government, and in his controversial defense of Christendom. In contrast, James Skillen argues that because the state is what he describes as "a differentiated political community," the implication of this is that "the state shows its direct submission to Christ by establishing and upholding public justice, not by constitutionally professing its submission to the church."[160] God does not give judicial authority to the state only in its capacity as a servant of the church. Hauerwas and Fodor argue this more forcefully and differ from O'Donovan to the extent to which he thinks "resurrection and ascension make it possible for Christians to be more than God's wandering people."[161] For however much Christendom may have represented the church's faithful and unfaithful witness, "wilderness, not rule, is where we presently dwell as Christians."[162] A further criticism is leveled by Andrew

---

[158] O'Donovan, "Deliberation, History and Reading," 133.

[159] Barth, "The Christian Community and the Civil Community," in *Against the Stream*, 21.

[160] James W. Skillen, "Acting Politically in Biblical Obedience?" in *A Royal Priesthood?* 415.

[161] Hauerwas and Fodor, "Remaining in Babylon," 31.

[162] Ibid., 54.

Shanks who suggests that a weakness of O'Donovan's work is that it does not tell us what to make of this "largely new mode of being-the-church."[163]

This understanding of the political authority of the church, as subscribed to by O'Donovan, does present a degree of conflict with Jürgen Moltmann's portrayal of Christ's servanthood. As Moltmann points out, although Jesus Christ undertook his ministry as Lord, he also undertook it as a servant. The concept of servanthood is indeed intrinsic to the mission of the incarnate Word, who is consistently depicted in Scripture as the Servant of the Lord. This concept of servanthood, however, is relatively absent in O'Donovan's account of the mission of the church and of its political authority. Mark Noll provides further insight vis-à-vis these discussions and augments Moltmann's understanding of servanthood in Christian political action in *Adding Cross to Crown*. Exploring what difference it might make for Christian politics to supplement images of Christ's kingly rule with images of his suffering on the cross, Noll declares:

> A properly Christian politics will display humility, a willingness to question one's own motives, and the expectation that reform of political vision will always be needed because even Christian politics is carried out by individuals who know they are still sinners, however glad they are to be sinners saved by grace.[164]

While O'Donovan has indeed surfaced a contentious issue in his defense of Christendom, this is not without a degree of justification, as found in the doctrine of grace. In responding to the divine work, the mission of the church is to fulfill the will of God, as God's covenant-partner. This is the point Colin Greene makes, who states that rather than seeking to defend Christendom as a witness to the power of the gospel, as Hauerwas claimed O'Donovan was trying to achieve, "he has defended the Christendom settlement as a viable, valid and courageous expression of Christian mission."[165] Unsurprisingly, from our analysis in the previous chapter, Lesslie Newbigin provides corroboration to O'Donovan's position of the church's mission. Reflecting upon Christendom, Newbigin states that although with hindsight it is easy to see how quickly the church fell into the temptations of worldly power, "yet we have to ask, would God's purpose as it is revealed in Scripture have been better served if the church had refused all political responsibility?"[166] For the reign of God means that the church cannot only be concerned with the private and domestic aspects of life: "To be faithful to a message which concerns the kingdom of God, his rule over all things and all peoples, the church has to claim the high ground of public

---

[163] Andrew Shanks, "Response to *The Desire of the Nations*," *Studies in Christian Ethics*, vol. 11/2, 90.

[164] Mark A. Noll, *Adding Cross to Crown: The Political Significance of Christ's Passion* (Washington D.C.: Centre for Public Justice, 1996), 20.

[165] Colin J.D. Greene, "Revisiting Christendom: A Crisis of Legitimization," in *A Royal Priesthood?* 332.

[166] Newbigin, *Foolishness to the Greeks*, 101.

truth."[167] It is a view endorsed by Joseph Oldham who argues that the Christian ethic cannot be accepted and acted on without consequences in the political field.[168] Such is the nature of grace and being called to be in covenant-partnership with God.

Covenant and Kingship as Political Concepts

In emphasizing the concept of the kingdom in his political theology, O'Donovan draws our attention to an integral feature of the doctrine of grace; it is resolutely theocentric. Yet although he discerns the kingdom as being the unifying theme in both the Old and New Testaments, it is slightly peculiar that O'Donovan makes little use of covenant in his theological ethics. For, as we have seen, it is precisely the kingdom of God that ties the covenant time line together. Victor Furnish identifies this lack of a covenant theme and suggests that it is questionable whether Israel's experience of divine rule was definitive for her understanding of God. Moreover, in *The Desire of the Nations*, Furnish observes, there are only passing references to Israel as being God's covenant people, from which truly derives Israel's understanding of God. "Arguably, the constitutive elements of this covenant, which are God's grace and faithfulness," he claims, "are more specifically and pervasively biblical than O'Donovan's three 'concepts' of power, judgment, and possession."[169]

Why there is an apparent neglect of covenant in O'Donovan's work may have something to do with how O'Donovan construes the relationship between the Old and New Testament. This is evident in *The Desire of the Nations* in which appeal to the Old Testament far exceeds an appeal to the New Testament. A contrast can be seen here between O'Donovan's and Walter Kaiser's understandings of the unity of biblical ethics. Claiming that few aspects of Old Testament study have proven to be so difficult as Old Testament ethics,[170] Kaiser shares O'Donovan's appreciation of Old Testament ethics as being profoundly theistic: "To know the God of Israel was to know and practice righteousness and justice."[171] Yet while endorsing O'Donovan's assumptions an ethicist makes when using an ethical text from the past for moral decisions in the present, namely, universalizable, consistent, and prescriptive,[172] he takes exception to O'Donovan's claim "that the continuity of ethical content is discernible only from the point of view of a certain strand of New Testament theology."[173] Rather than imposing "the New Testament grid of doctrine and ethics over an Old Testament in order to gain consistency or harmony," Kaiser appeals for the use of an "informing theology" or "informing ethic." Such an approach recognizes that the Old Testament text "contains within it some facet of

---

[167] Lesslie Newbigin, *The Gospel in a Pluralist Society* (London: SPCK, 2000), 222.

[168] Oldham, "The Function of the Church in Society," 214.

[169] Victor P. Furnish, "How Firm a Foundation? Some Questions about Scripture in *The Desire of the Nations*," *Studies in Christian Ethics*, vol. 11/2, 21.

[170] Walter C. Kaiser, *Toward Old Testament Ethics* (Grand Rapids: Zondervan, 1983), 1.

[171] Ibid., 5.

[172] O'Donovan, "The Possibility of a Biblical Ethic," 15-23.

[173] Ibid., 20.

ethics that already was part and parcel of the received inspired teaching in the community of faith and formed the backdrop against which this new word was heard and received."[174] There are limitations to Old Testament morality however. For although it is to be taken seriously by contemporary ethicists, "this testament reaches out beyond itself for fulfillment in Jesus Christ and the New Testament."[175]

Engaging with the theological problem of how the Scriptures ought to shape the ethical norms and practices of the church in our time is also found in the work of Richard Hays. In *The Moral Vision of the New Testament* Hays argues for a unified ethical vision in the biblical witness, centred in the themes of community, cross, and new creation. Hays declares: "Reading the diverse New Testament texts through these focal images will enable us to see them all more clearly within Scripture's overarching story of God's grace."[176] It is a task that involves explicating the messages of the individual writings in the canon, "without prematurely harmonizing them."[177] Indeed, as Hays is at pains to stress: "The New Testament is intelligible only as a hermeneutical appropriation of Israel's Scriptures."[178] This canonical approach to Scripture is most widely associated with the work of Brevard Childs. Biblical theology, Childs affirms, has the task of reflecting on the whole Christian Bible, both of which the church confesses bear witness to Christ:

> The challenge of biblical theology is to engage in the continual activity of theological reflection which studies the canonical text in detailed exegesis, and seeks to do justice to the witness of both testaments in the light of its subject matter who is Jesus Christ.[179]

Questioning if an architectonic hermeneutic of Scripture as a whole is genuinely present in O'Donovan's work, Walter Moberly states: "At the very least, any architectonic scriptural hermeneutic should surely present a dialectic between the two testaments." This involves, in the light of Christ, rereading and rethinking that history which preceded him. Moberly continues: "The concern here is not to impose a flat christomonism upon the whole of Scripture, but rather to seek a truly mutual and dialectical relationship between the Testaments."[180] Yet he also acknowledges the rightful place of God's reign in O'Donovan's work. For had he given greater weight to the Mosaic Torah in addition to using the Psalms, "this would indeed have rooted his exposition more deeply within foundational Old Testament texts, but it would not have suggested a shift of focus away from the reign of God."[181]

---

[174] Kaiser, *Toward Old Testament Ethics*, 28.

[175] Ibid., 34.

[176] Hays, *The Moral Vision of the New Testament*, 196.

[177] Ibid., 3.

[178] Ibid., 9.

[179] Childs, *Biblical Theology of the Old and New Testaments*, 78-79.

[180] R. Walter L. Moberly, "The Use of Scripture in *The Desire of the Nations*," in *A Royal Priesthood?* 58.

[181] Ibid., 62.

Gordon McConville echoes Moberly's claim that covenant has a surprisingly small part in *The Desire of the Nations*, due to its prominence in the Old Testament, and its usefulness as a concept for the commitment of a community under the authority of law and committed to justice. McConville states: "It furnishes a paradigm for consent to be governed that is more far-reaching than that which is entailed in Israel's confession '*yhwh malak*' as understood by O'Donovan."[182] This has arisen not least in that the Pentateuch is under-represented at the expense of the Psalms and the Prophets. Thus the concept of covenant may have featured more prominently had O'Donovan employed a more integrative approach to Old Testament theology. In proposing that the profile of Deuteronomy be raised in the discussion of *The Desire of the Nations*, McConville argues: "The 'political categories' of historical Israel are best identified by an approach that gives due weight to the canonical shaping of the Old Testament." In doing so, the reader seeks "to understand texts both in their entirety and in relation to each other."[183] Central to the message of Deuteronomy is Israel's "perpetual recommitment to covenant with Yahweh, whose substance is Torah."[184] It demonstrates Israel's distinctive understanding of kingship among those living in the surrounding ancient Near East:

> In this rapprochement of a concept of creational order with a politics based on a people's covenantal relationship with God in willing obedience to the Torah, Deuteronomy challenges profoundly the ancient Near Eastern concept of a political order with fixed hierarchical forms based on analogous hierarchies in the divine realm.[185]

So in summary, "Deuteronomy's provision for the political organization of the people," McConville states, "arises out of a belief in a fundamental moral order, which is rooted in the character of God, expressed in his creation, and applied in his making of a covenant with Israel."[186] Indeed the best models for the acceptance of political authority are in the covenantal texts (e.g. Exodus 19-24; Deuteronomy 26:17-19).[187] In response to McConville, O'Donovan does admittedly recognize this relative absence of covenant in his theological works. In his defense, he considered "on the one hand, that it was accounted for within the category of law, and on the other that it was a temptation to the modern mind, for which the slide from 'covenant' to 'contract' was a fatally easy one."[188]

---

[182] J. Gordon McConville, "Law and Morality in the Old Testament," in *A Royal Priesthood?* 81.

[183] Ibid., 72.

[184] Ibid., 77.

[185] Ibid., 78.

[186] Ibid., 80.

[187] Ibid., 81. Cf. Bartholomew, "A Time for War, and a Time for Peace," 108. Bartholomew suggests that covenant with its foundation in creation and its clear sense of historical development, also provides a valid biblical link between order and history.

[188] Oliver O'Donovan, "Response to Gordon McConville," in *A Royal Priesthood?* 89.

The Gospel and the Eschatological Hope of World Justice

The eschatological transformation of the world is a central theme in both O'Donovan's and Moltmann's theology. Both perceive this hope to derive from the death and resurrection of Jesus Christ. Yet there are distinct differences of understandings of the Christ-event. For Moltmann, the cross is primarily the demonstration of divine solidarity with the outcast and marginalized of society. O'Donovan does not contradict this aspect of the cross, but draws out its fuller meaning particularly in his earlier work *Resurrection and Moral Order*, in which he explicates the eschatological significance of the atonement and the multidimensional redemption this historical event brings to the world and the created order.[189]

Despite these differences, though, the eschatological hope of world justice is a pervasive theme running through the works of both theologians. It is a hope grounded in God's all-sovereign rule, as is intrinsic to a theology of grace. Augustine shared such a vision and claimed that true justice will be fully realized only in the coming City of God, and cannot be present in a broken and sinful world: "There is not any true justice in any commonwealth whatsoever, but in that whereof Christ is the founder and the ruler."[190] Chaplin describes the position O'Donovan advocates of governments, as articulated also by Augustine and continued by Martin Luther, which highlights the impact of this hope upon the dynamics of governing authorities. What O'Donovan offers, he declares "is a radically christological reading of Western political thought."[191] Government is seen to be "a post-lapsarian, remedial institution providentially established by God to curb human sinfulness and enforce a measure of 'earthly' justice until the return of Christ." At Christ's return a new order of peace will be ushered in, in which political authority will be redundant. O'Donovan supplements this patristic conception, Chaplin asserts, with the pronouncement that "after the exaltation of Christ, God now commands governments publicly to lay down their own pretensions to supreme authority and concede sovereignty to him upon whom all authority in heaven and earth has been conferred."[192]

It is this eschatological turning point with the coming of Christ, Chaplin notes, that "precipitates an awesome moment of decision for all who bear political authority *Anno Domini*."[193] The decision they are faced with is whether they will acknowledge their responsibility to the exalted Christ and the legitimacy of the church as witness to a higher sovereignty. Chaplin asserts: "This eschatologically charged notion of 'responsible' government, then, is the core of the political legacy of Christendom that has come to be crystallized in the early-modern liberalism which O'Donovan

---

[189] In summing up *Resurrection and Moral Order*, Hauerwas states: "Too much moral order, not enough resurrection." Quoted in Cavanaugh, "Stan the Man," 25.

[190] St. Augustine of Hippo, *The City of God*, ed. Randolph V.G. Tasker, trans. John Healey, vol. 1 (London: Dent, 1945), 64.

[191] Chaplin, "Political Eschatology and Responsible Government," 269.

[192] Ibid., 276-277.

[193] Ibid., 277.

presents as the distinctive political contribution of the gospel."[194] O'Donovan elaborates on his understanding of government and law by advocating the subordination of each branch of government to the definitive governmental task of judgment: "The court is the central paradigm of government – all government, in all its branches."[195] In doing so, Chaplin suggests, "the act of judgment is so accentuated because O'Donovan wishes to present political authority as an expression of God's providential will, of which political institutions are merely the contingent, historically variable, channels."[196] Yet Chaplin differs from O'Donovan in that the coming of Christ was not specifically a turning point for governments. "Christ calls government to what it has always been called to – if indeed with renewed eschatological urgency," claims Chaplin, "namely, the establishment of justice in the public realm of society."[197] Hence Christ's triumph does not reorder the essential functions of government:

> Power and tradition were from the beginning always supposed to be subservient to justice, and that triumph amounts to the decisive reaffirmation of that original ranking. If so, then government does not stand in need of an eschatological re-authorization by Christ nor an ecclesiocentric re-legitimation, but rather a humble acceptance of its calling to "public right action," not only for the church but for every person and community under its stewardship. If this is the case, then a political theology should not be "dispensational," but simply "restorative."[198]

It is this vision of eschatological justice that gives hope to the church in its mission to the world. As Moltmann espoused, it is to anticipate the coming kingdom of God. The church is therefore not to be served by the state in light of the gospel of grace, but, as Charles Dodd also affirms, the church is entirely subordinate to ends beyond itself, which are the ends of Christ: "Those ends transcend the interest of the church, for Christ is the Saviour not of the church alone, but of the world."[199] In short, as Christ's body on earth, the church is concerned with the salvation of the world and in no lesser end. It exists for the glory of God on the earth of which God's concern for universal justice is so intrinsically interrelated.

Conclusion

In this chapter we have sought to provide a critique of O'Donovan's political theology analyzing to what extent a theology of grace is evident in his theological project. The biblical concept of the kingdom of God has been a particularly dominant contribution of O'Donovan's theological works. God's unified kingly

---

[194] Ibid.

[195] Oliver O'Donovan, "Government as Judgment," *First Things*, vol. 92 (April 1999), 39.

[196] Chaplin, "Political Eschatology and Responsible Government," 291.

[197] Ibid., 303.

[198] Ibid., 303-304.

[199] Dodd, *Gospel and Law*, 35-36.

reign causes the church to actively engage with the social and political concerns of the world, guided by a holistic vision of a moral order restored in Jesus Christ. There are also areas of his work, however, that appear to lack theological justification and which neglects integral biblical concepts such as the covenant of grace. Additionally, there are questions as to core aspects of his political theology in that the state is reauthorized in order to serve the mission of the church. Despite these apparent deficiencies, O'Donovan's works are significant for developing the theological discussion as to what should constitute the mission of the Christian community in its socio-political aspect in the contemporary world.

PART 3

The Test Case

CHAPTER 6

Power and the Dynamics of Global Transformations

Having surveyed the extent to which a theology of grace is evident in the political theologies of leading contemporary thinkers, we now turn to the task of penetrating beyond merely formal considerations vis-à-vis the church's socio-political involvement and material theological concerns, by making specific judgments about its mission in the context of a globalized world. In order to apply our theological analysis in a constructive and informed manner to this specific context, we will devote this chapter wholly to evaluating the phenomenon of globalization, before returning to our theological engagement in chapter 7. Thus, this chapter is an integral constituent of our interdisciplinary study, and in particular, for answering our second fundamental theological question: *what are the implications of the church's distinctiveness for its socio-political mission in an age of globalization?* In particular, this chapter will include discussing the globalization debate, assessing the three main forces of global transformation, and focusing on the implications of diminished nation-states and the challenges for global justice in the midst of transforming power relations.

Introduction

As we move into the twenty-first century, virtually all areas of human life are changing. Of significant influence behind these changes is the multidimensional phenomenon of globalization, which is characterized by power transformations in the contemporary world. Although there have been different milestones throughout world history in the road towards globalization, the extent of the interaction and interdependence between peoples on a global basis has only arisen in comparatively recent years.[1] Ian Shapiro and Lea Brilmayer draw our attention to these

---

[1] For a comparison of the new wave of globalization from previous years, see David Dollar and Paul Collier (ed.), *Globalization, Growth, and Poverty: Building an Inclusive World Economy* (New York: Oxford University Press/ The World Bank, 2002), 23-52. The authors note that the first wave took place from 1870 to 1914. Advances in transportation and reductions of barriers led to some countries using their abundant land more productively. At this time, flows of goods, capital, and labour also increased dramatically. The years from 1950 to 1980 saw a second wave, which focused on integration among rich countries, namely Europe, North America, and Japan. The third wave started around 1980 and continues today. For a further historical overview of how the world has become increasingly integrated, see Philippe Legrain, *Open World: The Truth about Globalization* (London: Abacus, 2003), 80-

contemporary realities: "Globalization may well be in its infancy, yet its impact to date must be judged dramatic when compared with any previous era in human history."[2] Impacting on all spheres of human life, including the cultural, economic, political, religious, and social, globalization has led to a distinctly different global order, bringing with it new opportunities, and additionally, not insignificant challenges. Indeed, following the end of the Cold War, many scholars believe that a new world political system has emerged as a result of globalization.[3] It is also described as having led to a compression of the world.[4]

Yet despite the general acknowledgement that there is an apparent increased interconnectedness across the globe, there is also considerable disagreement within the academic community and in the public sphere about how best to conceptualize this contemporary issue and its diverse impact. There remains a degree of uncertainty about the actual causes of globalization and the future direction of this present reality.[5] It is our aim in this chapter, therefore, to clarify the issues pertaining to this phenomenon and its transforming impact across the world, in order to identify the specific challenges presented for ecclesial witness in the twenty-first century.

The Globalization Debate

The Hyperglobalizers, the Sceptics, and the Transformationalists

Sceptics of globalization abound. And the reason why this is so, is because globalization is a much used and frequently overused word in contemporary socio-political debate. Consequently, in seeking to understand and explain this multidimensional issue, a vibrant debate has developed in the public and academic sphere. Essentially there are three main schools of thought, which seek to describe the extent, form, and impact of contemporary globalization. These schools of thought have been referred to by David Held et al as "the hyperglobalizers," "the sceptics," and "the transformationalists."[6] We will retain these helpful terms and critique each of the three positions in turn in our analysis of the ongoing globalization debate.

117; and Jeffrey Frankel, "Globalization of the Economy," in *Governance in a Globalizing World*, 45-71.

[2] Ian Shapiro and Lea Brilmayer, "Introduction," in *Global Justice*, ed. Ian Shapiro and Lea Brilmayer (New York: New York University Press, 1999), 1.

[3] John Baylis and Steve Smith, "Globalization and its Precursors," in *The Globalization of World Politics: An Introduction to International Relations*, ed. John Baylis and Steve Smith, 2nd edn (Oxford: Oxford University Press, 2001), 7.

[4] Roland Robertson, "Globalization and the Future of 'Traditional Religion,'" in *God and Globalization*, vol. 1: *Religion and the Powers of the Common Life*, 53.

[5] Zygmunt Bauman, *Globalization: The Human Consequences* (New York: Columbia University Press, 1998), 57.

[6] David Held, et al, *Global Transformations: Politics, Economics and Culture* (Oxford: Polity Press, 1999), 2-10. For a concise interpretation of these debates, see David Held and Anthony McGrew, *Globalization/ Anti-Globalization* (Cambridge: Polity Press, 2002).

First, hyperglobalizers argue that we live in an increasingly global world in which states are being subject to massive economic and political processes of change. These forces of change are eroding and fragmenting nation-states that consequently have diminished the power of politicians. This emerging unitary global economy marks the beginning of a radically new era. Kenichi Ohmae holds such a view and claims "traditional nation-states have become unnatural, even impossible, business units in a global economy."[7] For in a borderless world, hyperglobalizers assert, power resides in global finance and corporate capital rather than in nation-states.[8] Yet within the hyperglobalist framework there is significant divergence of views. On the one hand, there are the neo-liberals who welcome the market principle over state power, as advocated by the Enlightenment's metanarrative of progress. On the other hand, the radical neo-Marxists regard globalization as the triumph of an oppressive global capitalism. Despite the divergent ideological convictions, however, among hyperglobalizers there exists a primary belief that globalization is essentially an economic phenomenon and that politics is being reduced to economic management.[9]

At the other end of the globalization debate, the sceptics strongly resist the views held by hyperglobalizers and insist that contemporary global circumstances are not unprecedented, but have occurred in different stages throughout world history. This is exemplified in the era of the gold standard in the late nineteenth century.[10] In their account, sceptics assert that globalization is essentially a myth, which conceals the true reality of an international economy. Yet in arguing that globalization is a myth sceptics rely on a completely economistic conception of globalization. Paul Hirst and Grahame Thompson argue this position, which emphasizes the centrality of the economy.[11] Hirst and Thompson claim that while there has indeed been an intensification of international and social activity in recent times, this has not led to a perfectly integrated worldwide economy. Rather than weakening the power of nation-states, the heightened interactions between predominately national economies has actually reinforced and enhanced state powers. For the forces of internationalization themselves, depend on the decision-making of national governments to ensure continued economic liberalization. Thus sceptics dispute the

---

[7] Kenichi Ohmae, *The End of the Nation State: The Rise of Regional Economies* (New York: Free Press, 1995), 5.

[8] For example, see Walter B. Wriston, *The Twilight of Sovereignty: How the Information Revolution is Transforming Our World* (New York: Scribner, 1992); and Jean-Marie Guehenno, *The End of the Nation-State*, trans. Victoria Elliot (Minneapolis: University of Minnesota Press, 1995).

[9] Held, et al, *Global Transformations*, 3-4.

[10] For example, see Robert Boyer and Daniel Drache, *States Against Markets: The Limits of Globalization* (London: Routledge, 1996).

[11] Paul Q. Hirst and Grahame Thompson, *Globalization in Question: The International Economy and the Possibilities of Governance*, 2nd edn (Cambridge: Polity Press, 1999).

hyperglobalizer's thesis and assert that the extent of globalization is misleading and exaggerated.[12]

The third main school of thought is the transformationalist position. Central to their thesis is the conviction that globalization is creating new economic, political and social dynamics, which are reshaping modern societies and world order.[13] Although globalization is not an entirely new phenomenon, transformationalists claim that the level of interdependency that has occurred is unprecedented in world history. Through a process of complex transnational networks a new form of sovereignty is displacing traditional patterns of statehood.[14] There is no longer a clear distinction between international and domestic, external, and internal affairs.[15] For however unevenly globalization is experienced throughout the world, the forces associated with this phenomenon are serving to transform state powers and the context in which states operate. Politics is now no longer simply being based on nation-states. In holding this position, they reject both the hyperglobalizer's rhetoric of a world that has actually witnessed the end of the nation-state, and they reject the sceptics' claim that globalization is a myth.[16] Yet transformationalists claim there remains uncertainty as to where globalization might be leading. Anthony Giddens articulates this belief: "We are being propelled into a global order that no one fully understands, but which is making its effects felt upon all of us."[17]

Contemporary Globalization and the Transformation of Power

In our thesis, we agree essentially with the transformationalist view, as espoused by scholars such as Held, that globalization is to be conceived as a powerful transformative force in the contemporary world. These increasing interdependencies and integrations are leading to changes in the global order, bringing not only

---

[12] For example, see Paul Q. Hirst, "The Global Economy: Myths and Realities," *International Affairs*, vol. 73/3 (July 1997), 409-425; and Justin Rosenberg, *The Follies of Globalization Theory: Polemical Essays* (London: Verso, 2000).

[13] For example, see Anthony Giddens, *The Consequences of Modernity* (Cambridge: Polity Press, 1990); Jan Aart Scholte, *International Relations of Social Change* (Buckingham: Open University Press, 1993); and Manuel Castells, *The Rise of the Network Society*, 2nd edn (Oxford: Blackwell, 2000).

[14] For example, see James N. Rosenau, *Turbulence in World Politics: A Theory of Change and Continuity* (London: Harvester Wheatsheaf, 1990); Joseph A. Camilleri and James Falk, *The End of Sovereignty?: The Politics of a Shrinking and Fragmenting World* (Aldershot: Edward Elgar, 1992); and Saskia Sassen, *Losing Control?: Sovereignty in an Age of Globalization* (New York: Columbia University Press, 1996).

[15] John MacMillan and Andrew Linklater, "Boundaries in Question," in *Boundaries in Question: New Directions in International Relations*, ed. John MacMillan and Andrew Linklater (London: Pinter, 1995), 1-16.

[16] Held, et al, *Global Transformations*, 9.

[17] Anthony Giddens, *Runaway World: How Globalization is Reshaping our Lives* (London: Profile, 1999), 7.

opportunities, but also unprecedented socio-political challenges, as we will discover in subsequent sections of this chapter. Despite globalization being an over-used term in both the academic sphere and in the public arena, when it is properly formulated, globalization does capture important features of the contemporary world.[18]

Although globalization reveals a great deal about continuity and change in the twenty-first century world, due to its multidimensional nature, it is particularly problematic in defining this contemporary issue. Ulrich Beck, however, helpfully describes its essential features. Globalization, Beck claims, "denotes the processes, through which sovereign national states are criss-crossed and undermined by transnational actors with varying prospects of power, orientations, identities and networks."[19] Held et al provide a further clarification. Fundamentally, globalization can be described as "the widening, deepening and speeding up of worldwide interconnectedness in all aspects of contemporary social life."[20] The pervasive impact of globalization as described highlights the weakness of the sceptics' approach in analyzing this phenomenon in relation to a single ideal globalized world, whether this is a single global market or a global civilization. In contrast, globalization is inherently multidimensional. Thus globalization cannot be reduced to a narrow form of conceptualization, as few areas of social life have escaped its transforming impact.

While we acknowledge the existence of a single world system, this does not mean the arrival of a single world society. On the contrary, globalization has led to new patterns of global stratification in which some states and communities are becoming increasingly caught up in the world system, while others are becoming increasingly marginalized.[21] Additionally, one of the paradoxes of globalization is that it also involves fragmentation and a certain type of localization. Roland Robertson discusses this issue further in *Global Modernities*. Robertson argues against a tendency to perceive globalization as involving large-scale macro-sociological issues and processes, which at the same time neglects the way in which globalization is localized. Coining the unattractive word "glocalization," Robertson asserts that globalization always takes place in some locality, while locality is absorbed and produced by the forces of globalization. A core feature of this society is the manipulation of locality and tradition to suit the needs of the global marketplace.[22]

Yet despite this fragmentation, which is one of the paradoxes of globalization, the forces of interdependence and integration are being felt across the globe. Of

---

[18] David Held, "Cosmopolitanism: Ideas, Realities and Deficits," in *Governing Globalization: Power, Authority and Global Governance*, ed. David Held and Anthony G. McGrew (Cambridge: Polity Press, 2002), 305-307.

[19] Ulrich Beck, *What is Globalization?* trans. Patrick Camiller (Cambridge: Polity Press, 2000), 11.

[20] Held, et al, *Global Transformations*, 2.

[21] See Dollar and Collier (ed.), *Globalization, Growth, and Poverty*.

[22] Roland Robertson, "Glocalization: Time-Space and Homogeneity-Heterogeneity," in *Global Modernities*, ed. Mike Featherstone, Scott Lash and Roland Robertson (London: Sage, 1995), 25-44.

significance is the global stratification linked with the changes in economic activity due to trade, production, and finance increasingly acquiring a global dimension. In this interconnected global system, the exercise of power through the decisions of agencies on one continent can have profound consequences for communities on other continents. Hence power is a fundamental attribute of globalization. The pervasive nature of power is articulated by Walter Wink, who describes the "Powers that Be" as "the systems themselves, the institutions and structures that weave society into an intricate fabric of power and relationships."[23] In defining the concept of power, Leslie Green declares: "Power involves the capacity to produce or prevent change."[24] Moreover, what is becoming evident is that power transformations are inherently embedded in the dynamics of our globalized world order.[25]

Consequently, one of the most significant changes which globalization has brought is that this phenomenon is intrinsically associated with the emergence of powerful new non-territorial forms of economic and political organization in the global domain. These new entrants to the making up of the contemporary global order include multinational corporations (MNCs),[26] transnational social movements, and international regulatory agencies. Power transformations in the socio-political arena have meant that the new global order can no longer be conceived as purely state-centric or even primarily state governed. For in an age of globalization, assert Held et al, "authority has become increasingly diffused among public and private agencies at the local, national, regional and global levels."[27] The causes of these global transformations will now be assessed in more detail.

Forces of Global Transformation in the Contemporary World

The Post-War World Economy

In analyzing the root causes of globalization, we have to go back to July 1944 at Bretton Woods, New Hampshire, in the United States of America.[28] It was at Bretton Woods, where policy-makers gathered at the United Nations Monetary and Financial Conference with the immediate task of seeking to rebuild the economies of Europe

---

[23] Walter Wink, *The Powers that Be: Theology for a New Millennium* (London: Doubleday, 1998), 1.

[24] Leslie Green, "Power," in *Routledge Encyclopedia of Philosophy*, vol. 7, 610.

[25] John H. Dunning concurs with these views, and claims in a personal correspondence that it is "right to consider globalization as an ongoing structural transformation process."

[26] For a theological analysis of MNCs, see Michael Novak, "Toward a Theology of the Corporation," in *On Moral Business: Classical and Contemporary Resources for Ethics in Economic Life*, ed. Max L. Stackhouse, Dennis P. McCann, and Shirely J. Roels (Grand Rapids: Eerdmans, 1995), 776.

[27] Held, et al, *Global Transformations*, 9.

[28] For a further discussion, see Robert S. Walters and David H. Blake, *The Politics of Global Economic Relations*, 4th edn (Englewood Cliffs, N.J.: Prentice-Hall, 1992), 64-102; and David N. Balaam and Michael Veseth, *Introduction to International Political Economy*, 2nd edn (Upper Saddle River, N.J.: Prentice-Hall, 2001), 146-154.

after the devastation of World War II. Additionally, policy-makers were keen to ensure that there would not be a recurrence of the Great Depression of the 1930s. At the conference, the major architects of the post-war strategy for the world economy included political leaders and key academic figures, such as John Maynard Keynes, a strong advocate of free trade.[29] Political decisions made and the international economic order that was developed not only had implications for the future of the world at that time, but were to be significant in shaping the global economy as we see it today. Stanley Hoffmann comments on these changes: "The postwar era has witnessed radical transformations in the elements, the uses, and the achievements of power."[30] Describing the outcome of the establishment of this economic system, Craig Murphy and Roger Tooze state: "The liberal system clearly did facilitate the enormous growth of the world economy and thereby created the context for the globalization of economic activity that is so much a part of economic life today."[31]

Three institutions were created at Bretton Woods that would eventually become dominant influences in the dynamics of globalization. The International Monetary Fund (IMF) had responsibility for seeking to ensure exchange rate stability, and also provide assistance to nations facing difficulties in their balance of payments regimes. The International Bank for Reconstruction and Development (IBRD), subsequently renamed the World Bank, was created to facilitate the increase in private investment and the reconstruction in war-torn Europe. A final agreement was signed in 1947 called the General Agreement on Trade and Tariffs (GATT), which became a forum for negotiation on trade liberalization. The plans for the world economy, however, were postponed due to the priority of seeking to contain the Soviet Union. Additionally, with the emergence of weaknesses in the United States of America's economy in the 1960s, the rising costs of the Vietnam War, and urban redevelopment programs, the rules of the international monetary system were changed in 1971.

During this period, the growth of global capital markets were buoyed by the investments derived from the oil price rise of 1973. This money was offered as loans to developing countries that were soon unable to repay following the rise in interest rates in 1979.[32] This changed the role of the IMF as it was no longer at the heart of the international monetary and financial system, but was focused on helping to prevent any country from defaulting on their loans. The intention was to avoid a perceived global financial crisis caused by these defaults. Similarly, the World Bank

---

[29] For a biography of Keynes written by a contemporary, see Henry R.F. Harrod, *The Life of John Maynard Keynes* (London: Macmillan, 1951).

[30] Stanley Hoffmann, "Notes on the Elusiveness of Modern Power," *International Journal*, vol. 30 (Spring 1975), 183.

[31] Craig N. Murphy and Roger Tooze, *The New International Political Economy* (Boulder, Colo.: Rienner, 1991), 3.

[32] For a review of this practice, which led to crippling debt being acquired by developing countries, see Andre Gunder Frank, *Crisis: In the Third World* (London: Heinemann, 1981), 132-156; and Peter Nunnenkamp, *The International Debt Crisis of the Third World: Causes and Consequences for the World Economy* (Brighton: Wheatsheaf, 1986).

had been given a change of role and was becoming primarily a development agency, making loans to developing countries. Joan Spero and Jeffrey Hart highlight that in addition to its traditional support for infrastructure projects, the bank began to make loans for basic human need projects, such as the development of subsistence farming, and rudimentary healthcare.[33] GATT had also failed in its role, as it was unable to prevent the new protectionism of the 1970s. The result of these changes was that globalization would not truly become a reality until after the ending of the Cold War.

Trade Liberalization and a New Global Framework

Since the end of the Cold War, a new framework for understanding the world has developed, which is seen powerfully in the liberalization of trade across the globe. Essentially this new framework is characterized by the closer interdependence and integration of the countries of the world. This has been brought about by the enormous reduction in transportation and communication costs, combined with the breaking down of artificial barriers to the flows of goods, services, capital knowledge, and people across national borders. Over the past fifty years in particular, the international community has reduced trade barriers in the form of customs or duties to minimal levels.[34] With the demise of communist economic systems in much of the world this has further led to economies becoming open to foreign business. For example, Central Europeans have been eager to create more competitive economies as they prepared to join the European Union at the start of the twenty-first century. Thus Kofi Annan states: "Globalization is only partly the result of technological change. Equally important have been decisions, taken by states, to reduce the controls and restrictions they formerly imposed on the economic life of their citizens."[35]

An influential institution in the shaping of globalization is the World Trade Organization (WTO). The WTO was created by the "Uruguay Round" of talks held by member nations of GATT and is a powerful advocate of deregulation and trade liberalization. It came into existence in January 1995 and is comprised of 149 member nations.[36] The influence of the WTO and the benefits that international trade can bring to a nation has resulted in countries such as China being committed to continue its economic opening now that it has signed up to the WTO's rules.[37] The

---

[33] Joan E. Spero and Jeffrey A. Hart, *The Politics of International Economic Relations*, 5th edn (London: Routledge, 1997), 178.

[34] For an overview of the changes that have occurred in the post-World War II trade system, see Balaam and Veseth, *Introduction to International Political Economy*, 110-132.

[35] A speech delivered by Kofi A. Annan, entitled "The Role of the State in the Age of Globalization," at the Conference on Globalization and International Relations in the 21st Century on June 2002.

[36] World Trade Organization website (www.wto.org).

[37] See Daniel Franklin, "Globalization's New Boom," in *The World in* 2003, ed. Dudley Fishburn and Stephen Green (London: The Economist, 2002), 112.

WTO demonstrated the benefits of international trade when it reported that in the 1990s China's trade growth was three times faster than global trade, and between 2000 and 2002 its exports and imports rose by 30 percent while world trade stagnated.[38] The result of these influences and changes in the global economy is that as barriers to trade have fallen across the world, global markets have emerged for a significant number of manufactured goods, and also increasingly, services.

Liberalization has occurred not only between countries but across regions as well. For example, the European Union has profoundly changed businesses located in this region through the drive to create barrier-free trade.[39] The formation of other free trade agreements, such as NAFTA in North America, LAFTA in Latin America, and ASEAN in Asia, have all led to the liberalization of trade throughout the regions of the world. As well as the liberalization of trade, the recent desire in many countries to deregulate entire industry sectors has opened up the market to MNCs. This has resulted in international trade growing to unprecedented levels in world history.[40] Leading corporate strategist Jean-Pierre Jeannet, who advises many MNCs on their global business strategies, declares that we are witnessing a historic sea change in the global economy and the global trading system. Jeannet states: "As individual country-based economic systems become submerged in the larger, more prevalent global economy, this creates new imperatives for management."[41] It is a form of managerial and strategic thinking necessitated by a globalized world.

Despite the level of hostility towards globalization, which has gained much recognition in recent years due to the violent anti-globalization demonstrations at summit meetings of political leaders, there have been significant economic benefits brought to some deprived areas of the world as a result of the liberalization of trade. Opening up to international trade can lead to economic development, which has resulted in many countries' economies growing far more quickly than they would have done otherwise. This is evident in countries such as China as has already been noted. Liberalization of trade has meant that greater efficiencies have been achieved, and many people in the developing world have been given access to knowledge well beyond the reach of even the wealthiest in any country just a century ago.[42]

Yet although many countries have benefited from this new global framework, Raphael Kaplinsky points out that the distribution of gains is very uneven between

---

[38] World Trade Organization, *International Trade Statistics 2003* (Geneva: World Trade Organization, 2003).

[39] The European Union was further enlarged in 2004 when ten mostly ex-communist countries joined as members.

[40] Held, et al, *Global Transformations*, 149-188. In comparison with the late nineteenth century, which was an era of rapid trade growth, export levels today (measured as a share of GDP) are much greater for Organization for Economic Co-operation and Development states. Cf. *OECD in Figures: Statistics on the Member Countries* (Paris: OECD, 2004).

[41] Jean-Pierre Jeannet, *Managing with a Global Mindset* (London: Financial Times Management, 2000), 7. Cf. Christopher A. Bartlett and Sumantra Ghoshal, *Managing Across Borders: The Transnational Solution* (Boston: Harvard Business School, 1998).

[42] Joseph E. Stiglitz, *Globalization and Its Discontents* (London: Allen Lane, 2002), 4.

countries and also within countries.[43] For although markets may be global, regulation remains largely national. This exposes a weakness of globalization due to global opportunities and global risks outpacing global policy.[44] Regulation differences can therefore lead to international friction. Typically, trade liberalization proceeds in favouring the interests of those who have power, which are the developed nations. Highlighting this characteristic, the World Bank reports that industrial country tariffs on manufactures from developing countries are five times higher than they are on manufactures from other industrial countries.[45] Joseph Stiglitz describes this as a "special privilege" agenda of the rich nations of the world. This is seen in the asymmetries incorporated into trade agreements where developed countries have pushed poorer countries to eliminate trade barriers and trade subsidies, and yet did not reciprocate, keeping up their own barriers depriving developing countries of export income. Protections are maintained in those areas where developing countries have comparative advantage and would benefit greatly if these barriers were reduced.[46]

The unjust use of power in this new framework is seen most prominently in relation to the trade in agriculture. Since the more advanced industrial countries have continued to subsidize agriculture, this has resulted in some developing countries finding it difficult to compete. According to World Bank figures, the extent of this pressure is due to rich nations spending $350 billion a year on subsidies to their farmers, which is roughly seven times that spent on development aid and more than the entire Gross Domestic Product (GDP) of sub-Saharan Africa.[47] Because most of the world's poor people live in rural areas – estimated to be 73 percent - trade barriers in agriculture are among the most important to poverty reduction. It is calculated that reducing protection in agriculture alone would produce roughly two-thirds of the gains from full global liberalization of all merchandise trade.[48] Freeing up farm trade is therefore essential for farmers in the developing world whose lives have been negatively influenced by western protectionism. This is one of the key objectives of the Doha round of trade liberalization that was launched in Qatar in 2001, but which has as yet failed to succeed in achieving its aims.[49] Hence it is

---

[43] Raphael Kaplinsky, "Is Globalization All it is Cracked Up to be?" *Review of International Political Economy*, vol. 8/1 (Spring 2001), 45.

[44] Dollar and Collier (ed.), *Globalization, Growth, and Poverty*, 1.

[45] World Bank, *Global Economic Prospects 2004: Realizing the Development Promise of the Doha Agenda* (Washington D.C.: World Bank, 2003), 64.

[46] A speech delivered by Joseph E. Stiglitz, entitled *"Future of Globalization: In the Light of Recent Turbulence,"* at Yale University on 10 October 2003.

[47] Dollar and Collier (ed.), *Globalization, Growth, and Poverty*, 53-84.

[48] World Bank, *Global Economic Prospects 2004*, 103-141.

[49] See Ernesto Zedillo, "Doha or Die," in *The World in 2004*, ed. Daniel Franklin (London: The Economist, 2003), 93. It is estimated that the Doha Development Round of WTO negotiations could reduce the number of people living on less than $2 a day by 144 million, with sub-Saharan Africa seeing the greatest reduction. For a further analysis, see Department of Trade and Industry, *Trade and Investment White Paper 2004: Making*

evident that the liberalization of trade, despite its undeniable benefits to many people throughout the world, has frequently prospered those who have power at the expense of those who lack power and influence in the transforming global economy.

World Financial Markets and Global Interconnectedness

A further dynamic force of global transformations, are the world financial markets. In describing the nature of the international political economy in the twenty-first century, Robert Gilpin claims that globalization of finance has become a crucial and distinctive feature of the world economy.[50] As with the liberalization of trade, the growing influence of the world financial markets, as we see it today, can trace its roots back to Bretton Woods, which sought to create a liberal economic order. From the 1970s onwards in particular, the world has witnessed the phenomenon of highly mobile capital through unprecedented levels of international transactions. By the end of the 1990s, the daily turnover on the foreign exchange markets, involving the buying and selling of national currencies, reached approximately $1.5 trillion. This is an eightfold increase since 1986. By contrast the global volume of exports of goods and services for all of 1997 was $6.6 trillion, or $25 billion per day.[51] Furthermore, with the existence of 24-hour global financial markets, this has led to transactions now being virtually instantaneous. Thus the boundaries of the economy and the boundaries of the nation-state do not now appear to correspond.[52]

Similar to the other forces of globalization, power transformations are becoming increasingly evident in the financial world. John Goodman and Louis Pauly highlight this relationship between power and world financial markets and reveal that transformations in the structure of global production and international financial markets have led to further changes in government policies. Due to firms successfully exploiting these structures, government attempts to control capital movements have become more costly and less effective, resulting in national capital controls being made obsolete. It has also led to many countries adopting more liberal international financial policies.[53] Held et al point out that as worldwide trading of currencies and government bonds is a feature of contemporary global finance this means that exchange rates and interest rates, which are two critical variables in the

---

Globalization a Force for Good (London: The Stationery Office, 2004). Agriculture was singled out as being "a vital trade and development challenge" (87-91).

[50] Robert Gilpin, *Global Political Economy: Understanding the International Economic Order* (Princeton: Princeton University Press, 2001), 261.

[51] Ibid., 6.

[52] For a discussion of IPE schools of thought, see George T. Crane and Abla Amawi, *The Theoretical Evolution of International Political Economy - A Reader* (Oxford: Oxford University Press, 1991).

[53] John B. Goodman and Louis W. Pauly, "The Obsolescence of Capital Controls? Economic Management in an Age of Global Markets," in *International Political Economy: Perspectives on Global Power and Wealth*, ed. Jeffrey A. Frieden and David A. Lake, 4th edn (London: Routledge, 2000), 280-297.

formulation of national macroeconomic strategy, are determined in the context of global financial markets.[54] These impacts in the political and economic sphere display in a powerful way the interconnectedness of the international political economy that has increasingly become an internationalized world system.

Undoubtedly there are major benefits that can be realized for those living in both developed and developing nations through international financial transactions. Capital inflows can contribute to significant growth in a nation or region by stimulating investment and promoting financial development. Integrating with international financial markets enables advantages to be derived through trade in financial services. This potential positive outcome is supported by Robert Litan, Paul Masson, and Michael Pomerleano, who have provided statistical evidence demonstrating that opening domestic financial markets to foreign financial institutions brings increases in stability and efficiency to these markets.[55]

As with trade liberalization, however, the impact of world financial markets has not only brought benefits. A cause of concern with the growth of capital flows, particularly in low-income countries, is that where once international financial markets operated to finance long-term investment, a growing trend among financiers and international banks is to channel finances into short-term speculative ventures. This practice has led Susan Strange, in her aptly named work *Casino Capitalism*, comparing the world financial system to a vast casino:

> As in a casino, the world of high finance today offers the players a choice of games. Instead of roulette, blackjack, or poker there is dealing to be done - the foreign exchange market and all its variations; or in bonds, government securities or shares.[56]

The negative impact of speculative activity is that this form of investment can lead to volatile movements in asset prices and significantly increase the vulnerability of the international financial system.[57] The effects of speculative ventures in an economic region were dramatically seen in the financial crisis that hit East Asia in 1997.[58] George Soros argues that it is this destabilizing impact of global financial markets, which is where the Asian crisis actually emerged, rather than in the economies concerned.[59] Uncertainty surrounding market responses has also

---

[54] Held et al, *Global Transformations*, 189.

[55] Robert E. Litan, Paul Masson, and Michael Pomerleano, *Open Doors: Foreign Participation in Financial Systems in Developing Countries* (Washington: Brookings Institution Press, 2001).

[56] Susan Strange, *Casino Capitalism* (Oxford: Basil Blackwell, 1986), 1.

[57] See Jonathan Kirshner, "Keynes, Capital Mobility and the Crisis of Embedded Liberalism," *Review of International Political Economy*, vol. 6/3 (Autumn 1999), 313-337.

[58] See Norani Othman and Clive S. Kessler, "Capturing Globalization: Prospects and Projects," *Third World Quarterly*, vol. 21/6 (December 2000), 1013-1026.

[59] George Soros, "The New Global Financial Architecture," in *On the Edge: Living with Global Capitalism*, ed. Will Hutton and Anthony Giddens (London: Jonathan Cape, 2000), 86-92.

increased the difficulty of policymakers in developing effective macro-economic strategies. Thus due to these potentially harmful consequences of international financial transactions, Masson points out that appropriate incentives are required for capital to stay in a country and not flee at the first sign of trouble.[60] Such measures would be beneficial in protecting developing countries against the activities of financial speculators, who typically have only a short-term concern rather than a long-term desire to see growth in the country or a rise in living standards.

Production and the Changing Competitive Landscape for Business

In relatively recent years, as John Dunning has demonstrated through an analysis of historical, theoretical, and empirical material, the world has witnessed the unprecedented influence of MNCs, inaugurating a new era in the globalization of the world economy.[61] Concentrating on maximizing achievement of core business competencies has led many organizations to outsource non-core activities to low income countries in the southern hemisphere. In addition, with the desire to spread fixed costs over as wide a customer base as possible, the privatization of industries, and the proliferation of global mergers and acquisitions, the global firm is now becoming the norm. Although this phenomenon has been particularly evident in the manufacturing industry, it is also increasingly being felt in the service sector.[62]

Gary Hamel and C. K. Prahalad describe the opportunities and challenges anticipated by future changes in business operations and strategies, and claim that they are "inherently global." Global collaborations and global distribution reach will be required "to capture the rewards of leadership and fully amortize associated investments."[63] These changes taking place in the competitive landscape of business, Lowell Bryan predicts will entail geographic barriers to business virtually disappearing over the next thirty years, with at least 80 percent of world output being in global markets.[64] This integration has taken place at an unprecedented rate through the increasing mobility of capital, deregulation, and new communications and computing technologies, which Lowell claims, "have eliminated most of the barriers that formerly kept these economies distinct."[65] This "transition economy" has repercussions for a company's strategy, as "it results in the simultaneous

---

[60] Paul Masson, "Globalization: Facts and Figures," *International Monetary Fund Policy Discussion Paper* (October 2001), 10.

[61] See for example, John H. Dunning, *Multinational Enterprises and the Global Economy* (Wokingham: Addison-Wesley, 1993); and John H. Dunning (ed.), *United Nations Library on Transnational Corporations*, 20 vols. (London: Routledge, 1993-1994).

[62] For a discussion of the globalization of service activities, see John H. Dunning, *The Globalization of Business: The Challenge of the 1990s* (London: Routledge, 1993), 242-284.

[63] Gary Hamel and C. K. Prahalad, *Competing for the Future* (Boston, Mass.: Harvard Business School Press, 1994), 28.

[64] Lowell L. Bryan, *Race for the World: Strategies to Build a Great Global Firm* (Boston: Harvard Business School Press, 1999), 3.

[65] Ibid., xiii.

redefinition of value chains in the industry, the players, and their relative competitive positions."[66]

A helpful summary for analyzing how globalization is reshaping the business world is presented by George Yip, Johny Johansson, and Johan Roos who have identified four main types of globalization drivers. First, are market globalization drivers, which are indicated by commonality of customer tastes and the global transferability of marketing approaches. Second, are cost globalization drivers, which are indicated by global scale economies, experience curve effects, sourcing efficiencies, favourable logistics, product development costs, and differences in exchange rates. Third, are government globalization drivers, which are indicated by tariff and non-tariff barriers, compatible technical standards, and common marketing regulations. And fourth, are competitive globalization drivers, which are indicated by the extent to which competitors use global strategy.[67]

With the significant expansion of world trade this has led to increases in competitive intensity as companies strive to be among the two or three leaders in their industry. The spread of global business and the level of competitive intensity are evidenced in the large accountancy firms, which play an influential role in the global economy.[68] Accountancy firms do not limit their activities to auditing, but provide advice to MNCs involving mergers and acquisitions on a global scale. In their role as corporate financiers and tax consultants the top accountancy firms also play a key role in the world's financial structure. One of the top accountancy firms is Ernst & Young, which employs 100,000 people in over 140 countries worldwide. Similar to its competitors, Ernst &Young has placed maximizing the opportunities of globalization at the forefront of its business strategy. In striving to become globally integrated the ten largest Ernst & Young practices created a "Combined Practice," which represents over 90 percent of worldwide revenues.[69]

Maximizing the business opportunities presented by globalization led Jeannet to articulate what he calls the "global imperative." This is the "absolute necessity that forces companies to embrace globalization or face extinction."[70] Hence there are increasing pressures being exerted upon companies to globalize in order to remain competitive. The way organizations seek to respond to these changes is through global strategic positioning. Such competitive pressures do not only impact upon a company's market strategy. These shifts in strategic position have led to MNCs

---

[66] Ibid., 155.

[67] George S. Yip, Johny K. Johansson, and Johan Roos, "Effects of Nationality on Global Strategy," *Management International Review*, vol. 37/4 (October 1997), 365-386.

[68] Susan Strange, *The Retreat of the State: The Diffusion of Power in the World Economy* (Cambridge: Cambridge University Press, 1996), 135-146.

[69] Ernst & Young, *Global Vision 2002: Summary of Strategies* (London: Ernst & Young, 1998), 1.

[70] Jeannet, *Managing with a Global Mindset*, 5.

becoming driving forces behind further policies of deregulation and liberalization.[71] The increased power of MNCs relative to national governments is reflected in the widespread provision of subsidies to inward investment. Restrictions on MNC activity have also been substantially reduced since the 1980s. Commenting on these marketplace changes, Michael Porter claims: "By any measure, trade and foreign investment have risen significantly, and the shifts in strategic position that have accompanied industry evolution to global status are both dramatic and rapid."[72]

One of the primary ways MNCs are seeking to maintain a competitive edge in this global marketplace is through relocating substantial parts of the production process in developing and emerging economies in an effort to seek access to low cost resources and factors of production. This is demonstrated by General Electric, which has a presence in one hundred countries. Jeff Immelt, Chairman and CEO of General Electric, states that globalization is at the core of General Electric's identity going forward: "When our globalization initiative began in the late 1980s, the company derived more than 80 percent of its revenues within the US. Today we get 45 percent of our revenues from outside the US and that will keep climbing."[73] For the countries producing these goods, not only do their local populations increasingly consume goods from abroad, but also the production processes are dependent on components produced overseas. For example, Thomas Lawton and Kevin Michaels offer statistical findings, which indicate that over 40 percent of the exports of manufactured goods from Mexico involve assembly operations using components manufactured abroad.[74] Hence economic activity in any one country is strongly affected by economic activity in other countries of the world.

The positive impact that foreign direct investment (FDI) can have in a nation was demonstrated at a recent United Nations Conference on Trade and Development, when it was reported that the only developing countries that really are developing are those that have succeeded in attracting significant amounts of FDI.[75] FDI benefits host countries not only in the transfer of finance, but also due to the associated transfer of technology and knowledge. It was in connection with this surge of FDI by MNCs that led to the term "globalization" coming into popular usage in the second

---

[71] Winfried Ruigrok, "International Corporate Strategies and Restructuring," in *Political Economy and the Changing Global Order*, ed. Richard Stubbs and Geoffrey R.D. Underhill (Oxford: Oxford University Press, 2000), 320.

[72] Michael E. Porter, *Competitive Strategy: Techniques for Analysing Industries and Competitors* (New York: Free Press, 1980), 276.

[73] A speech delivered by Jeff Immelt, entitled *"The Changing Face of the Global Company,"* at the European Policy Centre in Brussels, Belgium on 28 January 2002.

[74] Thomas C. Lawton and Kevin P. Michaels, "The Evolving Global Production Structure: Implications for International Political Economy," in *Strange Power: Shaping the Parameters of International Relations and International Political Economy*, ed. Thomas C. Lawton, James N. Rosenau, and Amy C. Verdun (Aldershot: Ashgate, 2000), 65.

[75] United Nations, *United Nations Conference on Trade and Development. World Investment Report: FDI Policies for Development* (New York: United Nations, 2003), xiv.

half of the 1980s.[76] The growth of FDI was also dramatically seen in the 1990s when global FDI inflows soared from $160 billion in 1991 to $1.5 trillion in 2000, which was predominately due to investments of American and European firms.[77]

Global transformations in the corporate world have resulted in MNCs now being critical to the location, organization and distribution of productive power in the world economy.[78] Today MNCs account for at least 20 percent of world production and 70 percent of world trade. Despite MNCs typically accounting for a minority of national production this understates their strategic importance, due to being concentrated in the most technologically advanced economic sectors and in export industries. Especially in developing countries, even where independent firms produce for export, MNCs often control global distribution networks, resulting in MNCs exerting a powerful force within a nation-state. Beck indicates that dependencies are created not only for the economy, but also for society as a whole, since MNCs having it in their power to withdraw the material resources, such as capital, taxes and jobs, from society.[79] Thus a challenge brought by globalization, as Ben Knighton states, is that as the sovereignty of the nation-state is weakening under the dictate of MNCs and foreign investors, society becomes undermined and uncertainty increases.[80] For due to these dependencies created, as Noreena Hertz also notes, the ability of MNCs and financial institutions to change domestic policy becomes a real possibility.[81]

With the rise of multinational operations there is also a risk to developing nations of MNCs potentially employing unethical business practices and adhering to lax standards that would be rejected in the country where they are based. Naomi Klein comments on the emergence of what she calls the "new branded world," and anticipates an increased opposition to MNCs as people uncover secrets of the global activities of leading brand name organizations.[82] Risks can likewise arise in that opening up to free trade may undermine a local subsistence economy where a nation comes to rely upon only a few products.[83] The impact of abandoning these previously held socio-economic systems, assert Jane Collier and Rafael Esteban, is that they frequently lead to short-term benefits to those who hold power, while endangering the survival of the people in the longer term.[84] Thus what is clear from

---

[76] Gilpin, *Global Political Economy*, 7.

[77] Daniel Franklin, "Globalization's New Boom," 112.

[78] Held, et al. *Global Transformations*, 236-282.

[79] Beck, *What is Globalization?* 2.

[80] Ben Knighton, "Globalization: Implications of Violence, the Global Economy, and the Role of the State for Africa and Christian Mission," *Transformation*, vol. 18/4 (October 2001), 207-208.

[81] Noreena Hertz, *The Silent Takeover: Global Capitalism and the Death of Democracy* (London: Heinemann, 2001).

[82] Naomi Klein, *No Logo: No Space, No Choice, No Jobs* (London: Flamingo, 2001).

[83] Giddens, *Runaway World*, 17.

[84] Jane Collier and Rafael Esteban, *From Complicity to Encounter: The Church and the Culture of Economism* (Harrisburg: Trinity Press International, 1998), 28.

these changes in the competitive landscape for business is that they have strategic implications not only for corporations, but they bring fundamental challenges to national governments, and are leading to alterations in lifestyles and dependencies for people across the globe.

Transforming Power Relations and the Implications for Global Justice

Opportunities and Challenges of Globalization

Contrary to frequently held beliefs there is much to be said for the new global order. It is not all bad news. Advocates of the spread of globalization point to the opportunities closer interaction and interdependence between people from all over the world has brought. In offering us a list of the benefits an intertwined world brings, Philippe Legrain concludes: "Globalization has the potential to do immense good."[85] Greater effectiveness and efficiencies have been derived helping to protect some of the most vulnerable of society. For instance, global institutions, such as Oxfam, have addressed problems of rural development more effectively than state programs. Globalization is adding to the spread of more democratic governments and helping sustain the legitimacy of those newly created.[86] Despite the continued need for better management of foreign aid in addressing the health and geographic challenges of marginalized countries, aid has brought assistance to millions of people in desperate situations. Global pressure has led to the international landmines treaty.[87] Global markets have created more opportunities for women to enter employment raising their recognition in some societies. These are all positive outcomes of globalization.[88]

Advances brought by globalization have led to increased prosperity not only for individuals, but also for the wealth of nations. Flows of goods, capital, and information have allowed poorer countries to use modern technology in local production and public services. National governments have benefited from greater global integration due to increased tax revenues from the operations of MNCs. Benefits of this kind that can be realized are reflected in a recent worldwide poll that discovered views of globalization are distinctly more positive in low-income countries than in rich ones. For example, in sub-Saharan Africa 75 percent of households believed that MNCs were a positive influence in their country, compared to only 54 percent in rich countries. Why these views are expressed, claims David

---

[85] Legrain, *Open World*, 12.

[86] Merilee S. Grindle, "Ready or Not: The Developing World and Globalization," in *Governance in a Globalizing World*, 178.

[87] See Michael Bond, "The Backlash Against NGOs," in *The Globalization Reader*, ed. Frank J. Lechner and John Boli, 2nd edn (Malden, MA: Blackwell, 2004), 277.

[88] For a further comprehensive account of the positive benefits a globalized world brings, see Martin Wolf, *Why Globalization Works* (New Haven: Yale University Press, 2004).

Dollar, is due to the fact that the fast-growing economies of today are those of developing countries that are aggressively integrating with the world economy.[89]

In a study prepared by the World Bank, the opportunities presented by globalization were highlighted, providing a degree of justification as to why globalization is perceived in such a positive light in many developing countries. It was reported that twenty-four developing countries, which increased their integration into the world economy over two decades ending in the late 1990s, achieved higher growth in incomes, longer life expectancy, and better schooling. These countries, home to some three billion people, enjoyed an average 5 percent growth rate in income per capita in the 1990s compared to 2 percent in rich countries. The report describes how many of these countries, such as Brazil, China, India, Hungary, and Mexico, have adopted domestic policies and institutions that have enabled people to take advantage of global markets and hence have sharply increased the share of trade in their GDP.[90] This therefore does appear to lend support to Legrain's claim that "globalization offers a richer life – in the broadest sense – for people in rich countries and the only realistic route out of poverty for the world's poor."[91]

Yet this is not the whole account of globalization. While globalization has been a force for poverty reduction in some parts of the world, social consequences have resulted from uncontrolled market processes, which are not always benign in all their effects, and may have profound disruptive consequences.[92] Merilee Grindle notes the inherent dangers that globalization can bring: "In worst case scenarios, globalization has the potential to cause economic dislocation, destruction of important social safety nets, accelerated environmental damage, loss of cultural identities, increased conflict, and the spread of disease and crime."[93] Those most at risk are the poorest of society, which are those who lack power in the developing nations of the world. This is reflected in the growing worldwide divide resulting in many living in dire poverty while others live in comparative luxury. Today only 22 percent of global wealth belongs to developing countries, which account for 80 percent of the world's population.[94] The extent of the problem is brought home further in that it is estimated by the World Bank that 1.1 billion people live on less than $1 a day - equivalent to about one-fifth of the world's population living in extreme poverty. Added to this figure, it is calculated that 2.7 billion people continue to live on less than $2 a day.[95]

---

[89] David Dollar, "The Poor Like Globalization," *Yale Global Online* (June 2003). This report summarizes the findings of the poll undertaken by the Pew Global Attitude Survey. Of the 38,000 people in 44 nations surveyed, those in the developing world generally blamed their local governments for their country's ills rather than globalization.

[90] Dollar and Collier (ed.), *Globalization, Growth, and Poverty*, 5.

[91] Legrain, *Open World*, 24.

[92] R. J. Barry Jones, *The World Turned Upside Down?: Globalization and the Future of the State* (Manchester: Manchester University Press, 2000), 231.

[93] Grindle, "Ready or Not," 178-179.

[94] Bauman, *Globalization*, 70-71.

[95] James D. Wolfensohn, "*Fighting Poverty for Peace*," which was a report presented by the former President of the World Bank on 29 December 2003. Cf. World Commission on the

In the same report highlighting the benefits brought by globalization, the World Bank provides empirical evidence to demonstrate that not all countries have integrated successfully into the global economy. There is a disturbing global trend of the past two decades in which developing countries with a combined population of about two billion people, particularly in sub-Saharan Africa, the Middle East, and the former Soviet Union, are in danger of becoming marginalized in the world economy. In these countries incomes have been falling, poverty has been rising, and they participate less in trade today than they did twenty years ago. These countries have been unable to increase their integration with the world economy, which has meant that their ratio of trade to GDP either remained flat or actually declined. On average, the World Bank reports these economies have contracted, poverty has risen, and education levels have risen less rapidly than in the more globalized countries.[96] What this highlights, as David Smith points out, is that for a significant number of people in the world, globalization is not working. Rather than creating a homogenized world where differences are being overcome, globalization is resulting in new forms of social and economic division on a worldwide scale.[97]

Within the countries that are being marginalized in the integration of the global economy, there is typically a dire need for good delivery of education and health services. This exposes the basic problem that if people living in poverty have little or no access to health and education services, then it is extremely hard for them to benefit from the opportunities presented by globalization.[98] Desperately poor people are heavily preoccupied simply with the struggle to survive. This is reflected in an analysis of underdevelopment in the developing world undertaken by Howard Handelman, who claims that the most salient characteristic of these countries is their poverty.[99] Poverty has such a damaging effect not only for the people suffering, but also due to the environmental destruction that is caused, exacerbating the problem of poverty for future generations. Such is the nature of the vicious cycle of poverty in many developing countries. As parents rely on their children to support them in old age this leads to overpopulation. In turn overpopulation leads to malnourishment as well as the consumption and eventual destruction of any available food.

Because of these poverty levels, René Padilla claims that a secularist capitalist system is being globalized, which is "almost totally oriented to the accumulation of

---

Social Dimension of Globalization, *A Fair Globalization: Creating Opportunities for All* (Geneva: ILO, 2004). The report team summarize their findings: "Seen through the eyes of the vast majority of men and women, globalization has not met their simple and legitimate aspirations for decent jobs and a better future for their children" (x).

[96] Dollar and Collier (ed.), *Globalization, Growth, and Poverty*, 6-7.

[97] David Smith, *Mission After Christendom* (London: Darton, Longman & Todd, 2003), 94.

[98] See Dollar and Collier (ed.), *Globalization, Growth, and Poverty*, 19.

[99] Howard Handelman, *The Challenge of Third World Development* (Upper Saddle River, N.J.: Prentice Hall, 1996), 3.

wealth rather than to the satisfaction of basic human needs."[100] Yet although from our analysis of the forces driving globalization there is a degree of truth that the accrual of wealth is an over-riding concern for those who hold power, market forces can also bring benefits to society. For as we have seen the dynamics of a global market economic system does have the potential to benefit those living in poverty and in meeting their basic human needs.[101] Michael Novak, who seeks to demonstrate the economic benefits of capitalism, albeit somewhat overoptimistically, claims that of all the systems of political economy that have shaped world history, "none has so revolutionized ordinary expectations of human life – lengthened the life span, made the elimination of poverty and famine thinkable, enlarged the range of human choice – as democratic capitalism."[102] Arguing that MNCs provide an opportunity for great good, Novak claims: "Governments all around the world, especially the developing countries, are queuing up to attract multinationals."[103] Despite these positive assertions, however, what is undisputable as Padilla highlights is that there are both winners and losers from globalization in its current form.

Thus although many of the countries experiencing extreme poverty also suffer from debilitating problems such as being prone to disease, conflict, corruption, and poor governance, few would argue that globalization has impacted negatively upon many people living in these countries. Dollar comments: "It is increasingly clear that while this integration brings benefits, it also requires complementary institutions and policies in order to enhance the gains and cushion some of the risks of greater openness."[104] Coupled with this need to create the institutions and policies to help reduce the adverse effects of globalization, as Jagdish Bhagwati points out, is the requirement to assess the speed at which globalization is pursued.[105] These are challenges that must be overcome if the world's poorest and weakest citizens are to share in the benefits brought by a globalized world.

The Transforming Nature of Nation-States

Intrinsic to the contemporary issue of globalization is that this phenomenon is not simply a new economic dynamic, as is frequently perceived, but involves all facets

---

[100] René Padilla, "Mission at the Turn of the Century/ Millennium," *Evangel* (Spring 2001), 6-12.

[101] See for example, The Economist, "Poverty and Inequality: A Question of Justice?" *The Economist* (13 March 2004), 14.

[102] Michael Novak, *The Spirit of Democratic Capitalism* (Lanham, Maryland: Madison Books, 1991), 13. For a further theological discussion of the economy, see D. Stephen Long, *Divine Economy: Theology and the Market* (London: Routledge, 2000); Donald A. Hay, *Economics Today: A Christian Critique* (Leicester : Apollos, 1989); and J. Philip Wogaman, *Economics and Ethics: A Christian Enquiry* (London: SCM Press, 1986).

[103] Novak, "Toward a Theology of the Corporation," 785.

[104] Dollar, "The Poor Like Globalization."

[105] Jagdish Bhagwati, *In Defense of Globalization* (Oxford: Oxford University Press, 2004), 34-35.

of political and societal life. Growing integration of economies and societies across the globe has not only brought change to individuals' prosperity levels, but has brought unprecedented change to the contemporary world order. For this new global marketplace is exerting an inexorable force upon the dynamics within individual nation-states. An evaluation of how nation-states traditionally operated supports this conclusion, which prior to the advent of globalization as it is recognized today, was chiefly organized on the basis of the so-called Westphalian system. It is a framework of governance derived from the Peace of Westphalia in 1648.

How the world came to be organized into sovereign states is discussed by Daniel Philpott in *Revolutions and Sovereignty*, in which he presents a powerful case for the central role of ideas, and especially religious ideas, in how the world was shaped into a system of sovereign states. Philpott's core thesis is: "Revolutions in sovereignty result from prior revolutions in ideas about justice and political authority."[106] Central to his argument, two historical ideas are perceived as being responsible for how the world came to be organized into sovereign states. First, the Protestant Reformation ended medieval Christendom and brought a system of sovereign states in Europe. Philpott declares: "Sovereignty, in substance if not in name, comes directly out of the very propositions of Protestant theology, in all of its variants."[107] Second, ideas of equality and colonial nationalism brought to an end the colonial empires around 1960, which spread the sovereign state system to the rest of the globe. It was this new constitution of international society, consummated through the 1960 United Nations (UN) declaration on colonial independence, which "was the terminus of the long campaign of the state to capture the territory of the globe."[108] Philpott comments upon the impact of the sovereign state system post-Westphalia:

> What is remarkable about this form of polity, the sovereign state, is how thoroughly it spread. Westphalia began and colonial independence completed an unprecedented feat – the extension of the sovereign state to the entire land surface of the globe. It is the only form of polity in history to attain such universality. The two revolutions in sovereignty, as diverse as they may be, form a common story, a single movement that culminated in this exceptional state of affairs.[109]

The system of sovereign states was a system that provided a means of formulating, implementing, monitoring, and enforcing rules within a particular nation. Principles of statehood and sovereignty were at the centre of this mode of governance. Sovereignty is thus an essential feature of statehood and is to be defined, states Philpott, as "supreme authority within a territory."[110] With the Westphalian system, statehood meant the world was divided into different territories,

---

[106] Daniel Philpott, *Revolutions in Sovereignty: How Ideas Shaped Modern International Relations* (Princeton: Princeton University Press, 2001), 4.

[107] Ibid., 108.

[108] Ibid., 153.

[109] Ibid., 255.

[110] Ibid., 16.

and a separate government ruled each territory. This has typically been the case post-Westphalian era, where "constitutions of international society have bestowed sovereignty upon the state while leaving open the question of who holds sovereignty within the state."[111] This concept of the state as being supreme within its borders meant that it was to remain independent from outside interference, and was deemed to be sovereign in its affairs. Philpott illustrates the pervasiveness of this form of government: "The sovereign state, a polity in which a single authority reigns supreme over a people within a bounded territory, is the only form of political organization ever to cover the entire land surface of the globe."[112] Jan Aart Scholte supports this description of government post-Westphalia in which the nation-state "exercised comprehensive, supreme, unqualified and exclusive control over its designated territorial domain."[113]

With the rise of globalization, however, the Westphalian norm of sovereignty is in the midst of another transformation. Annan makes this point clear: "State sovereignty, in its most basic sense, is being redefined – not least by the forces of globalization and international co-operation."[114] Shapiro and Brilmayer lend support to this analysis of the changing nature and role of the nation-state:

> We are evolving toward a world in which authorities and jurisdictions overlap in increasingly complex and intricate ways, perhaps more like Europe before the rise of the nation-state system and less like the world most of us have known in the twentieth century.[115]

The ramifications of these adjustments, James Rosenau argues, is that nation-states are no longer the sole centres or the principal forms of governance or authority in the world.[116] Governments do not now exercise total and exclusive authority over a specified territorial domain. For in today's world, clearly demarcated territorial borders do not separate jurisdictions. The extent of this phenomenon is evident in that of the one hundred largest economies in the world today over half are run by MNCs and less than half are nation-states.[117] A key factor in this new role of the

---

[111] Ibid., 19. Philpott highlights two exceptions to the sovereignty of nation-states. These are the impact of the European Union and the United Nations, which "show that the state is not the only possible holder of sovereignty, nor is its sovereignty necessarily absolute."

[112] Daniel Philpott, "The Ethics of Boundaries: A Question of Partial Commitments," in *Boundaries and Justice: Diverse Ethical Perspectives*, ed. David Miller and Sohail H. Hashmi (Princeton: Princeton University Press, 2001), 335.

[113] Jan Aart Scholte, "The Globalization of World Politics," in *The Globalization of World Politics*, 20.

[114] Kofi A. Annan, "Two Concepts of Sovereignty," *The Economist* (18 September 1999), 81.

[115] Shapiro and Brilmayer, "Introduction," 2.

[116] James N. Rosenau, *Along the Domestic-Foreign Frontier: Exploring Governance in a Turbulent World* (Cambridge: Cambridge University Press, 1997).

[117] Hertz, *The Silent Takeover*, 7.

state, as Philip Cerny notes, lies in the changes brought by economic competition.[118] Presenting a graphic image of these existing realities, Beck declares: "A globally disorganized capitalism is continually spreading out."[119] Yet despite the demise of sovereignty of the nation-state, Strange argues that heads of governments are some of the last people to recognize that they have lost the authority they formerly had.[120]

Along with the transforming forces of globalization, Rosenau argues that people are unsettled by the realization that deep changes are unfolding in every sphere of life. Concerns are raised due to the fact that events in any part of the world can have consequences for developments in every other part of the world. With the sovereignty and boundaries of nation-states becoming increasingly porous, the world has moved into a period of extraordinary complexity.[121] Yet although globalization has led to the transcending of borders, this does not mean it has augured the demise of the nation-state itself, as is mistakenly claimed by hyperglobalizers. Rather, it is more accurate to say that the role of the nation-state is changing and transforming power relations are becoming integral to the shaping of the new global order. It is these power transformations and the implications for global justice that presents new challenges to the socio-political mission of the church in the twenty-first century.

Power and the Contemporary Global Order

With the transformation of power among non-territorial forms of authority in the new global order, the form and functions of the state are being forced to adapt and develop coherent strategies in response to these changes. This has resulted in the development of regional and global organizations and institutions, and the emergence of regional and global law. Robert Keohane and Joseph Nye describe the effect of this change in *Power and Interdependence*, in which they claim that the link between effective government, self-government, and a bounded territory is being broken. The authors begin their widely acclaimed work by stating categorically: "We live in an era of interdependence."[122] Existing now are complex networks of political power at both the regional and global levels; Keohane and Nye thus coin the term "complex interdependence" for understanding world politics.[123] Because it is an inherently multidimensional phenomenon, what is criticized is a definition of globalization in strictly economic terms "as if the world economy defined globalism."[124]

---

[118] Philip G. Cerny, "What Next for the State?" in *Globalization: Theory and Practice*, ed. Eleonore Kofman and Gillian Youngs (London: Pinter, 1996), 124.

[119] Beck, *What is Globalization?* 13.

[120] Strange, *The Retreat of the State*, 3.

[121] James N. Rosenau, "Governance in a New Global Order," in *Governing Globalization*, 70.

[122] Robert O. Keohane and Joseph S. Nye, *Power and Interdependence*, 3rd edn (New York: Longman, 2001), 3.

[123] Ibid., 20.

[124] Ibid., 230.

It can no longer be presupposed that the locus of effective political power is synonymous with national governments and the nation-state. The contemporary nation-state now finds itself at the intersection of a vast array of international regimes and organizations that have been established to manage issues of collective global policy. Even if it were desired, globalization has advanced to such an extent that opting out of the processes of greater global interdependence is not a realistic option for national governments. As Ciaran Cronin and Pablo de Greiff state, were nation-states to pursue isolationist policies, this would effectively mean self-imposed exclusion from the process of shaping an increasingly pervasive global order.[125]

With the changing nature of the nation-state, a distinctive feature of the state is that it now advances transborder as well as national causes, leading to more frequent and intensive multilateral consultations among different countries in addressing transborder issues. For example, the Group of 8 (G8), which is comprised of Canada, France, Germany, Italy, Japan, Russia, the United Kingdom, and the United States of America, have met frequently since the mid-1970s to seek to coordinate policy, particularly on macro-economic issues.[126] Greater interaction between national governments has, however, led to the marginalizing of much of the world's populations, as people do not have equal opportunities to participate in global relations. There is also a concern of a narrow elite holding control of a country's future, resulting in the exploitation of those who lack power, which raises critical moral issues for the global order and global governance in the twenty-first century.

Of significance as to how globalization is managed are the developed nations of the world and various international institutions and corporations.[127] Currently the three main institutions that govern globalization are the IMF, the World Bank, and the WTO. All three institutions, though, have come under much criticism. Peter Singer states: "If there is one organization that critics of globalization point to as responsible for pushing the process onward—and in the wrong way—it is the World Trade Organization."[128] In his analysis of the criticisms directed against the WTO, Singer identifies four main charges. First, the WTO places economic considerations ahead of all other concerns. Second, the WTO erodes national sovereignty. Third,

---

[125] Ciaran Cronin and Pablo De Greiff, *Global Justice and Transnational Politics: Essays on the Moral and Political Challenges of Globalization* (Cambridge, Mass.: MIT Press, 2002), 3. Cf. Wolf, *Why Globalization Works*, 194-199. In rejecting "localization," Wolf states: "This attempt to fragment markets – the global into the regional, the regional into the national and the national into the local – raises three questions: the first is why anybody would regard this as a sensible idea; the second is how, in practice, it could be done; and the third is why anybody would consider the consequences for economic security, prosperity, the environment and development to be desirable" (195).

[126] Russia joined the G7 in 1998, making it the G8.

[127] In our communications, Dunning pointed out that along with the responsibilities of supranational entities, likewise, individuals, firms, NGOs and national governments have a critical role to play in ensuring the transformation process is both efficient and just.

[128] Peter Singer, *One World: The Ethics of Globalization* (New Haven: Yale University Press, 2002), 51.

the WTO is undemocratic. Fourth, the WTO increases inequality by making the rich richer and leaving the world's poorest people even worse off than they would otherwise have been.[129] Tony Clarke endorses some of these criticisms and argues that the WTO provided "the mechanisms for accelerating and extending the transfer of peoples' sovereignty from nation-states to global corporations."[130]

The influence of power is evident due to poor countries not having the same share of representatives or expertise at the WTO meetings compared to well-funded nations such as the United States of America and the European Union. For as Philip McMichael asserts, the WTO is not a state, but "a disembodied executive." The key crisis facing the WTO, he argues, centres on the issue of representation and ultimately that of power. McMichael continues his attack: "Comprised of member states, the WTO not only instrumentalizes the competitive and hierarchical relations among those states, but it also denies full representation from civil society."[131] Hertz claims that the cumulative result of these international negotiations is a highly uneven and unfair global economic system in which the interests of the global poor are not given a high priority.[132] It is a system where the developed nations of the world reap the benefits of global economic growth at the expense of those nations that lack power.

Barry Jones exposes the dangers caused by this erosion of the capacities of states without the emergence of their functional equivalents at regional and global level. If state-based governance is insufficient for the new global economy, then "a serious vacuum threatens to emerge at the heart of the global system."[133] There is a risk that other agencies will impose themselves upon the world stage, or may be forced to assume responsibilities for which they are not prepared.[134] The absence of such coercive institutions to create international justice, claims Brian Barry and Matt Matravers, has meant that the populations of rich countries have had "little self-interested motivation" to correct the situations that have arisen due to the abuse of power.[135] Cronin and de Greiff concur with these sentiments, and declare that a world characterized by increasing interdependence is one in which theorizing about politics and justice cannot be pursued exclusively in the traditional state-centric

---

[129] Ibid., 55.

[130] Tony Clarke, *By What Authority!: Unmasking and Challenging the Global Corporations' Assault on Democracy through the World Trade Organization* (Ottawa: Polaris Institute/ International Forum on Globalization, 1999), 14. And yet as Singer points out in *One World*, that is not in itself grounds for condemning the WTO. The loss of national sovereignty might be a price worth paying for the benefits the WTO brings. (73-74).

[131] Philip McMichael, "Sleepless Since Seattle: What is the WTO About?" *Review of International Political Economy*, vol. 7/3 (Autumn 2000), 467.

[132] Hertz, *The Silent Takeover*, 83-85.

[133] Jones, *The World Turned Upside Down?* 209.

[134] Ibid., 114.

[135] Brian Barry and Matt Matravers, "Justice, International," in *Routledge Encyclopedia of Philosophy*, vol. 5, 156.

fashion. Instead, "it calls for deliberation about the appropriate interpretation and institutional realization of democracy and justice at the transnational level."[136]

Furthermore, the challenge this contemporary issue brings to theologians is in articulating a biblically based response to the transformations taking place in the socio-political arena. Jonathan Sacks asserts that there is a danger of succumbing to the temptation in the face of challenges as complicated as those presented by globalization to abdicate responsibility to experts. Yet none of us can stand aside from critical reflection on what is happening as a result of the interconnectedness and fragility of the global age. Faced with these challenges, Sacks claims, great responsibility now lies with the world's religious communities. Yet we must do more than simply protest against injustice, for "protest is only a prelude to, not a substitute for, nuanced argument and the building of consensus between conflicting interests."[137]

Indeed, in addressing this complex contemporary issue, Sacks is surely correct that the challenge for the church, in being a community defined by grace, is not only to provide a critique of globalization, but also to develop an informed and respected voice. Specifically, there is a need for robust theological scholarship to engage with this phenomenon and the challenges it presents for issues of global justice in the twenty-first century world.

Conclusion

In this chapter we have evaluated the three primary schools of thought in the globalization debate, and have discovered that power is embedded within the process of globalization. The exercise of power is transforming the role of nation-states with profound implications for the new global order. Although there are undeniably significant benefits to be gained from these global transformations, there are also pressing challenges to be confronted, which have been highlighted by the increasing gap between the rich and poor across the globe. The underlying problem of much of these adverse effects of a globalized world is the abuse of power, and the exploitation of those who do not hold the same levels of power. Accordingly, in its current form, globalization is a system that must be changed. The task presented to the church is how it interprets its thoughts and policies in response to this multidimensional phenomenon. That is the theological task we will now turn to in our next chapter.

---

[136] Cronin and Greiff, *Global Justice and Transnational Politics*, 29.

[137] Jonathan Sacks, *The Dignity of Difference: How to Avoid the Clash of Civilizations* (London: Continuum, 2002), 16-17.

CHAPTER 7

Grace and Agents of Justice in a Globalized World

In being a community defined by grace, how is the church to conceive of its mission in a globalized world? That is the final task we will seek to address in this study. Orientated to practical considerations, this chapter will unfold in two parts. First, as it is our desire to contribute to interdisciplinary discussions in developing an informed response to globalization, we engage initially with international political theory and the growing influence of cosmopolitan theories of justice.[1] This chapter begins, therefore, by looking at what a straightforwardly secular analysis of globalization looks like, and assesses whether the questions raised are the right ones. Second, we shall then evaluate the implications for the church's social and political witness in an age of globalization, moving from considerations of international ethics to explicitly theological ethics. By integrating the theological insights derived from Jürgen Moltmann's, Stanley Hauerwas', and Oliver O'Donovan's distinctive political theologies we will seek to bring the concerns of this study into practical focus.

Introduction

Globalization in its current form must be reshaped. This is the oft-repeated message coming from leaders who have been instrumental in the management of globalization in recent years.[2] But the question that then subsequently arises is: how exactly should globalization be reshaped? And furthermore, what precisely are the criteria that we will use for determining our response to the pressing challenges of global justice brought by the world's increasing interdependence and integration?

How we come to answer these fundamental questions vis-à-vis global justice in a globalized society will depend on whether we hold to a purely secular worldview, or whether our thinking is shaped by acknowledging the priority of God's gracious self-revelation and the attendant imperatives of human response to the divine work.

---

[1] International political theory is the name given to the intertwining of ethics and world politics.

[2] For example, see Department of Trade and Industry, *Making Globalization a Force for Good*; and Lael Brainard and Vinca LaFleur, *America's Role in the Fight Against Global Poverty: A Project of the Richard C. Blum Roundtable* (July 2004). This latter publication follows a meeting of forty leaders from the public, private, and non-profit sectors, including Al Gore, Mary Robinson, George Soros, and Kumi Naidoo, who sought to explore the issue of global poverty in the contemporary world.

When we come to consider notions of justice in world politics, we find that there is a wide variety of social, political, and moral thought in the context of international affairs. Making sense of these different positions is therefore a prerequisite in understanding how such debates illuminate the moral framing of world politics. Yet in approaching questions of justice in a globalized society from a straightforwardly secular position, this brings with it not insignificant weaknesses. These failings become increasingly apparent when we consider the differing perspectives held of human rights and an understanding of how these rights shape critical decision-making in contemporary world affairs.

But what expressly is the impact for the "holistic" mission of the body of Christ, this community of grace, in being confronted with the increasingly complex and multidimensional challenges inherent in an interconnected world? In contrast to a purely secular approach to questions of international ethics, when we turn to questions of theological ethics rooted in a theology of grace, we find a clear mandate for the mission of the church in the specific context of a globalized world. For if the Christian community is to conceive of itself as a community defined by the covenant of grace, the church is challenged not only with understanding the dynamics of this multifaceted reality, but is presented with a vision of being an agent of God's justice in the transforming socio-political arena. For in addition to traditional discussions surrounding social justice in biblical and theological debate, the transforming global order and its impact upon the sovereignty of nation-states, presents Christians, as members of this grace-defined counter-cultural community, with the opportunity of serving as a unique voice for the marginalized of contemporary society. It will achieve this aim through being an integral influence in the decision-making process as to the shaping of the future direction of globalization in seeking to achieve greater global justice in the ever-more interdependent world of the twenty-first century.

International Political Theory and Global Justice

Recognizing the Need for an "Ethical Globalization"[3]

Critics of globalization are not hard to find. One of the most outspoken and influential of these critics is Joseph Stiglitz, who was previously the chairman of the Council of Economic Advisers under President Clinton. Stiglitz argues the imperative for there to be a radical change of direction if the adverse effects of globalization are not to be repeated in the future. It is not just a question of changing institutional structures. Rather, the mindset around globalization itself must change. For the problem is not with globalization, but with how it has been managed. In his widely acclaimed work *Globalization and its Discontents*, Stiglitz declares:

---

[3] In a speech delivered by Mary Robinson, former UN High Commissioner on Human Rights, entitled *"Building an Ethical Globalization,"* at Yale University on 8 October 2002, she claimed that one of the most important questions facing the world today is "how do we build an ethical globalization which bridges the current divides between north and south, rich and poor, secular and religious?"

If globalization continues to be conducted in the way that it has been in the past, if we continue to fail to learn from our mistakes, globalization will not only not succeed in promoting development but will continue to create poverty and instability.[4]

Stiglitz's comments reflect a growing recognition of the need to develop an "ethical globalization." In becoming more aware of the acute impact globalization can have on the powerless of society, national governments, business corporations, academic institutions, and religious groups are recognizing that globalization is fast becoming the key agenda that must be analyzed and understood in terms of its transforming effects upon the peoples of the world. For example, James Wolfensohn, former President of the World Bank states: "We are convinced that globalization can and does contribute to development, but we cannot ignore those who are left out, nor can we fail to recognize how much better development progress could be."[5] Similarly, William Schweiker ponders over this heightened recognition in the academy and in the wider society: "The fact of world poverty raises profound questions of distributive justice. Little wonder, then, that from the papacy to Wall Street there has been intense concern about and reflection on the moral, political, and economic features of global developments."[6] Global economic inequality has indeed increased at a rapid pace. Ian Shapiro and Lea Brilmayer describe this particular concern of globalization:

Globalization has done little, if anything, to promote justice, if this is understood to require substantial redistribution from rich to poor. The world's few wealthiest countries continue to control and consume the vast bulk of its resources while billions live below the poverty line.[7]

Specifically, the challenge presented for those who shape public policy is to capture a vision of global justice in the twenty-first century. For global justice and global order are inextricably intertwined. But as we will discover in this chapter, how we approach questions of justice will differ markedly according to the extent to which our deliberations are rooted in an understanding of divine grace, or whether they are driven by purely secular considerations. Furthermore, this opportunity of developing a vision of global justice has regrettably been missed in how globalization has been managed so far, as Stiglitz points out:

---

[4] Stiglitz, *Globalization and Its Discontents*, 248.

[5] James D. Wolfensohn, "Global Links," in *2002 World Development Indicators* (Washington D.C.: World Bank, 2002), 331. Cf. Ethan B. Kapstein, "Does Globalization have an Ethical Problem?" in *Ethics and International Affairs: Extent and Limits*, ed. Jean-Marc Coicaud and Daniel Warner (New York: United Nations University Press, 2001). Ethan Kapstein declares: "Globalization can only be welfare enhancing when it promotes the life chances of all members of the international community" (262).

[6] William Schweiker, "Responsibility in the World of Mammon: Theology, Justice, and Transnational Corporations," in *God and Globalization*, vol. 1, 105-106.

[7] Shapiro and Brilmayer, "Introduction," 2.

The end of the Cold War opened up new opportunities to try to create a new, global economic order – a global economic order that was based more on a set of principles, on ideology, on ideas of social justice...We missed that opportunity. I think most people – policy makers, academics and most of the public alike – did not have a clear enough vision of what we wanted or what should have been created.[8]

Dominant among the concerns of our globalized world is the marginalizing of the powerless, which has led to a situation of vulnerability to exploitation by those who do have power. Jonathan Sacks captures well this predicament, and argues that the economics and politics of globalization have an inescapable moral dimension. Sacks comments: "Markets serve those who pay, but what of those who cannot pay? Politics is about the balance of power, but what of those who have no power?"[9] Although markets are the best way we know of structuring exchanges, such as goods to be bought or sold, Sacks maintains "they are far from the best way of ordering relationships or preserving goods whose value is not identical with their price. Inevitably, societies face choices that cannot be resolved by economics alone."[10]

In tackling the adverse effects of globalization, a quandary to be overcome derives from people in the West living in extreme isolation from severe poverty. Thomas Pogge draws our attention to this reality and argues forcefully that our global economic order has adapted to make us appear disconnected from massive poverty abroad. Our insulated world "surrounds us with affluent, civilized people for whom the poor abroad are a remote good cause alongside the spotted owl."[11] One of Pogge's most striking claims is that most rich people are not merely failing to help those who are in desperate need, but are actually responsible for grave injustices. The present global economic order is unethical precisely because of its role in perpetuating inequality. But in this world of disconnection from extreme poverty, Pogge states:

> The thought that we are involved in a monumental crime against these people, that we must fight to stop their dying and suffering, will appear so cold, so strained, and ridiculous, that we cannot find it in our heart to reflect on it any farther.[12]

Although Pogge is undoubtedly correct that people in the West are to a large extent shielded from severe poverty, globalization is today being challenged throughout the world. Revealing this desire to see change occur, Kofi Annan, the UN Secretary-General, encouraged business leaders to join an international initiative entitled a "Global Compact." This initiative would take the form of partnerships between businesses, international organizations, and governments in addressing the

---

[8] Stiglitz, *"Future of Globalization."*

[9] Sacks, *The Dignity of Difference*, 4.

[10] Ibid., 88.

[11] Thomas W. Pogge, *World Poverty and Human Rights: Cosmopolitan Responsibilities and Reforms* (Cambridge: Polity Press, 2002), 26.

[12] Ibid.

adverse effects of globalization.[13] Why such initiatives are being introduced is that despite globalization making life more pleasant for those with the resources to benefit from this phenomenon, significant segments of the world's population do not have the resources to maximize the opportunities presented. On the contrary, the functioning of the globalized economy would appear to have further impoverished many people.

Recognition of the need for a global ethic was evident in a public address given by Bill Clinton, former President of the United States of America in 2003. In stating that our interdependence is more than economic, he stressed that for all of its promise, the interdependent world is unsustainable because it is unstable. We cannot continue to live in a world of increasing interdependence, while not having an over-arching system to have the positive elements outweigh the negative ones. Building systems for developing countries is required that will enable them to build sustainable economies within their borders. In confronting this state of affairs, Clinton presents a challenge as to what is our vision of the twenty-first century world. His own view is that "the great mission of the twenty-first century world is to make it a genuine global community." This will involve moving from mere interdependence to comprehensive integration, which means sharing the benefits of an interdependent world.[14]

Expecting us to be the people we think we are, Peter Singer shares this growing sentiment of the necessity for the ethical management of an interconnected world.

---

[13] A speech delivered by Kofi A. Annan, entitled "Global Compact," at the World Economic Forum in Davos on 31 January 1999. For a critical examination of the UN Global Compact, see Diane Elson, "Human Rights and Corporate Profits: The UN Global Compact – Part of the Solution or Part of the Problem?" in *Global Tensions*, 45-64. Various other suggestions have been put forward. For example, see Dollar and Collier (ed.), *Globalization, Growth, and Poverty*, 18-22. Seven areas for action in helping to address issues of injustice in a globalized world are identified: a development round of trade negotiations; improving the investment climate in developing countries; good delivery of education and health services; social protection tailored to the more dynamic labour market in an open economy; greater volume of foreign aid, better managed; debt relief; and tackling greenhouse gases and global warming. Cf. Beck, *What is Globalization?* 129-155; Legrain, *Open World*, 320-334; and the three articles in *Ethics and International Affairs*, vol. 17/1 (April 2003) under the heading "Achieving Global Economic Justice, " namely: Vivien Collingwood, "Assistance with Fewer Strings Attached," 55-68; Ngaire Woods, "Holding Intergovernmental Institutions to Account," 69-80; and Sanjay G. Reddy, "Developing Just Monetary Arrangements," 81-93. The need for dealing justly with debt is reviewed further in Ann Pettifor, "Resolving International Debt Crises Fairly," *Ethics and International Affairs*, vol. 17/2 (October 2003), 2-9. For a more radical alternative to globalization, see John Cavanagh, et al., *Alternatives to Economic Globalization* (San Francisco, CA: Berrett-Koehler, 2002).

[14] A speech delivered by William J. Clinton, entitled "*Global Challenges*," at Yale University on 31 October 2003. Cf. Gordon Brown, "Governments and Supranational Agencies: A New Consensus? in *Making Globalization Good*, 320-333. Gordon Brown, the UK Chancellor of the Exchequer shares these sentiments, and argues that for global prosperity to be sustained, it has to be fairly shared.

Instead of looking back on the Westphalian era with nostalgia, "we should be developing the ethical foundations of the coming era of a single world community."[15] Developing a suitable form of government for this century, he asserts, "is a daunting moral and intellectual challenge, but one we cannot refuse to take up."[16] Such a challenge has indeed raised fundamental questions vis-à-vis issues of justice and world politics. We will now consider how these questions are being answered from a secular standpoint, before turning our attention in the next part of this chapter to how the church as a community of grace can respond to the phenomenon of globalization.

The Question of Justice

Throughout history, people have debated the question of justice. It is a central question of all life in society, as Serge-Christophe Kolm notes: "Facing the question of justice is in fact a condition for the very existence of a society."[17] But it is a debate that has often led to intractable positions as Duncan Forrester also points out:

> Knowing what justice is and doing justice are inherently and deeply problematic. Human beings have an in-built propensity to distort ideas of justice and manipulate them so that they are compatible with our interests and desires, and, at the extreme, disguise our selfishness and exploitation as morally acceptable.[18]

In the context of international political theory, as also in other contexts, the word *justice* has been perceived to derive from the Latin *iustitia*, which is interpreted as pertaining to a juridical concept concerned with authoritative rules and rights and with the duties derived from them. As such, Terry Nardin declares that in society, "conduct that disregards moral or legal limits is open to the charge of being unjust."[19] Brian Barry and Matt Matravers elaborate on this conception, and claim that in the history of thought about justice, appeal has been made to an external, usually divine authority for justifying a given set of laws or practices. In the natural law tradition, though, in order to claim that an act is just it is not enough that it complies with the society's positive law. The positive law must itself be in accordance with a natural law, which is knowable through the faculty of human

---

[15] Singer, *One World*, 197-198.

[16] Ibid., 200-201. Cf. Ian Clark, "Globalization and the Post-Cold War Order," in *The Globalization of World Politics*, 645. Ian Clark calls for "a globalized international order."

[17] Serge-Christophe Kolm, *Modern Theories of Justice* (Cambridge, Mass.: The MIT Press, 1998), 4.

[18] Forrester, *Christian Justice and Public Policy*, 1. Cf. E. Clinton Gardner, *Justice and Christian Ethics* (Cambridge: Cambridge University Press, 1995), 1. Clinton Gardner declares: "Justice is the fundamental moral requirement of human life in community."

[19] Terry Nardin, *Law, Morality, and the Relations of States* (Princeton: Princeton University Press, 1983), 257.

reason.[20] Thus not only does this comprehension of justice fail to begin with God; the Enlightenment vision of a morality grounded in reason would appear to be an illusion in our pluralistic world.

It is precisely this question of how to make sense of justice in a global context which is at the centre of current political and philosophical debates. As we have seen in our analysis of the dynamics of globalization, the issue of justice in world politics has been brought to prominence due to the marginalizing of the powerless in our increasingly interconnected world. Pogge highlights this intertwined relationship between power and justice, and argues that issues of justice are "associated with the morally appropriate and, in particular, equitable treatment of persons and groups."[21] International political theory, therefore, has become keenly concerned in assessing how the exercise of power can be subordinated to the imperative of global justice.

Debates concerning issues of justice flourished in the latter decades of the twentieth century. The *locus classicus* of these debates was John Rawls' *A Theory of Justice*, in which his stated aim is to provide considered judgments of justice that "constitutes the most appropriate moral basis for a democratic society."[22] Highly influential for international political theorists in debating principles of justice as it relates to a globalized society, Rawls presents a liberal, egalitarian, moral conception of "justice as fairness," which he uses to justify the institutions of a constitutional democracy.[23] Yet his principles of justice are not only applied to laws and the constitution. Applying these principles to other basic social institutions that regulate the distribution of wealth and opportunities to achieve favourable social positions is also his aim. Proceduralist accounts of justice are subsequently challenged with its focus on impartial rules impartially applied.[24] Instead, with his distributive notions of justice, Rawls has been instrumental in shifting the focus on outcomes rather than the rules that have generated those outcomes.[25] In doing so, Rawls gave many a great confidence in the idea that we can create justice in a liberal democratic state.

Beginning his theory of justice with a normative conception of persons, whom he describes as free, equal and rational, Rawls claims we have been endowed with a moral capacity for a sense of justice: "We acquire a skill in judging things to be just and unjust, and in supporting these judgments by reasons."[26] What is noticeable, though, is that because he approaches issues of justice from a non-theocentric worldview, Rawls, as is characteristic of post-Enlightenment thought, fails at the outset of his considerations to provide a robust explanation of where our moral

---

[20] Brian Barry and Matt Matravers, "Justice," in *Routledge Encyclopedia of Philosophy*, vol. 5, 143.

[21] Pogge, *World Poverty and Human Rights*, 31.

[22] John Rawls, *A Theory of Justice* (Oxford: Oxford University Press, 1996), viii.

[23] For a philosophical critique of Rawls' position, see Samuel Freeman, "Rawls, John," in *Routledge Encyclopedia of Philosophy*, vol. 8, 106-110.

[24] Rawls, *A Theory of Justice*, 83-90.

[25] See Chris Brown, *Sovereignty, Rights and Justice* (Cambridge: Polity Press, 2002), 167-170.

[26] Rawls, *A Theory of Justice*, 46.

capacity originates. As we have previously argued, our moral capacity derives from a theology of grace, where God communicates his desire for justice in the world, mediated through the Spirit, to those whom he has made in his image and with whom he is in covenant-partnership. This is the privileged epistemic access of the church.

Our conception of the good, Rawls states, will differ depending on our knowledge and personal situations. It has the effect that to pursue their good, free persons will make conflicting claims on scarce resources. This suggests to Rawls that the appropriate way to decide principles for a democratic society is by conjecturing what principles free persons would agree to among themselves to regulate basic social institutions.[27] Central to this approach is the concept of an "original position."

In essence, the original position is a hypothetical state of equality in which the persons involved in the exercise do not yet know who they are going to be. Rawls states: "No one knows his place in society, his class position or social status, nor does any one know his fortune in the distribution of natural assets and abilities, his intelligence, strength, and the like."[28] They are placed behind a complete "veil of ignorance" so none can take advantage of their social circumstances, talents or individual conceptions of the good, which ensures that this agreement is fair. With this move, Samuel Freeman notes, he "carries to the limit the ideal of equality behind democratic contractualism."[29] Rawls' argument is that given complete ignorance of everyone's position, it would be irrational to jeopardize one's good to gain whatever marginal advantages might be promised by other alternatives. The conception of justice that would be agreed to in the original position is neither utilitarian nor perfectionist, but is a Kantian account of justice as fairness.[30]

The resulting conception of justice as fairness, as articulated by Rawls, accords priority to a principle guaranteeing certain basic individual rights and liberties to all citizens equally. Once these rights have been secured, this provides his central premise for an egalitarian principle of distributive justice. He argues for two main principles of justice for such societies. The first principle echoes the libertarian view that all persons should have equal and maximal liberties. This principle affirms that positions and offices be open to all on the basis of fair equality of opportunity. Secondly, Rawls advocates the so-called difference principle, which qualifies the

---

[27] For a contrasting approach, see William A. Galston, *Liberal Purposes: Goods, Virtues and Diversity in the Liberal State* (Cambridge: Cambridge University Press, 1991). He challenges theorist, such as Rawls, who believe the essence of liberalism is that it should remain neutral concerning different ways of life and individual conceptions of what is good.

[28] Rawls, *A Theory of Justice*, 12.

[29] Samuel Freeman, "Contractarianism," in *Routledge Encyclopedia of Philosophy*, vol. 2, 663.

[30] Rawls, *A Theory of Justice*, 251-257. Typical of Kant's approach is found in "Essay on Theory and Practice," in *International Relations in Political Thought*, ed. Chris Brown, Terry Nardin, and Nicholas Rengger (Cambridge: Cambridge University Press, 2002). It is an essay in which Kant stresses the concept of duty: "The hope for better times to come, without which an earnest desire to do something useful for the common good would never have inspired the human heart, has always influenced the activities of right-thinking men" (429).

first principle with the requirement that inequalities be permitted only where they would be to the advantage of the "representative worst-off person."

It is evident, therefore, that Rawls' theory of justice benefits those who lack power as it gives primary attention to those least advantaged in society. Of importance to discussions of global justice, however, is that since Rawls' theory assumes the framework of a closed society, his conception of the representative worst-off person is not thought of as representing the worst-off of the whole world. Singer demurs at this absence in Rawls' work:

> If he [John Rawls] accepted that to choose justly, people must also be ignorant of their citizenship, his theory would become a forceful argument for improving the prospects of the worst-off people in the world. But in the most influential work on justice written in twentieth-century America, the question never even arises.[31]

Significantly, therefore, not only is Rawls' theory of justice lacking in that it presents no absolute foundation for debating questions of justice, which is in marked contrast to the mission of the church in being in covenant-partnership with a righteous God; but it also raises the question from a straightforwardly secular standpoint as to whether it is adequate as a response to the challenges of the existing global order.

Human Rights and International Distributive Justice

It is in engaging with issues of justice in the modern world that the concept of distributive justice, which was a central feature of Rawls' theory, has become the engine of growth in international political theory. Principles of distributive justice serve to generate just distributions of the earth's valued resources to seek the equitable treatment of persons and groups. This may require the redistribution of wealth from the wealthy within the state to the less advantaged members of society.[32] Stanley Hoffmann highlights the importance of distributive justice, which he claims "goes to the essence of politics."[33] At the heart of these debates are human rights and the implication of recognizing these rights in how policies are developed for different societies throughout the world.[34] By contrast with approaches deriving human dignity from an individualistic concept of human rights, the covenant of grace affirms humankind's worth due to being made to be in relationship with God, others,

---

[31] Singer, *One World*, 9.

[32] Simon Caney, "International Distributive Justice," *Political Studies*, vol. 49/5 (December 2001), 974.

[33] Stanley Hoffmann, *Duties Beyond Borders: On the Limits and Possibilities of Ethical International Politics* (Syracuse, NY: Syracuse University Press, 1981), 141.

[34] See also Martha C. Nussbaum, *The Therapy of Desire: Theory and Practice in Hellenistic Ethics* (Princeton: Princeton University Press, 1994). Martha Nussbaum prefers to speak of what she describes as the "capabilities" required for living a good life.

and the rest of creation.[35] Thus, here again, we shall see that in approaching issues of justice from a non-theocentric foundation, this is inherently problematic for theologians.[36]

A principal figure in the discussion of human rights is Michael Ignatieff, who expresses his frustration concerning the disjointing between academics and practice. Ignatieff's claim is that the philosophical literature has been focused on the grounds for human rights, yet this is disconnected from the real world. Rather than being concerned with the philosophical foundation, we should now interpret how to apply human rights in the world today. Sceptical of the role religion plays in defining and protecting human rights, Ignatieff states:

> People who do not believe in God must either reject that human beings are sacred or believe they are sacred on the basis of a secular use of religious metaphor that a religious person will find unconvincing. Foundational claims of this sort divide, and these divisions cannot be resolved in the way humans usually resolve their arguments, by means of discussion and compromise. Far better, I would argue, to forgo these kinds of foundational arguments altogether and seek to build support for human rights on the basis of what such rights actually do for human beings.[37]

While Ignatieff rightly recognizes the need for practical action to follow theological and philosophical debate, it is also evident that the two cannot legitimately be divorced from each other. Demonstrating the essential nature of a theoretical base for socio-political action, particularly in addressing issues of world poverty, Onora O'Neill in *Faces of Hunger* argues that most modern ethical theories deny that human needs make any special claims on us. It is a claim that has a direct impact on how we respond to contemporary issues in the world. O'Neill declares in surveying the issue of poverty: "Philosophical reflection is notoriously late on the intellectual scene, but it will not be redundant if it can show agents and agencies who affect poverty and hunger more urgent reasons to perceive and to treat the poor differently."[38]

---

[35] For a further discussion, see Howard Taylor, *Human Rights: Its Culture and Moral Confusions* (Edinburgh: Rutherford House, 2004).

[36] See, for example, Alasdair MacIntyre, *Whose Justice? Which Rationality?* (London: Duckworth, 1988), 351. Alasdair MacIntyre argues there are now no ways of resolving fundamental intellectual disputes among secular theorists about the nature of justice, as they all claim to be proceeding according to purely rational considerations, without appealing to fundamental axioms about the nature of things. Cf. Lesslie Newbigin, "Whose Justice?" *Ecumenical Review*, vol. 44/3 (July 1992), 310.

[37] Michael Ignatieff, *Human Rights as Politics and Idolatry* (Princeton: Princeton University Press, 2001), 54.

[38] Onora O'Neill, *Faces of Hunger: An Essay on Poverty, Justice and Development* (London: Allen & Unwin, 1986), 8. This need to oscillate between theory and practice is found in Henry Shue, *Basic Rights: Subsistence, Affluence, and US Foreign Policy*, 2nd edn (Princeton: Princeton University Press, 1996). "Basic rights," Henry Shue contends, "are

Yet despite the noteworthy advances that have been achieved in addressing matters of social and political concern, the individualistic concept of human rights for issues pertaining to distributive justice has a critical weakness. Sparking a vigorous debate, and accentuating the intrinsic problems associated with this thought, was one of Rawls' most prominent critics, Robert Nozick. Nozick contributed to the justice debate in his statement of libertarianism in *Anarchy, State, and Utopia* where he begins with the words: "Individuals have rights, and there are things no person or group may do to them without violating their rights."[39] At its core, he advocates a fully voluntary society, in which people cooperate only on terms that do not violate anyone's rights. Conjuring up the fear of redistribution, where some authority will come and take away part of what you own in order to devote it to some purpose it deems worthy, Nozick's thesis of the entitlement theory involves a defense of the minimal state being consistent with individual rights to life, liberty, and property.[40]

Taking an opposing perspective of distributive justice from Nozick is Pogge - although he concurs with Nozick's view that human rights are vital to questions of justice. Distinctive to Pogge's theory of justice is a universalistic conception of human rights, which include rights to economic resources. Pogge champions the case of the world's poor and claims that most of the current under-fulfillment of human rights today is directly connected to poverty: "That a large segment of humankind lives in extreme poverty is nothing new. What is comparatively new, however, is that another large segment is living in considerable affluence."[41] Because the decisive variable for realizing human rights is bound up with the existing global order, the responsibility for the realization of these rights must rest with those who impose this order.[42] Yet Pogge does not advocate a path of greater mutual isolation. Instead he seeks a path of globalization that will involve political as well as economic integration to afford all people an opportunity to share the benefits of global economic growth.[43]

---

everyone's minimum reasonable demands upon the rest of humanity" (19). The three basic rights he identifies are subsistence, security, and liberty.

[39] Robert Nozick, *Anarchy, State, and Utopia* (Oxford: Blackwell, 1974), ix.

[40] Yet in defending his thesis Nozick fails to justify the initial acquisition of individual property rights. For a further analysis, see Jonathan Wolff, "Nozick, Robert," in *Routledge Encyclopedia of Philosophy*, vol. 7, 44-47.

[41] Thomas W. Pogge, "Human Rights and Human Responsibilities," in *Global Justice and Transnational Politics: Essays on the Moral and Political Challenges of Globalization*, ed. Pablo de Greiff and Ciaran Cronin (Cambridge, Mass.: The MIT Press, 2002), 152.

[42] Ibid., 185. See also Thomas W. Pogge, "Priorities of Global Justice," in *Global Justice*, ed. Thomas W. Pogge (Oxford: Blackwell, 2001), 22. Noticeably, Pogge argues not primarily for a positive duty of helping those in need, but rather a negative duty not to harm: "Because our responsibility is negative and because so much harm can be prevented at so little cost to ourselves, the reduction of severe global poverty should be our foremost moral priority."

[43] Pogge, *World Poverty and Human Rights*, 20. Cf. Charles Jones, *Global Justice: Defending Cosmopolitanism* (Oxford: Oxford University Press, 1999). In addressing the

Following from these claims, therefore, in our evaluation of international ethics in the context of a globalized world, we will now consider the arguments for a cosmopolitan understanding of distributive justice and its moral demands.

The Moral Demands of Cosmopolitanism

Significantly, as we have discovered, Rawls' theory of justice is developed within the context of a bounded society. When Rawls did finally produce a work on international justice in *The Law of Peoples*, much to the frustration of many international political theorists, he argues only for selected principles of international justice. Rawls concludes his somewhat restrictive and conservative approach: "What is important to the law of peoples is the justice and stability for the right reasons of liberal and decent societies, living as members of a society of well-ordered peoples."[44] The law of peoples therefore does not support a cosmopolitan regime that operates on a global scale to redistribute wealth from wealthy to poorer nations in accordance with a global difference principle. Instead, he advocates only a voluntary confederation of liberal and decent peoples that recognizes a duty to assist people living in societies burdened by unfavourable conditions. Voluntary action of this kind has a specific aim, which is the establishment of liberal or decent social institutions.[45]

Redistribution among peoples in different societies, Rawls argues, would be unacceptable because it would not respect peoples' political autonomy. In defending his thesis, Rawls asks us to imagine two societies, initially equally prosperous. The first society decides to industrialize and increase its real rate of savings. In contrast, the second hypothetical society prefers a more leisurely existence, resulting in it being less prosperous. It would be inappropriate, Rawls claims, to tax the first society and redistribute the proceeds to the second. If we were to take this course of action we would not be respecting each society's right to self-determination.[46] Yet although there is an inherent logic in Rawls' argument that differential efforts should bring differential rewards, as we shall discuss later, it fails to recognize that there is a fundamental responsibility placed upon those who have been advantaged in the global economy to assist those who are not able to maximize the opportunities presented.[47]

---

issue of what obligations the world's wealthy have to the world's poor, Charles Jones argues for what he calls "qualified sovereigntism" in which states retain elements of sovereign authority, with legitimate scope for higher-level overriding of that authority when it fails to meet minimal cosmopolitan requirements (214-216).

[44] John Rawls, *The Law of Peoples* (Cambridge, Mass.: Harvard University Press, 1999), 120.

[45] Ibid., 105-113.

[46] Ibid., 117-118.

[47] See also Leif Wenar, "The Legitimacy of Peoples," in *Global Justice and Transnational Politics*, 58. Leif Wenar points out that background institutions should be in

In recent years, in assessing how to respond to globalization, several scholars have challenged Rawls' original position, and the stance advocated by political theorists such as Nardin that principles of distributive justice should only apply to the state or nation-level.[48] This alternative has come to be known as the cosmopolitan position, which derives from the Greek compound term *Kosmou-polites* meaning "citizen of the universe." As "one of the more diffuse but influential movements to have come to prominence," Nicholas Rengger notes, cosmopolitanism can trace its roots to the Hellenistic period of ancient Greek thought, and yet has developed "a distinct modern character."[49] The nebulous core shared by cosmopolitans is that the proper scope of moral principles extends to include all humans wherever they live. Christien van den Anker suggests that the widest definition we can use is that it takes "the scope of justice to be global."[50] According to this position, duties of distributive justice apply to all human beings.[51] A just society will be a fair system of cooperation among global citizens all of whom are regarded as free and equal. For the basic idea lying behind cosmopolitanism, as Charles Jones declares, is that "each person affected by an institutional arrangement should be given equal consideration."[52]

Debates among international political theorists vis-à-vis global justice in a globalized world highlight the philosophical interest in cosmopolitanism, which lies in its challenge to commonly recognized attachments to fellow-citizens of a particular nation. Distinctive to contemporary cosmopolitan accounts of distributive justice is precisely that it affirms duties are owed to individuals, and not simply to states. Mark Amstutz notes that in effect, "they [cosmopolitanists] assume that international morality requires the subordination of state boundaries to human dignity." This is in contrast with communitarianism, which contends that the quest for human dignity is best achieved within and through each distinct political society.

---

place to prevent the overall distribution of wealth and resources "from reflecting factors arbitrary from a moral point of view."

[48] Nardin, *Law, Morality, and the Relations of States*, 255-277

[49] Nicholas Rengger, "Cosmopolitanism," in *Understanding Democratic Politics*, ed. Roland Axtmann (London: Sage, 2003), 321-323.

[50] Christien van den Anker, "Introduction: The Need for an Integrated Cosmopolitan Agenda," in *Global Society*, vol. 14/4 (October 2000), 479.

[51] See Caney, "International Distributive Justice," 974-997. Caney distinguishes between "radical" and "mild" cosmopolitanism. Radical cosmopolitanism claims that there are both global principles of distributive justice (the positive claim) and also that there are no nation-wide principles of distributive justice (the negative claim). Mild cosmopolitanism simply affirms the positive claim, and accepts the claim that people have special obligations of distributive justice to fellow nationals or fellow citizens.

[52] Jones, *Global Justice*, 15. Cf. Brian Barry, *The Liberal Theory of Justice: A Critical Examination of the Principal Doctrines in 'A Theory of Justice'* (Oxford: Clarendon Press, 1973). Barry supports this firmly egalitarian theoretical position by drawing on Thomas Scanlon's model of contractualism, and declares that Rawls' refusal to allow for principles of international distributive justice produces results that are intuitively wrong.

Amstutz summarizes these differences of approach: "Whereas communitarianism accepts the legitimacy of the existing international order, the cosmopolitan approach denies the moral significance of the structures of the existing neo-Westphalian order."[53]

Amartya Sen advocates such a position and criticizes Rawls' exclusive focus on peoples in his interpretation of ethics and world politics. Since diverse identities are a vital feature of today's world, a theory of global justice must take account of the full scope of our multiple identities and interconnections across borders.[54] Focusing on the freedoms to be enjoyed by all the world's citizens, Sen asserts: "Development requires the removal of major sources of unfreedom: poverty as well as tyranny, poor economic opportunities as well as systematic social deprivation, neglect of public facilities as well as intolerance or over-activity of repressive states."[55] Thus Sen admits to being attracted to this "grand universalism" in which "the domain of the exercise of fairness is all people everywhere taken together...seen without distinction of nationality and other classifications."[56] But in spite of its ethical interest and its comprehensive coverage, he shares Rawls' scepticism about the application of the contractualist approach to all human beings since we currently lack the global political institutions required to implement such universal principles.[57]

This lack of will and vision among governments and statesmen to bring about institutional arrangements for promoting global justice, Pogge argues, means that these leaders bear a special responsibility for the injustice in the world today. In confronting this situation, Pogge states: "In view of such massive deprivations and unprecedented inequalities, we cannot decently avoid reflection on global institutional reform."[58] Voicing similar sentiments, Singer emphasizes that absolute poverty is "the situation that prevails on our planet all the time."[59] In his approach to the global justice debate from a utilitarian position, Singer calls our attention to the ethical obligations placed upon those who have wealth to use their wealth to help

---

[53] Mark R. Amstutz, *International Ethics: Concepts, Theories, and Cases in Global Politics* (Lanham, Maryland: Rowman & Littlefield, 1999), 179.

[54] Amartya Sen, "Justice Across Borders," in *Global Justice and Transnational Politics*, 50.

[55] Amartya Sen, *Development as Freedom* (Oxford: Oxford University Press, 1999), 3.

[56] Sen, "Justice Across Borders," 39.

[57] Ibid., 40. Cf. Amstutz, *International Ethics*, 83. Although "one of the basic ethical norms of global society is that moral obligations are not defined by territorial boundaries," Amstutz notes, "it is much less evident how such moral obligations should be fulfilled."

[58] Pogge, *World Poverty and Human Rights*, 195. Although he defends certain core ideas of Rawls' theory of justice, Pogge differs in arguing that all principles of justice should have a universal scope. See Thomas W. Pogge, *Realizing Rawls* (Ithaca: Cornell University Press, 1989), 211-280. Cf. Charles R. Beitz, *Political Theory and International Relations* (Princeton: Princeton University Press, 1999).

[59] Peter Singer, *Practical Ethics*, 2nd edn (Cambridge: Cambridge University Press, 1993), 220.

benefit the poor of our global society. Controversially, Singer argues that failing to assist those living in poverty is actually the moral equivalent of murder: "If, then, allowing someone to die is not intrinsically different from killing someone, it would seem that we are all murderers."[60] This assertion strikingly exposes a core feature of Singer's moral theory in his commitment to equality, which requires that principles of justice incorporate every person's utility irrespective of their citizenship. Singer asserts: "If it is in our power to prevent something bad from happening, without thereby sacrificing anything of comparable moral importance, we ought, morally, to do it."[61]

In *Democracy and the Global Order*, Held contributes to the international ethics debate in the contemporary context, and provides an account of democratic theory as it applies to a world of intensifying global relations. With the rapid growth of complex interrelations between states and societies, he claims, this presents a need for the establishment of a new global order. Espousing the cosmopolitan virtues, Held is adamant that all persons have a right to autonomy: "Persons should enjoy equal rights and, accordingly, equal obligations in the specification of the political framework which generates and limits the opportunities available to them."[62] In a similar approach to that of Rawls, Held articulates the implications of an ideal autonomy through a "democratic thought experiment" in which we ask what free and equal persons would agree to.[63] Yet he displays a wider vision of justice and calls for the creation of a new set of regional and global rules and procedures for a globalized world: "In the contemporary world, democracy can only be fully sustained by ensuring the accountability of all related and interconnected power systems, from economics to politics."[64] It is this cosmopolitan model of democracy that introduces fundamental issues vis-à-vis state boundaries and global justice in international ethics.

State Boundaries and Agents of Justice in a Globalized World

Boundaries are an integral feature of international law. This is the point Robert McCorquodale makes in declaring: "They are a cause of conflict and a reason for peace. They establish order and lead to disorder. They provide a protection and a weapon. They include and exclude. They define and divide. They are real and imagined."[65] Daniel Philpott elucidates further on the far-reaching implication of state boundaries for considerations of justice and moral obligations:

---

[60] Singer, *Practical Ethics*, 222.

[61] Peter Singer, "Famine, Affluence, and Morality," in *International Ethics*, ed. Charles R. Beitz, et al. (Princeton: Princeton University Press, 1985), 249.

[62] David Held, *Democracy and the Global Order: From the Modern State to Cosmopolitan Governance* (Cambridge: Polity Press, 1995), 147.

[63] Ibid., 160-167.

[64] Ibid., 267.

[65] Robert McCorquodale, "International Law, Boundaries, and Imagination," in *Boundaries and Justice*, 136.

As borders have so formidably fenced the world's populations, the state's most ardent philosophical enthusiasts, along with many citizens of many actual states, have arrived at a corresponding ethical notion – that their obligations of justice are exclusive to, or at least may heavily favour, their fellow members.[66]

Philosophers have referred to this position, Philpott notes, as "partial commitments." They are the type of commitments that borders tend to create. And yet, they are commitments that "have never rested easy with universalistic systems of ethics."[67] Singer exemplifies this disagreement, and forthrightly refutes the notion of boundaries and partial commitments: "A global ethic should not stop at, or give great significance to, national boundaries. National sovereignty has no intrinsic moral weight."[68] Yet despite recognizing that there are global issues that demand global responses, Singer reluctantly acknowledges that there is little political support for ideas at present, such as a world community with its own directly elected legislature, perhaps evolving along the lines of the European Union. Undeterred by this lack of interest, and in seeking to respond to criticisms that world government would be cumbersome and ultimately ineffective, he declares:

> The European Union is a federal body that has adopted the principle that decisions should always be taken at the lowest level capable of dealing with the problem. The application of this principle, known as subsidiarity, is still being tested. But if it works for Europe, it is not impossible that it might work for the world.[69]

Singer has much in common with O'Neill vis-à-vis considerations about justice in a globalized world. This is reflected in O'Neill's significant work *Bounds of Justice*, in which she endorses the concept of global distributive justice, and claims it will entail setting out a form of universalism for ethics and politics in order to be "relevant for a world in which state boundaries are increasingly porous to movements of goods, capital, ideas and people, and in which state sovereignty is increasingly circumscribed." Yet O'Neill points out the difficulty of such an endeavour: "This will not be easy because conceptions of justice which were devised with the thought that states are the primary context of justice may need a lot of stretching and remodelling if they are to do global duty."[70] For although the images of a "global village" may be sentimental slogans, O'Neill declares, the view that

---

[66] Philpott, "The Ethics of Boundaries," 335.

[67] Ibid. See Robert McKim and Jeff McMahon, *The Morality of Nationalism* (Oxford: Oxford University Press, 1997) for an exploration of partial commitments in the context of nationalism and the state.

[68] Singer, *One World*, 148. Global ethical demands led Singer to advocate giving a 1 percent donation of our annual income "to overcome world poverty as the minimum that one must do to lead a morally decent life" (194). Cf. Pogge, *World Poverty and Human Rights*, 196-215. Pogge argues for a Global Resources Dividend where 1 percent of global income would be put in a fund to equip the global poor.

[69] Singer, *One World*, 199-200.

[70] Onora O'Neill, *Bounds of Justice* (Cambridge: Cambridge University Press, 2000), 3.

boundaries of actual communities or states are impervious is "sheer idealizing nostalgia."[71]

O'Neill develops the cosmopolitan position further and makes the argument that the global realities of political and economic life raise the critical question of who are the agents who will bring about justice in a globalized world, which has led to considerations as to whether institutions can be treated as moral agents. In discussing how we might work towards a global conception of justice, O'Neill declares: "We may do well not to presuppose that the sole context and guarantors of justice should be a set of mutually exclusive...territorial units, each claiming monopoly of the legitimate use of force within its territory." Instead, "we might do better to consider a much wider range of institutions which exercise substantial power, including some that are not intrinsically territorial."[72] O'Neill distinguishes between "primary agents of justice" which are those "with capacities to determine how principles of justice are to be institutionalized within a certain domain," and "secondary agents of justice," which are those who primarily contribute to justice, "by meeting the demands of primary agents, most evidently by conforming to any legal requirements they establish."[73] Agents of justice and their capacities or abilities to act will be multiple and diverse. It will include states and also non-state actors, such as international nongovernmental organizations that operate across borders, MNCs, and numerous transnational social, political, and epistemic movements.[74]

O'Neill has indeed raised interesting questions vis-à-vis the dilemma as to who will be the agents of justice in a globalized world. It is a question that challenges the church as to how it will respond to the issues of global justice in the historical and cultural context of the twenty-first century. What will become apparent, however, is that as the church is a community defined by grace, when we come to consider questions of explicitly theological ethics, the foundation and decisive motivation for this community's engagement with the social and political challenges of a globalized world will differ sharply from that offered by secular theories of justice.

Consequently, although international political theorists have successfully identified some of the current public concerns presented in a world of transforming global dynamics, the starting point for determining a Christian response to this contemporary issue is emphatically shaped by the gospel of grace.

The final theological task, therefore, that we will turn to in our study is concerned with identifying the attendant implications a theology of grace brings for the socio-

---

[71] Ibid., 121.

[72] Ibid., 182. Cf. two essays in *Governance in a Globalizing World*: L. David Brown, et al., "Globalization, NGOs, and Multisectoral Relations," 271- 296; and Cary Coglianese, "Globalization and the Design of International Institutions," 297-318. See also Nicholas Rengger, "On 'Good Global Governance,' Institutional Design, and the Practices of Moral Agency," in *Can Institutions Have Responsibilities?: Collective Moral Agency and International Relations*, ed. Toni Erskine (Basingstoke: Palgrave Macmillan, 2003), 214, in which Rengger identifies additional challenges for the shaping of this complex global order.

[73] Onora O'Neill, "Agents of Justice," in *Global Justice*, 189.

[74] Ibid., 196-201.

political mission of the church in an age of globalization. Expressly, we have found in part 2 of this book that Jürgen Moltmann, Stanley Hauerwas, and Oliver O'Donovan each develop a distinctive appreciation of divine grace in their political theologies that can be instrumental in overcoming some of the weaknesses of a straightforwardly secular understanding of how to approach questions of global justice in an age of globalization. We will now examine in turn the questions raised by these theologians for determining an appropriate Christian response to the social and political concerns inherent with this multidimensional contemporary issue.

Grace and Servant-Leadership in the Globalized Socio-Political Arena

Servanthood in a Power Dominated World

So we have surveyed some of the core arguments espoused by international political theorists in the debate as to what should constitute an ethical response to the challenges presented by a world of increasing interdependence. And we have found that the direction of the questions being asked, although they have been successful in helping to raise the dilemma facing many of the world's populations living in abject poverty, are nonetheless to a large extent theologically lacking. The root reason why the questions being asked are essentially problematic for those standing in the Reformational theological position is because, at their core, they ignore questions that are intrinsic to a theology of grace.[75] Rather then starting from an anthropocentrically understanding of ethical concerns in a globalized society, where the realization of human rights becomes the driving concern, the church in being a community defined by grace in every facet of its being, asks questions of a fundamentally different nature.

Let's start our examination of how the Christian community may address the challenges presented in a world of global power transformations by focusing on the theology of Moltmann. What in essence is the driving concern of Moltmann's work? It is to urge the church, as a voluntary fellowship of committed disciples to become more involved in meeting the full range of society's multidimensional needs, as it anticipates the eschatological kingdom of God in which all things will be made anew. And the church undertakes this task by recognizing that its mandate is to participate in Christ's messianic mission here on earth.[76] Thus although a concept of human rights does feature in Moltmann's theology, his focus still remains one of being resolutely theocentric. As such, a primary question that Moltmann's theology raises at this juncture is: *as christology and christopraxis are integrally related, how will the life and teachings of Christ shape Christian public involvement in an integrated world?*

---

[75] It is theological insight shared by Newbigin: "At the centre of the Christian understanding of justice there stands the cross, not a symbol but a historic deed in which the justice of God was manifested in his covenant faithfulness right through to the point where the just died for the unjust." See Newbigin, "Whose Justice?" 310.

[76] See chapter 3.

In answering this question, an overriding characteristic that will be displayed by the church in the twenty-first century context of a power dominated world, is one of servanthood.[77] Indeed the concept of servanthood in the world is central to the Reformational theological position. A brief historical survey will demonstrate this distinguishing trait.[78] In preparing the way for the Reformation in Northern Europe, an influential movement arose called the Devotio Moderna, meaning "the modern way of serving God." The character who most epitomizes the faith of the Devotio Moderna is Thomas à Kempis. Thomas wrote several devotional works although his principal work is *The Imitation of Christ*, which has become a classic devotional for the church.[79] Primarily, the purpose of this book is to teach Christians to imitate Christ's servanthood. Thomas challengingly enunciates: "True greatness can only be reckoned in terms of charity; the really great man is one who doesn't think much of himself, and doesn't think much of rank or precedence either."[80]

In more recent history, the influence of Philip Jakob Spener and John Wesley were instrumental in motivating the church to recapture its social conscience. As a reaction against current trends, Spener wrote *Pia Desideria*, which set out proposals for the revitalization of the church of his day. Influenced by Pietism, on 2 April 1739, Wesley preached the gospel to the poor in a way that broke with conventions of his time. Wesley records in his journals: "I submitted to be more vile, and proclaimed in the highways the glad tidings of salvation."[81] Mark Noll asserts that the Wesleys were the most effective proponents of the Reformation's message since Protestantism began. They kept alive the message of God's grace and were at the forefront of social change.[82] In a historical survey of Wesley's life, Bruce Hindmarsh distinguishes the concerns of this notable Christian leader from contemporary church activity:

---

[77] Cf. Thomas W. Manson, *The Church's Ministry* (London: Hodder & Stoughton, 1948), 27. Thomas Manson states: "In the kingdom of God service is not a stepping-stone to nobility: it is nobility, the only kind of nobility that is recognized."

[78] Throughout the entire history of the church there have been prominent individuals who have displayed a remarkable example of servanthood. In its earlier history, such an individual was St. Francis of Assisi. St. Francis was the founder of the Franciscans, which were one of the most significant groups of monks in the Middle Ages, and who were devoted to poverty and service to the poor. For a further analysis, see Clemens Jockle, *Encyclopedia of Saints* (London: Parkgate, 1997), 165-169. Also of particular note is St. Bonaventure, who was head of the Order of Friars Minor, and who wrote *The Character of a Christian Leader* in which he similarly articulated the need for servanthood. See St. Bonaventure, *The Character of a Christian Leader*, trans. Philip O'Mara (Ann Arbor, Mich.: Servant Books, 1978), 4-5.

[79] James D. Douglas and Philip W. Comfort, *Who's Who in Christian History* (Wheaton: Tyndale House, 1992), 672.

[80] Thomas à Kempis, *The Imitation of Christ*, trans. Ronald Knox and Michael Oakley (New York: Sheed and Ward, 1959), 22.

[81] John Wesley, *The Journal of the Rev. John Wesley, A.M. Sometime Fellow of Lincoln College, Oxford: From October 14th, 1735 to October 24th, 1790*, vol. 1 (London: John Mason, 1864), 174.

[82] Mark A. Noll, *Turning Points*, 2nd edn. (Grand Rapids: Baker, 2000), 223-224.

The evangelical sense of what it meant to proclaim and live the gospel, to announce God's salvation to the world, embraced a broader perspective than we might have expected given the characterization today that evangelicals are concerned only with saving souls.[83]

The concept of servanthood, Moltmann notes, is deeply embedded in the compassion of the triune God as supremely displayed in the crucified Christ. On the cross, Christ himself shares the suffering of the outcast and rejected of society, which is indeed a distinguishing contribution of Moltmann's theological works. It is a concept of divine solidarity with the marginalized and powerless of this world that is consolidated by a vision of universal transformation grounded in the resurrection hope. Thus, if the Christian community is to recognize the lordship of Christ over his church, as Moltmann insists, then this implies it will have a multidimensional vision of liberation of the oppressed in the contemporary world. In particular, for a church that displays the servanthood of Christ in a globalized society, this will mean standing in solidarity with the approximately two billion people living in the developing world, particularly in sub-Saharan Africa, the Middle East, and the former Soviet Union, who are in danger of becoming marginalized in the world economy. In essence, it is to be an agent of God's justice in a world characterized by injustice.[84]

Taking the concept of servanthood further than Moltmann, however, in accepting that forms of Christian leadership and power are required to address current social and political concerns, Tom Sine comments on the challenge facing the contemporary church in an age of globalization: "In a world changing as rapidly as ours, it is essential that we learn to lead with foresight."[85] John Stott highlights the many kinds and degrees of servant-leadership in the world, and notes that sociopolitical involvement is not restricted to a small minority of world statesmen, but includes members of the church. Senior executives in business and industry, judges, doctors, politicians, social workers, lecturers, students, and opinion formers in the

---

[83] D. Bruce Hindmarsh, "Let Us See Thy Great Salvation," in *What Does it Mean to be Saved?*, 63.

[84] Cf. Newbigin, "Whose Justice?" 311. In being "an agency of God's justice," Newbigin remarks, the church "can continually nourish a combination of realism and hope which finds expression in concrete actions which can be taken in the local community and more widely, which reflect and embody the justice of God." See also Bob Goudzwaard and Harry de Lange, *Beyond Poverty and Affluence: Toward an Economy of Care*, ed. and trans. Mark R. Vander Vennen (Grand Rapids: Eerdmans, 1995), which offers a twelve-step program for economic recovery based on an 'economy of care' for the earth and its people.

[85] Tom W. Sine, "Globalization, Creation of Global Culture of Consumption and the Impact on the Church and its Mission," in *Evangelical Review of Theology*, vol. 27/4 (October 2003), 355-356. Cf. George Monbiot, *The Age of Consent: A Manifesto for a New World Order* (London: Flamingo, 2003), 14. George Monbiot states: "The notion that power can be dissolved and replaced by something called "anti-power" has some currency among anarchists in the rich world, but it is recognized as fabulous nonsense by most campaigners in the poor world, where the realities of power are keenly felt."

media are all called to serve in witness to the world.[86] Richard Mouw draws specific attention to the need for the church to relate as servants to the world through leadership in the political sphere: "At the very least the call to servanthood requires us to be able to communicate about and within actual political processes."[87]

Yet a noticeable feature of Moltmann's work is that the church engages in socio-political action to serve the outcast of a globalized society not principally because it is guaranteed to lead to comprehensive advances in the conditions of those living in the developing world. Rather it is because we share with all human beings, irrespective of our nationality, a horizontal relationship due to being created by the creator God. This egalitarian understanding of the common humanity of all people "precedes every society and every established system of rule."[88] It is just such a relationship that causes the church to serve those who can give nothing back in return. George Hunsinger makes much the same claim: "The rule for social witness is that faithfulness is a higher virtue than effectiveness. Some things ought indeed to be done regardless of whether by human calculations they promise to be effective."[89] Rather than being judged by "immediate consequences alone," the validity of Christian social witness must be judged, "primarily, by the quality of its correspondence to God's compassion as revealed and embodied in Jesus Christ."[90]

In summary, we can say that, in contrast to a purely secular approach to the question of global ethics based fundamentally on a foundationless concept of human rights, Moltmann has effectively emphasized the priority of recognizing the centrality of Jesus Christ in formulating the necessary questions that must be initially asked in developing a theological valid response to the multidimensional challenges of the contemporary world, where millions of people still live in extreme poverty. Such a holistic understanding of ecclesial mission and servanthood in the world is a key component of the Christian community's response to the indicatives of grace.

Faithful Christian Witness in a Culture of Economism

Presenting a differing perspective of ecclesial witness in the world from Moltmann, yet who nonetheless raises vital theological questions in addressing the social and political challenges presented by the phenomenon of globalization, is Hauerwas. Foremost amongst Hauerwas' theological concerns, as we have seen, is his passionate desire to offer a church-orientated social ethics, which accentuates the need for the church to display authentic Christian witness in a world that is hostile to the gospel.[91] It is an understanding of Christian ethics that is immediately

---

[86] Stott, *Issues Facing Christians Today*, 327. Cf. Chaplin, "Prospects for an 'Evangelical Political Philosophy,'" 368. Chaplin likewise notes that the state does not have exclusive responsibility for justice; justice is the duty of all people.

[87] Mouw, *Politics and the Biblical Drama*, 69-70.

[88] Moltmann, *The Church in the Power of the Spirit*, 179.

[89] Hunsinger, "Social Witness in Generous Orthodoxy," 45.

[90] Ibid., 48-49.

[91] See chapter 4.

distinguishable from secular theories of justice, as we have discussed earlier in this chapter, derived from the individualistic rationalism of post-Enlightenment thought. Thus in essence, a key question that Hauerwas' theology raises is: *what does it mean to be a faithful Christian community in a world that demonstrates values and behaviour that are, at their core, counter-cultural to the message of the gospel?*

In their examination of Western culture, Jane Collier and Rafael Esteban present a disturbing critique and argue that the West is obsessed by the "culture of economism," in which economic factors become the main source of cultural meanings and values. Such economism, Collier and Esteban point out, perpetrates inequality and injustice.[92] From our analysis of the forces driving contemporary globalization, there does indeed appear to be evidence supporting these conclusions. Therefore it follows that due to about one-fifth of the world's current population living on less than $1 per day, the opinions and lives of people living in the developing world are perceived to be of significantly less value than those living in the developed world.

It is in such an environment, Hauerwas argues, that the Christian community should get on with being the church, which will mean exhibiting a behavior that is increasingly counter-cultural in a world characterized by a culture of economism. As Hauerwas points out, the Christian community is to be a people in whom the kingdom of God is made visible in the world. For in being devoted to a particular God and a particular way of life that follows Jesus Christ, the church will hold to an understanding of ethics that does not simply conform to our preconceptions of right living. Rather, as Hauerwas insists, if we hold to a theocentric worldview, our moral guidance comes from Scripture, which gives direction in terms of how the world is to be changed. Indeed it is this repeated emphasis on the importance of character and virtues for the Christian community that is such a distinguishing trait of Hauerwas' works. With this focus on virtue ethics, Hauerwas reminds Christians the life they are committed to living in recognizing that their lives are not their own but God's.[93]

This concept of being a counter-cultural community, as stressed by Hauerwas, is especially pertinent for ecclesial witness in an age of globalization. Pointing out the

---

[92] Collier and Esteban, *From Complicity to Encounter*, 28. For a further theological critique of the consumer culture, see Peter Selby, *Grace and Mortgage* (London: Darton, Longman & Todd, 1997); and Ulrich Duchrow, *Alternatives to Global Capitalism: Drawn from Biblical History, Designed for Political Action*, trans. Elaine Griffiths, et al. (Utrecht: International Books, 1995). In his more radical denouncement of the capitalist global system, Ulrich Duchrow declares: "The accumulation of money assets is now the absolute, immutable yardstick for all economic, social, ecological and political decisions" (71).

[93] Cf. Hays, *The Moral Vision of the New Testament*, 196. Richard Hays likewise identifies this inescapable responsibility that rests with the church: "The church is a countercultural community of discipleship, and this community is the primary addressee of God's imperatives. The biblical story focuses on God's design for forming a covenant people." See also John I. Durham, *Exodus. Word Biblical Commentary* (Waco, TX: Word Books, 1987), 263. John Durham describes the church as "a display-people, a showcase to the world of how being in covenant with Yahweh changes a people."

danger of Christians failing to resist the wider social and political trends of a globalized society as the world fractures along cultural and civilizational lines, David Smith echoes these calls for the church to display faithful Christian witness in the world, and claims that Christian theology and mission are inevitably counter-cultural in a globalized world that is being shaped by materialist and economic values.[94] An associated concern, Smith points out, is that because the majority of the churches in the South will be churches of the poor, they are likely to become increasingly restive about the injustice of the contemporary global system.[95]

Characteristic of the negative aspects of globalization, the abuse of power was not unknown in the first century world either. This is particularly apparent in Paul's letter to the Corinthians.[96] The influence of hierarchy and power in Corinth provides an explanation of the factionalism, which Paul opposed so strongly (1 Corinthians 1:10-31).[97] Within Corinth, society was strongly biased in favour of those who were already privileged, which is a visible trait of our globalized world. Andrew Clarke asserts: "Wealth was of supreme value, the rich were of far greater importance than the poor and esteem far more highly sought than justice alone."[98] Not immune from these social pressures, the Christian church was heavily influenced by this culture.[99] As a result, Paul charges the Christians for being "worldly" in their behaviour (1 Corinthians 3:3). Gordon Fee states that Paul's concern is "to get them to stop

---

[94] Smith, *Against the Stream*, 8.

[95] Ibid., 17. Cf. Philip Jenkins, *The Next Christendom: The Coming of Global Christianity* (Oxford: Oxford University Press, 2002). Although "over the past five centuries or so, the story of Christianity has been inextricably bound up with that of Europe and European-derived civilizations overseas, above all in North America," Jenkins points out, "over the past century, however, the centre of gravity in the Christian world has shifted inexorably southward, to Africa, Asia, and Latin America" (1-2).

[96] A comprehensive survey of the Greco-Roman world, and especially Corinth, is offered in: Bruce W. Winter, *After Paul Left Corinth: The Influence of Secular Ethics and Social Change* (Grand Rapids: Eerdmans, 2001); Bruce J. Malina, *The New Testament World: Insights from Cultural Anthropology*, 3rd edn (Louisville, KY: Westminster John Knox Press, 2001); Gerd Theissen, *The Social Setting of Pauline Christianity: Essays on Corinth*, ed. and trans. John H. Schütz (Edinburgh: T&T Clark, 1982); A. Duane Litfin, *St. Paul's Theology of Proclamation: 1 Corinthians 1-4 and Greco-Roman Rhetoric* (Cambridge: Cambridge University Press, 1994); and Shelton, Jo-Ann, *As the Romans Did: A Sourcebook in Roman Social History*, 2nd edn. (Oxford: Oxford University Press, 1998).

[97] Stephen C. Barton, "Social Values and Structures," in *Dictionary of New Testament Background*, ed. Craig A. Evans and Stanley E. Porter (Leicester: InterVarsity, 2000), 1129. The dichotomy between the powerful and powerless is typified where patricians developed ties of responsibility with their social inferiors. The plebs became clients to their patrons and they owed the patricians deference. For a further discussion, see James S. Jeffers, *Conflict at Rome: Social Order and Hierarchy in Early Christianity* (Minneapolis: Fortress, 1991), 131.

[98] Andrew D. Clarke, *Secular and Christian Leadership in Corinth: A Socio-Historical and Exegetical Study of 1 Corinthians 1-6* (Leiden: E.J. Brill, 1993), 25.

[99] John K. Chow, *Patronage and Power: A Study of Social Networks in Corinth - in JSNT Supplement Series,* vol. 75 (Sheffield: JSOT Press, 1992), 83-112.

thinking like the people of the present age."[100] Greatest importance was attached in responding to those who were using their power as a tool to alienate the poor.[101]

Consequently, we can see that the similarities found in first century Corinth are remarkably striking to the twenty-first century world in which global power transformations have led to the marginalization of much of the world's poor. As such, there is particular relevance in the contemporary context in Hauerwas' call for the church to be a counter-cultural community in a world that is hostile to the ethics of the gospel. In doing so, as Hauerwas articulates, the faithful church will be authentically demonstrating the truthfulness of Christian convictions "in a society of unbelief."

Global Integration and the Unified Kingdom of God

So we have established that the church in response to the covenant of grace is to be characterized by servant-leadership in standing in solidarity with the outcast and marginalized of the world's citizens, and is to be a counter-cultural community in a globalized world where the dominant culture is one of economism. But there is a further dimension of global integration that we have not yet considered in this chapter from a distinctly Reformational theological position. And it is brought out most fully in O'Donovan's political theology. The fundamental question arising from the works of this theologian, which is inherent to a theology of grace is: *with the world becoming increasingly integrated, how are we to conceive of globalization in relation to God's unified kingdom reign in his world, and what are the implications of this reign for the mission of the church in this contemporary context?*

Being in covenant-partnership with God in anticipation of this eschatological kingdom, of which God's justice for the whole world is so central, does indeed have far-reaching implications for the church in an age where the role and boundaries of nation-states are progressively changing. As O'Donovan enunciated, the kingly reign of God, which is inextricably tied to the concept of authority, causes the church to be actively engaged in the socio-political sphere as the vindication and restoration of the entire created order is foundational to the divine plan of world redemption. Where the kingdom of God is ushered in is found in the resurrection of Christ from the dead. It is this divine act that both leads to the reaffirmation of creation's order and coherence, and also provides the impetus to the church in its mission to the world. It is therefore to recognize that the word of the gospel must be our starting point for addressing society's concerns. Integral to this holistic message of the

---

[100] Gordon D. Fee, *The First Epistle to the Corinthians* (Grand Rapids: Eerdmans, 1987), 122. Such a transformation of relations is found in Paul's redefinition of what it means to be a servant, which was a particularly low class in Roman society. See Everett Ferguson, *Backgrounds of Early Christianity*, 2nd edn. (Grand Rapids: Eerdmans, 1993), 56-59.

[101] Andrew D. Clarke, *Serve the Community of the Church: Christians as Leaders and Ministers* (Grand Rapids: Eerdmans, 2000), 185.

gospel, the church has a crucial role to play as a political society in the unfolding of God's all-sovereign rule.[102]

Yet a root cause of tension with this biblical portrayal of God's kingdom and a globalized world is due to developing countries holding considerably less levels of power than the richer nations.[103] Sine comments on the danger existing in that those who do have power will exploit the powerless for economic gain, which is opposed to the kingdom of God: "The rapid movement of peoples into a new one world economic order is shaping their aspirations and values in ways that are often at counter-point to the aspirations and values of God's kingdom."[104] In being confronted with these realities in an age of globalization, Ben Knighton calls upon churches, "to become a prophetic community of hope and resistance guided by the vision of the kingdom of God. To arrive at this goal, churches need to opt for the poor and empower them."[105]

Expressly, when we consider Christian witness in the context of a globalized world vis-à-vis God's unified kingly reign, the answer which it invites is that national boundaries are only of contingent moral significance for a community of grace. Insofar as the autonomous nation-state stands in the way of redistribution that would be required to promote global justice, boundaries are of secondary importance. Despite arguably having a legitimate particular interest in issues of justice in one's own nation, as O'Donovan points out, a Christian vision of justice, grounded in an acknowledgment of the universal reign of God in his created world, causes the church to have a universal understanding of justice. Therefore, although cosmopolitan theories of justice have flourished in an age where traditional nation-state boundaries are becoming transformed, the doctrine of grace means geographical boundaries have never been supremely the criteria for questions of justice for ecclesial witness.

---

[102] See chapter 5.

[103] Carl Henry elaborates on this disparity between God's justice and the injustice found in the world: "The God of the Bible…gives the lie to modern notions that injustice is strength, that rectitude is weakness." See Carl F.H. Henry, *The God Who Shows Himself* (Waco, TX: Word, 1966), 11. A concern for the just use of power is also found in the Reformation era. Human beings "steal," wrote John Calvin, "not only when they secretly take the property of others, but also when they make money by injuring others, accumulate wealth in objectionable ways, or are more concerned with their own advantage than with justice." See John Calvin, "Commentary on Exodus 20:15/Deuteronomy 5:19," in *Calvin: Commentaries*, ed. Joseph Haroutunian (London: SCM Press, 1958), 328-329.

[104] Sine, "Globalization, Creation of Global Culture of Consumption," 354. For a comparison of the contemporary abuse of power with the great Babylon in the book of Revelation, see Bauckham, *The Bible in Politics*, 85-102. Bauckham illustrates how the Roman Empire is opposed to God's kingdom and has a "single-minded pursuit of her own power and economic advantage." In contrast, Christians witnessed to a different kind of rule, "a kingdom founded not on exploitative power but on sacrificial service" (101). Cf. Richard J. Bauckham, *The Theology of the Book of Revelation* (Cambridge: Cambridge University, 1993), 159.

[105] Knighton, "Globalization," 212.

In analyzing how we think about boundaries in relation to theological ethics, Richard Miller captures this vision of God's unified rule in stressing the cosmopolitan aspects of Christianity. Miller states: "Central to this priority is the belief that God is the highest good, a source of love and order in this-worldly affairs, requiring loyalty that transcends the divisions of political life."[106] Even though some Christians provide a clear rationale for boundaries and regional loyalties, Miller articulates that it is a rationale that stands in tension with obligations to love the neighbour irrespective of political affiliation and distance: "Borders ask us to privilege local solidarities, but Christian agape, exemplified by Jesus' teaching and example, is altruistic and cosmopolitan."[107] It is a conception of boundaries, which accentuates the priority of the metaphysical over the geographical vis-à-vis ethical and political questions:

> This priority has theological and ethical dimensions. Theologically, it implies a hierarchy of being and value according to which God is to receive unconditional loyalty. All lesser loyalties are subordinate to a fundamental love of God, bound as they are by finitude and dependence upon the deity as the author of good. Ethically, this priority assigns at most a provisional and qualified value to regional boundaries, a value that is corrigible when measured against the requirements of a universal neighbour-love.[108]

To summarize our analysis of God's unified kingly reign in an age of globalization, we can say that borders have always been of secondary importance for the community of grace. A theocentric vision of God's eschatological kingdom rule, as O'Donovan compellingly stressed, causes the church in being a sign of this future hope to have an unambiguously universal and holistic vision of global justice. As such, an integral aspect of the Christian community's witness in the globalized socio-political arena is to be an agent of justice, not because it is based on any secular theory of justice, but because it is based on a holistic understanding of divine grace, which leads to living in accordance with God's design for human existence.

Being a Community of Grace in the Globalized Socio-Political Arena

By way of drawing together our conclusions in this final section, we have seen that it is when the church grasps the unconditional nature and significance of God's covenant relationship with himself that she is most effectively motivated to be an agent of God's justice in the globalized socio-political arena. In short, it is an understanding of God's grace that guides the Christian community in resisting the

---

[106] Richard B. Miller, "Christian Attitudes toward Boundaries," in *Boundaries and Justice*, 15. Cf. Hollenbach, *The Common Good and Christian Ethics*, 212. David Hollenbach argues that in an interdependent world the idea of the common good must take on a more universal definition.

[107] Ibid., 17.

[108] Ibid., 33.

status quo in the pursuit of global justice in an age of globalization. It is thus a righteousness that goes beyond merely secular models of justice. In each of the theologies presented by Moltmann, Hauerwas, and O'Donovan, each of these leading contemporary thinkers brings out in their distinctive manner core facets of this central Christian doctrine. As a way of summarizing the combined contributions of these three Reformational theologians, we can say that the doctrine of grace leads us to a more holistic understanding of salvation. It generates a theology that presents the church with a holistic vision of God's kingdom reign in the contemporary world.

Globalization does indeed have the potential to be a powerful force for good. Gordon Brown notes the benefits that can be realized if we were to share prosperity throughout an increasingly interdependent world: "This generation has in its power – if it so chooses – to finally free the world from want."[109] Amstutz emphasizes these opportunities, while simultaneously observing the "many sorrows" to be found on earth due to a large portion of the developing world's population living in conditions of abject destitution. Yet in comparing two alternative theories of the poverty and wealth of nations, he rejects the structural thesis frequently endorsed by the church.[110] This model assumes not only that poverty is the result of unjust structures and exploitative economic policies, but also that wealth creation is exploitative. Instead, Amstutz advocates the modernization thesis, claiming the expansion of economic production is the sole means by which living standards can be improved in the long-term. Wealth in one state need not result in the decline in wealth of another.

---

[109] Brown, "Governments and Supranational Agencies," 331.

[110] Mark R. Amstutz, "The Churches and Third World Poverty," in *On Moral Business*, 819-824. Amstutz identifies four reasons why churches should be wary of adopting a structuralist approach in dealing with issues of global justice. First, free enterprise strategies have been more successful in creating wealth than socialist systems. Second, socialist systems appear to be no more effective at establishing social justice and economic equality than capitalist systems. Third, the structural approach neglects job creation, and yet it is essential for an economy to expand at the same rate or higher rate than its population growth. Fourth, governments in developing countries are frequently an obstacle to the alleviation of poverty and the promotion of social justice, due to the pervasiveness of corruption. Cf. Keith Slack, "Sharing the Riches of the Earth: Democratizing Natural Resource-Led Development," *Ethics and International Affairs*, vol. 18/1 (April 2004), 47-62. Keith Slack offers empirical support for these claims. Contrasting the economic histories of developed countries such as the United States, Canada, and Australia, which had significant natural resource sectors during the early stages of their industrialization, and successfully converted their mineral wealth into long-term economic development, he notes the actual experience of developing countries with resource-led economic development has not progressed in the way that this theory would predict. This is due to rents from natural resources accruing in most cases to elites rather than workers or landowners: "Resource dependence is now linked to a long list of problems. Among these are corruption; low human capital investment; slower economic growth; retarded economic reform; increased inequality; weakened institutions; authoritarianism; and higher poverty" (48).

In summary, Amstutz argues, churches can and must contribute to the alleviation of poverty in the developing world, by modeling the habits and virtues that contribute to job creation and sharing. This can be achieved in a humanitarian way to meet immediate basic human needs, such as providing food, shelter, and health care. Additionally, the church can contribute through establishing the preconditions for long-term economic expansion, which will involve teaching and modeling practices essential to economic expansion.[111] Yet although there are weaknesses of the structuralist thesis, as Amstutz has exposed, a resolute division between both theses cannot now be maintained in a world of intensifying global interconnectedness. For as we have seen the structure of the global economy would appear to have contributed to the growing disparity between the rich and the poor throughout the world.

In examining how this Christian vision of global justice may be worked out practically in the context of a globalized world, a good example to look at is that offered by the "Micah Challenge." The Micah Challenge is facilitated by the World Evangelical Alliance and the Micah Network, and draws its council members from the leadership of Evangelical Alliances and Christian relief and development agencies from around the globe.[112] The Micah Network, which brings together more than two hundred and fifty Christian organizations providing relief, development, and justice activities throughout the world, developed the *Declaration on Integral Mission* at its first International Consultation in Oxford in September 2001. The *Declaration* sets out the biblical and theological basis for the Micah Challenge:

> Integral mission or holistic transformation is the proclamation and demonstration of the gospel. It is not simply that evangelism and social involvement are to be done alongside each other. Rather, in integral mission our proclamation has social consequences as we call people to love and repentance in all areas of life. And our social involvement has evangelistic consequences as we bear witness to the transforming grace of Jesus Christ.

In facilitating a global campaign to mobilize Christians against poverty, the World Evangelical Alliance and the Micah Network aims to deepen Christian engagement with the poor and to influence leaders of rich and poor nations to fulfill their commitment to achieve the Millennium Development Goals, and so halve absolute global poverty by 2015. All one hundred and ninety-one members states of the

---

[111] For an example of a long-term approach to social transformation, see Joe Kapolyo, "Social Transformation as a Missional Imperative: Evangelicals and Development since Lausanne," in *Movement for Change*, 146. Joe Kapolyo notes the ventures initiated by Stott, which gives individuals in less affluent regions the opportunity via study to develop in order to take a leadership position in their own nations. Cf. Joseph E. Stiglitz, "Towards a New Paradigm of Development," in *Making Globalization Good*, 76-107.

[112] Cf. T. Howland Sanks, S.J. "Globalization and the Church's Social Mission," in *Theological Studies*, vol. 60/4 (December 1999), 644-645. Since globalization has changed the context in which the church carries out its social mission, Howland Sanks notes that the church may have to foster new transnational structures to deal with matters of global justice.

United Nations have promised to achieve the Millennium Development Goals by 2015, which include measurable, time-bound targets addressing poverty and hunger, education, maternal and child health, the prevalence of diseases including HIV/AIDS, gender equality, the environment, debt, trade justice and aid.[113] It is a holistic Christian response to some of the core social and political challenges inextricably linked with globalization, which is grounded in an appreciation of divine grace.

Commenting on the critical global challenges related to political and ideological oppression and conflict, Gary Edmonds, former Secretary General of the World Evangelical Alliance declares: "Evangelicals must learn how to be peacemakers in a pluralistic society and how to negotiate for justice in more monolithic societies." This will involve, Edmonds states, learning how to train and influence the business professionals to act with justice rather than for profit margin. It will mean a form of development of communities by investing in people and not simply the infrastructure, which so often leads to the gentrification of a community. Combined with these challenges for the church in being an agent of God's justice, Edmonds points out the need for evangelicals to learn how to advocate on behalf of the poor and the marginalized of a globalized society, at the local levels, national levels, and on regional or international levels. The big opportunity for evangelicals, however, Edmonds suggests, will be to be the bridge builders between Catholics, World Council of Churches, Orthodox and other faith communities:

> There will need to be multi-lateral decision making that brings together diverse faith communities for interaction with societal sectors of leadership such as business, education, government, arts and media. These cross-sector partnerships will be the only way to create a just society that 'seeks to do good to all people.' Evangelicals will be given an opportunity to play this role if they will rise up and take it. However, if evangelicals hide or stay entrenched in a narrow fundamentalist view of the faith they will miss out on the opportunity as they will not be viewed as advocates for the common good.[114]

When such greater global justice is incorporated into the development of a new global order, there is significantly more scope for creating a society where the marginalized will benefit from the fruits of globalization. For global integration not only presents challenges to be overcome. Globalization has the potential to be a powerful force for poverty reduction, particularly for those living in the developing world. That is the challenge presented to the community of grace in being the agent of transformative action in the socio-political arena of the twenty-first century.

---

[113] Micah Challenge website (www.micahchallenge.org).

[114] Gary Edmonds highlighted these specific social and political challenges presented to the evangelical church in an age of globalization in a personal correspondence.

Conclusion

In this chapter we have engaged with international political theory and have outlined how approaching issues of global justice from a straightforwardly secular position is inherently problematic for those adopting the central theological affirmations for which the Reformers argued. While a cosmopolitan understanding of global justice has contributed in motivating some within the developed world to work on behalf of the most marginalized in our globalized society, it has not provided the theological warrant for directing a more "holistic" vision of the church's mission. Central to the Christian community's response to the social and political challenges presented by globalization is the fact that the church is defined by grace. Every facet of the church's life is indeed defined by this central Christian doctrine. In answering the question posed in the introduction to this book, we have argued that to the extent that a Christian community seeks to be true to the Reformation's emphasis on God's covenantal relationship with his people, it must see itself as called to be an agent of God's justice through demonstrating servant-leadership in an age of global power transformations, to enable the world's marginalized citizens to benefit from the fruits of globalization. We will now reflect on these findings in our concluding chapter.

CHAPTER 8

Conclusion

In this interdisciplinary project, we have sought to identify key concerns inherent in an interconnected and interdependent world, and offer a theological analysis of these concerns and their implications for the mission of the church. In exploring the fundamental theological questions of this study, we have discovered that the doctrine of grace, which is central to the Reformation tradition and which defines every facet of the life of the church, has profound social and political significance for ecclesial witness in the contemporary world. At this point we will make some final conclusions as a way of summarizing the main argument of this book vis-à-vis the implications of this central integrative motif of Scripture for the existence of the church as a community of grace in an age of globalization.

First, the starting point for discussing and debating issues relating to ecclesial social and political involvement in the historical and cultural context of a globalized world is the gospel of Jesus Christ. The heart of the church's creed is the affirmation that the gospel sets the agenda for ecclesial life and witness. Inextricably related to God's reconciliation with humankind in Christ is divine self-revelation. Crucial here is the role of Scripture, which as the ultimate source and criterion of Christian theology, is the narrative of God's gracious self-disclosure in the history of Israel culminating in the person and work of Jesus Christ. And significantly, in not only coming to this earth as the Messiah, but as the Servant, Jesus Christ challenges the church in carrying out its mission on earth by way of the servant.

Second, as the covenant of grace is inextricably linked with the kingdom of God, the church as a community of grace has an unambiguously trinitarian theocentric mission encompassing God's reign in the world. It is a kingly reign that includes not only the personal and spiritual dimensions, but also the social and political realities of human existence. The significance of God's universal reign is that the church is to be engaged in multidimensional liberating activity in the contemporary world. Hence a theology of grace is foundational to a biblical understanding of the holistic mission of the church. Consequently, national boundaries are of secondary importance in its task of making specific judgments about ethical issues in the context of a globalized world. Although cosmopolitan theories of global justice have become increasingly popular in a world of escalating interconnectedness, the theocentric nature of a theology of grace causes the church to have a cosmopolitan understanding of global justice irrespective of changes in geographic and political boundaries. What attention to issues of global justice has facilitated, however, is providing the Christian community with the opportunity of being an informed and valued contributor in the globalization debate.

Third, with regard to a theology of grace in its concern for the transformation of the entire world for the glory of God, this eschatological vision causes the church to hold in balance the concept of anticipation, which is fundamental to the New Testament's understanding of the new creation. It is to live patiently in this period of anticipation – always realizing that the eschatological kingdom is not yet, but simultaneously, refusing to resign oneself to the status quo. The church as a community of grace is thus not lulled into a premature utopian expectation of present reality. That is why there is an element of truth in the international political theorists' claim that an unwavering cosmopolitan understanding of global justice is unrealistic. Notwithstanding these assertions, however, the concept of anticipation and the vision it engenders, provides the Christian hope for the world's transformation, and directs the church as to its socio-political mission in the contemporary world.

Fourth, in contrast to moral systems espoused by liberal political theorists based on an Enlightenment rationalism, and hence which critically suffers through lacking an absolute foundation for debating questions of justice, the community of grace actively engages with issues of justice principally as a direct human response to the divine work. It is the demonstration of grace seen supremely in the person and work of Jesus Christ that provides the motivation for the church's involvement in the global challenges of the twenty-first century. The cross causes the church not only to identify with the marginalized of a globalized society, but also as the atoning act of reconciliation, provides the basis to respond to God's grace shown in being an agent of justice in the modern world. And it is the resurrection that imparts hope for the world's future transformation and inspires the church as it fulfils this mission.

Fifth, whereas globalization is inherently associated with power and the transformation of power relations on a global scale, the community of grace is a servant community. Thus a community defined by grace is to live counter-culturally in the contemporary world. The Christian community is called to embody the truth of the Word, and demonstrate through its life the reality of God's grace in our midst. Specifically, in a world of global power transformations, the socio-political mission of the church is to be an agent of God's justice through demonstrating servant-leadership. It fulfills this mission with the practical aim of contributing to the changes required in the new global order, which will enable the world's poorest and weakest citizens to share in the benefits brought by an increasingly interdependent world. Such is the mission of the church in the globalized socio-political arena to the extent that it conceives itself as a community defined by grace.

Bibliography

Aguilar, Mario I., *Current Issues on Theology and Religion in Latin America and Africa* (Lewiston, NY: Edwin Mellen, 2002).

Amstutz, Mark R., "The Churches and Third World Poverty," in *On Moral Business:Classical and Contemporary Resources for Ethics in Economic Life*, ed. Max L. Stackhouse, Dennis P. McCann, and Shirely J. Roels (Grand Rapids: Eerdmans, 1995).

Amstutz, Mark R., *International Ethics: Concepts, Theories, and Cases in Global Politics* (Lanham, Maryland: Rowman & Littlefield, 1999).

Anker, Christien van den, "Introduction: The Need for an Integrated Cosmopolitan Agenda," in *Global Society*, vol. 14/4 (October 2000), 479-485.

Annan, Kofi, A., "Global Compact," at the World Economic Forum in Davos, 31 January 1999.

Annan, Kofi A., "Two Concepts of Sovereignty," *The Economist* (18 September 1999), 81-82.

Annan, Kofi, A., "The Role of the State in the Age of Globalization," at the Conference on Globalization and International Relations in the 21st Century, June 2002.

Archer, Gleason L., "Covenant," in *Evangelical Dictionary of Theology*, ed. Walter A. Elwell, 2nd edn (Grand Rapids: Baker, 2001).

Assmann, Hugo, *Theology for a Nomad Church*, trans. Paul Burns (Maryknoll, NY: Orbis, 1976).

Audi, Robert and Nicholas Wolterstorff, *Religion in the Public Square: The Place of Religious Convictions in Political Debate* (Lanham, Maryland: Rowman & Littlefield, 1997).

Austin, Victor L., "Method in Oliver O'Donovan's Political Theology," in *Anglican Theological Review*, vol. 79/4 (Fall 1997), 583-594.

Balaam, David N. and Michael Veseth, *Introduction to International Political Economy*, 2nd edn (Upper Saddle River, N.J.: Prentice-Hall, 2001).

Balthasar, Hans Urs von, *The Theology of Karl Barth: Exposition and Interpretation,* trans. Edward T. Oakes (San Francisco: Ignatius Press, 1992).

Barr, James, *The Semantics of Biblical Language* (London: Oxford University Press, 1961).

Barry, Brian, *The Liberal Theory of Justice: A Critical Examination of the Principal Doctrines* in 'A Theory of Justice' (Oxford: Clarendon Press, 1973).

Barry, Brian and Matt Matravers, "Justice," in *Routledge Encyclopedia of Philosophy*, vol. 5, ed. Edward Craig (London: Routledge, 1998).

Barry, Brian and Matt Matravers, "Justice, International," in *Routledge Encyclopedia of Philosophy*, vol. 5, ed. Edward Craig (London: Routledge, 1998).

Barth, Karl, *The Word of God and the Word of Man*, trans. Douglas Horton (London: Hodder & Stoughton, 1928).

Barth, Karl, *The Epistle to the Romans*, trans. Edwyn C. Hoskyns (London: Oxford University Press, 1933).

Barth, Karl, *Revelation*, ed. John Baillie and Hugh Martin (New York: Macmillan, 1937).

Barth, Karl, *The Knowledge of God and the Service of God According to the Teaching of the Reformation: Recalling the Scottish Confession of 1560* (London: Hodder and Stoughton, 1938).

Barth, Karl, *Dogmatics in Outline*, trans. George T. Thomson (London: SCM Press, 1949).

Barth, Karl, "Poverty," in *Against the Stream: Shorter Post-War Writings 1946-52*, ed. Ronald G. Smith, trans. E. M. Delacour and Stanley Godman (London: SCM Press, 1954).

Barth, Karl, "The Christian Community and the Civil Community," in *Against the Stream: Shorter Post-War Writings 1946-52*, ed. Ronald G. Smith, trans. E. M. Delacour and Stanley Godman (London: SCM Press, 1954).

Barth, Karl, "Gospel and Law," in *God, Grace and Gospel: Scottish Journal of Theology Occasional Papers*, No. 8, trans. James S. McNab (Edinburgh: Oliver & Boyd, 1959).

Barth, Karl, "The Humanity of God," in *God, Grace and Gospel: Scottish Journal of Theology Occasional Papers*, No. 8, trans. James S. McNab (Edinburgh: Oliver & Boyd, 1959).

Barth, Karl, *Anselm: Fides Quaerens Intellectum: Anselm's Proof of the Existence of God in the Context of his Theological Scheme*, trans. Ian W. Robertson (London: SCM Press, 1960).

Barth, Karl, *Evangelical Theology: An Introduction*, trans. Grover Foley (Edinburgh: T&T Clark, 1963).

Barth, Karl, *Community, State, and Church* (Gloucester, Mass.: Peter Smith, 1968).

Barth, Karl, *Church Dogmatics*, 4 vols., ed. Geoffrey W. Bromiley and Thomas F. Torrance, trans. Geoffrey W. Bromiley (Edinburgh, T&T Clark, 1956-1975).

Barth, Karl, "Barth's Reply to Wurm, 29 May 1947," in *Karl Barth/ Rudolf Bultmann Letters 1922-1966*, ed. Geoffrey W. Bromiley and Bernd Jaspert (Grand Rapids: Eerdmans, 1982).

Barth, Karl, *The Göttingen Dogmatics: Instruction in the Christian Religion*, vol. 1, ed. Hannelotte Reiffen, trans. Geoffrey W. Bromiley (Grand Rapids: Eerdmans, 1991).

Bartholomew, Craig G., "Introduction," in *A Royal Priesthood?: The Use of the Bible Ethically and Politically. A Dialogue with Oliver O'Donovan*, ed. Craig G. Bartholomew, et al. (Grand Rapids: Zondervan, 2002).

Bartholomew, Craig G., "A Time for War, and a Time for Peace: Old Testament Wisdom, Creation and O'Donovan's Theological Ethics," in *A Royal Priesthood?: The Use of the Bible Ethically and Politically. A Dialogue with Oliver O'Donovan*, ed. Craig G. Bartholomew, et al. (Grand Rapids: Zondervan, 2002).

Bartlett, Christopher A. and Sumantra Ghoshal, *Managing Across Borders: The Transnational Solution* (Boston: Harvard Business School, 1998).

Barton, Stephen C., "Social Values and Structures," in *Dictionary of New Testament Background*, ed. Craig A. Evans and Stanley E. Porter (Leicester: InterVarsity, 2000).

Bauckham, Richard J., *Moltmann: Messianic Theology in the Making* (Basingstoke, Hants: Marshall Pickering, 1987).

Bauckham, Richard J., *The Bible in Politics: How to Read the Bible Politically* (London: SPCK, 1989).

Bauckham, Richard J., et al. *Jesus 2000* (Oxford: Lion, 1989).

Bauckham, Richard J., *The Theology of the Book of Revelation* (Cambridge: Cambridge University, 1993).

Bauckham, Richard J., *The Theology of Jürgen Moltmann* (Edinburgh: T&T Clark, 1995).

Bauckham, Richard J., "Jürgen Moltmann," in *The Modern Theologians: An Introduction to Christian Theology in the Twentieth Century*, ed. David F. Ford, 2nd edn (Cambridge, MA: Blackwell, 1997).

Bauckham, Richard, J., "Time and Eternity," in *God Will Be All In All: The Eschatology of Jürgen Moltmann*, ed. Richard J. Bauckham (Edinburgh: T&T Clark, 1999).

Bauckham, Richard J. and Trevor A. Hart, *Hope Against Hope* (London: Darton, Longman & Todd, 1999).

Bauckham, Richard J., *James: Wisdom of James, Disciple of Jesus the Sage* (London: Routledge, 1999).

Bauckham, Richard J., "Jürgen Moltmann," in *The Dictionary of Historical Theology*, ed. Trevor A. Hart (Grand Rapids: Eerdmans, 2000).

Bauckham, Richard J., "Joining Creation's Praise of God," in *Ecotheology*, vol. 7/1 (July 2002), 45-59.

Bauckham, Richard J., *God and the Crisis of Freedom* (Louisville: Westminster John Knox Press, 2002).

Bauman, Zygmunt, *Globalization: The Human Consequences* (New York: Columbia University Press, 1998).

Baylis, John and Steve Smith, "Globalization and its Precursors," in *The Globalization of World Politics: An Introduction to International Relations*, ed. John Baylis and Steve Smith, 2nd edn (Oxford: Oxford University Press, 2001).

Bebbington, David, *Evangelicalism in Modern Britain* (London: Unwin Hyman, 1989).

Bebbington, David, "The Decline and Resurgence of Evangelical Social Concern 1918-1980," in *Evangelical Faith and Public Zeal: Evangelicals and Society in Britain 1780-1980*, ed. John Wolffe (London: SPCK, 1995).

Bebbington, David, "Evangelicals, Theology and Social Transformation," in *Movement for Change: Evangelicals and Social Transformation*, ed. David Hilborn (Carlisle: Paternoster, 2004).

Beck, Ulrich, *What is Globalization?* trans. Patrick Camiller (Cambridge: Polity Press, 2000).

Becker, Oswald, "Covenant," in *The New International Dictionary of New Testament Theology*, vol. 1, ed. Colin Brown (Exeter: Paternoster, 1975-1986).

Beitz, Charles R., *Political Theory and International Relations* (Princeton: Princeton University Press, 1999).

Bell, Daniel M., "Deliberating: Justice and Liberation," in *The Blackwell Companion to Christian Ethics*, ed. Stanley Hauerwas and Samuel Wells (Malden, MA: Blackwell, 2004).

Berkhof, Louis, *Systematic Theology* (Edinburgh: The Banner of Truth Trust, 1958).

Berkman, John, "An Introduction to the Hauerwas Reader," in *The Hauerwas Reader*, ed. John Berkman and Michael G. Cartwright (Durham: Duke University Press, 2001).

Berkouwer, Gerrit C., *The Triumph of Grace in the Theology of Karl Barth* (London: Paternoster, 1956).

Berkouwer, Gerrit C., *The Work of Christ*, trans. Cornelius Lambregtse (Grand Rapids: Eerdmans, 1965).

Berkouwer, Gerrit C., *General Revelation* (Grand Rapids: Eerdmans, 1968).

Berkouwer, Gerrit C., *The Return of Christ*, trans. James Van Oosterom (Grand Rapids: Eerdmans, 1972).

Berryman, Phillip, *Liberation Theology: Essential Facts about the Revolutionary Religious Movement in Latin America and Beyond* (London: Tauris, 1987).

Beyer, Peter, *Religion and Globalization* (London: SAGE, 1994).

Bhagwati, Jagdish, *In Defense of Globalization* (Oxford: Oxford University Press, 2004).

Biggar, Nigel, *The Hastening that Waits: Karl Barth's Ethics* (Oxford: Clarendon Press, 1993).

Biggar, Nigel, "Is Stanley Hauerwas Sectarian?" in *Faithfulness and Fortitude: In Conversation with the Theological Ethics of Stanley Hauerwas*, ed. Mark Thiessen Nation and Samuel Wells (Edinburgh: T&T Clark, 2000).

Bloesch, Donald G., "Forsyth, Peter Taylor," in *Evangelical Dictionary of Theology*, ed. Walter A. Elwell, 2nd edn (Grand Rapids: Baker, 2001).

Blount, Brian K., "Response to *The Desire of the Nations*," *Studies in Christian Ethics*, vol. 11/2 (August 1998), 8-17.

Bond, Michael, "The Backlash Against NGOs," in *The Globalization Reader*, ed. Frank J. Lechner and John Boli, 2nd edn (Malden, MA: Blackwell, 2004).

Bonhoeffer, Dietrich, *Ethics*, ed. Eberhard Bethge, trans. Neville H. Smith (London: SCM Press, 1955).

Bonhoeffer, Dietrich, *Christology*, trans. John Bowden (London: Collins, 1966).

Bonhoeffer, Dietrich, *Letters and Papers from Prison*, ed. Eberhard Bethge, trans. Reginald Fuller (London: SCM Press, 1967).

Bonino, José Míguez, *Doing Theology in a Revolutionary Situation* (Philadelphia: Fortress, 1975).

Bonsor, Jack A., "Rahner, Karl," in *Routledge Encyclopedia of Philosophy*, vol. 8, ed. Edward Craig (London: Routledge, 1998).

Bowden, John, *Karl Barth: Theologian* (London: SCM Press, 1983).

Boyer, Robert and Daniel Drache, *States Against Markets: The Limits of Globalization* (London: Routledge, 1996).

Brainard, Lael and Vinca LaFleur, *America's Role in the Fight Against Global Poverty: A Project of the Richard C. Blum Roundtable* (July 2004).

Bratt, James D. (ed.), *Abraham Kuyper: A Centennial Reader* (Grand Rapids: Eerdmans, 1998).

Bright, John, *The Kingdom of God in Bible and Church* (London: Lutterworth, 1955).

Bright, John, *Covenant and Promise* (London: SCM Press, 1977).

Brown, Chris, *Sovereignty, Rights and Justice* (Cambridge: Polity Press, 2002).

Brown, Delwin, *To Set at Liberty: Christian Faith and Human Freedom* (Maryknoll, NY: Orbis, 1981).

Brown, Gordon, "Governments and Supranational Agencies: A New Consensus? In *Making Globalization Good: The Moral Challenges of Global Capitalism*, ed. John H. Dunning (Oxford: Oxford University Press, 2003).

Brown, L. David, et al., "Globalization, NGOs, and Multisectoral Relations," in *Governance in a Globalizing World*, ed. Joseph S. Nye and John D. Donahue (Washington D.C.: Brookings, 2000).

Bruce, Frederick F., *The Books and the Parchments* (London: Marshall Pickering, 1991).

Bruce, Steve, *Politics and Religion* (Cambridge: Polity Press, 2003).

Bryan, Lowell L., *Race for the World: Strategies to Build a Great Global Firm* (Boston: Harvard Business School Press, 1999).

Bullinger, Heinrich, *One and Eternal Testament or Covenant* (1534).

Burns, James H., *The Cambridge History of Political Thought 1450-1700* (Cambridge: Cambridge University Press, 1991).

Busch, Eberhard, *Karl Barth: His Life from Letters and Autobiographical Texts*, trans. John Bowden (London: SCM Press, 1976).

Cairns, David, *The Image of God in Man* (London: Collins, 1973).

Calvin, John, *Commentary on a Harmony of the Evangelists, Matthew, Mark, and Luke*, vol. 3, trans. William Pringle (Grand Rapids: Eerdmans, 1956).

Calvin, John, "Commentary on Exodus 20:15/Deuteronomy 5:19," in *Calvin: Commentaries*, ed. Joseph Haroutunian (London: SCM Press, 1958).

Calvin, John, *Institutes of the Christian Religion*, vol. 1/6, ed. John T. McNeill, trans. Ford L. Battles (Philadelphia: Westminster Press, 1960).

Camilleri, Joseph A. and James Falk, *The End of Sovereignty?: The Politics of a Shrinking and Fragmenting World* (Aldershot: Edward Elgar, 1992).

Caney, Simon, "International Distributive Justice," *Political Studies*, vol. 49/5 (December 2001), 974-997.

Carr, Anne E., "Starting with the Human," in *A World of Grace: An Introduction to the Themes and Foundations of Karl Rahner's Theology*, ed. Leo J. O'Donovan (New York: Seabury Press, 1980).

Cartwright, Michael G., "Being Sent: Witness," in *The Blackwell Companion to Christian Ethics*, ed. Stanley Hauerwas and Samuel Wells (Malden, MA: Blackwell, 2004).

Casanova, José, *Public Religions in the Modern World* (Chicago: University of Chicago Press, 1994).

Castells, Manuel, *The Rise of the Network Society*, 2nd edn (Oxford: Blackwell, 2000).

Cavanagh, John, et al., *Alternatives to Economic Globalization* (San Francisco, CA: Berrett-Koehler, 2002).

Cavanaugh, William T., "Stan the Man: A Thoroughly Biased Account of a Completely Unobjective Person," in *The Hauerwas Reader*, ed. John Berkman and Michael G. Cartwright (Durham: Duke University Press, 2001).

Cavanaugh, William T. and Peter Scott, "Introduction," in *The Blackwell Companion to Political Theology*, ed. Peter Scott and William T. Cavanaugh (Malden, MA: Blackwell Publishing, 2004).

Cerny, Philip G., "What Next for the State?" in *Globalization: Theory and Practice*, ed. Eleonore Kofman and Gillian Youngs (London: Pinter, 1996).

Chaplin, Jonathan, "Prospects for an 'Evangelical Political Philosophy,'" *Evangelical Review of Theology*, vol. 24/4 (October 2000), 354-373.

Chaplin, Jonathan, "Political Eschatology and Responsible Government: Oliver O'Donovan's 'Christian Liberalism,'" in *A Royal Priesthood?: The Use of the Bible Ethically and Politically. A Dialogue with Oliver O'Donovan*, ed. Craig G. Bartholomew, et al. (Grand Rapids: Zondervan, 2002).

Cherry, Conrad, *The Theology of Jonathan Edwards: A Reappraisal* (Bloomington: Indiana University Press, 1990).

Childs, Brevard S., *Biblical Theology of the Old and New Testaments: Theological Reflection on the Christian Bible* (London: SCM Press, 1992).

Chow, John K., *Patronage and Power: A Study of Social Networks in Corinth – in JSNT Supplement Series*, vol. 75 (Sheffield: JSOT Press, 1992).

Clark, Ian, "Globalization and the Post-Cold War Order," in *The Globalization of World Politics: An Introduction to International Relations*, ed. John Baylis and Steve Smith, 2nd edn (Oxford: Oxford University Press, 2001).

Clarke, Andrew D., *Secular and Christian Leadership in Corinth: A Socio-Historical and Exegetical Study of 1 Corinthians 1-6* (Leiden: E.J. Brill, 1993).

Clarke, Andrew D., *Serve the Community of the Church: Christians as Leaders and Ministers* (Grand Rapids: Eerdmans, 2000).

Clarke, Tony, *By What Authority!: Unmasking and Challenging the Global Corporations' Assault on Democracy through the World Trade Organization* (Ottawa: Polaris Institute/ International Forum on Globalization, 1999).

Clements, Keith W., "P.T. Forsyth: A Political Theologian?" in *Justice the True and Only Mercy: Essays on the Life and Theology of Peter Taylor Forsyth*, ed. Trevor A. Hart (Edinburgh: T&T Clark, 1995).

Clinton, William J., "Global Challenges," at Yale University, 31 October 2003.

Coglianese, Cary, "Globalization and the Design of International Institutions," in *Governance in a Globalizing World*, ed. Joseph S. Nye and John D. Donahue (Washington D.C.: Brookings, 2000).

Collier, Jane and Rafael Esteban, *From Complicity to Encounter: The Church and the Culture of Economism* (Harrisburg: Trinity Press International, 1998).

Collingwood, Vivien, "Assistance with Fewer Strings Attached," *Ethics and International Affairs*, vol. 17/1 (April 2003), 55-68.

Consultation on the Relationship between Evangelism and Social Responsibility, *Evangelism and Social Responsibility: An Evangelical Commitment* (Grand Rapids: Reformed Bible College, 1982).

Costas, Orlando E., *Christ Outside the Gate: Mission Beyond Christendom* (Maryknoll, NY: Orbis, 1982).

Crane, George T. and Abla Amawi, *The Theoretical Evolution of International Political Economy - A Reader* (Oxford: Oxford University Press, 1991).

Cronin, Ciaran and Pablo de Greiff, *Global Justice and Transnational Politics: Essays on the Moral and Political Challenges of Globalization* (Cambridge, Mass.: MIT Press, 2002).

Davidson, Robert, "Covenant," in *The Oxford Companion to Christian Thought*, ed. Adrian Hastings, Alistair Mason, and Hugh Pyper (Oxford: Oxford University Press, 2000).

Demarest, Bruce A., *General Revelation: Historical Views and Contemporary Issues* (Grand Rapids: Zondervan, 1982).

Department of Trade and Industry, *Trade and Investment White Paper 2004: Making Globalization a Force for Good* (London: The Stationery Office, 2004).

Dodd, Charles H., *Gospel and Law: The Relation of Faith and Ethics in Early Christianity* (Cambridge: University Press, 1951).

Dodd, Charles H., *The Founder of Christianity* (New York: MacMillan, 1970).

Dollar, David and Paul Collier (ed.), *Globalization, Growth, and Poverty: Building an Inclusive World Economy* (New York: Oxford University Press/ The World Bank, 2002).

Dollar, David, "The Poor Like Globalization," *Yale Global Online* (June 2003).

Dorrien, Gary J., *Reconstructing the Common Good: Theology and the Social Order* (Maryknoll, NY: Orbis, 1990).

Douglas, James D. and Philip W. Comfort, *Who's Who in Christian History* (Wheaton: Tyndale House, 1992).

Duchrow, Ulrich, *Alternatives to Global Capitalism: Drawn from Biblical History, Designed for Political Action*, trans. Elaine Griffiths, et al. (Utrecht: International Books, 1995).

Dumbrell, William J., *Covenant and Creation: A Theology of the Old Testament Covenants* (Carlisle: Paternoster, 1997).

Dunning, John H., *Multinational Enterprises and the Global Economy* (Wokingham: Addison-Wesley, 1993).

Dunning, John H., *The Globalization of Business: The Challenge of the 1990s* (London: Routledge, 1993).

Dunning, John H. (ed.), *United Nations Library on Transnational Corporations*, 20 vols. (London: Routledge, 1993-1994).

Dunning, John H. (ed.), *Making Globalization Good: The Moral Challenges of Global Capitalism* (Oxford: Oxford University Press, 2003).

Durham, John I., *Exodus. Word Biblical Commentary* (Waco, TX: Word Books, 1987).

Eichrodt, Walther, *Theology of the Old Testament*, vol. 1, trans. John A. Baker (London: SCM Press, 1961).

Elshtain, Jean B., "Christian Contrarian," *Time*, vol. 158/11 (17 September 2001), 76-78.

Elson, Diane, "Human Rights and Corporate Profits: The UN Global Compact – Part of the Solution or Part of the Problem?" in *Global Tensions: Challenges and Opportunities in the World Economy*, ed. Lourdes Beneria and Savitri Bisnath (New York: Routledge, 2004).

Erickson, Millard, *Christian Theology*, 2nd edn (Grand Rapids: Baker, 2001).

Ernst & Young, *Global Vision 2002: Summary of Strategies* (London: Ernst & Young, 1998).

Escobar, Samuel, "Evangelization and Man's Search for Freedom, Justice and Fulfillment," in *Let the Earth Hear His Voice*, ed. James D. Douglas (Minneapolis: World Wide Publications, 1975).

Evangelical Alliance, *Uniting for Change: An Evangelical Vision for Transforming Society* (London: Evangelical Alliance, 2002).

Fee, Gordon D., *The First Epistle to the Corinthians* (Grand Rapids: Eerdmans, 1987).

Fensham, F. Charles, "Covenant, Alliance," in *New Bible Dictionary*, ed. James D. Douglas and Norman Hillyer, 2nd edn (Leicester: InterVarsity, 1982).

Fergusson, David, "Another Way of Reading Stanley Hauerwas?" in *Scottish Journal of Theology*, vol. 50/2 (May 1997), 242-249.

Fergusson, David, *Community, Liberalism and Christian Ethics* (Cambridge: Cambridge University Press, 1998).

Ferguson, Everett, *Backgrounds of Early Christianity*, 2nd edn. (Grand Rapids: Eerdmans, 1993).

Field, David H., "Ethics," in *New Dictionary of Theology*, ed. Sinclair B. Ferguson, David F. Wright, and James I. Packer (Leicester: InterVarsity, 1988).

Forell, George W. (ed.), *Christian Social Teachings: A Reader in Christian Ethics from the Bible to the Present* (Minneapolis: Augsburg, 1971).

Forrester, Duncan B., *Theology and Politics* (Oxford: Basil Blackwell, 1988).

Forrester, Duncan B., *Beliefs, Values and Policies: Conviction Politics in a Secular Age* (Oxford: Oxford University Press, 1989).

Forrester, Duncan B., *Christian Justice and Public Policy* (Cambridge: Cambridge University Press, 1997).

Forrester, Duncan B., "The Church and the Concentration Camp: Some Reflections of Moral Community," in *Faithfulness and Fortitude: In Conversation with the Theological Ethics of Stanley Hauerwas*, ed. Mark Thiessen Nation and Samuel Wells (Edinburgh: T&T Clark, 2000).

Forrester, Duncan B., *On Human Worth: A Christian Vindication of Equality* (London: SCM Press, 2001).

Forsyth, Peter T., *The Work of Christ* (London: Independent Press, 1952).

Forsyth, Peter T., *The Church and the Sacraments* (London: Independent Press, 1953).

Frank, Andre Gunder, *Crisis: In the Third World* (London: Heinemann, 1981).

Frankel, Jeffrey, "Globalization of the Economy," in *Governance in a Globalizing World*, ed. Joseph S. Nye and John D. Donahue (Washington D.C.: Brookings, 2000).

Franklin, Daniel, "Globalization's New Boom," in *The World in* 2003, ed. Dudley Fishburn and Stephen Green (London: The Economist, 2002).

Freeman, Samuel, "Contractarianism," in *Routledge Encyclopedia of Philosophy*, vol. 2, ed. Edward Craig (London: Routledge, 1998).

Freeman, Samuel, "Rawls, John," in *Routledge Encyclopedia of Philosophy*, vol. 8, ed. Edward Craig (London: Routledge, 1998).

Frei, Hans W., *The Eclipse of Biblical Narrative: A Study in Eighteenth and Nineteenth Century Hermeneutics* (New Haven: Yale University Press, 1974).

Furnish, Victor P., "How Firm a Foundation? Some Questions about Scripture in *The Desire of the Nations*," *Studies in Christian Ethics*, vol. 11/2 (August 1998), 18-23.

Garber, Daniel, "Descartes, René," in *Routledge Encyclopedia of Philosophy*, vol. 3, ed. Edward Craig (London: Routledge, 1998).

Gardner, E. Clinton, *Justice and Christian Ethics* (Cambridge: Cambridge University Press, 1995).

Giblet, Jean and Pierre Grelot, "Covenant," in *Dictionary of Biblical Theology*, ed. Xavier León-Dufour (London: Geoffrey Chapman, 1967).

Giddens, Anthony, *The Consequences of Modernity* (Cambridge: Polity Press, 1990).

Giddens, Anthony, *Runaway World: How Globalization is Reshaping our Lives* (London: Profile, 1999).

Gilpin, Robert, *Global Political Economy: Understanding the International Economic Order* (Princeton: Princeton University Press, 2001).

Goodman, John B. and Louis W. Pauly, "The Obsolescence of Capital Controls? Economic Management in an Age of Global Markets," in *International Political Economy: Perspectives on Global Power and Wealth*, ed. Jeffrey A. Frieden and David A. Lake, 4th edn (London: Routledge, 2000).

Gorringe, Timothy J., *God's Just Vengeance: Crime, Violence and the Rhetoric of Salvation* (Cambridge: Cambridge University Press, 1996).

Gorringe, Timothy J., "Invoking: Globalization and Power," in *The Blackwell Companion to Christian Ethics*, ed. Stanley Hauerwas and Samuel Wells (Malden, MA: Blackwell, 2004).

Goudzwaard, Bob and Harry de Lange, *Beyond Poverty and Affluence: Toward an Economy of Care*, ed. and trans. Mark R. Vander Vennen (Grand Rapids: Eerdmans, 1995).

Goudzwaard, Bob, *Globalization and the Kingdom of God* (Washington D.C.: Baker, 2001).

Graham, W. Fred, *The Constructive Revolutionary: John Calvin & His Socio Economic Impact* (Richmond: John Knox Press, 1971).

Green, Leslie, "Power," in *Routledge Encyclopedia of Philosophy*, vol. 7, ed. Edward Craig (London: Routledge, 1998).

Greene, Colin J.D., "Revisiting Christendom: A Crisis of Legitimization," in *A Royal Priesthood?: The Use of the Bible Ethically and Politically. A Dialogue with Oliver O'Donovan*, ed. Craig G. Bartholomew, et al. (Grand Rapids: Zondervan, 2002).

Greene, Mark, "The Road to Irrelevance: The Great Divide," *Idea* (March 2003), 20-23.

Grenz, Stanley J., *The Moral Quest: Foundations of Christian Ethics* (Downers Grove, Ill.: InterVarsity, 1997).

Grenz, Stanley J., *Theology for the Community of God* (Grand Rapids: Eerdmans, 2000).

Grenz, Stanley J., *The Social God and the Relational Self: A Trinitarian Theology of the Imago Dei* (London: Westminster John Knox Press, 2001).

Grindle, Merilee S., "Ready or Not: The Developing World and Globalization," in *Governance in a Globalizing World*, ed. Joseph S. Nye and John D. Donahue (Washington D.C.: Brookings, 2000).

Guehenno, Jean-Marie, *The End of the Nation-State*, trans. Victoria Elliot (Minneapolis: University of Minnesota Press, 1995).

Gunton, Colin E., *Enlightenment and Alienation: An Essay towards a Trinitarian Theology* (Basingstoke, Hants: Marshall, Morgan and Scott, 1985).

Gunton, Colin E., *Christ and Creation* (Carlisle: Paternoster, 1992).

Gunton, Colin E., "Historical and Systematic Theology," in *The Cambridge Companion to Christian Doctrine*, ed. Colin E. Gunton (Cambridge: Cambridge University Press, 1997).

Gunton, Colin E., "The Church as a School of Virtue? Human Formation in Trinitarian Framework," in *Faithfulness and Fortitude: In Conversation with the Theological Ethics of Stanley Hauerwas*, ed. Mark Thiessen Nation and Samuel Wells (Edinburgh: T&T Clark, 2000).

Gustafson, James M., "The Sectarian Temptation: Reflections on Theology, the Church, and the University," *Proceedings of the Catholic Theological Society*, vol. 40 (1985), 83-94.

Gutiérrez, Gustavo, *A Theology of Liberation*, trans. Sister Caridad Inda and John Eagleson (London: SCM Press, 1974).

Gutiérrez, Gustavo, "Toward a Theology of Liberation," in *Liberation Theology: A Documentary History*, ed. Alfred T. Hennelly (Maryknoll, NY: Orbis, 1992).

Hamel, Gary and C. K. Prahalad, *Competing for the Future* (Boston, Mass.: Harvard Business School Press, 1994).

Handelman, Howard, *The Challenge of Third World Development* (Upper Saddle River, N.J.: Prentice Hall, 1996).

Harrod, Henry R.F., *The Life of John Maynard Keynes* (London: Macmillan, 1951).

Hart, Trevor A., "Morality, Atonement and the Death of Jesus: The Crucial Focus of Forsyth's Theology," in *Justice the True and Only Mercy: Essays on the Life and Theology of Peter Taylor Forsyth*, ed. Trevor A. Hart (Edinburgh: T&T Clark, 1995).

Hart, Trevor A., "Imagination for the Kingdom of God?" in *God Will Be All In All: The Eschatology of Jürgen Moltmann*, ed. Richard J. Bauckham (Edinburgh: T&T Clark, 1999).

Hart, Trevor A., "Revelation," in *The Cambridge Companion to Karl Barth*, ed. John Webster (Cambridge: Cambridge University Press, 2000).

Hartwell, Herbert, *The Theology of Karl Barth: An Introduction* (London: Duckworth, 1964).

Hauerwas, Stanley M., *Vision and Virtue* (Notre Dame, Ind.: Fides, 1974).

Hauerwas, Stanley M., *Truthfulness and Tragedy: Further Investigations in Christian Ethics* (Notre Dame, Ind.: University of Notre Dame, 1977).

Hauerwas, Stanley M., *A Community of Character: Toward a Constructive Christian Social Ethic* (Notre Dame, Ind.: University of Notre Dame Press, 1981).

Hauerwas, Stanley M., "On Keeping Theological Ethics Theological," in *Revisions: Changing Perspectives in Moral Philosophy*, ed. Stanley M. Hauerwas and Alasdair MacIntyre (Notre Dame, Ind.: University of Notre Dame, 1983).

Hauerwas, Stanley M., *The Peaceable Kingdom: A Primer in Christian Ethics* (London: SCM Press, 1984).

Hauerwas, Stanley M., *Against the Nations: War and Survival in a Liberal Society* (Minneapolis: Winston Press, 1985).

Hauerwas, Stanley M., "Some Theological Reflections on Gutierrez's Use of 'Liberation' as a Theological Concept," *Modern Theology*, vol. 3/1 (October 1986), 67-76.

Hauerwas, Stanley M. and William H. Willimon, *Resident Aliens: A Provocative Christian Assessment of Culture and Ministry for People who Know that Something is Wrong* (Nashville: Abingdon Press, 1989).

Hauerwas, Stanley M., "The Testament of Friends," *The Christian Century*, vol. 107/7 (February 1990), 212-216.

Hauerwas, Stanley M., *After Christendom?: How the Church is to Behave if Freedom, Justice, and a Christian Nation are Bad Ideas* (Nashville: Abingdon Press, 1991).

Hauerwas, Stanley M., *Unleashing the Scriptures: Freeing the Bible from Captivity to America* (Nashville: Abingdon Press, 1993).

Hauerwas, Stanley M., *Character and the Christian Life: A Study in Theological Ethics* (Notre Dame, Ind.: University of Notre Dame Press, 1994).

Hauerwas, Stanley M., *Dispatches from the Front: Theological Engagements with the Secular* (Durham: Duke University Press, 1994).

Hauerwas, Stanley M., "The Church's One Foundation is Jesus Christ Her Lord; Or, In a World Without Foundations: All We Have is the Church," in *Theology Without Foundations: Religious Practice and the Future of Theological Truth*, ed. Stanley M. Hauerwas, Nancey C. Murphy, and Mark T. Nation (Nashville: Abingdon Press, 1994).

Hauerwas, Stanley M., *In Good Company: The Church as Polis* (Notre Dame, Ind.: University of Notre Dame, 1995).

Hauerwas, Stanley M., "What Could it Mean for the Church to be Christ's Body?: A Question Without a Clear Answer," in *Scottish Journal of Theology*, vol. 48/1 (February 1995), 1-21.

Hauerwas, Stanley, M. and Charles R. Pinches, *Christians Among the Virtues: Theological Conversations with Ancient and Modern Ethics* (Notre Dame, Ind.: University of Notre Dame Press, 1997).

Hauerwas, Stanley M., "On Doctrine and Ethics," in *The Cambridge Companion to Christian Doctrine*, ed. Colin E. Gunton (Cambridge: Cambridge University Press, 1997).

Hauerwas, Stanley M., *Sanctify Them in the Truth: Holiness Exemplified* (Nashville: Abingdon Press, 1998).

Hauerwas, Stanley M. and James Fodor, "Remaining in Babylon: Oliver O'Donovan's Defence of Christendom," *Studies in Christian Ethics*, vol. 11/2 (August 1998), 30-55.

Hauerwas, Stanley M. and Chris K. Huebner, "History, Theory, and Anabaptism: A Conversation on Theology after John Howard Yoder," in *The Wisdom of the Cross: Essays in Honour of John Howard Yoder*, ed. Stanley M. Hauerwas, et al (Grand Rapids: Eerdmans, 1999).

Hauerwas, Stanley M. and William H. Willimon, *The Truth About God: The Ten Commandments in Christian Life* (Nashville: Abingdon Press, 1999).

Hauerwas, Stanley M., *A Better Hope: Resources for a Church Confronting Capitalism, Democracy, and Postmodernity* (Grand Rapids: Brazos Press, 2000).

Hauerwas, Stanley M., *Wilderness Wanderings: Probing Twentieth-Century Theology and Philosophy* (London: SCM Press, 2001).

Hauerwas, Stanley M., *With the Grain of the Universe: The Church's Witness and Natural Theology: Being the Gifford Lectures Delivered at the University of St. Andrews in 2001* (Grand Rapids: Brazos Press, 2001).

Hay, Donald A., *Economics Today: A Christian Critique* (Leicester : Apollos, 1989).

Haynes, Jeff, *Religion in Global Politics* (Harlow: Longman, 1998).

Hays, Richard B., *The Moral Vision of the New Testament: A Contemporary Introduction to New Testament Ethics* (New York: HarperCollins, 1996).

Headlam, Arthur C., *Christian Theology* (Oxford: Clarendon, 1934).

Held, David, *Democracy and the Global Order: From the Modern State to Cosmopolitan Governance* (Cambridge: Polity Press, 1995).

Held, David, et al, *Global Transformations: Politics, Economics and Culture* (Oxford: Polity Press, 1999).

Held, David, "Cosmopolitanism: Ideas, Realities and Deficits," in *Governing Globalization: Power, Authority and Global Governance*, ed. David Held and Anthony G. McGrew (Cambridge: Polity Press, 2002).

Held, David and Anthony McGrew, *Globalization/ Anti-Globalization* (Cambridge: Polity Press, 2002).

Henry, Carl F.H., *The Uneasy Conscience of Modern Fundamentalism* (Grand Rapids: Eerdmans, 1947).

Henry, Carl F.H., *Aspects of Christian Social Ethics* (Grand Rapids: Eerdmans, 1964).

Henry, Carl F.H., *The God Who Shows Himself* (Waco, TX: Word, 1966).

Henry, Carl F.H., *God, Revelation, and Authority: The God Who Speaks and Shows*, vol. 1 (Waco, TX: Word, 1976).

Henry, Carl F.H., "Revelation, Special," in *Evangelical Dictionary of Theology*, ed. Walter A. Elwell, 2nd edn (Grand Rapids: Baker, 2001).

Herion, Gary A., "Covenant," in *Eerdmans Dictionary of the Bible*, ed. David N. Freedom (Grand Rapid: Eerdmans, 2000).

Hertz, Noreena, *The Silent Takeover: Global Capitalism and the Death of Democracy* (London: Heinemann, 2001).

Hexham, Irving, "Kuyper, Abraham," in *Evangelical Dictionary of Theology*, ed. Walter A. Elwell, 2nd edn (Grand Rapids: Baker, 2001).

Hilton, Boyd, *The Age of Atonement: The Influence of Evangelicalism on Social and Economic Thought, 1795-1865* (Oxford: Clarendon, 1988).

Hindmarsh, D. Bruce, "Let Us See Thy Great Salvation," in *What Does it Mean to be Saved?: Broadening Evangelical Horizons of Salvation*, ed. John G. Stackhouse (Grand Rapids: Baker, 2002).

Hirst, Paul Q., "The Global Economy: Myths and Realities," *International Affairs*, vol. 73/3 (July 1997), 409-425.

Hirst, Paul Q. and Grahame Thompson, *Globalization in Question: The International Economy and the Possibilities of Governance*, 2nd edn (Cambridge: Polity Press, 1999).

Hodge, Charles, *Systematic Theology*, vol. 1 (London: Thomas Nelson, 1871-1873).

Hoffmann, Stanley, "Notes on the Elusiveness of Modern Power," *International Journal*, vol. 30 (Spring 1975), 183-206.

Hoffmann, Stanley, *Duties Beyond Borders: On the Limits and Possibilities of Ethical International Politics* (Syracuse, New York: Syracuse University Press, 1981).

Hollenbach, S.J., David, *The Common Good and Christian Ethics* (Cambridge: Cambridge University Press, 2002).

Holmes, Stephen R., *God of Grace and God of Glory: An Account of the Theology of Jonathan Edwards* (Edinburgh: T&T Clark, 2000).

Hooker, C.A. "Laws, Natural," in *Routledge Encyclopedia of Philosophy*, vol. 5, ed. Edward Craig (London: Routledge, 1998).

Hunsinger, George, "What Can Evangelicals and Postliberals Learn From Each Other? The Carl Henry-Hans Frei Exchange Reconsidered," in *The Nature of Confession: Evangelicals and Postliberals in Conversation*, ed. Timothy R. Phillips and Dennis L. Okholm (Downers Grove, Ill.: InterVarsity, 1996).

Hunsinger, George, "Social Witness in Generous Orthodoxy," *Princeton Seminary Bulletin*, vol. 21/1 (2000), 38-62.

Hunsinger, George, "Baptism and the Soteriology of Forgiveness," *International Journal of Systematic Theology*, vol. 2/3 (November 2000), 247-269.

Huntington, Samuel P., *The Clash of Civilizations and the Remaking of World Order* (London: Touchstone Books, 1998).

Ignatieff, Michael, *Human Rights as Politics and Idolatry* (Princeton: Princeton University Press, 2001).

Immelt, Jeff, "*The Changing Face of the Global Company*," at the European Policy Centre in Brussels, Belgium, 28 January 2002.

Jeannet, Jean-Pierre, *Managing with a Global Mindset* (London: Financial Times Management, 2000).

Jeffers, James S., *Conflict at Rome: Social Order and Hierarchy in Early Christianity* (Minneapolis: Fortress, 1991).

Jenkins, Philip, *The Next Christendom: The Coming of Global Christianity* (Oxford: Oxford University Press, 2002).

Jenson, Robert W., "The Hauerwas Project," *Modern Theology*, vol. 8/3 (July 1992), 285-295.

Jenson, Robert W., "The Church and the Sacraments," in *The Cambridge Companion to Christian Doctrine*, ed. Colin E. Gunton (Cambridge: Cambridge University Press, 1997).

Jockle, Clemens, *Encyclopedia of Saints* (London: Parkgate, 1997).

Johnson, William S., *The Mystery of God: Karl Barth and the Postmodern Foundations of Theology* (Louisville, Kentucky: Westminster John Knox Press, 1997).

Jones, Charles, *Global Justice: Defending Cosmopolitanism* (Oxford: Oxford University Press, 1999).

Jones, R. J. Barry, *The World Turned Upside Down?: Globalization and the Future of the State* (Manchester: Manchester University Press, 2000).

Jones, R. Tudor, "Reformation Theology," in *New Dictionary of Theology*, ed. Sinclair B. Ferguson, David F. Wright, and James I. Packer (Leicester: InterVarsity, 1988).

Kabeer, Nakila, "Labour Standards, Women's Rights, Basic Needs: Challenges to Collective Action in a Globalizing World," in *Global Tensions: Challenges and Opportunities in the World Economy*, ed. Lourdes Beneria and Savitri Bisnath (New York: Routledge, 2004).

Kaiser, Walter C., *Toward Old Testament Ethics* (Grand Rapids: Zondervan, 1983).

Kant, Immanuel, "Perpetual Peace," in *Kant's Political Writings*, ed. Hans Reiss, trans. Hugh B. Nisbet (London: Cambridge University Press, 1970).

Kant, Immanuel, "Essay on Theory and Practice," in *International Relations in Political Thought*, ed. Chris Brown, Terry Nardin, and Nicholas Rengger (Cambridge: Cambridge University Press, 2002).

Kaplinsky, Raphael, "Is Globalization All it is Cracked Up to be?" *Review of International Political Economy*, vol. 8/1 (Spring 2001), 45-65.

Kapolyo, Joe, "Social Transformation as a Missional Imperative: Evangelicals and Development since Lausanne," in *Movement for Change: Evangelicals and Social Transformation*, ed. David Hilborn (Carlisle: Paternoster, 2004).

Kapstein, Ethan B., "Does Globalization have an Ethical Problem?" in *Ethics and International Affairs: Extent and Limits*, ed. Jean-Marc Coicaud and Daniel Warner (New York: United Nations University Press, 2001).

Kasper, Walter, *Jesus the Christ*, trans. Verdont Green (London: Burns & Oates, 1976).

Katongole, Emmanuel, *Beyond Universal Reason: The Relation between Religion and Ethics in the Work of Stanley Hauerwas* (Notre Dame, Ind.: University of Notre Dame, 2000).

Keil, Carl F. and Franz Delitzsch, *Commentary on the Old Testament: Isaiah*, vol. 7, trans. James Martin (Grand Rapids: Eerdmans, 1983).

Keohane, Robert O. and Joseph S. Nye, *Power and Interdependence*, 3rd edn (New York: Longman, 2001).

Kirk, J. Andrew, "Christian Mission and the Epistemological Crisis of the West," in *To Stake a Claim: Mission and the Western Crisis of Knowledge*, ed. J. Andrew Kirk and Kevin J. Vanhoozer (Maryknoll, NY: Orbis, 1999).

Kirshner, Jonathan, "Keynes, Capital Mobility and the Crisis of Embedded Liberalism," *Review of International Political Economy*, vol. 6/3 (Autumn 1999), 313-337.

Klein, Naomi, *No Logo: No Space, No Choice, No Jobs* (London: Flamingo, 2001).

Kline, Meredith G., *Kingdom Prologue: Genesis Foundations for a Covenantal Worldview* (Overland Park, Kansas: Two Age Press, 2000).

Knighton, Ben, "Globalization: Implications of Violence, the Global Economy, and the Role of the State for Africa and Christian Mission," *Transformation*, vol. 18/4 (October 2001), 204-219.

Kolm, Serge-Christophe, *Modern Theories of Justice* (Cambridge, Mass.: The MIT Press, 1998).

Kruijf, Gerrit de, "The Function of Romans 13 in Christian Ethics," in *A Royal Priesthood?: The Use of the Bible Ethically and Politically. A Dialogue with Oliver O'Donovan*, ed. Craig G. Bartholomew, et al. (Grand Rapids: Zondervan, 2002).

Kuyper, Abraham, *Lectures on Calvinism* (Grand Rapids: Eerdmans, 1943).

LaCugna, Catherine M., *God for Us: The Trinity and Christian Life* (San Francisco: Harper, 1992).

Lawton, Thomas C. and Kevin P. Michaels, "The Evolving Global Production Structure: Implications for International Political Economy," in *Strange Power: Shaping the Parameters of International Relations and International Political Economy*, ed. Thomas C. Lawton, James N. Rosenau, and Amy C. Verdun (Aldershot: Ashgate, 2000).

Legrain, Philippe, *Open World: The Truth about Globalization* (London: Abacus, 2003).

Letham, Robert W.A., "Reformed Theology," in *New Dictionary of Theology*, ed. Sinclair B. Ferguson, David F. Wright, and James I. Packer (Leicester: InterVarsity, 1988).

Lewellen, Ted C., *The Anthropology of Globalization: Cultural Anthropology Enters the 21st Century* (Westport, Connecticut: Bergin and Garvey, 2002).

Lindbeck, George A., *The Nature of Doctrine: Religion and Theology in a Postliberal Age* (Philadelphia: Westminster Press, 1984).

Linder, Robert D., "The Reformation," in *The New International Dictionary of the Christian Church*, ed. James D. Douglas and Earle E. Cairns, 2nd edn (Grand Rapids: Zondervan, 1978).

Litan, Robert E., Paul Masson, and Michael Pomerleano, *Open Doors: Foreign Participation in Financial Systems in Developing Countries* (Washington: Brookings Institution Press, 2001).

Litfin, A. Duane, *St. Paul's Theology of Proclamation: 1 Corinthians 1-4 and Greco Roman Rhetoric* (Cambridge: Cambridge University Press, 1994).

Long, D. Stephen, *Divine Economy: Theology and the Market* (London: Routledge, 2000).

Longenecker, Richard N., *New Testament Social Ethics for Today* (Grand Rapids: Eerdmans, 1984).

Lossky, Vladimir, *In the Image and Likeness of God* (London: Mowbrays, 1975).

Lovin, Robin W., *Reinhold Niebuhr and Christian Realism* (Cambridge: Cambridge University Press, 1995).

Lull, Timothy F. (ed.), *Martin Luther's Basic Theological Writings* (Minneapolis: Fortress, 1989).

MacIntyre, Alasdair, *After Virtue: A Study in Moral Theory*, 2nd edn (London: Duckworth, 1985).

MacIntyre, Alasdair, *Whose Justice? Which Rationality?* (London: Duckworth, 1988).

MacMillan, John and Andrew Linklater, "Boundaries in Question," in *Boundaries in Question: New Directions in International Relations*, ed. John MacMillan and Andrew Linklater (London: Pinter, 1995).

Macmurray, John, *Persons in Relation: Being the Gifford Lectures Delivered in the University of Glasgow in 1954* (London: Faber, 1961).

Malina, Bruce J., *The New Testament World: Insights from Cultural Anthropology*, 3rd edn (Louisville, KY: Westminster John Knox Press, 2001).

Manson, Thomas W., *The Church's Ministry* (London: Hodder & Stoughton, 1948).

Manson, Thomas W., *The Servant Messiah: A Study of the Public Ministry of Jesus* (Cambridge: Cambridge University Press, 1977).

Marsden, George, *Fundamentalism and American Culture* (New York: Oxford University Press, 1980).

Marshall, I. Howard, "Using the Bible in Ethics," in *Essays in Evangelical Social Ethics*, ed. David F. Wright (Exeter: Paternoster, 1978).

Masson, Paul, "Globalization: Facts and Figures," *International Monetary Fund Policy Discussion Paper* (October 2001).

Matheson, Peter (ed.), *The Third Reich and the Christian Churches* (Edinburgh: T&T Clark, 1981).

Maury, Philippe, *Evangelism and Politics* (London: Lutterworth, 1959).

Mayer-Schönberger, Viktor and Deborah Hurley, "Globalization of Communication," in *Governance in a Globalizing World*, ed. Joseph S. Nye and John D. Donahue (Washington D.C.: Brookings, 2000).

McCarthy, Dennis J., *Treaty and Covenant: A Study in Form in the Ancient Oriental Documents and in the Old Testament* (Rome: Biblical Institute, 1978).

McConville, J. Gordon, "Law and Morality in the Old Testament," in *A Royal Priesthood?: The Use of the Bible Ethically and Politically. A Dialogue with Oliver O'Donovan*, ed. Craig G. Bartholomew, et al. (Grand Rapids: Zondervan, 2002).

McCormack, Bruce L., *Karl Barth's Critically Realistic Dialectical Theology* (Oxford: Oxford University Press, 1997).

McCorquodale, Robert, "International Law, Boundaries, and Imagination," in *Boundaries and Justice: Diverse Ethical Perspectives*, ed. David Miller and Sohail H. Hashmi (Princeton: Princeton University Press, 2001).

McFadyen, Alistair I., *The Call to Personhood: A Christian Theory of the Individual in Social Relationships* (Cambridge: Cambridge University Press, 1990).

McGrath, Alister E., *A Passion for Truth: The Intellectual Coherence of Evangelicalism* (Leicester: InterVarsity, 1996).

McGrath, Alister E., "An Evangelical Evaluation of Postliberalism," in *The Nature of Confession: Evangelicals and Postliberals in Conversation*, ed. Timothy R. Phillips and Dennis L. Okholm (Downers Grove, Ill.: InterVarsity, 1996).

McGrath, Alister E., *Christian Theology*, 2nd edn (Oxford: Blackwell, 1997).

McKim, Robert and Jeff McMahon, *The Morality of Nationalism* (Oxford: Oxford University Press, 1997).

McMichael, Philip, "Sleepless Since Seattle: What is the WTO About?" *Review of International Political Economy*, vol. 7/3 (Autumn 2000), 466-474.

McRay, John R., "Corinth," in *Dictionary of New Testament Background*, ed. Craig A. Evans and Stanley E. Porter (Leicester: InterVarsity, 2000).

Meeks, M. Douglas, *Origins of the Theology of Hope* (Philadelphia: Fortress, 1974).

Mendenhall, George E. and Gary A. Herion, "Covenant," in *The Anchor Bible Dictionary*, vol. 1, ed. David N. Freedman (New York: Doubleday, 1992).

Metz, Johann-Baptist and Jürgen Moltmann, *Faith and the Future* (Maryknoll, NY: Orbis, 1995).

Micah Challenge website (www.micahchallenge.org).

Michalowski, Piotr, "The Torch and the Censer," in *The Tablet and The Scroll*, ed. William W. Hallo (Maryland: CDL Press, 1993).

Miller, Richard B., "Christian Attitudes toward Boundaries," in *Boundaries and Justice: Diverse Ethical Perspectives*, ed. David Miller and Sohail H. Hashmi (Princeton: Princeton University Press, 2001).

Moberly, R. Walter L., "The Use of Scripture in *The Desire of the Nations*," in *A Royal Priesthood?: The Use of the Bible Ethically and Politically. A Dialogue with Oliver O'Donovan*, ed. Craig G. Bartholomew, et al. (Grand Rapids: Zondervan, 2002).

Moltmann, Jürgen, *Theology of Hope: On the Ground and the Implications of a Christian Eschatology* (London: SCM Press, 1967).

Moltmann, Jürgen, *Theology and Joy* (London: SCM Press, 1971).

Moltmann, Jürgen, *The Gospel of Liberation* (Waco, TX: Word, 1973).

Moltmann, Jürgen, *Man: Christian Anthropology in the Conflicts of the Present* (London: SPCK, 1974).

Moltmann, Jürgen, et al., *Religion and Political Society* (New York: Harper and Row, 1974).

Moltmann, Jürgen, *The Crucified God: The Cross of Christ as the Foundation and Criticism of Christian Theology* (London: SCM Press, 1974).

Moltmann, Jürgen, *The Church in the Power of the Spirit: A Contribution to Messianic Ecclesiology* (London: SCM Press, 1975).

Moltmann, Jürgen, *The Experiment Hope* (London: SCM Press, 1975).

Moltmann, Jürgen, *Hope for the Church: Moltmann in Dialogue with Practical Theology* (Nashville, Tennessee: Abingdon, 1979).

Moltmann, Jürgen, *The Future of Creation* (London: SCM Press, 1979).

Moltmann, Jürgen, *The Trinity and the Kingdom of God: The Doctrine of God* (London: SCM Press, 1981).

Moltmann, Jürgen, "The Challenge of Religion in the 1980s," in *Theologians in Transition: The Christian Century 'How My Mind Has Changed Series,'* ed. James M. Wall (New York: Crossroad, 1981).

Moltmann, Jürgen, *The Power of the Powerless* (London: SCM Press, 1983).

Moltmann, Jürgen, *On Human Dignity* (London: SCM Press, 1984).

Moltmann, Jürgen, *God in Creation: An Ecological Doctrine of Creation: The Gifford Lectures 1984-1985* (London: SCM Press, 1985).

Moltmann, Jürgen, *Theology Today* (London: SCM Press, 1988).

Moltmann, Jürgen, *The Way of Jesus Christ: Christology in Messianic Dimensions* (London: SCM Press, 1990).

Moltmann, Jürgen, *The Spirit of Life: A Universal Affirmation* (London: SCM Press, 1992).

Moltmann, Jürgen, *Jesus Christ for Today's World* (London: SCM Press, 1994).

Moltmann, Jürgen, "Covenant or Leviathan? Political Theology for Modern Times," in *Scottish Journal of Theology*, vol. 47/1 (February 1994), 19-41.

Moltmann, Jürgen, *The Coming of God: Christian Eschatology* (London: SCM Press, 1996).

Moltmann, Jürgen, *A Passion for God's Reign: Theology, Christian Learning and the Christian Self*, ed. Miroslav Volf (Grand Rapids: Eerdmans 1998).

Moltmann, Jürgen, *God for a Secular Society: The Public Relevance of Theology* (Minneapolis: Fortress, 1999).

Moltmann, Jürgen, "The Liberation of the Future and its Anticipations in History," in *God Will Be All In All: The Eschatology of Jürgen Moltmann*, ed. Richard J. Bauckham (Edinburgh: T&T Clark, 1999).

Moltmann, Jürgen, "What Has Happened to Our Utopias?" in *God Will Be All In All: The Eschatology of Jürgen Moltmann*, ed. Richard J. Bauckham (Edinburgh: T&T Clark, 1999).

Moltmann, Jürgen, *Experiences in Theology: Ways and Forms of Christian Theology* (London: SCM Press, 2000).

Monbiot, George, *The Age of Consent: A Manifesto for a New World Order* (London: Flamingo, 2003).

Moo, Douglas J., *The Epistle to the Romans* (Grand Rapids: Eerdmans, 1996).

Moreau, A. Scott, "Congress on the Church's Worldwide Mission," in *Evangelical Dictionary of World Missions*, ed. A. Scott Moreau (Grand Rapids: Baker, 2000).

Moreland, James P., *What is the Soul?: Recovering Human Personhood in a Scientific Age* (Norcross, Georgia: RZIM, 2002).

Morse, Christopher, *The Logic of Promise in Moltmann's Theology* (Philadelphia: Fortress, 1979).

Motyer, J. Alec, *The Prophecy of Isaiah* (Leicester: InterVarsity, 1993).

Mouw, Richard J., *Politics and the Biblical Drama* (Grand Rapids: Eerdmans, 1976).

Mouw, Richard J., *When the Kings Come Marching In: Isaiah and the New Jerusalem* (Grand Rapids: Eerdmans, 2002).

Müller-Fahrenholz, Geiko, *The Kingdom and the Power: The Theology of Jürgen Moltmann*, trans. John Bowden (London: SCM Press, 2000).

Murphy, Craig N. and Roger Tooze, *The New International Political Economy* (Boulder, Colo.: Rienner, 1991).

Murray, Robert S.J., *The Cosmic Covenant: Biblical Themes of Justice, Peace, and the Integrity of Creation* (London: Sheed and Ward, 1992).

Nanno, Edward L., "Narrative Theology," in *The Dictionary of Historical Theology*, ed. Trevor A. Hart (Grand Rapids: Eerdmans, 2000).

Nardin, Terry, *Law, Morality, and the Relations of States* (Princeton: Princeton University Press, 1983).

Nelson, Mark, "Ethics," in *The Oxford Companion to Christian Thought*, ed. Adrian Hastings, Alistair Mason, and Hugh Pyper (Oxford: Oxford University Press, 2000).

Nelson, Paul, *Narrative and Morality: A Theological Inquiry* (University Park: Pennsylvanian State University Press, 1987).

Neuhaus, Richard J., "Commentary on *The Desire of the Nations*," *Studies in Christian Ethics*, vol. 11/2 (August 1998), 56-61.

Newbigin, Lesslie, *Foolishness to the Greeks: The Gospel and Western Culture* (London: SPCK, 1986).

Newbigin, Lesslie, "Whose Justice?" *Ecumenical Review*, vol. 44/3 (July 1992), 308-311.

Newbigin, Lesslie, *The Gospel in a Pluralist Society* (London: SPCK, 2000).

Nicholson, Ernest W., *God and His People: Covenant and Theology in the Old Testament* (Oxford: Clarendon Press, 1986).

Niebuhr, H. Richard, "The Grace of Doing Nothing," *Christian Century*, vol. 49 (March 1932), 378-380.

Niebuhr, H. Richard, *Christ and Culture* (London: Faber, 1952).

Niebuhr, Reinhold, "Must We Do Nothing?" *Christian Century*, vol. 49 (March 1932), 415-417.

Niebuhr, Reinhold, *Moral Man and Immoral Society* (New York: Scribner's, 1934).

Niebuhr, Reinhold, *Nature and Destiny of Man*, 2 vols. (London: Nisbet, 1941-1943).

Niebuhr, Reinhold, *The Children of Light and the Children of Darkness* (London: Nisbet, 1945).

Noll, Mark A., *Adding Cross to Crown: The Political Significance of Christ's Passion* (Washington D.C.: Centre for Public Justice, 1996).

Noll, Mark A., *Turning Points*, 2nd edn. (Grand Rapids: Baker, 2000).

Noll, Mark A., "Niebuhr, H. Richard," in *Evangelical Dictionary of Theology*, ed. Walter A. Elwell, 2nd edn (Grand Rapids: Baker, 2001).

Northcott, Michael S., *The Environment and Christian Ethics* (New York: Cambridge University Press, 1996).

Novak, Michael, *The Spirit of Democratic Capitalism* (Lanham, Maryland: Madison Books, 1991).

Novak, Michael, "Toward a Theology of the Corporation," in *On Moral Business: Classical and Contemporary Resources for Ethics in Economic Life*, ed. Max L. Stackhouse, Dennis P. McCann, and Shirely J. Roels (Grand Rapids: Eerdmans, 1995).

Nozick, Robert, *Anarchy, State, and Utopia* (Oxford: Blackwell, 1974).

Nunnenkamp, Peter, *The International Debt Crisis of the Third World: Causes and Consequences for the World Economy* (Brighton: Wheatsheaf, 1986).

Nussbaum, Martha C., *The Therapy of Desire: Theory and Practice in Hellenistic Ethics* (Princeton: Princeton University Press, 1994).

Nussbaum, Martha C., "Promoting Women's Capabilities," in *Global Tensions: Challenges and Opportunities in the World Economy*, ed. Lourdes Beneria and Savitri Bisnath (New York: Routledge, 2004).

O'Donovan, Oliver, "The Possibility of a Biblical Ethic," *Theological Student Fellowship Bulletin*, vol. 67 (Autumn 1973), 15-23.

O'Donovan, Oliver, "The Natural Ethic," in *Essays in Evangelical Social Ethics*, ed. David F. Wright (Exeter: Paternoster, 1978).

O'Donovan, Oliver, *The Problem of Self-Love in St. Augustine* (New Haven: Yale University Press, 1980).

O'Donovan, Oliver, *Begotten or Made?* (Oxford: Clarendon Press, 1984).

O'Donovan, Oliver, *Resurrection and Moral Order: An Outline for Evangelical Ethics* (Leicester: InterVarsity, 1986).

O'Donovan, Oliver, "The Political Thought of the Book of Revelation," *Tyndale Bulletin* vol. 37 (1986), 61-94.

O'Donovan, Oliver, "Augustine's City of God XIX and Western Political Thought," *Dionysius*, vol. 11 (December 1987), 89-110.

O'Donovan, Oliver, *Peace and Certainty: A Theological Essay on Deterrence* (Oxford: Clarendon Press, 1989).

O'Donovan, Oliver, "Karl Barth and Ramsey's 'Uses of Power,'" *The Journal of Religious Ethics*, vol. 19/2 (Fall 1991), 1-30.

O'Donovan, Oliver, *Liturgy and Ethics* (Bramcote: Grove, 1993).

O'Donovan, Oliver, *The Desire of the Nations: Rediscovering the Roots of Political Theology* (Cambridge: Cambridge University Press, 1996).

O'Donovan, Oliver, "Response to Respondents: Behold, the Lamb!" *Studies in Christian Ethics*, vol. 11/2 (August 1998), 91-110.

O'Donovan, Oliver and Joan L. O'Donovan, *From Irenaeus to Grotius: A Sourcebook in Christian Political Thought, 100-1625* (Grand Rapids: Eerdmans, 1999).

O'Donovan, Oliver, "Political Theology, Tradition and Modernity," in *The Cambridge Companion to Liberation Theology*, ed. Christopher Rowland (Cambridge: Cambridge University Press, 1999).

O'Donovan, Oliver, "Government as Judgment," *First Things*, vol. 92 (April 1999), 36-44.

O'Donovan, Oliver, "Deliberation, History and Reading: A Response to Schweiker and Wolterstorff," in *Scottish Journal of Theology*, vol. 54/1 (February 2001), 127-144.

O'Donovan, Oliver, *Common Objects of Love: Moral Reflection and the Shaping of Community – The 2001 Stob Lectures* (Grand Rapids: Eerdmans, 2002).

O'Donovan, Oliver, "Response to Andrew Lincoln," in *A Royal Priesthood?: The Use of the Bible Ethically and Politically. A Dialogue with Oliver O'Donovan*, ed. Craig G. Bartholomew, et al. (Grand Rapids: Zondervan, 2002).

O'Donovan, Oliver, "Response to Craig Bartholomew," in *A Royal Priesthood?: The Use of the Bible Ethically and Politically. A Dialogue with Oliver O'Donovan*, ed. Craig G. Bartholomew, et al. (Grand Rapids: Zondervan, 2002).

O'Donovan, Oliver, "Response to Gordon McConville," in *A Royal Priesthood?: The Use of the Bible Ethically and Politically. A Dialogue with Oliver O'Donovan*, ed. Craig G. Bartholomew, et al. (Grand Rapids: Zondervan, 2002).

O'Donovan, Oliver, "Establishment," *Paper Submitted to the Commission of Inquiry on Faith and Nation* (2003).

O'Donovan, Oliver and Joan L. O'Donovan, *Bonds of Imperfection: Christian Politics, Past and Present* (Grand Rapids: Eerdmans, 2004).

Ohmae, Kenichi, *The End of the Nation State: The Rise of Regional Economies* (New York: Free Press, 1995).

Oldham, Joseph H., "The Function of the Church in Society," in *The Church and its Function in Society*, ed. Willem A. Visser't Hooft and Joseph H. Oldham (London: George Allen & Unwin, 1937).

O'Neill, Onora, *Faces of Hunger: An Essay on Poverty, Justice and Development* (London: Allen & Unwin, 1986).

O'Neill, Onora, *Bounds of Justice* (Cambridge: Cambridge University Press, 2000).

O'Neill, Onora, "Agents of Justice," in *Global Justice*, ed. Thomas W. Pogge (Oxford: Blackwell, 2001).

Organization for Economic Co-operation and Development, *OECD in Figures: Statistics on the Member Countries* (Paris: OECD, 2004).

Othman, Norani and Clive S. Kessler, "Capturing Globalization: Prospects and Projects," *Third World Quarterly*, vol. 21/6 (December 2000), 1013-1026.

Padilla, René, "Evangelism and the World," in *Let the Earth Hear His Voice*, ed. James D. Douglas (Minneapolis: World Wide Publications, 1975).

Padilla, René, "Mission at the Turn of the Century/ Millennium," *Evangel* (Spring 2001), 6-12.

Palmer, Leonard R., *The Latin Language* (London: Faber, 1954).

Pannenberg, Wolfhart, *What is Man?: Contemporary Anthropology in Theological Perspective*, trans. Duane A. Priebe (Philadelphia: Fortress, 1970).

Pannenberg, Wolfhart, *Systematic Theology*, vol. 1, trans. Geoffrey W. Bromiley (Edinburgh: T&T Clark, 1991).

Parker, Thomas H.L., *The Doctrine of the Knowledge of God: A Study in the Theology of John Calvin* (Edinburgh: Oliver and Boyd, 1952).

Peskett, Howard and Vinoth Ramachandra, *The Message of Mission: The Glory of Christ in All Time and Space* (Leicester: InterVarsity, 2003).

Pettifor, Ann, "Resolving International Debt Crises Fairly," *Ethics and International Affairs*, vol. 17/2 (October 2003), 2-9.

Phillips, Timothy R. and Dennis L. Okholm, "The Nature of Confession: Evangelicals and Postliberals," in *The Nature of Confession: Evangelicals and Postliberals in Conversation*, ed. Timothy R. Phillips and Dennis L. Okholm (Downers Grove, Ill.: InterVarsity, 1996).

Phillips, Timothy R., "Postliberal Theology," in *Evangelical Dictionary of Theology*, ed. Walter A. Elwell, 2nd edn (Grand Rapids: Baker, 2001).

Philpott, Daniel, *Revolutions in Sovereignty: How Ideas Shaped Modern International Relations* (Princeton: Princeton University Press, 2001).

Philpott, Daniel, "The Ethics of Boundaries: A Question of Partial Commitments," in *Boundaries and Justice: Diverse Ethical Perspectives*, ed. David Miller and Sohail H. Hashmi (Princeton: Princeton University Press, 2001).

Pinches, Charles R., *Theology and Action: After Theory in Christian Ethics* (Grand Rapids: Eerdmans, 2002).

Placher, William C., "Paul Ricoeur and Postliberal Theology: A Conflict of Interpretations," *Modern Theology*, vol. 4/1 (October 1987), 35-52.

Placher, William C., "Postliberal Theology," in *The Modern Theologians: An Introduction to Christian Theology in the Twentieth Century*, ed. David F. Ford, 2nd edn (Cambridge, MA: Blackwell, 1997).

Plant, Raymond, *Politics, Theology and History* (Cambridge: Cambridge University Press, 2001).

Plantinga, Alvin, "Religious Belief as 'Properly Basic,'" in *Philosophy of Religion: A Guide and Anthology*, ed. Brian Davies (Oxford: Oxford University Press, 2000).

Pogge, Thomas W., *Realizing Rawls* (Ithaca: Cornell University Press, 1989).

Pogge, Thomas W., "Priorities of Global Justice," in *Global Justice*, ed. Thomas W. Pogge (Oxford: Blackwell, 2001).

Pogge, Thomas W., "Human Rights and Human Responsibilities," in *Global Justice and Transnational Politics: Essays on the Moral and Political Challenges of Globalization*, ed. Pablo de Greiff and Ciaran Cronin (Cambridge, Mass.: The MIT Press, 2002).

Pogge, Thomas W., *World Poverty and Human Rights: Cosmopolitan Responsibilities and Reforms* (Cambridge: Polity Press, 2002).

Porter, Michael E., *Competitive Strategy: Techniques for Analysing Industries and Competitors* (New York: Free Press, 1980).

Rahner, Karl, *Foundations of Christian Faith: An Introduction to the Idea of Christianity*, trans. William V. Dych (London: Darton, Longman & Todd, 1984).

Rasmusson, Arne, *The Church as Polis: From Political Theology to Theological Politics as Exemplified by Jürgen Moltmann and Stanley Hauerwas* (Notre Dame, Ind.: University of Notre Dame, 1995).

Rasmusson, Arne, "Not All Justifications of Christendom are Created Equal: A Response to Oliver O'Donovan," *Studies in Christian Ethics*, vol. 11/2 (August 1998), 69-76.

Rawls, John, *A Theory of Justice* (Oxford: Oxford University Press, 1996).

Rawls, John, *The Law of Peoples* (Cambridge, Mass.: Harvard University Press, 1999).

Reddy, Sanjay G., "Developing Just Monetary Arrangements," *Ethics and International Affairs*, vol. 17/1 (April 2003), 81-93.

Rengger, Nicholas, "Cosmopolitanism," in *Understanding Democratic Politics*, ed. Roland Axtmann (London: Sage, 2003).

Rengger, Nicholas, "On 'Good Global Governance,' Institutional Design, and the Practices of Moral Agency," in *Can Institutions Have Responsibilities?: Collective Moral Agency and International Relations*, ed. Toni Erskine (Basingstoke: Palgrave Macmillan, 2003).

Richards, Lawrence O. and Gib Martin, *A Theology of Personal Ministry* (Grand Rapids: Zondervan, 1981).

Robertson, Roland, "Glocalization: Time-Space and Homogeneity-Heterogeneity," in *Global Modernities*, ed. Mike Featherstone, Scott Lash and Roland Robertson (London: Sage, 1995).

Robertson, Roland, "Globalization and the Future of 'Traditional Religion,'" in *God and Globalization*, vol. 1: *Religion and the Powers of the Common Life* (Harrisburg, Pa.: Trinity Press International, 2000).

Robinson, Mary, "Building an Ethical Globalization," at Yale University, 8 October 2002.

Rosenau, James N., *Turbulence in World Politics: A Theory of Change and Continuity* (London: Harvester Wheatsheaf, 1990).

Rosenau, James N., *Along the Domestic-Foreign Frontier: Exploring Governance in a Turbulent World* (Cambridge: Cambridge University Press, 1997).

Rosenau, James N., "Governance in a New Global Order," in *Governing Globalization: Power, Authority and Global Governance*, ed. David Held and Anthony G. McGrew (Cambridge: Polity Press, 2002).

Rosenberg, Justin, *The Follies of Globalization Theory: Polemical Essays* (London: Verso, 2000).

Rosendorf, Neal M., "Social and Cultural Globalization: Concepts, History, and America's Role," in *Governance in a Globalizing World*, ed. Joseph S. Nye and John D. Donahue (Washington D.C.: Brookings, 2000).

Ruigrok, Winfried, "International Corporate Strategies and Restructuring," in *Political Economy and the Changing Global Order*, ed. Richard Stubbs and Geoffrey R.D. Underhill (Oxford: Oxford University Press, 2000).

Sacks, Jonathan, *The Dignity of Difference: How to Avoid the Clash of Civilizations* (London: Continuum, 2002).

Samuel, Vinay K. and Christopher M.N. Sugden, "Toward a Theology of Social Change," in *Evangelicals and Development*, ed. Ronald J. Sider (Exeter: Paternoster, 1981).

Samuel, Vinay K. and Christopher M.N. Sugden, "God's Intention for the World," in *The Church in Response to Human Need*, ed. Vinay K. Samuel and Christopher M.N. Sugden (Grand Rapids: Eerdmans, 1987).

Sanks, S.J., T. Howland, "Globalization and the Church's Social Mission," in *Theological Studies*, vol. 60/4 (December 1999), 625-651.

Sassen, Saskia, *Losing Control?: Sovereignty in an Age of Globalization* (New York: Columbia University Press, 1996).

Scholte, Jan Aart, *International Relations of Social Change* (Buckingham: Open University Press, 1993).

Scholte, Jan Aart, "The Globalization of World Politics," in *The Globalization of World Politics: An Introduction to International Relations*, ed. John Baylis and Steve Smith, 2nd edn (Oxford: Oxford University Press, 2001).

Schweiker, William, "Responsibility in the World of Mammon: Theology, Justice, and Transnational Corporations," in *God and Globalization*, vol. 1: *Religion and the Powers of the Common Life* (Harrisburg, Pa.: Trinity Press International, 2000).

Schweiker, William, "Freedom and Authority in Political Theology: A Response to Oliver O'Donovan's *The Desire of the Nations*," in *Scottish Journal of Theology*, vol. 54/1 (February 2001), 110-126.

Schwöbel, Christoph, "The Creature of the Word: Recovering the Ecclesiology of the Reformers," in *On Being the Church: Essays on the Christian Community*, ed. Colin E. Gunton and Daniel W. Hardy (Edinburgh: T&T Clark, 1989).

Schwöbel, Christoph, "Grace," in *The Oxford Companion to Christian Thought*, ed. Adrian Hastings, Alistair Mason, and Hugh Pyper (Oxford: Oxford University Press, 2000).

Schwöbel, Christoph, "Theology," in *The Cambridge Companion to Karl Barth*, ed. John Webster (Cambridge: Cambridge University Press, 2000).

Sebam, Jean-Loup, "Barth, Karl," in *Routledge Encyclopedia of Philosophy*, vol. 1, ed. Edward Craig (London: Routledge, 1998).

Sedgwick, Peter, "Globalization," in *The Blackwell Companion to Political Theology*, ed. Peter Scott and William T. Cavanaugh (Malden, MA: Blackwell Publishing, 2004).

Selby, Peter, *Grace and Mortgage* (London: Darton, Longman & Todd, 1997).

Sen, Amartya, *Development as Freedom* (Oxford: Oxford University Press, 1999).

Sen, Amartya, "Justice Across Borders," in *Global Justice and Transnational Politics: Essays on the Moral and Political Challenges of Globalization*, ed. Pablo de Greiff and Ciaran Cronin (Cambridge, Mass.: The MIT Press, 2002).

Shanks, Andrew, "Response to *The Desire of the Nations*," *Studies in Christian Ethics*, vol. 11/2 (August 1998), 86-90.

Shapiro, Ian and Lea Brilmayer, "Introduction," in *Global Justice*, ed. Ian Shapiro and Lea Brilmayer (New York: New York University Press, 1999).

Shelton, Jo-Ann, *As the Romans Did: A Sourcebook in Roman Social History*, 2nd edn (Oxford: Oxford University Press, 1998).

Shue, Henry, *Basic Rights: Subsistence, Affluence, and US Foreign Policy*, 2nd edn (Princeton: Princeton University Press, 1996).

Sider, Ronald J., *Rich Christians in an Age of Hunger* (London: Hodder & Stoughton, 1990).

Sine, Tom W., "Globalization, Creation of Global Culture of Consumption and the Impact on the Church and its Mission," in *Evangelical Review of Theology*, vol. 27/4 (October 2003), 353-370.

Singer, Peter, "Famine, Affluence, and Morality," in *International Ethics*, ed. Charles R. Beitz, et al. (Princeton: Princeton University Press, 1985).

Singer, Peter, *Practical Ethics*, 2nd edn (Cambridge: Cambridge University Press, 1993).

Singer, Peter, *One World: The Ethics of Globalization* (New Haven: Yale University Press, 2002).

Skillen, James W., "Acting Politically in Biblical Obedience?" in *A Royal Priesthood?: The Use of the Bible Ethically and Politically. A Dialogue with Oliver O'Donovan*, ed. Craig G. Bartholomew, et al. (Grand Rapids: Zondervan, 2002).

Skinner, Quentin, *The Foundations of Modern Political Thought, vol. 2: The Age of Reformation* (Cambridge: Cambridge University Press, 1978).

Slack, Keith, "Sharing the Riches of the Earth: Democratizing Natural Resource-Led Development," *Ethics and International Affairs*, vol. 18/1 (April 2004), 47-62.

Smail, Tom, *Once and For All: A Confession of the Cross* (London: Darton, Longmann & Todd, 1998).

Smith, David W., *Against the Stream: Christianity and Mission in an Age of Globalization* (Leicester: InterVarsity, 2003).

Smith, David W., *Mission After Christendom* (London: Darton, Longman & Todd, 2003).

Smith, Michael J., *Realist Thought from Weber to Kissinger* (Baton Rouge: Louisiana State University Press, 1986).

Smith, Timothy L., *Revivalism and Social Reform in Mid-Nineteenth Century America* (Nashville: Abingdon Press, 1957).

Soros, George, "The New Global Financial Architecture," in *On the Edge: Living with Global Capitalism*, ed. Will Hutton and Anthony Giddens (London: Jonathan Cape, 2000).

Spero, Joan E. and Jeffrey A. Hart, *The Politics of International Economic Relations*, 5th edn (London: Routledge, 1997).

Spykman, Gordon J., *Reformational Theology: A New Paradigm for Doing Dogmatics* (Grand Rapids, Eerdmans, 1992).

St. Augustine of Hippo, *The City of God*, ed. Randolph V.G. Tasker, trans. John Healey, vol. 1 (London: Dent, 1945).

St. Augustine of Hippo, *Confessions*, vol. 1/1 (Oxford: Clarendon Press, 1992).

St. Bonaventure, *The Character of a Christian Leader*, trans. Philip O'Mara (Ann Arbor, Mich.: Servant Books, 1978).

Stackhouse, John G., "Evangelical Theology Should Be Evangelical," in *Evangelical Futures: A Conversation on Theological Method*, ed. John G. Stackhouse (Grand Rapids: Baker, 2000).

Stackhouse, Max L., "Public Theology and Civil Society in a Globalizing Era," *Bangalore Theological Forum*, vol. 32/1 (June 2000), 46-72.

Stackhouse, Max L. and Peter Paris (ed.), *God and Globalization*, 3 vols. (Harrisburg, Pa.: Trinity Press International, 2000-2002).

Stackhouse, Max L., "Public Theology and Political Economy in a Globalizing Era," in *Public Theology for the 21st Century: Essays in Honour of Duncan B. Forrester*, ed. William F. Storrar and Andrew R. Morton (Edinburgh: T&T Clark, 2004).

Stambaugh, John E., *The Ancient Roman City* (Baltimore: Johns Hopkins University Press, 1988).

Stek, John H., "What Says the Scripture?" in *Portraits of Creation: Biblical and Scientific Perspectives on the World's Formation*, ed. Howard J. Van Til (Grand Rapids, Eerdmans, 1990).

Stevenson, Leslie and David L. Haberman, *Ten Theories of Human Nature* (Oxford: Oxford University Press, 1998).

Stiglitz, Joseph E., *Globalization and Its Discontents* (London: Allen Lane, 2002).

Stiglitz, Joseph E., *"Future of Globalization: In the Light of Recent Turbulence,"* at Yale University, 10 October 2003.

Stiglitz, Joseph E., "Towards a New Paradigm of Development," in *Making Globalization Good: The Moral Challenges of Global Capitalism*, ed. John H. Dunning (Oxford: Oxford University Press, 2003).

Storkey, Alan, "The Bible's Politics," in *Witness to the World: Papers from the Second Oak Hill College Annual School of Theology*, ed. David Peterson (Carlisle: Paternoster, 1999).

Storrar, William F., "Where the Local and the Global Meet," in *Public Theology for the 21ˢᵗ Century: Essays in Honour of Duncan B. Forrester*, ed. William F. Storrar and Andrew R. Morton (London: T&T Clark, 2004).

Stott, John R.W., *Issues Facing Christians Today* (Basingstoke: Marshall, 1984).

Strange, Susan, *Casino Capitalism* (Oxford: Basil Blackwell, 1986).

Strange, Susan, *The Retreat of the State: The Diffusion of Power in the World Economy* (Cambridge: Cambridge University Press, 1996).

Sugden, Christopher M., "Social Gospel," in *New Dictionary of Christian Ethics and Pastoral Theology*, ed. David J. Atkinson and David H. Field (Leicester: InterVarsity, 1995).

Sykes, John, "Narrative Accounts of Biblical Authority: The Need for a Doctrine of Revelation," *Modern Theology*, vol. 5/4 (July 1989), 327-342.

Taylor, Charles, *Sources of the Self: The Making of the Modern Identity* (Cambridge: Cambridge University Press, 1989).

Taylor, Howard, *Human Rights: Its Culture and Moral Confusions* (Edinburgh: Rutherford House, 2004).

The Economist, "Poverty and Inequality: A Question of Justice?" *The Economist* (13 March 2004), 14.

Theissen, Gerd, *The Social Setting of Pauline Christianity: Essays on Corinth*, ed. and trans. John H. Schütz (Edinburgh: T&T Clark, 1982).

Thielicke, Helmut, *Theological Ethics, 1. Foundations*, ed. William H. Lazarerth (London: Black, 1968).

Thielicke, Helmut, *The Evangelical Faith*, vol. 1, trans. Geoffrey W. Bromiley (Edinburgh: T&T Clark, 1978).

Thomas à Kempis, *The Imitation of Christ*, trans. Ronald Knox and Michael Oakley (New York: Sheed and Ward, 1959).

Thomson, J. Arthur, "Covenant (OT)," in *The International Standard Bible Encyclopedia*, ed. Geoffrey W. Bromiley (Grand Rapids: Eerdmans, 1979-1988).

Torrance, Alan J., "Introduction," in *Christ and Context: The Confrontation between Gospel and Culture*, ed. Hilary Regan and Alan J. Torrance (Edinburgh: T&T Clark, 1992).

Torrance, Alan J., "Introductory Essay," in Eberhard Jüngel, *Christ, Justice and Peace: Toward a Theology of the State*, trans. D. Bruce Hamill and Alan J. Torrance (Edinburgh: T&T Clark, 1992).

Torrance, Alan J., *Persons in Communion: An Essay on Trinitarian Description and Human Participation* (Edinburgh: T&T Clark, 1996).

Torrance, Alan J., "The Trinity," in *The Cambridge Companion to Karl Barth*, ed. John Webster (Cambridge: Cambridge University Press, 2000).

Torrance, James B., "The Vicarious Humanity of Christ," in *The Incarnation: Ecumenical Studies in the Nicene-Constantinopolitan Creed AD381*, ed. Thomas F. Torrance (Edinburgh: Handsel, 1981).

Torrance, James B., "The Covenant Concept in Scottish Theology and Politics and its Legacy," in *Scottish Journal of Theology*, vol. 34/3 (June 1981), 225-243.

Torrance, James B., *Worship, Community and the Triune God of Grace* (Carlisle: Paternoster, 1996).

Torrance, Thomas F., *The Doctrine of Grace in the Apostolic Fathers* (Edinburgh: Oliver & Boyd, 1948).

Torrance, Thomas F., "Service in Jesus Christ," in *Service in Christ: Essays Presented to Karl Barth on his 80th Birthday*, ed. James I. McCord and Thomas H.L. Parker (London: Epworth Press, 1966).

Torrance, Thomas F., *Theological Science* (London: Oxford University Press, 1969).

Torrance, Thomas F., *God and Rationality* (London: Oxford University Press, 1971).

Troeltsch, Ernst, *The Social Teaching of the Christian Churches*, trans. Olive Wyon (London: George Allen & Unwin, 1931).

United Nations, *United Nations Conference on Trade and Development. World Investment Report: FDI Policies for Development* (New York: United Nations, 2003).

Vanhoozer, Kevin J., "Human Being, Individual and Social," in *The Cambridge Companion to Christian Doctrine*, ed. Colin E. Gunton (Cambridge: Cambridge University Press, 1997).

Vanhoozer, Kevin J., "The Voice and the Actor," in *Evangelical Futures: A Conversation on Theological Method*, ed. John G. Stackhouse (Grand Rapids: Baker, 2000).

Volf, Miroslav, *Exclusion and Embrace: A Theological Exploration of Identity, Otherness, and Reconciliation* (Nashville: Abingdon Press, 1996).

Volf, Miroslav, "Theology, Meaning and Power," in *The Nature of Confession: Evangelicals and Postliberals in Conversation*, ed. Timothy R. Phillips and Dennis L. Okholm (Downers Grove, Ill.: InterVarsity, 1996).

Vorgrimler, Herbert, *Karl Rahner: His Life, Thought and Works*, trans. Edward Quinn (London: Burns & Oates, 1965).

Walters, Robert S. and David H. Blake, *The Politics of Global Economic Relations*, 4th edn (Englewood Cliffs, N.J.: Prentice-Hall, 1992).

Walton, John, *Covenant: God's Purpose; God's Plan* (Grand Rapids: Zondervan, 1994).

Warfield, Benjamin B., *Revelation and Inspiration* (London: Oxford University Press, 1927).

Watson, Francis, "The Bible," in *The Cambridge Companion to Karl Barth*, ed. John Webster (Cambridge: Cambridge University Press, 2000).

Watson, Philip S., *The Concept of Grace: Essays on the Way of Divine Love in Human Life* (London: Epworth, 1959).

Webster, Douglas D., "Liberation Theology," in *Evangelical Dictionary of Theology*, ed. Walter A. Elwell, 2nd edn (Grand Rapids: Baker, 2001).

Webster, John, *Word and Church: Essays in Christian Dogmatics* (Edinburgh: T&T Clark, 2001).

Webster, John, "What's Evangelical about Evangelical Soteriology?" in *What Does it Mean to be Saved?: Broadening Evangelical Horizons of Salvation*, ed. John G. Stackhouse (Grand Rapids: Baker, 2002).

Webster, John, *Barth 'Outstanding Christian Thinkers Series'* (London: Continuum, 2003).

Weger, Karl-Heinz, *Karl Rahner: An Introduction to His Theology*, trans. David Smith (London: Burns & Oates, 1980).

Weinandy, Thomas G., *Does God Suffer?* (Edinburgh: T&T Clark, 2000).

Weinfeld, Moshe, "berit," in *Theological Dictionary of the Old Testament*, vol. 2, ed. G. Johannes Botterweck and Helmer Ringgren, trans. John T. Willis (Grand Rapids: Eerdmans, 1975).

Weinfeld, Moshe, "The Covenant of Grant in the Ancient Near East," in *Essential Papers on Israel and the Ancient Near East*, ed. Frederick E. Greenspahn (New York: New York University Press, 1991).

Wells, Samuel, *Transforming Fate into Destiny: The Theological Ethics of Stanley Hauerwas* (Carlisle: Paternoster, 1998).

Wells, Samuel, "Introduction to the Essays," in *Faithfulness and Fortitude: In Conversation with the Theological Ethics of Stanley Hauerwas*, ed. Mark Thiessen Nation and Samuel Wells (Edinburgh: T&T Clark, 2000).

Wenar, Leif, "The Legitimacy of Peoples," in *Global Justice and Transnational Politics: Essays on the Moral and Political Challenges of Globalization*, ed. Pablo de Greiff and Ciaran Cronin (Cambridge, Mass.: The MIT Press, 2002).

Wenham, Gordon, "Grace and Law in the Old Testament," in *Law, Morality and the Bible: A Symposium*, ed. Bruce Kaye and Gordon Wenham (Leicester: InterVarsity, 1978).

Werpehowski, William, "Theological Ethics," in *The Modern Theologians: An Introduction to Christian Theology in the Twentieth Century*, ed. David F. Ford, 2nd edn (Cambridge, MA: Blackwell, 1997).

Wesley, John, *The Journal of the Rev. John Wesley, A.M. Sometime Fellow of Lincoln College, Oxford: From October 14th, 1735 to October 24th, 1790*, vol. 1 (London: John Mason, 1864).

West, Gerald, "The Bible and the Poor: A New Way of Doing Theology," in *The Cambridge Companion to Liberation Theology*, ed. Christopher Rowland (Cambridge: Cambridge University Press, 1999).

White, Lynn, "The Historical Roots of our Ecological Crisis," in *Western Man and Environmental Ethics: Attitudes Toward Nature and Technology*, ed. Ian G. Barbour (Reading, Mass.: Addison-Wesley, 1973).

Whitehouse, Walter A., *The Authority of Grace: Essays in Response to Karl Barth*, ed. Ann Loades (Edinburgh: T&T Clark, 1981).

Willard, Dallas, *The Divine Conspiracy: Rediscovering Our Hidden Life in God* (San Francisco: Harper, 1998).

Williamson, Paul R., "Covenant," in *Dictionary of the Old Testament: Pentateuch*, ed. T. Desmond Alexander and David W. Baker (Downers Grove, Ill.: InterVarsity, 2003).

Wink, Walter, *The Powers that Be: Theology for a New Millennium* (London: Doubleday, 1998).

Winter, Bruce W., *After Paul Left Corinth: The Influence of Secular Ethics and Social Change* (Grand Rapids: Eerdmans, 2001).

Wirt, Sherwood E., *The Social Conscience of the Evangelical* (New York: Harper, 1968).

Wogaman, J. Philip, *Economics and Ethics: A Christian Enquiry* (London: SCM Press, 1986).

Wolf, Martin, *Why Globalization Works* (New Haven: Yale University Press, 2004).

Wolfensohn, James D., "Global Links," in *2002 World Development Indicators* (Washington D.C.: World Bank, 2002).

Wolfensohn, James D., "*Fighting Poverty for Peace*," 29 December 2003.

Wolff, Jonathan, "Nozick, Robert," in *Routledge Encyclopedia of Philosophy*, vol. 7, ed. Edward Craig (London: Routledge, 1998).

Wolffe, John, "Introduction," in *Evangelical Faith and Public Zeal: Evangelicals and Society in Britain 1780-1980*, ed. John Wolffe (London: SPCK, 1995).

Wolters, Albert M., *Creation Regained: Biblical Basics for a Reformational Worldview* (Grand Rapids: Eerdmans, 1985).

Wolterstorff, Nicholas, *Until Justice and Peace Embrace: The Kuyper Lectures for 1981 Delivered at The Free University of Amsterdam* (Grand Rapids: Eerdmans, 1983).

Wolterstorff, Nicholas, "A Discussion of Oliver O'Donovan's *The Desire of the Nations*," in *Scottish Journal of Theology*, vol. 54/1 (February 2001), 87-109.

Woods, Ngaire, "Holding Intergovernmental Institutions to Account," *Ethics and International Affairs*, vol. 17/1 (April 2003), 69-80.

World Bank, *Global Economic Prospects 2004: Realizing the Development Promise of the Doha Agenda* (Washington D.C.: World Bank, 2003).

World Trade Organization website (www.wto.org).

World Trade Organization, *International Trade Statistics 2003* (Geneva: World Trade Organization, 2003).

Wright, Christopher J.H., *Living as the People of God: The Relevance of Old Testament Ethics* (Leicester: InterVarsity, 1983).

Wright, Christopher J.H., *Walking in the Ways of the Lord: The Ethical Authority of the Old Testament* (Leicester: Apollos, 1995).

Wright, Christopher J.H., *God's People in God's Land: Family, Land and Property in the Old Testament* (Carlisle: Paternoster, 1997).

Wright, Christopher J.H., "Mission as a Matrix for Hermeneutics and Biblical Theology," August 2003.

Wright, David F. (ed.), *Essays in Evangelical Social Ethics* (Exeter: Paternoster, 1978).

Wright, Nicholas T., *Jesus and the Victory of God*, vol. 2 (London: SPCK, 1996).

Wriston, Walter B., *The Twilight of Sovereignty: How the Information Revolution is Transforming Our World* (New York: Scribner, 1992).

Yip, George S., Johny K. Johansson, and Johan Roos, "Effects of Nationality on Global Strategy," *Management International Review*, vol. 37/4 (October 1997), 365-386.

Yoder, John H., *The Politics of Jesus* (Grand Rapids: Eerdmans, 1972).

Zedillo, Ernesto, "Doha or Die," in *The World in 2004*, ed. Daniel Franklin (London: The Economist, 2003).

Zerner, Ruth, "Bonhoeffer, Dietrich," in *Evangelical Dictionary of Theology*, ed. Walter A. Elwell, 2nd edn (Grand Rapids: Baker, 2001).

Zizioulas, John D., "Human Capacity and Human Incapacity: A Theological Exploration of Personhood," in *Scottish Journal of Theology*, vol. 28/5 (October 1975), 401-448.

Zizioulas, John D., "On Being a Person: Towards an Ontology of Personhood," in *Persons, Divine and Human*, ed. Christoph Schwöbel and Colin E. Gunton (Edinburgh: T&T Clark, 1999).

General Index

Amstutz, Mark, 189-190, 203-204
Anabaptism, 12-13, 16, 93, 103
Anker, Christien van den, 189
Annan, Kofi, 158, 172, 180
Anticipation, 68-69, 83-86, 115, 147, 194, 200, 208
Aquinas, Thomas, 34, 40n, 101
Archer, Gleason, 51
Aristotle, 98, 101
ASEAN, 159
Assmann, Hugo, 36
Atonement, 24, 88-91, 146, 208
Audi, Robert, 14
Augustine of Hippo, St., 6, 55, 121-122, 128, 134, 146
Austin, Victor, 126

Barry, Brian, 175, 182, 189n
Barth, Karl, 16-18, 32-33, 37-44, 54, 56-57, 62, 66, 83n, 86-87, 88n, 97, 102, 105, 110-111, 113, 122-123, 141
Bartholomew, Craig, 122-123, 126, 145n
Bauckham, Richard, 4, 21-24, 33, 61, 65, 68, 78, 81, 83, 85-86, 116, 201n
Bebbington, David, 24
Beck, Ulrich, 155, 166, 173
Becker, Oswald, 51
Bell, Daniel, 27
Berit, 48, 50-52, 54n
Berkhof, Louis, 41-42, 44
Berkman, John, 92, 100
Berkouwer, G.C., 40, 45n, 54n, 83n
Berryman, Phillip, 36
Beyer, Peter, 27
Bhagwati, Jagdish, 170
Bible
  and ethics, 21, 37, 62, 99-100, 102, 114, 116, 122-124, 143-144, 198

authority of, 8, 24, 26, 44, 65-66, 75n, 81, 110-113, 116, 120-124, 129, 131, 139-140, 207
concern for the poor, 16-17, 36, 60, 89
holistic reading of, 4, 6, 15, 21-24, 52-53, 62n, 116-119, 132, 144, 200-201
requirements of God in, 13, 61, 142
self-revelation of God, 35, 40-43, 66, 141
theological method, 32-33
unity of, 47, 143-145
Biggar, Nigel, 111, 117
Blount, Brian, 122, 131, 139
Bonaventure, St., 195n
Bonhoeffer, Dietrich, 18, 45n
Bonino, José Míguez, 85
Bowden, John, 38
Brazil, 168
Bretton Woods, 156-157, 161
Brilmayer, Lea, 151-152, 172
Brown, Gordon, 181n, 203
Bruce, F.F., 47, 51, 55
Bryan, Lowell, 163
Bullinger, Heinrich, 47n

Calvin, John, 13, 43-44, 59, 96, 201n
Calvinism, 13-16
Canada, 174
Caney, Simon, 189n
Cavanaugh, William, 3, 92n
Central Europe, 158
Cerny, Philip, 173
Chaplin, Jonathan, 9n, 135, 137n, 138, 146-147, 197n
Cherry, Conrad, 31n
Childs, Brevard, 116, 144
China, 158-159, 168

Christendom, 103, 107, 137-138,
    141-142, 146, 171
Christian ethics
    See also Bible: and ethics
    application of theological practice,
        8-9, 74-75, 96, 103-104, 120,
        143
    doctrine of the Trinity, 57
    eschatology, 83-84, 125-126
    ethical religion, 27, 97, 114
    love, 127-129
    narrative, 5, 92-93, 96-102, 116-
        117, 119
    Reformational theology, 96
    sub-category of theology, 39, 130
    the resurrection, 124-127
    virtues, 100-102, 105, 109, 198
Christian realism, 18-21
Christopraxis, 65, 74-76
Church
    agent of transformation, 5, 15, 68-
        69, 79, 84, 119, 178, 193, 196,
        202, 205, 208
    as counter-culture, 13, 78, 82, 103-
        104, 110, 197-200, 208
    community defined by the covenant
        of grace, 6-7, 10, 30-62, 177-
        178, 184-185, 193-194, 202,
        206-208
    holistic mission, 4-6, 25, 49-50,
        61-62, 69-70, 74-75, 78-82, 83n,
        85, 91, 115, 118, 120, 135-137,
        142, 147-148, 178, 197, 200-208
    servanthood, 13, 17-18, 27, 46, 74-
        83, 90, 109, 142, 194-208
    sign of God's kingdom, 15, 62,
        136, 198
    voluntary fellowship, 78-81, 194
Church Dogmatics, 33, 40, 105
Cicero, 121
Clark, Ian, 182n
Clarke, Andrew, 199
Clarke, Tony, 175
Clements, Keith, 90
Clinton, William, 178, 181
Cold War, 152, 158, 180
Collier, Jane, 166, 198

Complexity
    of church's mission, 15
    of modern society, 4, 19, 21
Consultation on the Relationship
    between Evangelism and Social
    Responsibility (1982), 26
Contemporary world
    challenges of, 15, 22, 173, 176
    commitment of the church to, 8,
        30-31, 65-66, 80, 91, 119, 148,
        151-152, 182, 193-194, 204,
        207-208
    pluralism in, 30
Cosmopolitanism, 177, 188-191, 193,
    201-202, 206-208
Costas, Orlando, 25
Council of Nicea, 44
Covenant
    ancient Near East, 50-52
    and creation, 48-49, 57
    contractualism, 52, 58, 145
    kingdom of God, 47-52, 115, 143-
        145, 207
    nature of, 32, 47, 50-55, 133, 145
    New Covenant, 54-55
    Noahic covenant, 48-49
    obligations to, 53-54, 55n, 57n, 61-
        62, 88, 90, 142-145, 148, 176-
        177, 185, 193, 197, 200, 202-
        208
    Sinaitic covenant, 52-53
    unity of, 48-50
Cronin, Ciaran, 174-175

Demarest, Bruce, 35
Democracy
    church interaction, 109-110, 118
    establishment of, 20, 71, 167, 170,
        176, 183-185, 191
Descartes, René, 34, 40, 57, 60
Dikaiosune, 60
Divine mandate, 18
Dodd, Charles, 27, 61n, 147
Doha Development Round, 160
Dollar, David, 167-168, 170
Dorrien, Gary, 65
Duchrow, Ulrich, 198n

Duke University, 5
Dumbrell, William, 48-49, 53
Dunning, John, H. 28, 156n, 163,
    174n
Durham, John, 198n

East Asia, 162
Edmonds, Gary, 205
Eichrodt, Walther, 52
Enlightenment, 5, 16, 31-35, 38, 42,
    47, 60, 73, 93-95, 113, 130, 139,
    153, 183, 198, 208
Erickson, Millard, 33, 46
Ernst &Young, 164
Eschatology, 5, 32, 62, 65-74, 83-88,
    91, 115, 125-127, 135, 138, 146-
    147, 194, 200-202, 208
Escobar, Samuel, 25
Esteban, Rafael, 166, 198
European Union, 158-159, 166,
    172n, 192
Evangelical Revival, 25
Evangelicalism
    and postliberalism, 111n
    Christian theology, 7-8
    political philosophy, 9n
    socio-political action: 5-6, 11, 24-
    26, 28, 84-85, 120, 124, 127,
    129, 136, 196, 204-205

Fee, Gordon, 199-200
Fensham, Charles, 47n, 50
Fergusson, David, 112-113, 118
Field, David, 61, 114
Fodor, James, 139-141
Foreign direct investment, 165-166
Forell, George, 4
Forrester, Duncan, 15-17, 110n, 182
Forsyth, P.T., 88-90
France, 174
Francis of Assisi, St., 195n
Free University of Amsterdam, 14
Freeman, Samuel, 184
Frei, Hans, 98
Furnish, Victor, 143

G8, 174

Galston, William, 184n
Gardner, Clinton, 182n
General Agreement on Trade and
    Tariffs, 157-158
General Electric, 165
Germany, 174
Giddens, Anthony, 154
Gilpin, Robert, 161
Globalization
    impact on cultural uniformity, 10
    impact on the environment, 10
    impact on women, 10
    multidimensional phenomenon, 4,
    22, 81
    need for public theology, 8, 11, 27-
    29
    power transformations, 3, 9, 29, 71,
    151-208
Glocalization, 27
God
    as creator, 22, 35, 38, 41, 48-51,
    55-60, 70-73, 84-86, 113, 124-
    127, 139, 197
    doctrine of grace, 31
    glory of, 17, 45, 71-73, 84-86, 116,
    147, 208
    reign of, 131-135, 139-142, 144-
    148, 200-203, 207
    will for creation, 13, 15, 24, 30, 54,
    57-62, 71-73, 83, 86, 115, 142,
    200, 207-208
Goodman, John, 161
Gorringe, Timothy, 28, 51
Gospel
    and culture, 37, 103-104, 118, 200,
    207
    deliverance from sin, 89-90
    faithfulness to, 7, 102, 106, 120-
    121, 124, 132, 138, 147, 198
    grace defines, 31
    privatization of, 11
    wholeness of, 25-26, 135-136
Goudzwaard, Bob, 28, 196n
Grace
    church dependent on, 7, 88, 112-
    113, 129, 142
    definition of, 31, 55, 99

justification by, 38
knowledge of God, 35-44, 62, 112-
    113, 177, 207
Reformational theology, 6-8, 10,
    30-32, 37, 42, 52, 61-62, 88, 91,
    194, 200, 206-207
revelation and reconciliation, 44,
    56, 207
socio-political action, 37, 47, 50,
    60-62, 84, 87, 118-119, 143,
    193-208
Graham, Billy, 25
Great Depression, 157
Green, Leslie, 156
Greene, Colin, 142
Greene, Mark, 11
Greiff, Pablo de, 174-175
Grenz, Stanley, 8-9, 31, 34, 57, 61n
Grindle, Merilee, 168
Gunton, Colin, 6, 8-9, 31, 56, 100
Gustafson, James, 117
Gutiérrez, Gustavo, 36

Haberman, David, 58
Hamel, Gary, 163
Handelman, Howard, 169
Hart, Jeffrey, 158
Hart, Trevor, 41-42, 68, 85, 88-89
Hauerwas, Stanley, 5, 20, 30, 82n,
    92-119, 139-142, 146n, 194, 197-
    200, 203
Hays, Richard, 22n, 84, 116, 144,
    198n
Headlam, Arthur, 39-40
Held, David, 152-156, 161-162, 191
Henry, Carl, 8, 25, 43, 201n
Hertz, Noreena, 166, 175
Hexham, Irving, 14
Hindmarsh, Bruce, 195-196
Hirst, Paul, 153
Hodge, Charles, 43
Hoffmann, Stanley, 157, 185
Hollenbach, David, 28, 202n
Holy Spirit
    doctrine of grace, 31
    empowerment for mission, 22, 62,
        72-73, 76, 127, 136

facilitator of covenant community,
    56-58, 83
revelation of God, 38, 42, 184
Human freedom
    demonstration of, 73-76
    in relationship with God, 22, 127-
        129
Human rights, 69-71, 84, 108, 178,
    185-188, 194, 197
Hungary, 168
Hunsinger, George, 82, 89-91, 112,
    197
Huntington, Samuel, 10n

Ignatieff, Michael, 186
Imago Dei, 56-60, 70, 72
India, 168
Institutes of the Christian Religion,
    43
Interdisciplinary research, 4, 8-9, 29,
    151, 177, 207
International Monetary Fund, 157,
    174
International political theory, 9, 177,
    182, 185, 189, 193-194, 206, 208
International relations
    influence of Christian realism, 20
    traditional concepts of, 29
Israel
    economic structure of, 23
    history of, 44-46, 132-134, 207
    laws of justice, 60-61, 133, 143
    relationship with God, 23, 50-55,
        99, 132-136, 139-140, 143-145
Italy, 174
Iustitia, 60, 182

James, William, 105
Japan, 174
Jeannet, Jean-Pierre, 159, 164
Jenkins, Philip, 199n
Jenson, Robert, 31n, 95, 118
Jesus Christ
    compassion of, 25, 61, 197
    doctrine of grace, 31
    ethical teachings, 5, 75, 94, 96,
        103, 106, 119

lordship of, 14, 17, 37, 73-74, 84,
  116, 136
person and work of, 7, 12, 21, 24,
  26, 41-47, 54-58, 67-70, 72-86,
  88-91, 99, 102, 109-110, 112-
  115, 121, 124-129, 132, 134-
  136, 141-144, 146-148, 194-198,
  200, 207-208
revelation of God, 41-47, 81, 99
Spirit's witness to, 42
Johansson, Johny, 164
Jones, Barry, 175
Jones, Charles, 188n, 189
Jüngel, Eberhard, 35
Justice
  contemporary understanding of, 16,
    20, 27, 108-110, 138, 177-194
  function of state, 14, 140-141
  God's desire for, 13, 15, 60-62, 69-
    72, 83, 128, 145-147, 200
  in a globalized world, 9-10, 28-29,
    151, 173-208
  state sovereignty, 171

Kaiser, Walter, 143
Kant, Immanuel, 34, 129-130, 184
Kaplinsky, Raphael, 159
Kapstein, Ethan, 179n
Kasper, Walter, 46, 82
Katongole, Emmanuel, 95
Keohane, Robert, 173
Keynes, John Maynard, 157
Kingdom of God
  and the created order, 124-127,
    143, 146, 200
  eschatology, 5, 62, 65-74, 83-88,
    194, 200-202, 208
  priority of Jesus Christ, 5-6, 46, 61,
    117, 119, 140
  priority of the church, 14-16, 47,
    61-62, 66, 99-100, 103, 105-107,
    120-121, 133-137, 142-143,
    147-148, 198, 200-203, 207-208
Klein, Naomi, 166
Kline, Meredith, 49, 52, 54n
Knighton, Ben, 166, 201
Kolm, Serge-Christophe, 182

Kruijf, Gerrit de, 122
Kuyper, Abraham, 13-14

LaCugna, Catherine, 57
LAFTA, 159
Lange, Harry de, 196n
Latin America, 25n, 36n, 85
Lausanne Covenant, 25-26
Lawton, Thomas, 165
Legrain, Philippe, 167-168
Letham, Robert, 13
Lewellen, Ted, 10n
Liberation theology, 12n, 36, 85,
  115, 130, 132
Lindbeck, George, 95, 102
Litan, Robert, 162
Longenecker, Richard, 61-62
Lovin, Robin, 19-20
Luther, Martin, 17, 76, 96, 146

MacIntyre, Alasdair, 5, 93, 100-101,
  186n
Macmurray, John, 58
Manson, Thomas, 46, 195n
Marshall, Howard, 37
Masson, Paul, 162-163
Matravers, Matt, 175, 182
Maurice, Frederick Denison, 13
Maury, Philippe, 11
McCarthy, Dennis, 50n
McConville, Gordon, 145
McCormack, Bruce, 38
McCorquodale, Robert, 191
McFadyen, Alistair, 56
McGrath, Alister, 9, 75n, 94, 110-
  113
McMichael, Philip, 175
Meeks, Douglas, 83
Mexico, 165, 168
Micah Challenge, 204-205
Michaels, Kevin, 165
Michalowski, Piotr, 50n
Middle East, 169, 196
Milbank, John, 111n
Miller, Richard, 202
Milne, Bruce, 37n-38n
Mirandola, Pico della, 33

Moberly, Walter, 144-145
Moltmann, Jürgen, 5, 30, 65-91, 114-
    118, 142, 146-147, 194-197, 203
Monbiot, George, 196n
Moo, Douglas, 43
Moreland, James P., 59
Mouw, Richard, 14-15, 19, 84, 197
Müller-Fahrenholz, Geiko, 68
Multinational corporations, 9, 156,
    159, 163-167, 170, 172, 179, 193
Murphy, Craig, 157

NAFTA, 159
Nardin, Terry, 182, 189
Narrative
    Christian ethics, 5, 92-93, 96-102,
        116-117, 119
    divine self-communication, 99-100
Nation-states
    boundaries of, 3, 9, 173-176, 178,
        188-194, 200-202, 207-208
    function of, 4, 14, 20, 138, 140-
        141, 146-148, 151-208
    limitations of power, 16-17
Natural law, 20, 95, 182-183
Natural theology, 40-41, 44
Nazism, 16-18, 35, 39
Nelson, Mark, 114
Nelson, Paul, 97-98, 116
Neuhaus, Richard, 121
Newbigin, Lesslie, 118-119, 142,
    194n, 196n
Niebuhr, Reinhold, 18-21, 93, 105
Niebuhr, Richard, 18-19, 86, 93, 103
Noll, Mark, 19, 142, 195
Novak, Michael, 170
Nozick, Robert, 187
Nussbaum, Martha, 185n
Nye, Joseph, 173

O'Donovan, Joan, 11
O'Donovan, Oliver, 5, 11, 30, 117n,
    120-148, 194, 200-203
O'Neill, Onora, 9, 186, 192-193
Ohmae, Kenichi, 153
Okholm, Dennis, 110
Oldham, Joseph, 143

Organization for Economic Co-
    operation and Development, 159n
Oxfam, 167

Padilla, René, 25-26, 169
Pannenberg, Wolfhart, 39, 55
Paris, Peter, 28
Pauly, Louis, 161
Peace of Westphalia (1648), 171-
    172, 182, 190
Peskett, Howard, 62
Pew Global Attitude Survey, 167-168
Phillips, Timothy, 96, 110
Philpott, Daniel, 171-172, 191-192
Placher, William, 95, 102
Plant, Raymond, 11
Plantinga, Alvin, 40n-41n
Pogge, Thomas, 9, 180, 183, 187,
    190, 192n
Political authority, 128-135, 139-142,
    145, 171-172, 200
Political theology
    decision-making, 120
    defined, 3, 66, 106
    theological consistency, 30, 129
Pomerleano, Michael, 162
Porter, Michael, 165
Postliberalism, 94-96, 110-113, 116
Poverty
    awareness of, 180, 186
    dehumanization, 77-78
    reduction of, 167-170, 190, 203,
        207-208
    vicious circle, 70-71
Power
    dangers of, 20, 138, 176
    global transformations, 3-4, 9-10,
        151-176, 180, 191
    in Corinth, 199-200
    necessity of, 115, 128, 131, 133-
        134, 142, 147
    of the resurrection, 13
    rejection of, 12, 104, 106-107, 110,
        114, 117
Prahalad, C. K., 163
Princeton University, 14

Protestant Reformation, 6, 11n, 12,
80, 171, 195, 206
Rahner, Karl, 34-35, 56n
Ramachandra, Vinoth, 62
Ramsey, Paul, 122
Rasmusson, Arne, 82n, 93n, 117-118,
138
Rawls, John, 108, 183-185, 187-191
Reformation tradition
*See also Grace: Reformational
theology*
Christian ethics, 96
diversity of, 4-5, 8, 27, 117-118
doctrine of covenant, 47n
person of Christ, 12, 81
servanthood, 195-196
theocentricity, 33, 36, 113, 130,
139
theological scholarship, 12, 129,
203
Reformed theology, 13-16, 37
Renaissance, 31
Rengger, Nicholas, 189, 193n
Robertson, Roland, 155
Robinson, Mary, 177n-178n
Roman Empire, 21, 201n
Roos, Johan, 164
Rosenau, James, 172-173
Russia, 174

Sacks, Jonathan, 176, 180
Samuel, Vinay, 26, 85
Sanks, Howland, 204n
Schleiermacher, Friedrich, 40n
Scholte, Jan Aart, 172
Schweiker, William, 120, 179
Schwöbel, Christoph, 6
Scientific theology, 40
Scott, Peter, 3
Sedgwick, Peter, 28
Selby, Peter, 198n
Sen, Amartya, 190
Sermon on the Mount, 104, 114
Servanthood
*See also Church: servanthood and
Reformation tradition:
servanthood*

example of Jesus Christ, 45-47, 56,
61, 76, 82-83, 142, 195-196, 207
in vocations, 80
role of theology, 94
servant-leadership, 26, 83n, 115,
194-206, 208
to the powerless, 5, 15, 18, 25-26,
46, 60-62, 66, 73-85, 89
Shanks, Andrew, 141-142
Shapiro, Ian, 151-152, 172
Shue, Henry, 186n-187n
Sider, Ronald, 25n
Sine, Tom, 196, 201
Singer, Peter, 174, 175n, 181, 185,
190-192
Skillen, James, 141
Slack, Keith, 203n
Smail, Tom, 89
Smith, David, 28, 169, 199
Smith, Michael, 20
Smith, Timothy, 24-25
Social gospel, 19-20, 24-25, 90, 93
Soros, George, 162
South African apartheid, 18
Soviet Union, 157, 169, 196
Special revelation, 42-44
Spener, Philip Jakob, 195
Spero, Joan, 158
Spykman, Gordon, 8
Stackhouse, John, 25
Stackhouse, Max, 28
Stek, John, 49n
Stevenson, Leslie, 58
Stiglitz, Joseph, 160, 178-179
Storkey, Alan, 28-29
Storrar, William, 27
Stott, John, 24-26, 84-85, 196-197
Strange, Susan, 162, 173
Sub-Saharan Africa, 160, 167, 169,
196
Sugden, Christopher, 24, 26, 85
Sykes, John, 113

Taylor, Charles, 60
The Great Reversal, 24
Theocentric worldview, 18, 35, 40,
50, 59, 71-73, 84-85, 91, 113-114,

116, 130, 139, 143, 186, 194, 198, 202, 207
Theological method, 31-33, 50, 62
Thielicke, Helmut, 34, 83
Thomas à Kempis, 195
Thompson, Arthur, 48
Thompson, Grahame, 153
Tooze, Roger, 157
Torrance, Alan, 30, 36-37, 81
Torrance, James, 32, 52
Torrance, T.F., 39, 44, 46-47, 54-55
Trade liberalization, 3, 157-161, 165
Trinity
    doctrine of grace, 31, 47, 56-57, 62
    history of salvation, 78
    interpersonal relationship, 80-81
    relationship with creation, 6, 54
Tsedaqah, 60

United Kingdom, 174
United Nations Conference on Trade and Development, 165
United Nations Declaration on the Granting of Independence to Colonial Countries and Peoples (1960), 171
United States of America, 156-157, 166, 174, 181, 185
University of Edinburgh, 5
University of St. Andrews, 105
University of Tübingen, 5

Vanhoozer, Kevin, 44, 57n
Victim-oriented soteriology, 88-91
Vietnam War, 157
Volf, Miroslav, 76, 91, 115
Vorgriff, 35

Warfield, Benjamin, 42-43
Watson, Francis, 33
Watson, Philip, 6
Webster, John, 7, 37, 41, 59, 84
Weinfeld, Moshe, 50n
Wells, Samuel, 94n, 98, 111n, 113
Wenar, Leif, 188n-189n
Wenham, Gordon, 53
Werpehowski, William, 96, 107

Wesley, John, 195
West, Gerald, 36
Wheaton Declaration, 25
Williamson, Paul, 48, 49n
Willimon, William, 103-104
Wink, Walter, 156
Wirt, Sherwood, 25
Wolf, Martin, 174n
Wolfensohn, James, 179
Wolffe, John, 24
Wolters, Albert, 33n
Wolterstorff, Nicholas, 14, 84, 121, 139-141
World Bank, 157-158, 160, 168-169, 174, 179
World financial markets, 161-163
World Trade Organization, 158-159, 174-175
World War II, 156-157, 158n
World-formative Christianity, 14
Wright, Christopher, 22-24, 53, 60-61, 62n
Wright, David, F. 11
Wright, N.T., 55n

Yale University, 93-94
Yip, George, 164
Yoder, John Howard, 5, 12-13, 93, 139

Zizioulas, John, 58

Paternoster Biblical Monographs

(All titles uniform with this volume)
Dates in bold are of projected publication

Joseph Abraham
Eve: Accused or Acquitted?
A Reconsideration of Feminist Readings of the Creation Narrative Texts in Genesis 1–3
Two contrary views dominate contemporary feminist biblical scholarship. One finds in the Bible an unequivocal equality between the sexes from the very creation of humanity, whilst the other sees the biblical text as irredeemably patriarchal and androcentric. Dr Abraham enters into dialogue with both camps as well as introducing his own method of approach. An invaluable tool for any one who is interested in this contemporary debate.
2002 / 0-85364-971-5 / xxiv + 272pp

Octavian D. Baban
Mimesis and Luke's on the Road Encounters in Luke-Acts
Luke's Theology of the Way and its Literary Representation
The book argues on theological and literary (mimetic) grounds that Luke's on-the-road encounters, especially those belonging to the post-Easter period, are part of his complex theology of the Way. Jesus' teaching and that of the apostles is presented by Luke as a challenging answer to the Hellenistic reader's thirst for adventure, good literature, and existential paradigms.
2005 */ 1-84227-253-5 / approx. 374pp*

Paul Barker
The Triumph of Grace in Deuteronomy
This book is a textual and theological analysis of the interaction between the sin and faithlessness of Israel and the grace of Yahweh in response, looking especially at Deuteronomy chapters 1–3, 8–10 and 29–30. The author argues that the grace of Yahweh is determinative for the ongoing relationship between Yahweh and Israel and that Deuteronomy anticipates and fully expects Israel to be faithless.
2004 / 1-84227-226-8 / xxii + 270pp

Jonathan F. Bayes
The Weakness of the Law
God's Law and the Christian in New Testament Perspective
A study of the four New Testament books which refer to the law as weak (Acts, Romans, Galatians, Hebrews) leads to a defence of the third use in the Reformed debate about the law in the life of the believer.
2000 / 0-85364-957-X / xii + 244pp

Mark Bonnington
The Antioch Episode of Galatians 2:11-14 in Historical and Cultural Context
The Galatians 2 'incident' in Antioch over table-fellowship suggests significant disagreement between the leading apostles. This book analyses the background to the disagreement by locating the incident within the dynamics of social interaction between Jews and Gentiles. It proposes a new way of understanding the relationship between the individuals and issues involved.
2005 / 1-84227-050-8 / approx. 350pp

David Bostock
A Portrayal of Trust
The Theme of Faith in the Hezekiah Narratives
This study provides detailed and sensitive readings of the Hezekiah narratives (2 Kings 18–20 and Isaiah 36–39) from a theological perspective. It concentrates on the theme of faith, using narrative criticism as its methodology. Attention is paid especially to setting, plot, point of view and characterization within the narratives. A largely positive portrayal of Hezekiah emerges that underlines the importance and relevance of scripture.
2005 / 1-84227-314-0 / approx. 300pp

Mark Bredin
Jesus, Revolutionary of Peace
A Non-violent Christology in the Book of Revelation
This book aims to demonstrate that the figure of Jesus in the Book of Revelation can best be understood as an active non-violent revolutionary.
2003 / 1-84227-153-9 / xviii + 262pp

Robinson Butarbutar
Paul and Conflict Resolution
An Exegetical Study of Paul's Apostolic Paradigm in 1 Corinthians 9
The author sees the apostolic paradigm in 1 Corinthians 9 as part of Paul's unified arguments in 1 Corinthians 8–10 in which he seeks to mediate in the dispute over the issue of food offered to idols. The book also sees its relevance for dispute-resolution today, taking the conflict within the author's church as an example.
2006 / 1-84227-315-9 / approx. 280pp

Daniel J-S Chae
Paul as Apostle to the Gentiles
His Apostolic Self-awareness and its Influence on the Soteriological Argument in Romans
Opposing 'the post-Holocaust interpretation of Romans', Daniel Chae competently demonstrates that Paul argues for the equality of Jew and Gentile in Romans. Chae's fresh exegetical interpretation is academically outstanding and spiritually encouraging.
1997 / 0-85364-829-8 / xiv + 378pp

Luke L. Cheung
The Genre, Composition and Hermeneutics of the Epistle of James
The present work examines the employment of the wisdom genre with a certain compositional structure and the interpretation of the law through the Jesus tradition of the double love command by the author of the Epistle of James to serve his purpose in promoting perfection and warning against doubleness among the eschatologically renewed people of God in the Diaspora.
2003 / 1-84227-062-1 / xvi + 372pp

Youngmo Cho
Spirit and Kingdom in the Writings of Luke and Paul
The relationship between Spirit and Kingdom is a relatively unexplored area in Lukan and Pauline studies. This book offers a fresh perspective of two biblical writers on the subject. It explores the difference between Luke's and Paul's understanding of the Spirit by examining the specific question of the relationship of the concept of the Spirit to the concept of the Kingdom of God in each writer.
2005 / 1-84227-316-7 / approx. 270pp

Andrew C. Clark
Parallel Lives
The Relation of Paul to the Apostles in the Lucan Perspective
This study of the Peter-Paul parallels in Acts argues that their purpose was to emphasize the themes of continuity in salvation history and the unity of the Jewish and Gentile missions. New light is shed on Luke's literary techniques, partly through a comparison with Plutarch.
2001 / 1-84227-035-4 / xviii + 386pp

Andrew D. Clarke
Secular and Christian Leadership in Corinth
A Socio-Historical and Exegetical Study of 1 Corinthians 1–6
This volume is an investigation into the leadership structures and dynamics of first-century Roman Corinth. These are compared with the practice of leadership in the Corinthian Christian community which are reflected in 1 Corinthians 1–6, and contrasted with Paul's own principles of Christian leadership.
2005 / 1-84227-229-2 / 200pp

Stephen Finamore
God, Order and Chaos
René Girard and the Apocalypse
Readers are often disturbed by the images of destruction in the book of Revelation and unsure why they are unleashed after the exaltation of Jesus. This book examines past approaches to these texts and uses René Girard's theories to revive some old ideas and propose some new ones.
2005 / 1-84227-197-0 / approx. 344pp

David G. Firth
Surrendering Retribution in the Psalms
Responses to Violence in the Individual Complaints
In *Surrendering Retribution in the Psalms*, David Firth examines the ways in which the book of Psalms inculcates a model response to violence through the repetition of standard patterns of prayer. Rather than seeking justification for retributive violence, Psalms encourages not only a surrender of the right of retribution to Yahweh, but also sets limits on the retribution that can be sought in imprecations. Arising initially from the author's experience in South Africa, the possibilities of this model to a particular context of violence is then briefly explored.
2005 / 1-84227-337-X / xviii + 154pp

Scott J. Hafemann
Suffering and Ministry in the Spirit
Paul's Defence of His Ministry in II Corinthians 2:14–3:3
Shedding new light on the way Paul defended his apostleship, the author offers a careful, detailed study of 2 Corinthians 2:14–3:3 linked with other key passages throughout 1 and 2 Corinthians. Demonstrating the unity and coherence of Paul's argument in this passage, the author shows that Paul's suffering served as the vehicle for revealing God's power and glory through the Spirit.
2000 / 0-85364-967-7 / xiv + 262pp

Scott J. Hafemann
Paul, Moses and the History of Israel
The Letter/Spirit Contrast and the Argument from Scripture in 2 Corinthians 3
An exegetical study of the call of Moses, the second giving of the Law (Exodus 32–34), the new covenant, and the prophetic understanding of the history of Israel in 2 Corinthians 3. Hafemann's work demonstrates Paul's contextual use of the Old Testament and the essential unity between the Law and the Gospel within the context of the distinctive ministries of Moses and Paul.
2005 / 1-84227-317-5 / xii + 498pp

Douglas S. McComiskey
Lukan Theology in the Light of the Gospel's Literary Structure
Luke's Gospel was purposefully written with theology embedded in its patterned literary structure. A critical analysis of this cyclical structure provides new windows into Luke's interpretation of the individual pericopes comprising the Gospel and illuminates several of his theological interests.
2004 / 1-84227-148-2 / xviii + 388pp

Stephen Motyer
Your Father the Devil?
A New Approach to John and 'The Jews'
Who are 'the Jews' in John's Gospel? Defending John against the charge of antisemitism, Motyer argues that, far from demonising the Jews, the Gospel seeks to present Jesus as 'Good News for Jews' in a late first century setting.
1997 / 0-85364-832-8 / xiv + 260pp

Esther Ng
Reconstructing Christian Origins?
The Feminist Theology of Elizabeth Schüssler Fiorenza: An Evaluation
In a detailed evaluation, the author challenges Elizabeth Schüssler Fiorenza's reconstruction of early Christian origins and her underlying presuppositions. The author also presents her own views on women's roles both then and now.
2002 / 1-84227-055-9 / xxiv + 468pp

Robin Parry
Old Testament Story and Christian Ethics
The Rape of Dinah as a Case Study

What is the role of story in ethics and, more particularly, what is the role of Old Testament story in Christian ethics? This book, drawing on the work of contemporary philosophers, argues that narrative is crucial in the ethical shaping of people and, drawing on the work of contemporary Old Testament scholars, that story plays a key role in Old Testament ethics. Parry then argues that when situated in canonical context Old Testament stories can be reappropriated by Christian readers in their own ethical formation. The shocking story of the rape of Dinah and the massacre of the Shechemites provides a fascinating case study for exploring the parameters within which Christian ethical appropriations of Old Testament stories can live.

2004 / 1-84227-210-1 / xx + 350pp

Ian Paul
Power to See the World Anew
The Value of Paul Ricoeur's Hermeneutic of Metaphor in Interpreting the Symbolism of Revelation 12 and 13

This book is a study of the hermeneutics of metaphor of Paul Ricoeur, one of the most important writers on hermeneutics and metaphor of the last century. It sets out the key points of his theory, important criticisms of his work, and how his approach, modified in the light of these criticisms, offers a methodological framework for reading apocalyptic texts.

2006 / 1-84227-056-7 / approx. 350pp

Robert L. Plummer
Paul's Understanding of the Church's Mission
Did the Apostle Paul Expect the Early Christian Communities to Evangelize?

This book engages in a careful study of Paul's letters to determine if the apostle expected the communities to which he wrote to engage in missionary activity. It helpfully summarizes the discussion on this debated issue, judiciously handling contested texts, and provides a way forward in addressing this critical question. While admitting that Paul rarely explicitly commands the communities he founded to evangelize, Plummer amasses significant incidental data to provide a convincing case that Paul did indeed expect his churches to engage in mission activity. Throughout the study, Plummer progressively builds a theological basis for the church's mission that is both distinctively Pauline and compelling.

2006 / 1-84227-333-7 / approx. 324pp

David Powys
'Hell': A Hard Look at a Hard Question
The Fate of the Unrighteous in New Testament Thought
This comprehensive treatment seeks to unlock the original meaning of terms and phrases long thought to support the traditional doctrine of hell. It concludes that there is an alternative—one which is more biblical, and which can positively revive the rationale for Christian mission.
1997 / 0-85364-831-X / xxii + 478pp

Sorin Sabou
Between Horror and Hope
Paul's Metaphorical Language of Death in Romans 6.1-11
This book argues that Paul's metaphorical language of death in Romans 6.1-11 conveys two aspects: horror and hope. The 'horror' aspect is conveyed by the 'crucifixion' language, and the 'hope' aspect by 'burial' language. The life of the Christian believer is understood, as relationship with sin is concerned ('death to sin'), between these two realities: horror and hope.
2005 / 1-84227-322-1 / approx. 224pp

Rosalind Selby
The Comical Doctrine
The Epistemology of New Testament Hermeneutics
This book argues that the gospel breaks through postmodernity's critique of truth and the referential possibilities of textuality with its gift of grace. With a rigorous, philosophical challenge to modernist and postmodernist assumptions, Selby offers an alternative epistemology to all who would still read with faith *and* with academic credibility.
2005 / 1-84227-212-8 / approx. 350pp

Kiwoong Son
Zion Symbolism in Hebrews
Hebrews 12.18-24 as a Hermeneutical Key to the Epistle
This book challenges the general tendency of understanding the Epistle to the Hebrews against a Hellenistic background and suggests that the Epistle should be understood in the light of the Jewish apocalyptic tradition. The author especially argues for the importance of the theological symbolism of Sinai and Zion (Heb. 12:18-24) as it provides the Epistle's theological background as well as the rhetorical basis of the superiority motif of Jesus throughout the Epistle.
2005 / 1-84227-368-X / approx. 280pp

Kevin Walton
Thou Traveller Unknown
The Presence and Absence of God in the Jacob Narrative
The author offers a fresh reading of the story of Jacob in the book of Genesis through the paradox of divine presence and absence. The work also seeks to make a contribution to Pentateuchal studies by bringing together a close reading of the final text with historical critical insights, doing justice to the text's historical depth, final form and canonical status.
2003 / 1-84227-059-1 / xvi + 238pp

George M. Wieland
The Significance of Salvation
A Study of Salvation Language in the Pastoral Epistles
The language and ideas of salvation pervade the three Pastoral Epistles. This study offers a close examination of their soteriological statements. In all three letters the idea of salvation is found to play a vital paraenetic role, but each also exhibits distinctive soteriological emphases. The results challenge common assumptions about the Pastoral Epistles as a corpus.
2005 / 1-84227-257-8 / approx. 324pp

Alistair Wilson
When Will These Things Happen?
A Study of Jesus as Judge in Matthew 21–25
This study seeks to allow Matthew's carefully constructed presentation of Jesus to be given full weight in the modern evaluation of Jesus' eschatology. Careful analysis of the text of Matthew 21–25 reveals Jesus to be standing firmly in the Jewish prophetic and wisdom traditions as he proclaims and enacts imminent judgement on the Jewish authorities then boldly claims the central role in the final and universal judgement.
2004 / 1-84227-146-6 / xxii + 272pp

Lindsay Wilson
Joseph Wise and Otherwise
The Intersection of Covenant and Wisdom in Genesis 37–50
This book offers a careful literary reading of Genesis 37–50 that argues that the Joseph story contains both strong covenant themes and many wisdom-like elements. The connections between the two helps to explore how covenant and wisdom might intersect in an integrated biblical theology.
2004 / 1-84227-140-7 / xvi + 340pp

Stephen I. Wright
The Voice of Jesus
Studies in the Interpretation of Six Gospel Parables
This literary study considers how the 'voice' of Jesus has been heard in different periods of parable interpretation, and how the categories of figure and trope may help us towards a sensitive reading of the parables today.
2000 / 0-85364-975-8 / xiv + 280pp

Paternoster
9 Holdom Avenue,
Bletchley,
Milton Keynes MK1 1QR,
United Kingdom
Web: www.authenticmedia.co.uk/paternoster

Paternoster Theological Monographs

(All titles uniform with this volume)
Dates in bold are of projected publication

Emil Bartos
Deification in Eastern Orthodox Theology
An Evaluation and Critique of the Theology of Dumitru Staniloae
Bartos studies a fundamental yet neglected aspect of Orthodox theology:
deification. By examining the doctrines of anthropology, christology, soteriology and ecclesiology as they relate to deification, he provides an important
contribution to contemporary dialogue between Eastern and Western
theologians.

1999 / 0-85364-956-1 / xii + 370pp

Graham Buxton
The Trinity, Creation and Pastoral Ministry
Imaging the Perichoretic God
In this book the author proposes a three-way conversation between theology,
science and pastoral ministry. His approach draws on a Trinitarian
understanding of God as a relational being of love, whose life 'spills over' into
all created reality, human and non-human. By locating human meaning and
purpose within God's 'creation-community' this book offers the possibility of a
transforming engagement between those in pastoral ministry and the scientific
community.

2005 / 1-84227-369-8 / approx. 380 pp

Iain D. Campbell
Fixing the Indemnity
The Life and Work of George Adam Smith
When Old Testament scholar George Adam Smith (1856–1942) delivered the
Lyman Beecher lectures at Yale University in 1899, he confidently declared that
'modern criticism has won its war against traditional theories. It only remains to
fix the amount of the indemnity.' In this biography, Iain D. Campbell assesses
Smith's critical approach to the Old Testament and evaluates its consequences,
showing that Smith's life and work still raises questions about the relationship
between biblical scholarship and evangelical faith.

2004 / 1-84227-228-4 / xx + 256pp

Tim Chester
Mission and the Coming of God
Eschatology, the Trinity and Mission in the Theology of Jürgen Moltmann
This book explores the theology and missiology of the influential contemporary theologian, Jürgen Moltmann. It highlights the important contribution Moltmann has made while offering a critique of his thought from an evangelical perspective. In so doing, it touches on pertinent issues for evangelical missiology. The conclusion takes Calvin as a starting point, proposing 'an eschatology of the cross' which offers a critique of the over-realised eschatologies in liberation theology and certain forms of evangelicalism.
2006 / 1-84227-320-5 / approx. 224pp

Sylvia Wilkey Collinson
Making Disciples
The Significance of Jesus' Educational Strategy for Today's Church
This study examines the biblical practice of discipling, formulates a definition, and makes comparisons with modern models of education. A recommendation is made for greater attention to its practice today.
2004 / 1-84227-116-4 / xiv + 278pp

Darrell Cosden
A Theology of Work
Work and the New Creation
Through dialogue with Moltmann, Pope John Paul II and others, this book develops a genitive 'theology of work', presenting a theological definition of work and a model for a theological ethics of work that shows work's nature, value and meaning now and eschatologically. Work is shown to be a transformative activity consisting of three dynamically inter-related dimensions: the instrumental, relational and ontological.
2005 / 1-84227-332-9 / xvi + 208pp

Stephen M. Dunning
The Crisis and the Quest
A Kierkegaardian Reading of Charles Williams
Employing Kierkegaardian categories and analysis, this study investigates both the central crisis in Charles Williams's authorship between hermetism and Christianity (Kierkegaard's Religions A and B), and the quest to resolve this crisis, a quest that ultimately presses the bounds of orthodoxy.
2000 / 0-85364-985-5 / xxiv + 254pp

Keith Ferdinando
The Triumph of Christ in African Perspective
A Study of Demonology and Redemption in the African Context
The book explores the implications of the gospel for traditional African fears of occult aggression. It analyses such traditional approaches to suffering and biblical responses to fears of demonic evil, concluding with an evaluation of African beliefs from the perspective of the gospel.
1999 / 0-85364-830-1 / xviii + 450pp

Andrew Goddard
Living the Word, Resisting the World
The Life and Thought of Jacques Ellul
This work offers a definitive study of both the life and thought of the French Reformed thinker Jacques Ellul (1912-1994). It will prove an indispensable resource for those interested in this influential theologian and sociologist and for Christian ethics and political thought generally.
2002 / 1-84227-053-2 / xxiv + 378pp

David Hilborn
The Words of our Lips
Language-Use in Free Church Worship
Studies of liturgical language have tended to focus on the written canons of Roman Catholic and Anglican communities. By contrast, David Hilborn analyses the more extemporary approach of English Nonconformity. Drawing on recent developments in linguistic pragmatics, he explores similarities and differences between 'fixed' and 'free' worship, and argues for the interdependence of each.
2006 / 0-85364-977-4 / approx. 350pp

Roger Hitching
The Church and Deaf People
A Study of Identity, Communication and Relationships with Special Reference to the Ecclesiology of Jürgen Moltmann
In *The Church and Deaf People* Roger Hitching sensitively examines the history and present experience of deaf people and finds similarities between aspects of sign language and Moltmann's theological method that 'open up' new ways of understanding theological concepts.
2003 / 1-84227-222-5 / xxii + 236pp

John G. Kelly
One God, One People
The Differentiated Unity of the People of God in the Theology of
Jürgen Moltmann
The author expounds and critiques Moltmann's doctrine of God and highlights the systematic connections between it and Moltmann's influential discussion of Israel. He then proposes a fresh approach to Jewish–Christian relations building on Moltmann's work using insights from Habermas and Rawls.
2005 / 0-85346-969-3 / approx. 350pp

Mark F.W. Lovatt
Confronting the Will-to-Power
A Reconsideration of the Theology of Reinhold Niebuhr
Confronting the Will-to-Power is an analysis of the theology of Reinhold Niebuhr, arguing that his work is an attempt to identify, and provide a practical theological answer to, the existence and nature of human evil.
2001 / 1-84227-054-0 / xviii + 216pp

Neil B. MacDonald
Karl Barth and the Strange New World within the Bible
Barth, Wittgenstein, and the Metadilemmas of the Enlightenment
Barth's discovery of the strange new world within the Bible is examined in the context of Kant, Hume, Overbeck, and, most importantly, Wittgenstein. MacDonald covers some fundamental issues in theology today: epistemology, the final form of the text and biblical truth-claims.
2000 / 0-85364-970-7 / xxvi + 374pp

Keith A. Mascord
Alvin Plantinga and Christian Apologetics
This book draws together the contributions of the philosopher Alvin Plantinga to the major contemporary challenges to Christian belief, highlighting in particular his ground-breaking work in epistemology and the problem of evil. Plantinga's theory that both theistic and Christian belief is warrantedly basic is explored and critiqued, and an assessment offered as to the significance of his work for apologetic theory and practice.
2005 / 1-84227-256-X / approx. 304pp

Gillian McCulloch
The Deconstruction of Dualism in Theology
With Reference to Ecofeminist Theology and New Age Spirituality
This book challenges eco-theological anti-dualism in Christian theology, arguing that dualism has a twofold function in Christian religious discourse. Firstly, it enables us to express the discontinuities and divisions that are part of the process of reality. Secondly, dualistic language allows us to express the mysteries of divine transcendence/immanence and the survival of the soul without collapsing into monism and materialism, both of which are problematic for Christian epistemology.
2002 / 1-84227-044-3 / xii + 282pp

Leslie McCurdy
Attributes and Atonement
The Holy Love of God in the Theology of P.T. Forsyth
Attributes and Atonement is an intriguing full-length study of P.T. Forsyth's doctrine of the cross as it relates particularly to God's holy love. It includes an unparalleled bibliography of both primary and secondary material relating to Forsyth.
1999 / 0-85364-833-6 / xiv + 328pp

Nozomu Miyahira
Towards a Theology of the Concord of God
A Japanese Perspective on the Trinity
This book introduces a new Japanese theology and a unique Trinitarian formula based on the Japanese intellectual climate: three betweennesses and one concord. It also presents a new interpretation of the Trinity, a co-subordinationism, which is in line with orthodox Trinitarianism; each single person of the Trinity is eternally and equally subordinate (or serviceable) to the other persons, so that they retain the mutual dynamic equality.
2000 / 0-85364-863-8 / xiv + 256pp

Eddy José Muskus
The Origins and Early Development of Liberation Theology in Latin America
With Particular Reference to Gustavo Gutiérrez
This work challenges the fundamental premise of Liberation Theology, 'opting for the poor', and its claim that Christ is found in them. It also argues that Liberation Theology emerged as a direct result of the failure of the Roman Catholic Church in Latin America.
2002 / 0-85364-974-X / xiv + 296pp

Jim Purves
The Triune God and the Charismatic Movement
A Critical Appraisal from a Scottish Perspective
All emotion and no theology? Or a fundamental challenge to reappraise and realign our trinitarian theology in the light of Christian experience? This study of charismatic renewal as it found expression within Scotland at the end of the twentieth century evaluates the use of Patristic, Reformed and contemporary models of the Trinity in explaining the workings of the Holy Spirit.

2004 / 1-84227-321-3 / xxiv + 246pp

Anna Robbins
Methods in the Madness
Diversity in Twentieth-Century Christian Social Ethics
The author compares the ethical methods of Walter Rauschenbusch, Reinhold Niebuhr and others. She argues that unless Christians are clear about the ways that theology and philosophy are expressed practically they may lose the ability to discuss social ethics across contexts, let alone reach effective agreements.

2004 / 1-84227-211-X / xx + 294pp

Ed Rybarczyk
Beyond Salvation
Eastern Orthodoxy and Classical Pentecostalism on Becoming Like Christ
At first glance eastern Orthodoxy and classical Pentecostalism seem quite distinct. This ground-breaking study shows they share much in common, especially as it concerns the experiential elements of following Christ. Both traditions assert that authentic Christianity transcends the wooden categories of modernism.

2004 / 1-84227-144-X / xii + 356pp

Signe Sandsmark
Is World View Neutral Education Possible and Desirable?
A Christian Response to Liberal Arguments
(Published jointly with The Stapleford Centre)
This book discusses reasons for belief in world view neutrality, and argues that 'neutral' education will have a hidden, but strong world view influence. It discusses the place for Christian education in the common school.

2000 / 0-85364-973-1 / xiv + 182pp

Hazel Sherman
Reading Zechariah
The Allegorical Tradition of Biblical Interpretation through the Commentary of Didymus the Blind and Theodore of Mopsuestia
A close reading of the commentary on Zechariah by Didymus the Blind alongside that of Theodore of Mopsuestia suggests that popular categorising of Antiochene and Alexandrian biblical exegesis as 'historical' or 'allegorical' is inadequate and misleading.
2005 / 1-84227-213-6 / approx. 280pp

Andrew Sloane
On Being a Christian in the Academy
Nicholas Wolterstorff and the Practice of Christian Scholarship
An exposition and critical appraisal of Nicholas Wolterstorff's epistemology in the light of the philosophy of science, and an application of his thought to the practice of Christian scholarship.
2003 / 1-84227-058-3 / xvi + 274pp

Damon W.K. So
Jesus' Revelation of His Father
A Narrative-Conceptual Study of the Trinity with Special Reference to Karl Barth
This book explores the trinitarian dynamics in the context of Jesus' revelation of his Father in his earthly ministry with references to key passages in Matthew's Gospel. It develops from the exegeses of these passages a non-linear concept of revelation which links Jesus' communion with his Father to his revelatory words and actions through a nuanced understanding of the Holy Spirit, with references to K. Barth, G.W.H. Lampe, J.D.G. Dunn and E. Irving.
2005 / 1-84227-323-X / approx. 380pp

Daniel Strange
The Possibility of Salvation Among the Unevangelised
An Analysis of Inclusivism in Recent Evangelical Theology
For evangelical theologians the 'fate of the unevangelised' impinges upon fundamental tenets of evangelical identity. The position known as 'inclusivism', defined by the belief that the unevangelised can be ontologically saved by Christ whilst being epistemologically unaware of him, has been defended most vigorously by the Canadian evangelical Clark H. Pinnock. Through a detailed analysis and critique of Pinnock's work, this book examines a cluster of issues surrounding the unevangelised and its implications for christology, soteriology and the doctrine of revelation.
2002 / 1-84227-047-8 / xviii + 362pp

Scott Swain
God According to the Gospel
Biblical Narrative and the Identity of God in the Theology of Robert W. Jenson
Robert W. Jenson is one of the leading voices in contemporary Trinitarian theology. His boldest contribution in this area concerns his use of biblical narrative both to ground and explicate the Christian doctrine of God. *God According to the Gospel* critically examines Jenson's proposal and suggests an alternative way of reading the biblical portrayal of the triune God.
2006 / 1-84227-258-6 / approx. 180pp

Justyn Terry
The Justifying Judgement of God
A Reassessment of the Place of Judgement in the Saving Work of Christ
The argument of this book is that judgement, understood as the whole process of bringing justice, is the primary metaphor of atonement, with others, such as victory, redemption and sacrifice, subordinate to it. Judgement also provides the proper context for understanding penal substitution and the call to repentance, baptism, eucharist and holiness.
2005 / 1-84227-370-1 / approx. 274 pp

Graham Tomlin
The Power of the Cross
Theology and the Death of Christ in Paul, Luther and Pascal
This book explores the theology of the cross in St Paul, Luther and Pascal. It offers new perspectives on the theology of each, and some implications for the nature of power, apologetics, theology and church life in a postmodern context.
1999 / 0-85364-984-7 / xiv + 344pp

Adonis Vidu
Postliberal Theological Method
A Critical Study
The postliberal theology of Hans Frei, George Lindbeck, Ronald Thiemann, John Milbank and others is one of the more influential contemporary options. This book focuses on several aspects pertaining to its theological method, specifically its understanding of background, hermeneutics, epistemic justification, ontology, the nature of doctrine and, finally, Christological method.
2005 / 1-84227-395-7 / approx. 324pp

Graham J. Watts
Revelation and the Spirit
*A Comparative Study of the Relationship between the Doctrine of Revelation
and Pneumatology in the Theology of Eberhard Jüngel and of
Wolfhart Pannenberg*
The relationship between revelation and pneumatology is relatively unexplored.
This approach offers a fresh angle on two important twentieth century
theologians and raises pneumatological questions which are theologically crucial
and relevant to mission in a postmodern culture.
2005 / 1-84227-104-0 / xxii + 232pp

Nigel G. Wright
Disavowing Constantine
*Mission, Church and the Social Order in the Theologies of John Howard Yoder
and Jürgen Moltmann*
This book is a timely restatement of a radical theology of church and state in the
Anabaptist and Baptist tradition. Dr Wright constructs his argument in dialogue
and debate with Yoder and Moltmann, major contributors to a free church
perspective.
2000 / 0-85364-978-2 / xvi + 252pp

Paternoster
9 Holdom Avenue,
Bletchley,
Milton Keynes MK1 1QR,
United Kingdom
Web: www.authenticmedia.co.uk/paternoster

July 2005